Rebels in Groups

Rebels in Groups

Dissent, Deviance, Difference and Defiance

Edited by

Jolanda Jetten and Matthew J. Hornsey

WILEY-BLACKWELL
A John Wiley & Sons, Ltd., Publication

This edition first published 2011

Blackwell Publishing was acquired by John Wiley & Sons in February 2007. Blackwell's publishing program has been merged with Wiley's global Scientific, Technical, and Medical business to form Wiley-Blackwell.

Registered Office
John Wiley & Sons Ltd, The Atrium, Southern Gate, Chichester, West Sussex, PO19 8SQ, United Kingdom

Editorial Offices
350 Main Street, Malden, MA 02148-5020, USA
9600 Garsington Road, Oxford, OX4 2DQ, UK
The Atrium, Southern Gate, Chichester, West Sussex, PO19 8SQ, UK

For details of our global editorial offices, for customer services, and for information about how to apply for permission to reuse the copyright material in this book please see our website at www.wiley.com/wiley-blackwell.

Library of Congress Cataloging-in-Publication data is available for this book.

HB: 9781405196857

A catalogue record for this book is available from the British Library.
Set in 10.5/13pt Minion by Thomson Digital, Noida, India
Printed and bound in Malaysia by Vivar Printing Sdn Bhd
1 2011

To Helen and Sophie – rebellion at its best (JJ)
To my little deviants Rosa and Sophie (MJH)

Contents

About the Editors

Jolanda Jetten is Professor of Social Psychology at the University of Queensland, Australia. She has published on topics relating to peripheral and marginal group membership; deviance within groups; normative influence and conformity; the role of perceptions of intergroup distinctiveness in intergroup discrimination; coping with devalued group membership; and identity change processes. She is currently Chief Editor of the *British Journal of Social Psychology* and Associate Editor of *Social Psychology*.

Matthew J. Hornsey is an Associate Professor of Social Psychology and Associate Dean (Research) at the University of Queensland, Australia. His research focuses on the social psychology of intergroup relations, identity threat, criticism, dissent, collective forgiveness, and the tension between individual and group will. He is currently Associate Editor for the journal *Group Processes and Intergroup Relations*, and the *Australian Journal of Psychology*.

About the Contributors

Dominic Abrams is Professor of Social Psychology at the University of Kent (UK). His research focuses on social identity, social exclusion and discrimination as well as group decisions and influence. His work spans basic and applied research in social and developmental psychology in areas including deviance, leadership, stereotype threat, cooperation and prosociality, social cohesion, intergroup contact, ageing, and equality and human rights. He is the Director of the Center for the Study of Group Processes and co-editor of the journal *Group Processes and Intergroup Relations.*

Fabrizio Butera is Professor of Social Psychology at the University of Lausanne (Switzerland). His research is concerned with social comparison and social influence, and focuses in particular on how social comparison may represent a threat in social influence situations. He has been Associate Editor with the *European Journal of Social Psychology* and is currently member of the Executive Committee of the European Association of Social Psychology.

Hoon-Seok Choi is an Associate Professor of Psychology at Sungkyunkwan University in Seoul, Korea. His research focuses on newcomer dynamics in work groups, group creativity, social exclusion, self-regulation, cultural dynamics in individual and collective behaviour, inter-cultural contact and stereotyping, and game behaviour. He was Editor of the *Korean Journal of Social and Personality Psychology.*

Céline Darnon is Assistant Professor of Social Psychology at Clermont University (France). Her main research field is social psychology of education. Her research focuses in particular on the social value of achievement goals in educational settings as well as their effects on individual (e.g., performance) and social outcomes (e.g., conflict regulation). She is also interested in social status as a moderator of goals effects.

Cory Davenport is a graduate student of psychology at San Diego State University. His research interests include attitudes and persuasion, social influence and political psychology.

Naomi Ellemers is Professor of Social and Organisational Psychology at Leiden University. After completing her studies at the University of California at Berkeley and the University of Groningen, where she obtained her PhD, she was Assistant Professor and Associate Professor at the Free University of Amsterdam. Her research addresses a range of topics in group processes and intergroup relations, and includes experimental studies as well as more applied research in organisations. She has co-edited several books, for instance on stereotyping, social identity theory and social identity processes in organisations.

Jack A. Goncalo joined the Cornell University, School of Industrial and Labor Relations as an Assistant Professor in August 2004. He received his PhD in Business Administration in 2004, from the University of California at Berkeley. Although most research in organisational behaviour emphasises the value of being a 'team player' his research suggests that in order to spark creativity, organisations should emphasise individualistic norms and individual achievement. His research has been published in *Organizational Behavior and Human Decision Processes, Management Science, Journal of Experimental Social Psychology* and the *European Journal of Social Psychology*. He also co-edited the book, *Research on Managing Groups and Teams: Creativity in Groups.*

S. Alexander Haslam is Professor of Social Psychology at the University of Exeter (UK) whose research focuses on group processes in social and organisational contexts. His most recent book is *The New Psychology of Leadership: Identity, Influence and Power* (co-authored with Stephen Reicher and Michael Platow; Psychology Press, London, 2010). He is a fellow of the Canadian Institute for Advanced Research and a former Chief Editor of the *European Journal of Social Psychology.*

Paul Hutchison is a Senior Lecturer in Social Psychology at London Metropolitan University. His research focuses on group processes and intergroup relations; prejudice and discrimination; identity maintenance, identity change and identity loss; and conformity and deviance in groups.

Aarti Iyer is a Senior Lecturer in Social Psychology at the University of Queensland, Australia. Her research investigates: individuals' emotional and political responses to inequality and injustice; the implementation of affirmative action and equal opportunity programmes in employment; and social identity processes during life transitions. She serves on the Editorial Boards of *Personality and Social Psychology Bulletin*, the *European Journal of Social Psychology* and the *British Journal of Social Psychology*.

John M. Levine is Professor of Psychology and Senior Scientist at the Learning Research and Development Center at the University of Pittsburgh. His work focuses on small-group processes, including innovation in work teams, reaction to deviance and disloyalty, conflict and learning, and social processes in online groups. Dr Levine is a Fellow of the American Psychological Association and the American Psychological Society and has served as Editor of the *Journal of Experimental Social Psychology* and Chair of the Society of Experimental Social Psychology. He is an Honorary Professor of Psychology at the University of Kent, Canterbury, UK.

José M. Marques is Professor of Social Psychology at the University of Porto, Portugal. He has published on the black sheep effect and more recently has developed the subjective group dynamics theory.

Marcia P. Miceli is Professor of Management in the McDonough School of Business at Georgetown University, Washington, DC. She has published on topics relating to whistle-blowing (employees' reporting of perceived wrongdoing in organisations), compensation in organisations and recruiting.

John Michalak is a graduate student of psychology at San Diego State University. His research interests include goal attainment and motivation in the group context.

Dale T. Miller is Professor of Organizational Behavior at the Graduate School of Business at Stanford University. His research focuses on intragroup processes, especially peer misperception, social influence and minority status. He also is interested in the role of identity in political and group decisions. He directs the Center for Social Innovation at Stanford University.

Benoît Monin is an Associate Professor of Organizational Behavior and Psychology at Stanford University. His work focuses on self-image concerns, in particular how they pertain to morality. He has published on topics such as cognitive dissonance, discrimination, norm perception and moral credentials. He is currently an Associate Editor for the *Journal of Experimental Social Psychology.*

Thomas A. Morton is a Senior Lecturer in the School of Psychology at the University of Exeter, UK. His research focuses on the ways in which people experience and express their identities in relation to others and the role of strategic considerations and reality constraints in guiding these processes. His work on this theme covers topics such as deviance, intergroup relations, collective forgiveness, essentialism, prejudice and stereotypes.

Gabriel Mugny is Professor of Social Psychology at the University of Geneva (Switzerland). He has published on topics relating to the role of conflict and identity stakes in social influence processes; the social construction and development of knowledge; normative influences in discrimination; the interplay between social influence and social representations. He has been Chief Editor of the *Swiss Journal of Psychology* and is currently Chief Editor of the *International Review of Social Psychology.*

Janet P. Near is the Dale M. Coleman Chair of Management and the Chairperson of the Department of Management & Entrepreneurship in the Kelley School of Business at Indiana University. Her research focuses on two topics: antecedents and outcomes of whistle-blowing in organisations; and the relationship between work and non-work areas of life, especially variables that predict job satisfaction, life satisfaction and their interrelationship.

Charlan J. Nemeth is Professor of Psychology at the University of California, Berkeley. Her research centres on influence and decision making in small groups and has been broadly applied to law and to business. Her focus has been the value of dissent, the open airing of conflicting views, for the stimulation of information processing, problem solving and creativity. Her work of over 100 publications has influenced the discourse on diversity and dissent, on decision making in juries and on corporate cultures for innovation. She was a Visiting Professor at London Business School and has given numerous invited addresses at universities around the world and was the holder of the prestigious Leverhulme Fellowship in the UK.

Kieran O'Connor is a doctoral student in Organizational Behavior at the Stanford University Graduate School of Business. His research focuses on the social psychology of morality and justice, including reactions to moral rebels, vicarious processes of moral credentials and rule violations as a means to restore justice.

Dominic J. Packer has been an Assistant Professor of Psychology at Lehigh University since 2009. He received his PhD in 2007 from the University of Toronto, after which he was a Post-Doctoral Fellow at The Ohio State University. His scholarly work focuses on the psychology of collective life, with particular attention to processes underlying conformity and dissent, as well as ingroup biases.

Deborah A. Prentice is Alexander Stewart 1886 Professor of Psychology and Chair of the Psychology Department at Princeton University. She has published articles, chapters and essays on the psychology of social norms, social identities, the phenomenology of self, behaviour change and related topics. She is currently Associate Editor for the journal *Personality and Social Psychology Review*. Last year, she was Visiting Faculty in the School of Social Sciences at the Institute for Advanced Study in Princeton, and in 2009 she was an Invited Professor at the University Paris Descartes, France.

Radmila Prislin is Professor of Psychology and Associate Dean of Graduate Affairs at San Diego State University. Her research interests are in the areas of attitudes and persuasion, social influence, social change and group dynamics in the aftermath of social change.

Georgina Randsley de Moura is a Lecturer in Social Psychology at the Centre for the Study of Group Processes, School of Psychology, University of Kent (UK). Her research interests are predominantly in the field of intra- and intergroup dynamics, specifically leadership, deviance, collective political action and applying research to organisations.

Stephen D. Reicher is Professor of Social Psychology at the University of St Andrews (UK) whose research examines the role of social identity and group processes in shaping and changing society. He is a Fellow of the Royal Society of Edinburgh and a former Chief Editor of the *British Journal of Social Psychology*. His most recent book is *The New Psychology of Leadership: Identity, Influence and Power* (co-authored with Alexander Haslam and Michael Platow; Psychology Press, London, 2010).

Floor Rink obtained her PhD in Social and Organisational Psychology from Leiden University. She is currently employed as Associate Professor at the Faculty of Economics and Management of the University of Groningen, the Netherlands, as a Fellow in the Rosalind Franklin programme. She has been awarded several prizes (e.g., an APA dissertation award) and obtained substantial grants for her research, which she has published in top-tier journals and edited books. Her research interests include the psychology of the diversity and mobility in work groups, the effects of social identity processes in work teams, and the psychology of information sharing and innovation.

Kimberly Rios Morrison is an Assistant Professor of Social Psychology at the University of Chicago. Her research focuses on the self-concept, social identity, social influence and intergroup relations. She is particularly interested in what motivates people *not* to conform to others' opinions and behaviours.

Adam Rutland is Professor of Developmental Psychology at the University of Kent, UK. His research focuses on the development of social identity and prejudice during middle childhood and adolescence. This includes basic and applied studies on children's self-presentation, normative influences on peer exclusion, effects of extended contact on prejudice, children's implicit and explicit prejudice, and techniques for reducing interethnic prejudice. With Professor Melanie Killen he is author of *Children and Social Exclusion: Morality, Prejudice, and Group Identity.*

Jessica Salvatore received her PhD from Princeton University after which she took up a postdoctoral fellowship at the University of Exeter (UK). She is currently employed as a Five College Mellon Postdoctoral Fellow at Amherst College and Mount Holyoke College. Her research concerns issues of social stigmatisation, social influence and self-regulation, and particularly how these processes operate at the interface between personal and collective identities.

1

The Many Faces of Rebels

Jolanda Jetten and Matthew J. Hornsey

To illustrate a principle you must exaggerate much and you must omit much
(Walter Bagehot)

Serge Moscovici started his 1976 book, *Social Influence and Social Change*, with the above quote. Even though it is not immediately clear for the naive reader how this quote relates to the content of the book, it quickly becomes apparent that Moscovici is not referring to processes relating to understanding conformity, dependence and minority influence. Instead, he is commenting on our practices when conducting research in this field. What is the exaggeration that Moscovici is referring to?

Before answering this question, it is important to assess what Moscovici's book was trying to achieve. One of the main aims of his book was to examine the tension between the pressure of conforming versus the forces pushing for innovation and change. Of course, no one will dispute the omnipresence of these two opposing forces that guide our individual and group behaviour on a daily basis. Given this, why is it that social scientists have been more interested in what makes people conform than in what makes them defy authority and group pressure? Or as Moscovici put it: why do we exaggerate conformity and downplay processes relating to rebellion?

We do not have to look far to understand what Moscovici is referring to. For example, why is it that we are more interested in understanding why 12 per cent of participants in the classic Asch line study conformed on all trials than in the 24 per cent of participants who never conformed at all (Asch, 1951)? Why do we focus on explaining the 63 per cent of participants taking part in Milgram's study in 1963 who delivered what they thought was the maximum shock of 450 volts to a learner, and not on the 37 per cent of participants who insisted at some stage in the study that they did not want to

Rebels in Groups: Dissent, Deviance, Difference and Defiance Jolanda Jetten and Matthew J. Hornsey

continue shocking the learner? Finally, why is our theorising geared towards understanding why groups do not appreciate 'black sheep' and the conditions under which such 'black sheep' are evaluated most negatively? Why do we not instead focus on our liking for rebels and mavericks who challenge group norms and do not appear to be afraid of standing out (Bellah *et al.*, 1985; Hornsey & Jetten, 2004)?

Many of the most famous figures in psychology (e.g., Asch, Milgram, Zimbardo) spent their careers examining conformity and obedience pressures within groups. It is true that these studies have captured the attention of a generation of researchers for a good reason. These researchers tried to understand how obedience and conformity could lead to the destructive consequences witnessed during World War II. Coming to terms with the Holocaust, these studies reveal many important insights in the psychology of dissent, deviance, difference and defiance within groups and have clearly enhanced our understanding of the consequences of conformity (Farr, 1996).

However, some of the conclusions from these classic studies have been taken out of context; they have been interpreted as showing that conformity is the default in groups and that rebellion is generally not welcomed, is suppressed, and at times is actively punished by others in the groups. This has led to a psychology that has focused on the positive value that groups place on loyalty and uniformity and it paints a rather dark picture of groups' perceptions of dissent, deviance, difference and defiance: as detrimental forces within groups, as reflections of a lack of group loyalty, as a sign of disengagement, or as delinquent behaviour.

Still, this general message would not be a problem if it was accurate. But is that the case? Or is it, as Moscovici suggests, that we may have exaggerated the extent to which individuals and group members conform, are obedient, and are intolerant of difference and deviance of others? In Moscovici's words: 'It is difficult to explain why social psychology has been so obsessed with dependence' (Moscovici, 1976, p.18). Or on a lighter note: 'The French say "cherchez la femme"; social psychologists say "look for the dependence, and everything will be explained"' (Moscovici, 1976, p.19).

The main objective of this edited book is to provide a counterforce to the dominant message emerging from social psychological research that groups strive for conformity, homogeneity and sameness, with little respect for deviance, dissent, difference or defiance. Even though the pressure for conformity is without doubt a dominant force in group life, we have perhaps exaggerated the extent to which it affects group processes. That is, in our desire to understand conformity, we have perhaps unavoidably neglected and downplayed the important role played by those who are dissenting, deviant, different or defiant in group life. These individuals are not just a nuisance and trouble-makers. In many cases they are just as important for the functioning of the group as members who are trying hard to fit in and work for the group – indeed, they are often the same person. But why is it that we have been so captured by conformity in groups and why have we developed a dogma that deviance is detrimental for groups?

Do Social Psychologists have a Problem with Rebels?

Compared to other social scientists, it appears that social psychologists appear to be especially concerned about the negative effects of rebels in groups. For example, sociologists often point to the important function that deviance plays in group life and the beneficial effects of deviance. Emile Durkheim (1958) highlighted that deviance and crime are important activities within any healthy society. He argued that, in the process of responding to deviance, group members come together and bonds become tighter. It also enhances an understanding of the collective consciousness of a community, demarcates group boundaries, provides structure to groups, and clarifies important rules and norms that guide collective behaviour. In responding to deviance, groups' perceptions of being in control and being in charge of the way social change manifests itself are enhanced. It is therefore not surprising that sociologists like Erikson (1966) emphasise that groups need deviants. What is more, he argues that societies often develop institutions to sustain some level of deviance in society. At times, societies even 'recruit' deviants because they fulfil an important function. Rather than perceiving deviants as threats to the social order, deviants are part and parcel of the society and their presence stabilises society because it keeps these societies vibrant. If one takes this as a starting point, societies' behaviour is aimed at keeping deviance *within bounds*, rather than eroding it completely. Erikson (1966) quotes Aldous Huxley to make this point:

> Now tidiness is undeniably good – but a good of which it is easily possible to have too much and at too high a price. . . The good life can only be lived in a society in which tidiness is preached and practised, but not too fanatically, and where efficiency is always haloed, as it were, by a tolerated margin of mess (Erikson, 1966, p.13).

This view is very different from the way social psychologists approach deviance. In the latter view, deviants undermine stability and, in order to restore stability, groups would be better off to get rid of these individuals as quickly as possible. The differences between these views may appear subtle, but they point to a fundamentally different assumption: sociologists perceive deviants *as part of* a healthy society – even nourishing this society – whereas social psychologists perceive them as *separate* from it. Indeed, in the latter view, healthy group life can only resume without deviants.

As a final comparison, sociologists are quick to point out that the broader contexts in which behaviour occurs affect whether the act is perceived as deviance or not and that there are no objective criteria in establishing whether an act is deviant. Erikson highlights that 'behaviour which qualifies one man for prison may qualify another for sainthood' (1966, p.5). Sociologists will point out that there are more similarities than differences between the deviant and conforming group members because they both operate in the same community, culture or group, guided by the same rules and principles. Research on witchcraft hysteria has, for instance, revealed that those who were identified and accused of witchcraft held very similar norms and values as their prosecutors (Mather, 1866). Social psychologists, on the other hand, study deviance in settings where deviance is clearly defined; both the deviant and the conforming member will have no difficulty knowing who is who and where they each stand within the group.

The Consequences of an Analysis Defining Rebels as Problems

In noting that social psychologists and sociologists appear to approach and theorise the issue of deviance in a different way, the basic assumptions underlying the study of rebels in groups become salient. More specifically, and contrasting from sociology, social psychological literature has tended to lead to the suggestion that: (a) conformity is the default within groups and that dissent and deviance rarely occur; (b) dissent, deviance and defiance are the opposite of conformity and loyalty; and (c) those who depart from the status quo are perceived as trouble-makers, and that groups feel they would be better off without them. Let's examine these points in greater detail.

When looking at the way social psychologists have described the way groups respond to deviance, we often highlight that deviants are threatening to the group's identity and cohesion. The underlying assumption appears to be that the group's goal is to make everyone similar. People being out of step, being different and breaking group rules is not just a nuisance, it also undermines the group identity and group equilibrium. No wonder group members are predicted to be harsh on those who dissent and are different.

But is this really what happens? We think that rebels may indeed often be downgraded, if not outright rejected and excluded, but this is certainly not an automatic group response. Looking around us, the groups that we find ourselves in on a daily basis are full of individuals who disagree with others in the group (even challenge key norms of groups). They consist of people who speak their mind and at times throw a tantrum because they just do not agree with the group's course of action. Indeed, people may speak up and dissent from important group norms not because they want to be difficult and destructive, but because they care for the group and its future (Hornsey, 2006; Packer, 2008). Importantly too, this is not just one or two, or even a handful of individuals in a group who can be conceived of as engaging in rebellious behaviour, it is all of us who behave in this way (albeit perhaps not all of the time). So, rather than assuming that the majority of group members are conformist and that the group negatively evaluates anyone who is not, we actually all appear to be dissenters, deviants, different and defiant at least part of the time while being in groups that matter to us. So, when are we deviant and when are we a loyal group member? Are the two all that easy to distinguish?

To illustrate to what extent there appears to be a mismatch between the social psychological portrayal of group member behaviour and reality, just consider what the world would look like if we placed such a strong emphasis on conformity as suggested in the literature. That is, groups would consist of sheep anxiously avoiding deviating from the majority opinion, too afraid to share their personal opinions with others in the group for fear of facing rejection. They would want to show their loyalty to the group by downplaying their individuality and by emphasising that they would fight and die for the group and follow the group wherever it would lead them. It is not just that we personally have never been in such an Orwellian or sect-like group, it is probably fair to say that such groups appear to be the exception rather than the rule. These types of groups are more likely to be found in horror or science fiction movies than matching any kind of reality. What is more, and as Durkheim (1958) argues, even if such groups were commonly found, members would very quickly want to find someone breaking the rules, because groups *need* rebels:

> Imagine a society of saints, a perfect cloister of exemplary individuals. Crimes, properly so called, will there be unknown; but faults which appear venial to the layman will create there the same scandal that the ordinary defence does in ordinary consciousness. If, then, this society has the power to judge and punish, it will define these acts as criminal and will treat them as such (1958, pp. 68–9).

If we accept that conformity is not the default within groups – that group members may at times be harsh towards deviants, but at other times admire them, enjoy their company and like to hear their thoughts – and that we have all been rebels within some of our most valued groups, why does the psychological theorising about rebels appear to be separate and distinct from group process research? Put differently, why is our reasoning about dissent, deviance, difference or defiance not better integrated with our theorising on group processes in general? As outlined above, there may be good historical reasons for this. However, aside from the fact that we paint a picture of group life that seems removed from reality, there are at least three broader consequences of this development that are cause for concern.

First, by assuming that the reduction of deviance is the goal of most groups, we fail to understand social change. Indeed, social change would not be possible if there were no rebels and deviants: groups need deviants to move forward. By developing a psychology where deviance is the exception, detrimental to group life, and conformity is adaptive and normative, we can explain only stability and the process of restoring the current status quo (Moscovici, 1976). As Turner (2006) argues, this is consequential:

> Social psychology spends too much of its time explaining how society is reproduced, how the present recapitulates the past and very little on the other half of the problem, how and why society changes, how the future is created in the social present. Such a huge distortion of the defining problem cannot but harm the science and indeed it does (p. 45).

Second, by focusing on groups being intolerant of deviance, dissent, difference and defiance, we paint a rather dark picture of group life. In this view, groups are portrayed as being intolerant and dogmatic (see Spears, 2010, for a recent discussion). Groups are certainly not seen as places where creativity can flourish, critical self-examination can ever be encouraged or respect for difference will be commonplace. The view of groups as negative, oppressive and limiting influences on individual expression is too simplistic and has for too long stood in the way of developing a proper understanding of how individuality can be the result of group life rather than being harmed by it (see Hornsey & Jetten, 2004; Jetten & Postmes, 2006).

Finally, and related to the previous points, a psychology that perceives conformity and sameness as the norm and rebellion and deviance as the problem fails to take into account individual group members' agency. Individual group members are not passive bystanders when their groups punish deviant group members. They are active agents who make decisions on how they want to act within groups and how they position themselves within these groups. It is only when we abandon the idea that groups want their members first and foremost to blindly conform that we come to understand not only how individual agency is possible within groups, but also how it is formed, shaped and achieved within groups (see Reicher & Haslam, 2006).

The Present Book

In the last few years, there is a renewed interest in processes relating to dissent, deviance, difference and defiance within groups. Interestingly, much of this research tends to break with traditional views portraying groups as stifling evil forces that undermine individual agency. Instead, these recent accounts have focused on expressions of dissent, deviance, difference and defiance as normal and often healthy aspects of group life. Researchers have emphasised that group members actively engage with other group members, strive for individual distinctiveness within the group, and negotiate and challenge the group norms. Indeed, many researchers argue that a lack of difference and dissent can lead to stagnant and suboptimal group culture, with potentially disastrous consequences. In short, research has moved away from the view that deviance, dissent and defiance in groups are problematic and unwelcome by definition. Instead, researchers have developed a more refined and complete account of these processes by highlighting the negative as well as the positive functions of dissent, deviance, difference and defiance in groups.

The aim of this book is to bring together researchers at the forefront of this development. Indeed, in many ways, what we aim to achieve is precisely what Moscovici set out to do more than 30 years ago. We build on his theorising, and our contributors have developed some of these insights in new and exciting ways. However, it is also fair to say that we aim to do more than re-examining questions and re-opening this debate. We also noticed that some of these ideas have developed, at times quite independently, in many different domains of social, developmental and organisational psychology. This has led to the development of new questions and new insights. It is time to take stock of these insights and to bring together these new approaches to the study of rebels and integrate them with classic views on rebels in groups. Such an approach has the potential to help us develop a refined research agenda, one where rebels are firmly positioned *within* the psychology of group life.

Structure of this Book

This book consists of four sections concerned, respectively, with: (a) dissent; (b) deviance; (c) difference; and (d) defiance within groups. Even though we recognise that the boundaries between these four types of deviants are blurred, we chose to bring them together under these headers to do justice to the diverse ways in which rebels have been examined.

Part I: Dissent in groups

In the first section we bring together contributions that examine dissent within groups, with a particular focus on the positive function of dissent. Dissent can contribute to a diverse range of outcomes. *Charlan Nemeth* and *Jack Goncalo* give a historical overview of minority research. They provide a counterpoint to the idea that dissenting group members are detrimental to the group and offer compelling evidence that dissent in groups can, under some conditions, enhance group creativity and productivity. They conclude that rogues and rebels 'liberate us from conformity and, more importantly, they stimulate us to think more divergently and creatively'.

Fabrizio Butera, Céline Darnon and *Gabriel Mugny* challenge the prominent assumption in social psychology that dissent rarely occurs. They review their recent research on effective learning and examine the conditions under which dissent can promote learning. They show that dissent is beneficial for learning when mastery goals are activated. In contrast, performance goals seem to be associated with mostly negative learning outcomes. These findings have important practical implications for the way learning contexts should ideally be structured.

Floor Rink and *Naomi Ellemers* highlight how newcomers in groups are perceived. They focus on the reasons why, and the conditions under which, new group members are inclined to adapt to existing ways instead of voicing their dissent. Additionally, they examine some of the factors that are likely to make existing group members more or less open to the dissent and change represented by new group members. Their chapter is a compelling demonstration of the idea that there is no blanket rejection of newcomers; group members may be influenced by newcomers' views, even though they may not evaluate the newcomer positively and have no further interest in them.

John Levine and *Hoon-Seok Choi* also examine the conditions under which newcomers are able to change the groups they enter. They offer an opportunity/threat analysis, based on group socialisation theory, of the conditions that are likely to facilitate and inhibit such influence. They then summarise several studies showing that new members can indeed serve as agents of minority influence by changing the task strategies of the groups they enter and, in some cases, the performance of these groups. These findings sensitise us to the fact that people on the periphery of a group can, in some cases, be important sources of innovation and social change.

Part II: Deviance in groups

The second section brings together researchers that have examined deviance and in particular how deviance is perceived by other group members. In addition to recent research on responding to so-called 'black sheep', other types of deviance within groups are discussed. Importantly, the contributions in this section focus on groups in different contexts (e.g., organisations, political settings, ideology-based groups) and a range of samples including children, employees and small task groups.

The section starts with a chapter by *Thomas Morton*, who provides a powerful demonstration that, at times, group members can embrace deviants when they bring a strategic advantage for the group. Starting from the observation that groups realise at times they will need to change to survive, Thomas reviews research showing that those who deviate from traditionally held beliefs are ideally placed to lead a group in new directions. Deviance is not only tolerated in such contexts, it is even rewarded by other group members with a higher likelihood that group members will endorse such deviants for leadership positions.

The chapter by *Jolanda Jetten, Aarti Iyer, Paul Hutchison* and *Matthew Hornsey* also shows the important role of the broader context in determining responses to deviance. They point to the *a priori* moral stance of the group and identify the conditions when high identifiers are most likely to want to downplay the negative consequences of serious rule violations by other ingroup members. These authors focus on the ways groups that take the moral high ground turn a blind eye to deviance and thereby defy pressure from outsiders to punish those who have been in the wrong.

Dominic Abrams and *Adam Rutland* focus on social inclusion and exclusion during childhood and investigate how children become aware of, and interpret, deviance in intergroup relationships. They set out a developmental model of subjective group dynamics which holds that, as children get older, they also become more responsive to prescriptive norms and cues that these norms are relevant in a particular situation. They use this understanding to reflect on how other ingroup members will respond to deviants, reflections that go on to affect their own responses to deviance.

In the final chapter of this section, *Matthew Hornsey* and *Jolanda Jetten* discuss impostors within groups; that is, people who make public claims for group membership that are contested or even outright fraudulent. They identify different types of impostors and outline the psychological motivations behind these varied forms of impostorism. Literature is reviewed emphasising the dark side of impostors in terms of their potential to cause psychological and material damage to the group. It is also noted, however, that by pretending to be something they are not impostors can serve a purpose in terms of flushing out people's hidden prejudices, pretensions and vanities.

Part III: Difference in groups

The researchers brought together in the third section examine the interplay between standing out from the group versus conforming to the group.

Radmila Prislin, Cory Davenport and *John Michalak* show that perceptions of others within groups are affected not just by whether people have a majority or minority opinion, but also by whether this position was only recently acquired. For instance, it was found that those who previously took a minority position had little tolerance for different positions once they were themselves in the majority. In other words, today's rebel can become tomorrow's authoritarian enforcer of group norms. In so doing, they demonstrate the fluid, dynamic and temporal nature of group dynamics.

The next chapter by *Jessica Salvatore* and *Deborah Prentice* is concerned with the way self-expressions as an individual can be consistent or not with broader contextual and cultural influences. They make the important point that what may look like independence may, rather paradoxically, be an expression of self-definitions that are conforming to broader cultural values. In that way, their chapter illustrates the power of the context in defining conformity and non-conformity.

Working from the perspective that minority opinion expression can have both positive consequences (e.g., reduction of decision-making biases) and negative consequences (e.g., ideological extremism) for the group as a whole, *Kimberly Morrison* and *Dale Miller* focus on factors that are likely to trigger minority opinion expression. They introduce a model that distinguishes those minorities who deviate in a direction consistent with the group prototype ('descriptive norm deviants') from those who deviate in a direction inconsistent with the group prototype ('prescriptive norm deviants'). They go on to argue that descriptive norm deviants, because of their greater conformity to the prototype, may think of themselves as superior to other group members and are *more* willing to express their opinions than non-deviants or prescriptive norm deviants. This provides an interesting counterpoint to the standard assumption that minority opinion holders will bite their tongue in the face of majority opposition.

Finally, *Georgina Randsley de Moura, Dominic Abrams, José Marques* and *Paul Hutchison* discuss the effects of being different and standing out in the context of responding to leaders. They differentiate future leaders from current and ex-leaders and report research findings suggesting that anti-normative behaviour is accepted more from future leaders than from other types of leaders. In their analysis, they draw attention to group members' perceptions that future leaders are often most suited to facilitate social change and that non-normative behaviour is under such conditions rewarded rather than punished.

Part IV: Defiance in groups

In the final section, contributions are brought together which examine the way that individuals within groups or groups as a whole stand up and show defiance. This is an area of research that examines most explicitly the conditions under which individuals rebel against authority and when groups defy societal pressures because they believe it is their moral obligation to do so. The chapters in this section include the examination of responses to those who are defiant but also the processes that lead individuals to engage in rebellion.

The first chapter by *Benoît Monin* and *Kieran O'Connor* discusses responses to moral rebels. They show that those who resist pressures to conform are, at times, resented by those who chose to be obedient. This is because moral rebels threaten those who did conform on previous occasions. Moral rebels arouse cognitive dissonance among those who would conform and they are unwanted reminders of the fact that those who conformed also had the opportunity to rebel. This chapter nicely illustrates that when we downgrade rebels, it is not so much their behaviour that is the problem. Rather, their behaviour threatens the self and makes us very aware of our own inability to stand up for our moral beliefs.

In the next chapter, *Dominic Packer* emphasises that defiance of the status quo can be motivated by group loyalty and that high group commitment does not always mean blindly following group norms. In particular, highly committed group members may resort to defiance when they are concerned about the group's course of action or the behaviour of other group members. The chapter nicely illustrates the diverse ways in which group members express their group loyalty and how individual agency is part of that process.

Janet Near and *Marcia Miceli* examine responses to those who take a moral stance against corrupt or inappropriate elements of the group culture. While previous models of whistle-blowing in organisations have identified some variables that may cause observers of perceived wrongdoing to report it, these models often overlook that whistle-blowing can only occur when employees first decide that the organisational activity that they observed constitutes wrongdoing, and label it as such. In this chapter, an integrated model of whistle-blowing is presented as well as a series of propositions for empirical testing. These have the potential to inform our research agenda enhancing our understanding of when whistle-blowing behaviour is most likely to occur.

The final chapter by *Alexander Haslam* and *Stephen Reicher* examines the perspective of those who defy conformity pressures. They make the important point that our theorising in social psychology has been informed by the assumption that conformity is the dominant response to group pressure. However, they not only note that defiance is more prevalent than we may think, but also point out how people's propensity to stand up for their beliefs is inherent to any social change process. Some of the dynamics observed in the BBC prison experiment are testament to these points. This chapter finishes with the conclusion that in many ways encapsulates the core message of this book; that as researchers we appear to have become prisoners of our own theorising that has focused on conformity and not enough on individuals' ability, need and motivation to rebel.

References

Asch, S.E. (1951). Effects of group pressure upon the modification and distortion of judgment. In H. Guetzkow (ed.), *Groups, Leadership, and Men.* Pittsburgh: Carnegie Press.

Bellah, R.N., Madsen, R., Sullivan, W.M., Swidler, A. & Tipton, S.M. (1985). *Habits of the Heart: Individualism and Commitment in American Life.* New York: Harper. & Row.

Durkheim, E. (1958). *Les Règles de la méthode sociologique* [The rules of sociological method]. Glencoe, IL: Free Press.

Erikson, K.T. (1966). *Wayward Puritans: A Study in the Sociology of Deviance.* New York: John Wiley & Sons.

Farr, R.M. (1996). *The Roots of Modern Social Psychology.* Oxford: Blackwell.

Hornsey, M.J. (2006). Ingroup critics and their influence on groups. In T. Postmes & J. Jetten (eds), *Individuality and the Group: Advances in Social Identity* (pp. 74–91). London: Sage.

Hornsey, M.J. & Jetten, J. (2004). The individual within the group: balancing the need to belong with the need to be different. *Personality and Social Psychology Review, 8,* 248–64.

Jetten, J. & Postmes, T. (2006). 'I did it my way': collective expressions of individualism. In T. Postmes and J. Jetten (eds), *Individuality and the Group: Advances in Social Identity* (pp. 116–38). London: Sage.

Mather, C. (1866). Wonders of the invisible world. In S.G. Drake (ed.), *The Witchcraft Delusion in New England* (pp. 201–3). Roxbury, MA: W. Elliot Woodward.

Milgram, S. (1963). Behavioral study of obedience. *Journal of Abnormal and Social Psychology, 67,* 371–8.

Moscovici, S. (1976). *Social Influence and Social Change.* New York: Academic Press.

Packer, D.J. (2008). On being both with us and against us: a normative conflict model of dissent in social groups. *Personality and Social Psychology Review, 12,* 50–72.

Reicher, S.D. & Haslam, S.A. (2006). Rethinking the psychology of tyranny: the BBC Prison Study. *British Journal of Social Psychology, 45,* 1–40.

Spears, R. (2010). Group rationale, collective sense: beyond intergroup bias. *British Journal of Social Psychology, 49,* 1–20.

Turner, J.C. (2006). Tyranny, freedom and social structure: escaping our theoretical prisons. *British Journal of Social Psychology, 45,* 41–6.

Part I

Dissent in Groups

2

Rogues and Heroes: Finding Value in Dissent

Charlan J. Nemeth and Jack A. Goncalo

The late 1960s was a period of debate and conflict. Especially in 1968, minority voices were raised against the Vietnam War and various civil rights issues. And the ensuing 'debate' was often angry, even violent. Though these minority voices did not have the advantages of power or even numbers, they stood up and told the truth as they saw it. And many of those ideas prevailed and changed the nature of the discourse. Yet, at the same time, social psychology portrayed influence as synonymous with attitude change and we were taught that influence flowed from the strong to the weak. It was the highly credible or high-status individual that influenced the lower-status person. It was the majority that influenced the minority. The people holding a minority viewpoint were viewed as vulnerable and lacking in the ability to influence.

The power of the majority was well documented by the conformity studies which showed that people, when faced with a unanimous majority, would abdicate information from their own senses and agree with the majority even when the majority was wrong. In the classic study by Asch (1956), people judged which of three lines was equivalent to a standard line. Alone, people had no difficulty. They chose the correct line 99 per cent of the time. However, when a majority of three or more individuals unanimously judged a different line to be correct, nearly 35 per cent of responses were in agreement with that majority even though the majority was incorrect. This phenomenon – and even this paradigm – has been replicated in many different countries (Bond & Smith, 1996). However, the same portrait of the minority remained. They were recipients rather than sources of influence and they had two choices: they could conform or

Rebels in Groups: Dissent, Deviance, Difference and Defiance Jolanda Jetten and Matthew J. Hornsey

remain independent. In part, this was due to the dependence on the Asch paradigm where the majority consisted of confederates and the minority was the participant population whose responses were confined to agreement with or resistance to the majority.

Of interest is that, in those days, conformity was viewed with concern. Were people sheep? And independence from that majority was seen as desirable. As time has gone on, we often see conformity portrayed as desirable. Instead of being sheep they are 'team players' while resistance is often viewed as an obstacle. This is especially true in writings on organisational behaviour where the emphasis is often on cooperation and harmony because managers assume that aligning employees with the vision of the company will improve firm performance (Collins & Porras, 1994).

In trying to understand why people conform to majority views, even when they are in error, two reasons have stood the test of time. First, people assume that truth lies in numbers and so they believe that the majority is probably correct. Second, they worry about 'sticking out like a sore thumb' because, should they maintain a differing point of view, they may be on the receiving end of ridicule and rejection. In the classic study of whether or not such fears are warranted, Schachter (1951) looked at the reactions to a persistent minority. When one person differed, communication was directed towards him in an attempt to change his mind. When these attempts proved unsuccessful, he was ignored but he was also rejected. What is interesting is that the author did not study the possible influence of that minority on the majority. It was assumed that the minority was the recipient, not the source of influence. It was the minority that was vulnerable and this study demonstrated just how vulnerable he was. Ironically, we were yet to learn that those holding minority views can be active and that such behaviour could well have influenced the majority to his position.

Minorities as Sources of Influence

The notion that minority views could be active rather than passive – that they could be the source rather than the target of influence – was first theorised by Moscovici and Faucheux (1972; Faucheux & Moscovici, 1967) and demonstrated experimentally by Moscovici, Lage and Naffrechoux (1969). In that study, a minority of two individuals repeatedly called blue slides 'green' and managed to get the majority of four individuals to say 'green' nearly 9 per cent of the time. Further, there was evidence of greater attitude change on a subsequent task. When categorising blue–green stimuli as 'blue' or 'green', those exposed to a consistent minority called these slides 'green' when a control would call them 'blue'. That study and those that followed (see Moscovici & Nemeth, 1974; Wood *et al.*, 1994) both replicated and developed the findings of the early study.

In contrast to a field that emphasised strength, whether that was power, status or numbers, this line of work showed the potential power of those without such benefits. As such, the question was raised as to why and how minorities exert influence. A major contribution, in our judgement, was the emphasis on behavioural style, the orchestration and patterning of the minority's views to understand attitude change. Prior to that, studies of influence tended not to look at the persuasive attempts over time; you could get adoption of the majority position (or the position of a high-status person) very quickly. Majorities benefited from an assumption that they were correct, and minorities were motivated to assume that majorities were correct because it permitted them to move from 'deviant' to 'belonging'.

A number of studies investigated the styles of persuasion by a minority over time. Perhaps the most significant findings demonstrated the importance of consistency. For a minority view to persuade, a necessary (if not sufficient) condition was that they were consistent both over time and with one another. So now we had a very different view of influence, one that emphasised persuasive styles over time. Minorities did not have the luxury of both 'winning friends' *and* influencing people. If they persisted, that is, remained consistent in their position, they would be disliked. If they were inconsistent or capitulated, they would be liked but would exercise no influence. There were also subtleties in being consistent. If their consistency was viewed as rigid rather than consistent, they were not effective (Moscovici *et al.*, 1969; Mugny, 1982; Nemeth, Swedlund & Kanki, 1974).

It was perhaps the fact that minorities exercise their influence primarily at the private or latent level that has changed our conceptions of influence. A number of researchers have found influence by the minority to be greater when asked privately or on new but related issues (Mugny & Papastamou, 1980; Mugny & Perez, 1991; Nemeth & Wachtler, 1974).

The Reaction: Dissenters are still 'Rogues' and 'Obstacles'

Though a good deal of evidence had demonstrated differential types of influence exerted by minorities relative to majorities, it is interesting to note the field's response to this body of evidence. Many researchers, rather than recognising the differential processes and effects, offered what is called a 'single process' theory. Influence is influence, regardless of the majority or minority status of the source except that minorities are weaker or less able to exert influence. For example, Latane (1981) theorised that influence was determined by 'social impact', that is, a multiplicative function of strength, immediacy and number of people who are the sources of influence. In that framework, minority influence is a weak version of majority influence but the same processes occur. To us diehards who were there in the early days, minority influence was always different. For a minority, influence is an uphill battle heavily governed by the ways in which they argue their position. They continually have to confront the fact that people are reluctant to accept or adopt a minority position even if it is correct. Thus, for a minority, consistency is required to exert influence but this tends to evoke dislike, even anger. The choice then was which the minority wanted: influence or being liked.

In addition to viewing minority influence as a weak version of majority influence, many researchers in social psychology still had pejorative views of the minority. They were 'obstacles' to group goals and some portrayed dissenters as persons seeking attention (Maslach, Stapp & Santee, 1985) or 'distinctiveness' (if they wanted to be kind). Many of us, on the contrary, viewed dissenters who maintained their position as courageous; it was the stuff of 'heroes' and of people with conviction.

The Shift to Cognition: Attitude Change

The demonstration of differential processes of influence became more evident with a shift to the cognitive activity induced by majorities or minorities. In the attitude change realm, this was exemplified in Moscovici's (1980) conversion theory which posited different types of attitude change. Majorities induced *compliance.* People would adopt the majority position publicly but not privately. By contrast, minorities induced a *conversion* process. People often showed little or no public movement but were influenced privately. The theory hypothesised that majorities create a conflict of 'responses' whereas minorities create a conflict of 'perceptions'. The former conforms without much scrutiny; the latter requires a validation process where the minority's position is scrutinised.

Studies testing this approach often used the distinctions between central (or systematic) versus peripheral (or heuristic) processing (Chaiken, 1980; Petty & Cacioppo, 1981). These theories, while different in substantial ways, both distinguish between a careful scrutiny of the message versus a more superficial or heuristic basis for adopting the message. Using these distinctions, there arose a sizeable literature showing that there is more careful scrutiny of the minority's message and therefore 'conversion' or private attitude change though there is also evidence of systematic processing in response to a majority (Baker & Petty, 1994; Erb *et al.*, 2002; Mackie, 1987). In a review of this work, Hewstone and Martin (2008) argue that, on balance, the research supports Moscovici's (1980) conversion theory that there is message processing only for a minority. Processing of the majority's message seems to occur when there is a motivation 'to pay closer attention to the content of the majority's arguments' (Hewstone & Martin, 2008). These approaches have helped us to understand a great deal more about when and why attitudes will change in response to a majority versus a minority. However, the general emphasis is still on influence in terms of attitude change and adoption of the source's position.

The Shift to Cognition: Quality of Performance and Decision Making

Our own work took a different focus that even further differentiated between minority and majority influence. Inspired by some work on jury decision making (Nemeth, 1977), we formulated a model suggesting that majorities and minorities induce very different thinking about the issue – not just a differential processing of the message (Nemeth, 1976, 1986; Nemeth & Nemeth-Brown, 2003). Majorities, it was hypothesised, stimulate thinking about the issue *from the perspective they pose.* We know that people are stressed and very uncomfortable when they are faced with a disagreeing majority and this, in general, is related to a narrowing of focus, a convergence of thought. However, majorities don't induce just any convergent thought. They stimulate thinking from the majority perspective. Partly this is due to the fact that people assume that truth lies in numbers; partly it is due to a motivation to find the majority to be correct since that would permit movement to the majority. The minority asks questions such as 'What are they seeing? They must be correct'; 'What am I missing'?

Minorities, on the other hand, stimulate thinking that is divergent; people consider multiple perspectives. Majorities start with an assumption that the minority is not correct but the persistence on the part of that minority suggests a complexity. 'How can they be so sure and yet so wrong?' We theorise that it stimulates a reappraisal of the situation and, in the process, people evidence divergent thinking, a consideration of multiple sources of information and ways of thinking about the issue. On balance, this aids the quality of decision making and the finding of creative solutions to problems (Nemeth, 1986, 1995).

There is now considerable evidence for these propositions. Our own experimental studies have found that minorities stimulate a search for information on all sides of the issue while majorities stimulate a search for information that corroborates the majority view (Nemeth & Rogers, 1996); minorities stimulate the use of multiple strategies in problem solving whereas majorities stimulate the use of the majority strategy (Nemeth & Kwan, 1987); minorities stimulate the detection of solutions that otherwise would have gone undetected whereas majorities stimulate adoption of the majority solution, right or wrong (Nemeth & Wachtler, 1983). Further, minorities stimulate more originality while majorities stimulate more conventionality of thought (Nemeth & Kwan, 1985). As a consequence, those exposed to minority views come up with more creative solutions to problems (Nemeth, Brown & Rogers, 2001).

This type of research has moved the discourse from minority as passive to active and perhaps more importantly, from obstacle to facilitator of quality thought, decision and performance. The minority is no longer a 'deviant' worthy of derision; it is an individual or small group of individuals who have the courage to maintain a position in the face of sizeable opposition, in spite of the likely negative consequences for themselves. And they provide value in the thought that they stimulate.

As an illustration of the importance of 'courage', Nemeth and Chiles (1988) conducted a study where individuals were exposed to a minority who consistently called blue slides 'green'. As demonstrated before, people thought little of the minority; they were seen to be incorrect and as having bad eyesight. However, subsequent to this situation, they were put in a typical conformity setting where three of four individuals called red slides 'orange'. Compared to a control group who had no exposure to a minority viewpoint in the first setting, those exposed to a consistent (though erroneous) minority had a dramatic decrease in conformity. They had less than 30 per cent conformity – compared to 70 per cent conformity by those with no prior exposure to a minority view. We believe that the minority 'influenced' individuals, not so much on the perception of colour but, rather, on the importance of saying what you believe. Individuals did not like the minority but they perceived them as 'having courage'. Here, we underscore that those who maintain a dissenting view can often be respected; they are seen as courageous though not especially likeable. But this is the stuff of heroes and such individuals are not easily relegated to those who seek attention and 'distinctiveness'.

Application to Social Issues Part I: Juries and 'Truth'

In applying this research to jury decision making, we have often argued for protection of minority views, not because they may be correct but because *even when they are wrong* they stimulate thinking that on balance leads to better decisions. It stops the rush to judgement by providing a counter to the majority view. But more importantly, there is evidence that people search for more information on all sides of the issue; they utilise more ways of looking at facts (Nemeth, 1981; Nemeth & Goncalo, 2005).

Unanimity becomes one way to protect minority views as, under that condition, the minority tends to maintain its position longer; the deliberation is more 'robust'; and participants feel that justice has been better served (Nemeth, 1977). In spite of these advantages and their importance for justice, however, many countries have attempted to change the requirement of unanimity to some form of majority rule for jury decision making. The reason is often efficiency but it often includes a pejorative view of the minority holder, the 'deviant'.

In 1970, these issues came before the US Supreme Court (*Apodaca, Cooper & Madder v. Oregon*; *Johnson v. Louisiana*) because Oregon and Louisiana did not require unanimity and those convicted by less than a unanimous vote appealed their convictions. The Court ruled that their rights had not been violated and the basic reasoning was that the majority would have won anyway plus they assumed that the minority views would only be outvoted after the minority 'ceased to have persuasive reasons in support of its position'. In other words, the minority position was without merit; they were just taking up time; and they wouldn't win anyway.

Much more recently in Sydney, Australia (Nemeth, 2003), there was a conference about the reform movements in both Australia and New Zealand to move to some form of majority rule in juries. The comments by the participants – judges, academics and practitioners – were notable for their language as well as their content. The minority holder, the 'deviant', was continually referred to as the 'rogue' juror. Images of an attention-seeking, rigid obstacle to an important decision reared its head. It was rewarding to see the discussion turn to the possibility of courage, to the importance of rigorous debate, to a decision-making process that considered more facts and more ways to view those facts – to a consideration of justice. However, the issue remains, usually under the phrasings of expediting and reducing expenses of the criminal justice system. It is perhaps a powerful reminder of the desire for consensus and that those who dissent, who persist in their minority views, are often punished. They are at least disliked and often ridiculed.

Application to Social Issues Part II: Innovation in Organisations

The research that dissent, even when wrong, can stimulate creativity has practical applications, especially for organisations who recognise that innovation is highly profitable. In fact, organisational scholars and management practitioners have become increasingly aware that creative ideas are the lifeblood of the most admired organisations (Amabile, 1996; Collins & Porras, 1994). It is not enough to stick with what works; there must be a continuous effort to stay at the forefront of the industry. Creative ideas are the raw material necessary for innovation, and a strong competitive advantage is conferred upon organisations that are adept at eliciting creative solutions from their employees (Kanter, 1988).

Under the right circumstances, a single creative idea may be hugely profitable. Take, for example, one employee's idea for a 'failed' adhesive that gave rise to the ubiquitous Post-it Note by the 3M Corporation (Collins & Porras, 1994). One insight gave rise to three new product lines and a complete change in the company's strategic approach to innovation, not to mention untold millions of dollars to the bottom line (Von Hippel, Thomke & Sonnack, 1999). Yet despite the best of intentions, many potentially creative ideas are rejected outright either because they are too risky or because they threaten business as usual (Staw, 1995). Many organisations, whether they choose to recognise this fact or not, desire creativity but reward conformity, cohesion and commitment (Nemeth, 1997).

The research on dissent that has been conducted in organisational settings has an advantage in that the participants are people from a wide range of settings, working in jobs that are ongoing and meaningful to them. Despite these differences from experiments, there are two interesting points to keep in mind. The first is that the basic phenomenon replicates (e.g. De Dreu & West, 2001; Gruenfeld, 1995; Simons & Peterson, 2000). The idea that dissenting opinions stimulate creative thought is a common thread that ties this work together. The second point is that harnessing the positive and inhibiting the negative consequences of dissent may be difficult and requires a complex set of tradeoffs (Nemeth & Staw, 1989). Despite these complexities, however, this line of research has highlighted a number of practical suggestions for capitalising on dissent to manage creativity and innovation.

Dissent conflict and innovation in organisations

There is now considerable evidence that the model of minority influence (Nemeth, 1986) is robust and well replicated in field settings. For instance, Van Dyne and Saavedra (1996) conducted a field study of natural work groups and utilised confederates (who were also permanent members of the ongoing, interacting groups) to serve as dissenters over the course of a 10-week period. As we would expect based on past research, the experimental groups in which one person was privately instructed to take on the role of dissenter engaged in more divergent thinking and came up with more original product ideas than did the control groups. Likewise, utilising a novel Q-sort methodology for studying historical cases, Peterson *et al.* (1998) found that dissent also had stimulating properties in elite decision-making groups. Using archival data, they conducted an in-depth analysis of the top management teams of seven 'Fortune 500' companies who were highly successful or unsuccessful at a particular point in time. They found that the most successful top management teams encouraged dissent in private meetings. Again, we see that even elite decision makers – people who are experts at what they do – can still profit from dissenting opinions.

Despite these benefits, the relationship between dissent and creativity may also be elusive and depend on whether groups can mitigate the potentially numerous and unintended negative consequences of conflict and controversy. As we would expect based on experimental research, the role of dissenter is stressful even when it is assigned and the group has a history together (Van Dyne & Saavedra, 1996). This is probably because dissenters are targeted by the majority for not being cooperative and for being unwilling to readily adopt the majority point of view (Schachter, 1951). There is also a danger that dissent can lead to conflict that escalates and becomes problematic. For instance, unsuccessful groups in the study by Peterson and his colleagues (1998) seemed to be characterised by internal strife to the point of splitting into hostile factions that threatened to permanently split the group.

In an attempt to offset these liabilities, research has provided some clues about what strategies might work. For example, Dooley and Fryxell (1999) found in a study of US hospitals that dissent was positively associated with high-quality decision-making teams. However, the benefits of dissent were only realised in teams that managed to preserve dissent while at the same time building towards a consensus. This was achieved when people felt some sense of loyalty to the groups to which they belonged.

A continual problem is that people may respond to conflicting opinions by just shutting down the conversation. The dissenter may find it easier to remain silent, even if that means suppressing one's true opinions. For instance, De Dreu and West (2001) conducted a field study of innovation using semi-autonomous teams from several different organisations. They measured the extent of minority dissent using a survey measure and then assessed team innovation using supervisor ratings. They found that innovation was high in groups with dissent, but only when there was also a high degree of participation in team decision making. In other words, dissent may spark creative thought, but such thoughts are of little use unless there are procedures for ensuring that these thoughts are openly expressed. And getting them expressed is not easy (Morrison & Milliken, 2000). Overall, however, the basic message has been received: in order to foster creativity and innovation in the workplace, it is necessary to preserve alternative points of view, provided there is an atmosphere of mutual respect and procedures ensuring full participation.

The research in organisational settings also demonstrates that not all forms of conflict are beneficial. In fact, a related line of research has shown that conflict may take on many forms and only certain types of conflict have the stimulating properties previously discussed. Relatively recently, Jehn (1995) has conceptualised intragroup conflict in terms of three distinct types. *Relationship* conflict refers to interpersonal incompatibilities among group members, including personality differences. *Task* conflict refers to disagreements between group members about the content of the task being performed. And *process* conflict involves different strategies for how a group should go about completing a shared task (Jehn, 1995, 1997). There are many ways to have conflict but only some have been found to be productive.

On non-routine tasks, there is evidence that task conflict can be beneficial (Jehn, 1995) as it may cause the group to evaluate information more critically (Postmes, Spears & Cihangir, 2001) and break the tendency of groups to try to achieve consensus before all available alternatives have been thoroughly considered (Janis, 1971, 1972). This form of conflict is similar to the relatively impersonal, task-related issues that research on dissent has shown to facilitate group decision making (Nemeth, 1995). The key difference is that in most of the applied settings, it is not just one person faced with a unanimous majority; the conflict is more diffuse. Nevertheless, the benefits of conflict are similar in terms of promoting a deeper understanding of the task (Amason & Schweiger, 1994), stimulating the consideration of new ideas (Baron, 1991), and it thus contributes to overall group performance (Jehn, Northcraft & Neale, 1999).

Task-related conflict, however, is not an easy one to separate from more destructive forms of relationship conflicts which are often related to personality differences and which can become very emotional. These can create tension, anger and frustration which are not generally beneficial for the group (Jehn & Bendersky, 2003). Even seemingly benign conflicts related to the process of getting work done can escalate into emotional conflicts (Greer, Jehn & Mannix, 2008). For instance, arguments over 'who does what' can be taken to reflect judgements of competence that can easily be taken personally, 'If you do not think that I can do this part of the assignment then you are also saying that I am stupid'.

In practice, the various types of conflict are often hopelessly entangled. Indeed, a recent meta-analysis revealed negative relationships between task conflict, group performance and satisfaction with the team. These negative effects were strongest when task conflict occurred in the presence of relationship conflict (De Dreu & Weingart, 2003). Thus, we are reminded of the tradeoffs between cognitive stimulation and lowered morale, the tradeoffs between creative thought and performance. And the consequences for the dissenter can be considerable if her position is seen as a personal attack.

Some suggestions for ameliorating the negative consequences include timing of the conflict. For example, longitudinal research has shown that high-performing groups had moderate levels of task conflict but, importantly, only at the midpoint between the group's inception and the deadline (Jehn & Mannix, 2001). The midpoint of a project is often the most critical moment during a group's lifecycle (Gersick, 1988). It is there, with a deadline looming, that the most productive discussions occur (Gersick & Hackman, 1990). By permitting, even welcoming task conflict at this point, groups are most likely to capture the benefits of such conflicts while containing the potentially negative effects. It is also likely the way in which the 'rogue' dissenter will be viewed in more favourable terms.

Encouraging voice and creating a culture of dissent

Up to now, we have extolled the virtues and value of dissent and the battle against perceptions of attention seeking, rogue and rebel. This is difficult enough in any setting but organisations, even those that claim to desire creativity, are often unwilling to do what is necessary to achieve it (Staw, 1995). And what prevents the voicing of dissent? Isn't ridicule and rejection enough to prevent 'voice'? Isn't the fact that the likelihood of winning is low? Isn't the fact that, even if 'voice' stimulates creative thought, no credit will follow? These are daunting considerations. Thus, for organisations truly committed to achieving open expression of dissenting opinions, the answer is not simple. Relative to laboratory settings, the pressures for conformity are probably magnified in organisational settings where there are real threats to one's livelihood for taking an unpopular stance. For instance, Sherron Watkins of the Enron Corporation took an enormous risk when she wrote a detailed seven-page letter to her boss basically saying that the company was a huge Ponzi scheme that was likely to implode at any moment.

What makes one employee stand up and speak the truth while others remain silent – to have 'voice' (Packer, 2008; Van Dyne, Ang & Botero, 2003)? And when is it beneficial? Innovation is best served when the 'voice' is prosocial and improvement oriented. It is here, with constructive input about task-related issues (Van Dyne & Lepine, 1998), that errors are corrected and learning occurs (Beer & Eisenstat, 2000; Butera & Mugny, 2001). But again, why would anyone do this? Apart from all the personal considerations, employees are in a more difficult situation because 'voice' often means speaking up to someone who has power over you, those who control your next pay raise or promotion (Detert & Trevino, 2010; Jetten *et al.*, 2010).

There appear to be some personality traits that relate to the likelihood of speaking up. People who are extraverted, conscientious and not very agreeable are more likely to voice conflict than are their shy co-workers who would rather get along with others even if it means poor workmanship (LePine & Van Dyne, 2001). People who are satisfied with their job, have a relatively high self-esteem and work in smaller groups are more likely to engage in voice than others (LePine & Van Dyne, 2001). But even with the 'right' personality traits, there are consequences. Workers who show a great deal of personal initiative are often viewed as being 'rebellious' (Freese & Fay, 2001, p. 141) and such trouble-makers are frequently isolated by both their peers and their supervisors.

The hope is that bosses and organisations signal to their employees that they are truly open to alternative points of view – and mean it. In part, this means changing the perception of 'voice' and dissent from trouble-maker to courageous individual, from obstacle to contributor. This may be easier in more individualistic as opposed to collectivistic cultures, for the latter tend to view conflict as destructive and tend to have stronger pressures for conformity (Bond & Smith, 1996). While some have argued that conformity could promote an objective of creativity (Flynn & Chatman, 2001), there is recent evidence suggesting the reverse. In a recent study, Goncalo and Staw (2006) experimentally manipulated an individualistic or collectivistic culture and then had groups generate new business ideas for a space left vacant by a mismanaged restaurant. The individualistic groups generated more novel ideas than collectivistic groups. Further, they were better at implementation. From the list of ideas they generated, these groups combined ideas to come up with something new whereas collectivistic groups simply chose one idea from their list.

Rogues or heroes: team player or conformist

Throughout this chapter, we have emphasised that the usual reaction to a dissenter is negative. They are annoying, wrong and unpredictable. They are not 'team players', a trait that a recent survey of American workers (Kahpor-Klein & Kahlon, 2004) ranked more highly than whether they had knowledge, skill and ability. Yet, we believe (and the research demonstrates) that these rogues and rebels, assuming they are authentically voicing their views, provide benefit. They liberate us from conformity and, more importantly, they stimulate us to think more divergently and creatively. We consider more facts and more possibilities; we find and devise solutions. Their gift to us comes at a cost to themselves and some discomfort to us. But groups, organisations and societies benefit from the open airing of competing truths (Mill, 1979) and it is time to recognise the contributions of those who dare to dissent.

Acknowledgements

This manuscript was supported by the Kauffman Foundation whose support is gratefully acknowledged. Requests for reprints should be addressed to Professor Charlan Nemeth, Department of Psychology, University of California, Berkeley, CA 94720-1650, USA.

References

Amabile, T.M. (1996). *Creativity in Context.* Boulder, CO: Westview.

Amason, A. & Schweiger, D.M. (1994). Resolving the paradox of conflict, strategic decision making, and organizational performance. *International Journal of Conflict Management, 5*, 239–53.

Apodaca, Cooper & Madder v. Oregon, 406, U.S., 404 (1972).

Asch, S.E. (1956). Studies of independence and conformity: a minority of one against a unanimous majority. *Psychological Monographs*, 70.

Baker, S. & Petty, R. (1994). Majority and minority influence: source-position imbalance as determinant of message scrutiny. *Journal of Personality and Social Psychology, 67*, 5–19.

Baron, R.A. (1991). Positive effects of conflict: a cognitive perspective. *Employee Responsibilities and Rights Journal, 4*, 25–36.

Beer, M. & Eisenstat, R.A. (2000). The silent killers of strategy implementation and learning. *Sloan Management Review*, summer, 29–40.

Bond, R. & Smith, P.B. (1996). Culture and conformity: a meta-analysis of studies using Asch's (1952b, 1956) line judgment task. *Psychological Bulletin, 119*, 111–37.

Butera, F. & Mugny, G. (2001). Conflicts and social influences in hypothesis testing. In C.K.W. De Dreu & N.K. De Vries (eds), *Group Consensus and Minority Influence. Implications for Innovation* (pp. 161–82). Oxford: Blackwell.

Chaiken, S. (1980). Heuristic versus systematic information processing and the use of source versus message cues in persuasion. *Journal of Personality and Social Psychology, 39*, 752–66.

Collins, J.C. & Porras, J.I. (1994). *Built to Last: Successful Habits of Visionary Companies.* New York: Harper Collins.

De Dreu, C.K.W. & Weingart, L.R. (2003). Task versus relationship conflict, team performance, and team member satisfaction: a meta-analysis. *Journal of Applied Psychology, 88,* 741–9.

De Dreu, C.K.W. & West, M.A. (2001). Minority dissent and team innovation: the importance of participation in decision making. *Journal of Applied Psychology, 86,* 1191–201.

Detert, J.R. & Trevino, L.K. (2010). Speaking up to higher ups: how supervisors and skip-level leaders influence employee voice. *Organization Science, 21,* 249–70.

Dooley, R. S. & Fryxell, G.E. (1999). Attaining decision quality and commitment from dissent: the moderating effects of loyalty and competence in strategic decision-making teams. *Academy of Management Journal, 42,* 389–402.

Erb, H-P., Bohner, G., Rank, S. & Einwiller, S. (2002). Processing minority and majority communications: the role of conflict with prior attitudes. *Personality and Social Psychology Bulletin, 28,* 1172–82.

Faucheux, C. & Moscovici, S. (1967). The style of behavior of a minority and its influence on majority responses. *Bulletin Du CERP, 16,* 337–61.

Flynn, F. & Chatman, J. (2001). Strong cultures and innovation: oxymoron or opportunity? In S. Cartwright *et al.* (eds), *International Handbook of Organizational Culture and Climate.* Chichester: John Wiley & Sons.

Freese, M. & Fay, D. (2001). Personal initiative (PI): an active performance concept for work in the 21st century. *Research in Organizational Behavior, 23,* 133–87.

Gersick, C. (1988). Time and transition in work teams: toward a new model of group development. *Academy of Management Journal, 32,* 274–309.

Gersick, C. & Hackman, J.R. (1990). Habitual routines in task-performing groups. *Organizational Behavior and Human Decision Processing, 47,* 65–97.

Goncalo, J.A. & Staw, B.M. (2006). Individualism-collectivism and group creativity. *Organizational Behavior and Human Decision Processes, 100,* 96–109.

Greer, L.L., Jehn, K.A. & Mannix, E.A. (2008). Conflict transformation: a longitudinal investigation of the relationships between different types of intragroup conflict and the moderating role of conflict resolution. *Small Group Research, 39,* 278–302.

Gruenfeld, D.H. (1995). Status, ideology and integrative complexity in the U.S. Supreme Court: rethinking the politics of political decision making. *Journal of Personality and Social Psychology, 68,* 5–20.

Hewstone, M. & Martin, R. (2008). Social influence. In M. Hewstone, W. Stroebe & K. Jonas (eds), *Introduction to Social Psychology* (4th edition, pp. 216–43). Malden, MA: Blackwell Publishing.

Janis, I.L. (1971). Groupthink. *Psychology Today, 5,* 308–17.

Janis, I.L. (1972). *Victims of Groupthink: A Psychological Study of Foreign-Policy Decisions and Fiascoes.* Oxford: Houghton Mifflin.

Jehn, K. (1995). A multi-method examination of the benefits and detriments of intragroup conflict. *Administrative Science Quarterly, 40,* 256–82.

Jehn, K. (1997). A qualitative analysis of conflict types and dimensions in organizational groups. *Administrative Science Quarterly, 42,* 530–57.

Jehn, K.A. & Bendersky, C. (2003). Intragroup conflict in organizations: a contingency perspective on the conflict-outcome relationship. In R.M. Kramer & B.M. Staw (eds), *Research in Organizational Behavior: An Annual Series of Analytical Essays and Critical Reviews. Research in Organizational Behavior* (Vol. 25, pp. 187–242). Oxford: Elsevier.

Jehn, K.A. & Mannix, E.A. (2001). The dynamic nature of conflict: a longitudinal study of intra-group conflict and group performance. *Academy of Management Journal, 44,* 238–51.

Jehn, K., Northcraft, G. & Neale, M. (1999). Why differences make a difference: a field study of diversity, conflict, and performance in workgroups. *Administrative Science Quarterly, 44,* 741–63.

Jetten, J., Hornsey, M.J., Spears, R., Haslam, S.A. & Cowell, E. (2010) Rule transgressions in groups: the conditional nature of newcomers' willingness to confront deviance. *European Journal of Social Psychology, 40,* 338–48.

Johnson v. Louisiana, 406, U.S., 356 (1972).

Kahpor-Klein, F. & Kahlon, M. (2004). Discrimination and Americans' dreams. *HOW FAIR.* Level Playing Field Institute and the University of Connecticut.

Kanter, R.M. (1988). When a thousand flowers bloom: structural, collective and social conditions for innovation in organizations. In B. Staw & L.L. Cummings (eds), *Research in Organizational Behavior* (Vol. 10, pp. 169–211). Greenwich, CT: JAI Press.

Latane, B. (1981). The psychology of social impact. *American Psychologist, 36,* 343–56.

LePine, J.A. & Van Dyne, L. (2001). Voice and cooperative behavior as contrasting forms of contextual performance: evidence of differential relationships with Big 5 personality characteristics and cognitive ability. *Journal of Applied Psychology, 86,* 326–36.

Mackie, D.M. (1987). Systematic and nonsystematic processing of majority and minority persuasive communications. *Journal of Personality and Social Psychology, 53,* 41–52.

Maslach, C., Stapp, J. & Santee, R. (1985). Individuation: conceptual analysis and assessment. *Journal of Personality and Social Psychology, 49,* 729–38.

Mill, J.S. (1979). *On Liberty.* New York: Penguin (originally published 1859).

Morrison, E.W. & Milliken, F.J. (2000). Organizational silence: a barrier to change and development in a pluralistic world. *Academy of Management Review, 25,* 706–25.

Moscovici, S. (1980). Toward a theory of conversion behavior. In L. Berkowitz (ed.), *Advances in Experimental Social Psychology* (Vol. 13) New York: Academic Press.

Moscovici, S. & Faucheux, C. (1972). Social Influence, conforming bias and the study of active minorities. In L. Berkowitz (ed.), *Advances in Experimental Social Psychology* (Vol. 13) New York: Academic Press.

Moscovici, S., Lage, E. & Naffrechoux, M. (1969). Influence of a consistent minority on the responses of a majority in a color perception task. *Sociometry, 32,* 365–80.

Moscovici, S. & Nemeth, C. (1974). *Social Influence: II. Minority Influence.* Oxford: Rand McNally.

Mugny, G. (1982). *The Power of Minorities.* London: Academic Press.

Mugny, G. & Papastamou, S. (1980). When rigidity does not fail: individualization and psychologization as resistances to the diffusion of minority innovations. *European Journal of Social Psychology, 10,* 43–61.

Mugny, G. & Perez, J.A. (1991). *The Social Psychology of Minority Influence.* New York: Cambridge University Press.

Nemeth, C. (1976). *A Comparison between Conformity and Minority Influence.* Paper presented to the International Congress of Psychology, Paris, France.

Nemeth, C. (1977). Interactions between jurors as a function of majority vs. unanimity decision rules. *Journal of Applied Social Psychology, 7,* 38–56.

Nemeth, C. (1981). Jury trials: psychology and the law. In L. Berkowitz (ed.), *Advances in Experimental Social Psychology* (Vol. 14, pp. 309–67). New York: Academic Press.

Nemeth, C. (1986). Differential contributions of majority and minority influence. *Psychological Review, 93,* 23–32.

Nemeth, C. (1995). Dissent as driving cognition, attitudes and judgments. *Social Cognition, 13,* 273–91.

Nemeth, C. (1997). Managing innovation: when less is more. *California Management Review, 40.*

Nemeth, C. (2003). The requirement of unanimity, protection of minority views and the quality of the decision making. Invited address Jury Research Conference, University of Sydney Law School, Australia, October 2003.

Nemeth, C., Brown, K. & Rogers, J. (2001). Devil's advocate versus authentic dissent: stimulating quantity and quality. *European Journal of Social Psychology, 31*, 707–20.

Nemeth, C. & Chiles, C. (1988). Modeling courage: the role of dissent in fostering independence. *European Journal of Social Psychology, 18*, 275–80.

Nemeth, C. & Goncalo, J.A. (2005). Influence and persuasion in small groups. In T.C. Brock & M.C. Green (eds), *Persuasion: Psychological Insights and Perspectives* (pp. 171–94). London: Sage.

Nemeth, C. & Kwan, J.L. (1985). Originality of word associations as a function of majority vs. minority influence. *Social Psychology Quarterly, 48*, 277–82.

Nemeth, C. & Kwan, J.L. (1987). Minority influence, divergent thinking and detection of correct solutions. *Journal of Applied Social Psychology, 17*, 788–99.

Nemeth, C.J. & Nemeth-Brown, B. (2003). Better than individuals? The potential benefits of dissent and diversity for group creativity. In P. Paulus & B. Nijstad (eds), *Group Creativity: Innovation through Collaboration* (pp. 63–84). Oxford: Oxford University Press.

Nemeth, C. & Rogers, J. (1996). Dissent and the search for information. *British Journal of Social Psychology. Special Issue: Minority Influences, 35*, 67–76.

Nemeth, C.J. & Staw, B.M. (1989). The tradeoffs of social control and innovation in small groups and organizations. In L. Berkowitz (ed.), *Advances in Experimental Social Psychology* (Vol. 22, pp. 175–210). New York: Academic Press.

Nemeth, C., Swedlund, M. & Kanki, B. (1974). Patterning of a minority's responses and their influence on the majority. *European Journal of Social Psychology, 4*, 53–64.

Nemeth, C. & Wachtler, J. (1974). Creating the perceptions of consistency and confidence: a necessary condition for minority influence. *Sociometry, 37*, 529–40.

Nemeth, C. & Wachtler, J. (1983). Creative problem solving as a result of majority vs. minority influence. *European Journal of Social Psychology, 13*, 45–55.

Packer, D.J. (2008). On being both with us and against us: a normative conflict model of dissent in social groups. *Personality and Social Psychology Review, 12*, 50–72.

Peterson, R.S., Owens, P.D., Tetlock, P.E., Fan, E.T. & Martorana, P.V. (1998). Group dynamics in top management teams: groupthink, vigilance and alternative models of organizational failure and success. *Organizational Behavior and Human Decision Processes, 73*, 272–305.

Petty, R.E. & Cacioppo, J.T. (1981). *Attitudes and Persuasion – Classic and Contemporary Approaches.* Dubuque, IA: William C. Brown.

Postmes, T., Spears, R. & Cihangir, S. (2001). Quality of group decision making and group norms. *Journal of Personality and Social Psychology, 80*, 918–30.

Schachter, S. (1951). Deviation, rejection and communication. *Journal of Abnormal and Social Psychology, 46*, 190–207.

Simons, T. & Peterson, R. (2000). Task conflict and relationship conflict in top management teams: the pivotal role of intragroup trust. *Journal of Applied Psychology, 83*, 102–11.

Staw, B.M (1995). Why no one really wants creativity. In C.M. Ford & D.A. Gioia (eds), *Creative Action in Organizations: Ivory Tower Visions and Real World Voices* (pp. 161–72). Thousand Oaks, CA: Sage.

Van Dyne, L., Ang, S. & Botero, I.C. (2003). Conceptualizing employee silence and employee voice as multi-dimensional constructs. *Journal of Management Studies, 40*, 1360–92.

Van Dyne, L. & LePine, J.A. (1998). Helping extra-role behavior: evidence of a construct and predictive validity. *Academy of Management Journal, 41*, 108–19.

Van Dyne, L. & Saavedra, R. (1996). A naturalistic minority influence experiment: effects of divergent thinking, conflict and originality in work groups. *British Journal of Social Psychology, 35*, 151–68.

Von Hippel, E., Thomke, S. & Sonnack, M. (1999). Creating breakthroughs at 3M. *Harvard Business Review, 77*, 47–57.

Wood, W., Lundgren, S., Ouellette, J.A., Busceme, S. & Blackstone, T. (1994). Minority influence: a meta-analytic review of social influence processes. *Psychological Bulletin, 115*, 323–45.

3

Learning from Conflict

Fabrizio Butera, Céline Darnon and Gabriel Mugny

Do only rebels induce dissent in groups? In the present chapter, we contend that dissent from others' points of view should not be the prerogative of some particularly committed individuals, but rather a customary and promoted activity whenever learning is concerned. Indeed, dissent occurring during group or peer learning favours cognitive development and knowledge acquisition. We present a theory of socio-cognitive conflict, which argues that dissent from one or several partners over a task in which learning is concerned may stimulate task-related cognitive activity and result in progress. Should, therefore, socio-cognitive conflict be prescribed in educational settings? We address these questions by drawing on research pointing out that socio-cognitive conflict is beneficial for learning to the extent that conflict is regulated in an epistemic manner; that is, by focusing on the task or on the knowledge at hand. On the contrary, socio-cognitive conflict can result in detrimental effects whenever conflict is regulated in a relational manner, that is, by focusing on status and on interpersonal dominance.

This distinction is of importance with respect to the question of the usability of socio-cognitive conflict, as recent research has shown that the two forms of conflict regulation are predicted by different achievement goals. Epistemic regulation is predicted by mastery goals (the will to acquire knowledge and develop competences), and relational regulation is predicted by performance goals (the will to demonstrate competence relative to others). We argue that, although mastery goals are inherent to education, educational organisations also promote performance goals through evaluation and selection. In this respect they create the conditions for conflicts

Rebels in Groups: Dissent, Deviance, Difference and Defiance Jolanda Jetten and Matthew J. Hornsey

to be regulated in a relational manner, which is detrimental for learning. We conclude the chapter by reflecting upon the goals promoted by educational organisations that may favour or hinder the constructive effects for learning of socio-cognitive conflict.

Socio-Cognitive Conflict

In the introduction to this book (see Chapter 1), it is argued that social psychology, by giving a prominent place to the study of such phenomena as obedience and conformity, conveys the notion that these behaviours are the default within groups and that dissent rarely occurs. Indeed, social psychology has repeatedly shown that confronting a point of view that differs from one's own is not comfortable. People usually prefer information that confirms their own views (Festinger, 1957; Freedman & Sears, 1965; Frey, 1986), being exposed to familiar arguments (Begg, Anas & Farinacci, 1992; Zajonc, 1968), and being surrounded by similar others (Brehm, 1992; Byrne, 1971; Newcomb, 1961) rather than facing difference. Dissent is often described as a disturbing behaviour. And indeed, research on group processes has shown that dissent is seen as a threat for group locomotion and, as a consequence, leads to rejection (Festinger, 1950; Schachter, 1951). This is why dissent is so often avoided in social interactions.

Unfortunately, learning settings – be they the classroom, the university system, or other forms of training – are no exception, and one must admit that conformity and obedience are indeed the norm. The vast majority of educational organisations rely upon a classic unilateral teaching structure, in which the learner is asked to assimilate a number of pieces of knowledge that are presented as true by the teacher. Little time and space are left to questioning and arguing, with the notable exception of a small minority of alternative pedagogical systems. Indeed, in most educational organisations, students encounter relatively few opportunities to endorse a counter-normative point of view. They are socialised in a way that favours conformity to their teachers' view (Dambrun *et al.*, 2009; Guimond & Palmer, 1990), and they are rarely encouraged to endorse dissenting points of views. If they do, they take the risk of being sanctioned (e.g., by receiving a low grade).

We have referred to this state of affairs as unfortunate because research in social psychology clearly points out that dissent is a particularly powerful tool to promote learning (Buchs *et al.*, 2004; Doise & Mugny, 1984; Johnson & Johnson, 1993). A great many studies have demonstrated that – although unpleasant – unfamiliar arguments (Garcia-Marques & Mackie, 2001), diverging evidence (Kruglanski, 1980), opposing views (Nemeth, 1986), disconfirmatory information (Toma & Butera, 2009) and counterintuitive findings (Berlyne, 1960; Piaget, 1985) can generate deeper information processing and more elaborate knowledge than being confronted by familiar arguments or confirmatory evidence. Thus, should dissent be promoted in environments that are designed to help people construct and develop knowledge?

In this section, we focus on socio-cognitive conflict theory, developed within the field of developmental social psychology (Doise & Mugny, 1984; Doise & Palmonari, 1984; Mugny, Perret-Clermont & Doise, 1981). The theory states that social interaction represents the very context for progress and learning, precisely because the diversity in training, knowledge and points of view across group or dyad members has the potential to create dissent and discussion. Dissent occurring during social interaction has been termed 'socio-cognitive conflict', because it is both social (it entails disagreement between two or more persons) and cognitive (as disagreement leads each individual to doubt her/his own answer).

Socio-cognitive conflict can promote learning, understanding and cognitive development for several reasons. Facing dissent may lead to the realisation that a different point of view than one's own is possible, and therefore produces uncertainty (Butera, Mugny & Tomei, 2000; Darnon *et al.*, 2007; Hardin & Higgins, 1996). Indeed, if more than one answer is possible, one can come to question the validity of one's own answer, resulting in a sort of 'cognitive conflict' (see Berlyne, 1960; Limon, 2001; Piaget, 1985). Questioning the validity of one's own answer may then lead one to 'decentre' from one's point of view and take seriously into account the other's position (cf. Butera & Buchs, 2005). To account for the existence of different points of view, one must process and understand the elements that might explain why another person holds another position, which can result in an increase in knowledge. In sum, socio-cognitive conflict prompts individuals to reconsider their own point of view and to integrate the others'.

This theory has received abundant empirical support, showing the benefit of socio-cognitive conflict on learning and on the quality of reasoning. For instance, in an early study, children were confronted with a conservation-of-equal-length task (Doise, Mugny & Perret-Clermont, 1976). In this task, two pieces of railway track equal in length were presented to each child. When the two pieces are aligned so that they start and finish at the same point, any child is capable of recognising that they are equal. Non-conserving children, however, consider that they are unequal when the experimenter pushes one of the pieces so that the two are no longer aligned, since perceptually one sticks out and seems to outmeasure the other. The experiment was conducted with non-conserving children only. The experimenter reacted to the non-conserving answer given by the child ('this piece is longer because it sticks out here') in two different ways, according to the experimental condition. In the 'same-level-conflict' condition, the experimenter used the same argument as the child ('this piece is longer because it sticks out here'), but pointing to the other piece of track. Thus, the experimenter disagreed with the child, but also gave a wrong answer based on the same non-conserving reasoning. In the 'higher-level-conflict' condition, the experimenter used a compensatory conservation argument and gave the right answer ('the two pieces are equal in length, as this one sticks out here, but the other one sticks out there'). In the control condition, the experimenter did not contradict the child. Results showed progress on a delayed post-test for the two conflict conditions, as compared to the control condition. In other words, the 'same-level-conflict' condition also induced a higher degree of progress than the control condition, although – unlike the 'higher-level-conflict' condition – the answer proposed was just as wrong as the child's. This shows the crucial role of conflict in promoting learning.

In the same vein, Ames and Murray (1982) found significant progress when dyads of non-conserving children were composed by pairing two children who had previously given different, incorrect, answers. It is then not necessary that one of the children knows the correct answer to observe progress; it is sufficient that they are in conflict. In sum, research has shown in the past 30 years that socio-cognitive conflict can be beneficial for learning and cognitive development (cf. Darnon, Butera & Mugny, 2008; Doise, Mugny & Pérez, 1998; Perret-Clermont & Nicolet, 2001; Quiamzade *et al.*, 2006).

Two Forms of Conflict Regulations

The above conclusion may have conveyed the idea that socio-cognitive conflict is an all-purpose remedy to foster learning and cognitive development. In this respect, it could be viewed as a solution to the aforementioned pervasiveness of pedagogical methods based on conformity and obedience. After all, this research has been available for a long time, as has cooperative learning research and practice, which also places an emphasis on the beneficial effects of conflict (named controversy in this research tradition; see Johnson & Johnson, 1985, 1993; Johnson, Johnson & Tjosvold, 2000). However, research also shows that conflict may result in detrimental effects on learning (e.g., Buchs *et al.*, 2010; Butera & Mugny, 2001; Darnon, Buchs & Butera, 2002; Quiamzade, Tomei & Butera, 2000). Thus, research has focused on the conditions under which socio-cognitive conflict can be beneficial or detrimental for learning.

The effects of socio-cognitive conflict on learning largely depend on the way the conflict is regulated by the partners (Mugny, De Paolis & Carugati, 1984). Indeed, socio-cognitive conflict during an interaction with a partner has two distinct facets. On the one hand, the existence of an alternative point of view casts doubt on the validity of one's own answer. On the other hand, this implies that the other person might be right and, as a consequence, she/he might be more competent than oneself. The result is that socio-cognitive conflict can yield two distinct consequences. It can make individuals doubt the validity of their own knowledge, which can represent an interesting potential for engagement in the task, epistemic curiosity and cognitive reconstruction (Berlyne, 1960; Ohlsson, 1996; Piaget, 1985). However, conflict can also threaten self-competence (Butera & Mugny, 2001; Pool, Wood & Leck, 1998; Quiamzade & Mugny, 2001). Thus, socio-cognitive conflict can be regulated in two distinct ways. If the focus is on the doubt raised about the validity or accuracy of different answers, individuals can try to work through the problem again and examine the validity of each proposition. Previous research has termed this form of regulation 'epistemic conflict regulation', as it is centred on the correctness or validity of knowledge (cf. Quiamzade & Mugny, 2001). If, however, the focus is on the possibility of being less competent than the partner – especially in tasks in which competence is highly valued (Mugny *et al.*, 2003) – lower competence can affect a person's perception of self-worth (Covington, 1984, 1992; Steele, 1988; Tesser, 1988), and lead the individual to defend his/her own competence, for example by demonstrating that he/she is right and that the partner is wrong. Previous research has termed this form of regulation 'relational conflict regulation', as it is centred on the relative status of the partners (Darnon *et al.*, 2002; Mugny *et al.*, 1984).

Over the years, research on socio-cognitive conflict has accumulated converging evidence that epistemic and relational conflict regulations are related to different perceptions of the task and the other person (Mugny *et al.*, 1984, 2003; Butera & Mugny, 2001; Quiamzade, 2007; Quiamzade & Mugny, 2001). For instance, it has been shown that epistemic regulation is favoured when individuals believe in the complementarity of their points of views (Butera *et al.*, 1998; Butera *et al.*, 2000; Butera & Mugny, 2001; Johnson, Johnson & Smith, 2000; Quiamzade, Mugny & Darnon, 2009). On the contrary, socio-cognitive conflict is regulated in a relational way when the other person has the potential to be a competitor (e.g., Butera & Mugny, 1995; Butera *et al.*, 1998, 2000; Darnon *et al.*, 2002; Johnson & Johnson, 1985; Quiamzade & Mugny, 2009) or is susceptible to upstage one's competence (Butera *et al.*, 2000; Quiamzade, Tomei & Butera, 2000; Tjosvold, Johnson & Fabrey, 1980).

A recent experiment illustrates these dynamics (Darnon, Doll & Butera, 2007). University students participated in a fictitious computer-mediated interaction about a text with a bogus partner who introduced through her/his rhetoric either an epistemic conflict (a conflict that referred to the content of the text), or a relational conflict (a conflict that questioned participants' competence). Results indicated that compared to the epistemic conflict, the relational conflict enhanced threat and reduced the perceived contribution of the partner. Moreover, after a relational conflict, participants were more assertive in their answers, justified them to a lower extent, and expressed less doubt than after an epistemic conflict. Results also indicated that the intensity of disagreement predicted different modes of regulation depending on the conflict type. When the conflict was epistemic, the stronger the perceived conflict, the more participants said they worked through the problem to understand it better and tried to integrate the two points of views, that is, the more they regulated the conflict in an epistemic way. On the contrary, after a relational conflict, the stronger the perceived conflict, the more participants said they tried to assert they were right and the other person was wrong, that is, the more they engaged in a relational regulation of the conflict. Finally, epistemic conflict elicited better learning than relational conflict. Thus, the above line of research specifies that socio-cognitive conflict is beneficial for learning to the extent that conflict is regulated in an epistemic manner, but it can result in detrimental effects whenever conflict is regulated in a relational manner.

Two Goals Predicting Conflict Regulations

The above research provides a caveat for the use of socio-cognitive conflict in educational organisations. Practitioners should be aware that the construction of teaching methods that rely upon interpersonal interaction, cooperation and confrontation of viewpoints is to be implemented in an environment that focuses pupils, students or trainees on the development of knowledge and not on a competitive social comparison of competences. This caveat might seem trivial, but a longstanding area of research has shown that several goals may be at work when learning. Indeed, achievement situations, such as those in which the individual must carry out a school-related or academic task, are situations in which competence is at stake (Nicholls, 1984; Pérez & Mugny, 1996). However, how do people establish their own competence? Making progress and improving one's mastery of the task is one way. Trying to appear superior to others is another. In the eyes of researchers on achievement goals, the choice between these options depends on the extent to which different types of goals are endorsed in a specific task. It seems that two main types of goals exist: mastery goals and performance goals (see for reviews Dweck, 1986; Pintrich & Schunk, 2002). Mastery goals – also called learning goals (Dweck, 1986, 1992) or task-involvement goals (Nicholls, 1984) – correspond to the desire to learn, to understand the problem, to acquire new knowledge or to increase task-mastery. Competence, in this context, is therefore defined in terms of personal progress. Performance goals, on the other hand – also called ego-involvement goals (Nicholls, 1984) or relative competence goals (Butler, 1992; Urdan, 1997) – correspond to the desire to promote one's capacities and competences, to engender a positive evaluation or to succeed and be better than others. In this case competence evaluation is a question of competitive social comparison.[1]

With such a characterisation of achievement goals, it appears that there might be a parallel between mastery goals and epistemic conflict regulation, on the one hand, and between performance goals and relational conflict regulation on the other hand. This hypothesis has been tested by Darnon *et al.* (2006). In a first study, French introductory psychology students – for whom mastery and performance self-set goals had been recorded – were asked to imagine a discussion with another person who disagreed with them about an experiment they had studied in class during the previous semester. They were then asked to report to what extent during this 'debate' they would try to regulate the conflict in an epistemic way or a relational way. Items related to epistemic regulation asked students to what extent when disagreements occurred they would try: (a) to think about the text again in order to understand better; (b) to examine the conditions under which each point of view could help them understand; and (c) to think of a solution that could integrate both points of view. Items related to relational regulation asked students to what extent when disagreements occurred they would try: (a) to show they were right; (b) to resist by maintaining their initial position; and (c) to show their partner was wrong. Results indicated that mastery goals positively predicted the reported amount of epistemic conflict regulation whereas performance goals positively predicted the reported amount of relational conflict regulation.

Although results of this study showed that endorsed goals do predict different modes of conflict regulation assessed using self-reported intentions, one could argue that conflict regulation is a less conscious process and that these measures of conflict regulation are perhaps too sensitive to social desirability effects. Moreover, participants were just led to imagine they interacted with another person who disagreed. It is possible to think that this situation, since it implies a fictitious interaction, does not reflect how people react when they have to face a real conflict. To examine these issues in a more realistic context, participants of a second study were placed in a real, standardised conflict situation to provide evidence of the link between achievement goals and conflict regulation strategies using a more subtle measure of conflict regulation; that is, the competence attributed to oneself and to the person who disagreed. The study was conducted with 10th grade French students. In a first stage, participants were asked to fill out a questionnaire assessing achievement goals. One week later, they were invited to participate in a 'computer-mediated cooperative learning study', a task inducing a conflict with a bogus partner. When this task was over, participants were asked to report their perceived self-competence as well as the 'partner's' competence. Two weeks later, participants had the opportunity to ask for some information about the experiment: a more detailed version of the text studied during this experiment, the grade they obtained on a test about it, or both. Results indicated that mastery goals positively predicted reports of the other's competence, whereas performance goals positively predicted reported self-competence. In addition, results also indicated that mastery goals significantly predicted the request for the text whereas performance goals predicted the request for the grade.

Taken together, the results of these two studies indicated that mastery and performance goals predicted different modes of conflict regulation. The first illustrated these links on a self-reported measure of conflict regulation, whereas the second study showed similar results on a different and more subtle measure of conflict regulation and in a real conflict situation. It also indicated that in an interpersonal situation, as was the case in individual situations (e.g., Butler, 1992), mastery goals favoured interest in 'instructive information' (the text), whereas performance goals favoured the search for 'normative evaluative information' (the grade).

Similar dynamics have been observed with manipulated goals. In one study (Darnon & Butera, 2007) participants interacted by discussing conflictual issues in a context enhancing either performance goals, mastery goals or no goals. Participants each received one text (one received Version A and the other received Version B), which contained four parts discussing a different psychological topic. For example, the first part of the texts was about coaction effects: Version A presented the social facilitation effect and Version B the social inhibition effect. Another part was about social judgement with Version A describing the assimilation effect and Version B the contrast effect. Thus, the experimental effects presented in the two texts seemed contradictory, although they were not incompatible. These texts were designed to enhance the opportunities of disagreement during the social interaction. Results indicated that the amount of disagreement during the interaction predicted epistemic conflict regulation in the mastery goal condition, but not in the two other conditions. Moreover, disagreement predicted relational conflict regulation in the performance goal condition, but not in the other two.

Importantly, achievement goals also interact with socio-cognitive conflict to predict actual learning. In a recent study (Darnon, Butera & Harackiewicz, 2007), participants were led to think they interacted with a partner via a computer, sharing opinions about a text that they were studying. Mastery and performance goals were manipulated. During the 'interaction', they received answers from this bogus partner either disagreeing or agreeing. Results showed that the condition in which mastery goals were induced led to better learning than the performance goals condition only when the partner disagreed. No differences between goal conditions were observed when the partner agreed. In other words, when conflict is elicited during interaction, mastery goals have the potential to make conflict constructive, and lead to better learning than performance goals.

The good news is that teachers can influence achievement goals by shaping classroom climate. Indeed, students are more likely to develop mastery goals when the intrinsic value of a task is explained to them, when the teacher does not engage in controlling behaviour, when there is recognition of effort, and when a reward structure based on personal progress is used (Ames, 1992; Ames & Ames, 1984; see Meece, Anderman & Anderman, 2006, for a review on the impact of classroom structure on student motivation and achievement). The knowledge generated by research on classroom climate provides teachers with the necessary information to set up an educational environment that fosters mastery goals, and therefore provides the ideal ground for socio-cognitive conflict to be regulated in an epistemic way that is conducive to improved learning. However, this research has also identified factors that enhance performance goals. Indeed, performance goals will be favoured in contexts characterised by extrinsic reward structures, controlling teacher behaviour or normative standards for assessment. The bad news is that these factors are commonplace in the majority of educational organisations. This means that, although most teachers would agree that education is about inducing mastery goals in students, educational organisations are structured in such a way as to promote performance goals as well, thereby confronting students with an ambivalent normative environment.

Two Functions of Educational Organisations

Numerous positive outcomes are thus associated with mastery goals, including a positive regulation of the conflict, whereas performance goals seem to represent mostly negative outcomes. Teachers should then promote mastery goals and discourage performance goals in classrooms, especially when they want to encourage exchanges between students and positive reaction to divergence. In the achievement goal literature, this is indeed what researchers recommend (e.g., Ames, 1992; Brophy, 2005). However, we have also pointed out that institutional goal promotion might not match these recommendations. Indeed, if educational organisations were solely concerned with learning, there is no doubt that mastery goals should be promoted, but not performance goals.

Another analysis leads to different predictions. Some sociologists have pointed out that in Western countries educational institutions have taken up the structuring role of assigning pupils and students to 'the place where they belong' in society by selecting them in such a way as to reproduce the social inequalities typical of liberal societies (see Bourdieu, Passeron & Nice, 1990). According to some economic analyses (see Arrow, 1973), universities serve as a 'filter' designed to determine the place one may occupy in the workplace. Indeed, many students enrol every year at university, but these large numbers will be heavily reduced before they reach the bachelor's or master's degree graduation level (OECD, 2006). Thus, it appears that the role of university is not only to educate people, but also to 'detect' who – among the millions of students who enrol every year – are the 'best' students, those who most 'deserve' a degree (Dornbusch, Glasgow & Lin, 1996). This means that if students are aware of this system, they might infer that in order to succeed they not only have to learn and improve their skills (i.e., mastery goals), but also have to make it through the 'filter' – that is, to perform better than their fellow students (i.e., performance goals).

Because of this very functioning, a profound ambivalence is embedded in achievement goal promotion in universities (Darnon *et al.*, 2009). Mastery goal promotion is recommended by most researchers. Thus, the student who strongly endorses mastery goals fulfils the teachers' motivations and aims and is consequently perceived as someone who is appreciated by teachers. This is not the case for performance goals, which are not valued by teachers in their discourse. However, the selection processes which the students have to go through in their university career implicitly indicate that, in order to succeed, they have not only to improve knowledge but also get better grades than other students. Thus, not only mastery goals but also performance goals are seen by students as effective tools to succeed at university (Darnon *et al.*, 2009; Dompnier *et al.*, 2008). In sum, it appears that students are aware of the two functions of university, namely education (apparent in teachers' official discourse) and selection (hidden in the university structure). This means that performance goals may interfere with mastery goals in shaping the students' social interactions and academic achievement.

Conclusions

Is socio-cognitive conflict a viable mechanism to implement in educational organisations characterised by the promotion of ambivalent norms? We have opened this chapter by presenting the theory of socio-cognitive conflict, as well as relevant research showing that dissent in learning settings may enhance the development of knowledge. However, we have also shown that socio-cognitive conflict is beneficial for learning only when conflict is regulated in an epistemic manner, since when it is regulated in a relational manner socio-cognitive conflict appears to result in detrimental effects. The question of the usability of socio-cognitive conflict is therefore linked to the means that educators have at their disposal to induce epistemic, and not relational, regulation. Research on achievement goals has pointed out that educators may have a grip on conflict regulation through the induction of achievement goals. Epistemic regulation is predicted by mastery goals, and relational regulation by performance goals. However, we have also shown that, notwithstanding the educators' intention, education takes place in organisations that are concerned with formation *and* selection. Since students seem to be aware of this double function of educational organisations, at least as far as university is concerned, teachers' attempts to promote mastery goals are doomed to be counteracted by the reality of selection devices, from normative grades to year-failing, from streaming to honour roll. Thus, while the mastery goals promoted by teachers may favour the constructive effects for learning of socio-cognitive conflict, the performance goals associated with the selection practices may represent a hindrance.

A few years ago, some of us ended an article by noting that 'it is important that teachers using conflict avoid performance issues (e.g., normative comparisons) and enhance epistemic issues (e.g., the construction of knowledge; Maehr & Midgley, 1991), in order to allow their students to benefit from this confrontation' (Darnon *et al.*, 2007, p. 68). In fact, there is not much more that teachers can do in their relationship with students. With some variations, teachers are already well committed to the promotion of mastery goals in their everyday practice. However, they can do more with respect to their acceptance and endorsement of the general structure with which educational organisations function. They can, indeed, put into question such structural devices as streaming, ranking or year-repetition, which will prompt performance goals whatever the teacher's ideology and teaching method. In such a context only, dissent will be perceived not as a threat but as a help, and thus promote learning, knowledge construction and development of new ideas.

Notes

1. Recent research suggests that each of these two types of goals can be further divided into approach and avoidance goals (Elliot & Harackiewicz, 1996; Elliot &

McGregor, 2001). In this chapter, however, we will focus on the approach form of performance and mastery goals, the two goals which have been the most examined in the literature and, paradoxically, the two goals whose effects are still the objects of much debate (cf. Darnon, Butera & Harackiewicz, 2008).

Acknowledgements

This work was supported by the Swiss National Science Foundation and a Young Investigator project of the French Agence Nationale pour la Recherche (ANR-08-JCJC-0065-01).

References

Ames, C. (1992). Classrooms: goals, structures, and students' motivation. *Journal of Educational Psychology, 84*, 261–71.

Ames, C. & Ames, R.E. (1984). *Research on Motivation in Education: The Classroom Milieu* (Vol. 2). San Diego: Academic Press.

Ames, G.J. & Murray, F.B. (1982). When two wrongs make a right: promoting cognitive change by social conflict. *Developmental Psychology, 18*, 894–7.

Arrow, K. (1973). Higher education as a filter. *Journal of Public Economics, 2*, 193–216.

Begg, I.M., Anas, A. & Farinacci, S. (1992). Dissociation of processes in belief: source recollection, statement familiarity, and the illusion of truth. *Journal of Experimental Psychology, 121*, 446–58.

Berlyne, D.E. (1960). *Conflict, Arousal, and Curiosity.* New York: McGraw-Hill.

Bourdieu, P., Passeron, J.C. & Nice, J.P. (1990). *Reproduction in Education, Society and Culture.* London: Sage.

Brehm, S.S. (1992). *Intimate Relationships*, 4th edition. New York: McGraw-Hill.

Brophy, J. (2005). Goal theorists should move on from performance goals. *Educational Psychologist, 40*, 167–76.

Buchs, C., Butera, F., Mugny, G. & Darnon, C. (2004). Conflict elaboration and cognitive outcomes. *Theory into Practice, 43*, 23–30.

Buchs, C., Pulfrey, C., Gabarrot, F. & Butera, F. (2010). Competitive conflict regulation and informational dependence in peer learning. *European Journal of Social Psychology, 40*, 418–35.

Butera, F. & Buchs, C. (2005). Reasoning together: from focussing to decentring. In V. Girotto & P.N. Johnson-Laird (eds), *The Shape of Reason* (pp. 193–203). Hove: Psychology Press.

Butera, F., Gardair, E., Maggi, J. & Mugny, G. (1998). Les paradoxes de l'expertise: influence sociale et (in)compétence de soi et d'autrui [The paradox of expertise: social influence and self and others' (in)competence]. In J. Py, A. Somat & J. Baillé (eds), *Psychologie Sociale et Formation Professionnelle: Propositions Et Regards Critiques* (pp. 111–23). Rennes: Presses Universitaires de Rennes.

Butera, F. & Mugny, G. (1995). Conflict between incompetences and influence of a low expertise source in hypothesis testing. *European Journal of Social Psychology, 25*, 457–62.

Butera, F. & Mugny, G. (2001). Conflicts and social influences in hypothesis testing. In C.K.W. De Dreu & N.K. De Vries (eds), *Group Consensus and Minority Influence. Implications for Innovation* (pp. 161–82). Oxford: Blackwell.

Butera, F., Mugny, G. & Tomei, A. (2000). Incertitude et enjeux identitaires dans l'influence sociale [Uncertainty and identity stakes in social influence]. In J.-L. Beauvois, R.-V. Joule & J.-M. Monteil (eds), *Perspectives Cognitives et Conduites Sociales* (Vol. 7, pp. 205–29). Rennes: Presses Universitaires de Rennes.

Butler, R. (1992). What young people want to know when: effects of mastery and ability goals on interest in different kinds of social comparisons. *Journal of Personality and Social Psychology, 62*, 934–43.

Byrne, D. (1971). *The Attraction Paradigm.* New York: Academic Press.

Covington, M.V. (1984). The self-worth theory of achievement motivation: findings and implications. *Elementary School Journal, 85*, 5–20.

Covington, M.V. (1992). *Making the Grade: A Self-Worth Perspective on Motivation and School Reform.* New York: Cambridge University Press.

Dambrun, M., Kamiejski, R., Haddadi, N. & Duarte, S. (2009). Why does social dominance orientation decrease with university exposure to the social sciences? The impact of institutional socialization and the mediating role of 'geneticism'. *European Journal of Social Psychology, 39*, 88–100.

Darnon, C., Buchs, C. & Butera, F. (2002). Epistemic and relational conflict in sharing information during cooperative learning. *Swiss Journal of Psychology, 61*, 139–51.

Darnon, C. & Butera, F. (2007). Learning or succeeding? Conflict regulation with mastery or performance goals. *Swiss Journal of Psychology, 66*, 145–52.

Darnon, C., Butera, F. & Harackiewicz, J. (2007). Achievement goals in social interactions: learning with mastery vs. performance goals. *Motivation and Emotion, 31*, 61–70.

Darnon, C., Butera, F. & Harackiewicz, J.M. (guest eds) (2008). Toward a clarification of the effects of achievement goals. *International Review of Social Psychology, 21*, 1–2.

Darnon, C., Butera, F. & Mugny, G. (2008). *Des Conflits pour Apprendre* [Conflicts for learning]. Grenoble: Presses Universitaires de Grenoble.

Darnon, C., Doll, S. & Butera, F. (2007). Dealing with a disagreeing partner: relational and epistemic conflict elaboration. *European Journal of Psychology of Education, 22*, 227–42.

Darnon, C., Dompnier, B., Delmas, F., Pulfrey, C. & Butera, F. (2009). Achievement goal promotion at university: social desirability and social utility of mastery and performance goals. *Journal of Personality and Social Psychology, 96*, 119–34.

Darnon, C., Harackiewicz, J., Butera, F., Mugny, G.,& Quiamzade, A. (2007). Performance-approach and performance-avoidance goals: when uncertainty makes a difference. *Personality and Social Psychology Bulletin, 33*, 813–27.

Darnon, C., Muller, D., Schrager, S.M., Pannuzzo, N. & Butera, F. (2006). Mastery and performance goals predict epistemic and relational conflict regulation. *Journal of Educational Psychology, 98*, 766–76.

Doise, W. & Mugny, G. (1984). *The Social Development of the Intellect.* Oxford: Pergamon.

Doise, W., Mugny, G. & Pérez, J.A. (1998). The social construction of knowledge: social marking and socio-cognitive conflict. In U. Flick (ed.), *The Psychology of the Social* (pp. 77–90). Cambridge: Cambridge University Press.

Doise, W., Mugny, G. & Perret-Clermont, A. N. (1976). Social interaction and cognitive development: further evidence. *European Journal of Social Psychology, 6*, 245–7.

Doise, W. & Palmonari, A. (eds) (1984). *Social Interaction in Individual Development.* Cambridge: Cambridge University Press.

Dompnier, B., Darnon, C., Delmas, F. & Butera, F. (2008). Achievement goals and social judgment: the performance-approach paradox. *International Review of Social Psychology, 21*, 247–71.

Dornbusch, S.M., Glasgow, K.L. & Lin, I-C. (1996). The social structure of schooling. *Annual Review of Psychology, 47*, 401–29.

Dweck, C.S. (1986). Motivational processes affecting learning. *American Psychologist, 41*, 1040–8.

Dweck, C.S. (1992). The study of goals in psychology. *Psychological Science, 3*, 165–7.

Elliot, A.J. & Harackiewicz, J.M. (1996). Approach and avoidance achievement goals and intrinsic motivation: a mediational analysis. *Journal of Personality and Social Psychology, 70*, 461–75.

Elliot, A.J. & McGregor, H.A. (2001). A 2*2 achievement goal framework. *Journal of Personality and Social Psychology, 80*, 501–19.

Festinger, L. (1950). Informal social communication. *Psychological Review, 57*, 271–82.

Festinger, L. (1957). *A Theory of Cognitive Dissonance*. Stanford: Stanford University Press.

Freedman, J.L. & Sears, D.O. (1965). Selective exposure. In L. Berkowitz (ed.), *Advances in Experimental Social Psychology* (Vol. 1, pp. 58–97). New York: Academic Press.

Frey, D. (1986). Recent research on selective exposure to information. In L. Berkowitz (ed.), *Advances in Experimental Social Psychology* (Vol. 19, pp. 41–80). San Diego, CA: Academic Press.

Garcia-Marques, T. & Mackie, D.M. (2001). The feeling of familiarity as a regulator of persuasive processing. *Social Cognition, 19*, 9–34.

Guimond, S. & Palmer, D.L. (1990). Type of academic training and causal attributions for social problems. *European Journal of Social Psychology, 20*, 61–75.

Hardin, C.D. & Higgins, E.T. (1996). Shared reality: how social verification makes the subjective objective. In R.M. Sorrentino & E.T. Higgins (eds), *Handbook of Motivation and Cognition* (Vol. 3, pp. 28–84). New York: Guilford Press.

Johnson, D.W. & Johnson, R.T. (1985). Classroom conflict: controversy versus debate in learning groups. *American Educational Research Journal, 22*, 237–56.

Johnson, D.W. & Johnson, R.T. (1993). Structuring academic controversy. In S. Sharan (ed.), *Handbook of Cooperative Learning Methods*. Westport: Greenwood.

Johnson, D.W., Johnson, R.T. & Smith, K. (2000). Constructive controversy: the educative power of intellectual conflict. *Change, 32*, 29–37.

Johnson, D.W., Johnson, R.T. & Tjosvold, D. (2000). Constructive controversy: the value of intellectual opposition. In M. Deutsch & P.T. Coleman (eds), *The Handbook of Conflict Resolution: Theory and Practice* (pp. 65–85). San Francisco: Jossey-Bass.

Kruglanski, A.W. (1980). Lay epistemo-logic-process and contents: another look at attribution theory. *Psychological Review, 87*, 70–87.

Limon, M. (2001). On the cognitive conflict as an instructional strategy for conceptual change: a critical appraisal. *Learning and Instruction, 11*, 357–80.

Maehr, M.L. & Midgley, C. (1991). Enhancing students' motivation: a schoolwide approach. *Educational Psychologist, 26*, 399–427.

Meece, J.L., Anderman, E.M. & Anderman, L.H. (2006). Classroom goal structure, student motivation and academic achievement. *Annual Review of Psychology, 57*, 487–503.

Mugny, G., Butera, F., Quiamzade, A., Dragulescu, A. & Tomei, A. (2003). Comparaisons sociales des compétences et dynamiques d'influence sociale dans les tâches d'aptitudes [Social comparison and social influence in aptitude tasks]. *L'Année Psychologique, 104*, 469–96.

Mugny, G., De Paolis, P. & Carugati, F. (1984). Social regulations in cognitive development. In W. Doise & A. Palmonari (eds), *Social Interaction in Individual Development* (pp. 127–46). Cambridge: Cambridge University Press.

Mugny, G., Perret-Clermont, A.N. & Doise, W. (1981). Interpersonal coordinations and sociological differences in the construction of the intellect. In G.M. Stephenson & J.H. Davis (eds), *Progress in Applied Social Psychology* (Vol. 1, pp. 315–43). Chichester: John Wiley & Sons.

Nemeth, C.J. (1986). The differential contributions of majority and minority influence. *Psychological Review, 93*, 23–32.

Newcomb, T.M. (1961). *The Acquaintance Process.* New York: Holt, Rinehart & Winston.

Nicholls, J.G. (1984). Achievement motivation: conceptions of ability, subjective experience, task choice, and performance. *Psychological Review, 91*, 328–46.

OECD (2006). *Education at a Glance. OECD Indicators, 2006.* OECD Publishing.

Ohlsson, S. (1996). Learning from performance errors. *Psychological Review, 103*, 241–62.

Pérez, J.A. & Mugny, G. (1996). The conflict elaboration theory of social influence. In E.H. Witte & J.H. Davis (eds), *Understanding Group Behavior: Small Group Processes and Interpersonal Relations* (Vol. 2, pp. 191–210). Hillsdale, NJ: Lawrence Erlbaum.

Perret-Clermont, A.N. & Nicolet, M. (eds) (2001). *Interagir et Connaître. Enjeux et Régulations Sociales dans le Développement Cognitif* [Interaction and Knowledge. Social Issues and Regulations in Cognitive Development] Paris: L'Harmattan.

Piaget, J. (1985). *The Equilibration of Cognitive Structures: The Central Problem of Intellectual Development.* Chicago: University of Chicago Press.

Pintrich, P. & Schunk, D. (2002). *Motivation in Education: Theory, Research, and Applications.* Upper Saddle River, NJ: Merrill Prentice-Hall.

Pool, G.J., Wood, W. & Leck, K. (1998). The self-esteem motive in social influence: agreeing with valued majorities and disagreeing with derogated minorities. *Journal of Personality and Social Psychology, 75*, 967–75.

Quiamzade, A. (2007). Imitation and performance in confrontations between competent peers: the role of the representation of the task. *European Journal of Psychology of Education, 22*, 243–58.

Quiamzade, A. & Mugny, G. (2001). Social influence dynamics in aptitude tasks. *Social Psychology of Education, 4*, 311–34.

Quiamzade, A. & Mugny, G. (2009). Social influence and threat in confrontations between competent peers. *Journal of Personality and Social Psychology, 97*, 652–66.

Quiamzade, A., Mugny, G. & Darnon, C. (2009). The coordination of problem-solving strategies: when low competence sources exert more influence than high competence sources. *British Journal of Social Psychology, 48*, 159–82.

Quiamzade, A., Mugny, G., Falomir, J.M. & Chatard, A. (2006). De la psychologie sociale développementale à l'influence sociale dans les tâches d'aptitudes [From developmental social psychology to social influence in aptitude tasks]: retour sur l'ontogénèse de la notion de conflit sociocognitif dans l'école genevoise. In R.-V. Joule & P. Huguet (eds), *Bilans et Perspectives en Psychologie Sociale* (Vol. 1, pp. 171–205). Grenoble: Presses Universitaires de Grenoble.

Quiamzade, A., Tomei, A. & Butera, F. (2000). Informational dependence and informational constraint: social comparison and social influences in an anagram resolution task. *International Review of Social Psychology, 15*, 123–50.

Schachter, S. (1951). Deviation, rejection, and communication. *Journal of Abnormal and Social Psychology, 46*, 190–207.

Steele, C.M. (1988). The psychology of self-affirmation: sustaining the integrity of the self. In L. Berkowitz (ed.), *Advances in Experimental Social Psychology* (Vol. 21, pp. 261–302). San Diego, CA: Academic Press.

Tesser, A. (1988). Toward a self-evaluation maintenance model of social behavior. In L. Berkowitz (ed.), *Advances in Experimental Social Psychology* (Vol. 21, 181–227). San Diego, CA: Academic Press.

Tjosvold, D., Johnson, D.W.,& Fabrey, L.J. (1980). Effect of controversy and defensiveness on cognitive perspective taking. *Psychological Reports, 47*, 1043–53.

Toma, C. & Butera, F. (2009). Hidden profiles and concealed information: strategic information sharing and use in group decision making. *Personality and Social Psychology Bulletin, 35*, 793–806.

Urdan, T. (1997). Achievement goal theory: past results, future directions. In M. Maehr & P. Pintrich (eds), *Advances in Motivation and Achievement* (Vol. 10, pp. 99–141). Greenwich, CT: JAI.

Zajonc, R.B. (1968). Attitudinal effects of mere exposure. *Journal of Personality and Social Psychology, 9*, 1–27.

4

From Current State to Desired Future

How Compositional Changes Affect Dissent and Innovation in Work Groups

Floor Rink and Naomi Ellemers

Differences between group members in the knowledge, expertise and information they bring to the group can be a crucial resource. If managed effectively, intragroup dissent can foster innovation and change (see Nemeth & Goncalo, this volume). However, such differences are often not acknowledged and deviant views are suppressed due to socialisation pressures and the desire to fit in (see also Levine & Choi, this volume). In this chapter we focus on the reasons why, and the conditions under which, new group members are inclined to adapt to existing ways instead of voicing their dissent. Additionally, we examine some of the factors that are likely to make existing group members more or less open to the dissent and change represented by new group members. These insights can help create conditions that increase the tolerance for dissent in work groups, as a way to optimally benefit from the opportunities for innovation offered by compositional changes in work groups.

Compositional changes are a fact of organisational life. While new employees enter the organisation to strengthen the work force, existing employees may change positions or find a job elsewhere. In this chapter, we address the notion that changes in work-group composition can have beneficial as well as detrimental effects on the level of dissent and innovation within such groups. We argue that the behaviours that are functional for individuals to gain or maintain their position within a changing work group (i.e. to display concordant behaviour and to inhibit dissent) may be counterproductive for the group as a whole (Rink & Ellemers, 2009). We will first review current insights on how changes in group composition

Rebels in Groups: Dissent, Deviance, Difference and Defiance Jolanda Jetten and Matthew J. Hornsey

relate to dissent and group innovation. Subsequently, we will present evidence from three recent strands of research showing that the consequences of group compositional changes depend on: (a) the performance attributions that groups make; (b) the expectations group members have of each other and of the newly created situation; and (c) the self-esteem of individual group members. We will conclude by outlining some practical implications that can be derived from these studies, and indicate directions for future theory development and research.

Changes in Group Composition

Most work groups acknowledge that change is inevitable in organisations, and in some cases a necessity for group progress or survival. Yet, at the same time, members of work groups tend to fear the disruption and insecurity that comes along with change. Indeed, it is not always self-evident how new group members, or changes in existing group positions, can be beneficial. This is an important reason why the desire for change does not automatically imply a tolerance for dissent and innovation. Yet, group innovation – or the origination and implementation of new ideas, products, services or processes in groups – is for a large part dependent on the effective use of the unique skills, abilities and knowledge that each individual group member possesses (De Dreu & West, 2001). It is therefore important to examine the conditions under which group compositional changes induce or prevent individual group members to speak up and challenge the status quo.

The introduction of newcomers

Previous research in this area has mainly focused on the effects of *newcomers* on dissent and innovation in work groups (see Levine & Choi, this volume). This work has shown that groups are more open to newcomer influence when such change is frequent so that they have become accustomed to changes in their group's composition (Ziller, 1965). Additionally, newcomer influence is more likely to be accepted in groups that have a history of failure, and in groups working according to a strategy that is assigned to them rather than chosen (Choi & Levine, 2004). Finally, newcomers are more likely to be influential when they can communicate their ongoing attachment to the group (Hornsey *et al.*, 2007) or share a superordinate identity with existing group members (Hornsey, Trembath & Gunthorpe, 2004; Kane, Argote & Levine, 2005). These findings illustrate that newcomers can indeed increase innovation within groups and thus have positive effects on group performance (e.g. Choi & Levine, 2004; Kane, Argote & Levine, 2005). Yet, this prior research also suggests that work groups prefer newcomers who are seen as similar to them and adapt to the group, while they are more open to newcomer influence when this is not seen as a threat to the group's unity. Indeed, the preference for newcomer assimilation turns out to be highly robust, and is retained even after teams have benefited from the unique input of a newcomer (Kane & Rink, 2009).

In work groups, individuals often credit successful performance to the group as a whole because it reflects well on its members and fosters cohesion (Leary & Forsyth, 1987; Sherman & Kim, 2005). This can explain why work groups tend to reject newcomers who openly express their unique knowledge. As long as newcomers are not seen as representing the group as a whole, existing members are likely to feel threatened by the success of their actions, because they cannot easily take credit for or attribute this success to themselves. This resonates with research showing that people tend to respond defensively to criticism coming from someone located outside the group, while they establish greater tolerance when the same criticism is voiced by those who are perceived to have a psychological investment in the group (the intergroup sensitivity effect; Hornsey & Imani, 2004; Hornsey, Oppes & Svensson, 2002; Hornsey, Trembath & Gunthorpe, 2004). In a similar vein, to the extent that existing group members tend to see newcomers as 'outsiders', they are likely to question their motives and wonder whether they are really devoted to group goals. This suggests that newcomers need to demonstrate group loyalty and commitment in order to be fully accepted by existing group members and to be able to impact on group innovation (see also Nemeth & Owens, 1996). Even when newcomers are not seen as core group members, there are likely to be differences in the extent to which they are able to influence the group and enhance group innovation, due to the characteristics that they possess relative to others (Bunderson, 2003; Cohen & Zhou, 1991). We will address the effects this may have in the following section.

Newcomer similarity and performance expectations

People have the tendency to make 'performance appraisals' and develop *expectations* of others they work with on the basis of *specific* cues (e.g. their education, or their role in the team) as well as *diffuse* person characteristics (e.g. gender, age; see expectation states theory, Berger & Zelditch, 1998; Rink

& Ellemers, 2007). Over time, after group members have had the opportunity to get to know each other well, specific characteristics generally become more important than diffuse characteristics (Ridgeway, 2001). Nevertheless, people tend to rely on more easily accessible, diffuse cues when they first start working with somebody, or when they try to make sense of changing situations (Bargh *et al.*, 1992). For example, Chaiken and Maheswaran (1994) showed that, in an ambiguous context, the surface level characteristics of a dissenting group member (i.e., diffuse cues) determined their perceived credibility and the persuasive impact of their message, independently of the actual quality of their unique input (specific cues).

Thus, there is a fairly large body of literature indicating that the attributions groups make, and the expectations they develop about newcomers on the basis of specific or diffuse cues, have a profound influence on the extent to which dissent is accepted from newcomers, and the likelihood that group innovation may result from this. This is why it is important to understand the impact of such cues on the expectations people develop about newcomers and their likely contributions to the task. We argue that the interplay between diffuse and specific cues impacts on the expectations existing group members develop about the likelihood that newcomers will be similar to and fit in with the group. This in turn not only determines their anticipations about the contributions newcomers have to offer, but also affects newcomers' actual input to the group task.

Changes in existing positions

As indicated above, compositional changes are not only caused by the entry of newcomers into a work group. Existing group members – 'old-timers' – may also leave the group, or switch roles, and cause a shift in group dynamics. Relatively little work has as yet been done in this specific domain. Importantly, though, Jetten, Branscombe and Spears (2002) showed that providing group members with information about the likely direction of change from their position within a group affects *self-related concerns*. When group members expect to become more prototypical over time – implying they can gain a more stable and secure position as core group members (Noel, Wann & Branscombe, 1995) – their self-esteem will be higher than when they expect to remain peripheral. Those members who are in a peripheral position within a team generally report lower levels of self-esteem and aim to consolidate their position in the group. Interestingly, this finding illustrates that positional changes do not necessarily affect group members' level of identification with the work group or their willingness to invest in the group (Ellemers, Kortekaas & Ouwerkerk, 1999). When existing members are in a peripheral position, they may nevertheless remain highly attached to the team and report a rise in self-related concerns instead (see also Sleebos, Ellemers & De Gilder, 2006a, 2006b). Importantly, up to now it remains relatively unclear whether these self-related concerns in turn influence the task behaviour displayed by existing team members, and if so, how. To the extent that the group remains important to them, are they inclined to behave in ways that are viewed as indicating 'good' group membership and assimilate to group norms? Or will they believe that their chances of acceptance will increase when they show off their usefulness and value to the group by explicitly offering unique and divergent contributions (Phillips *et al.*, 2004)?

Overview of our research

In the next sections, we will discuss three research strands in which we have examined the questions raised above. In a first series of studies, we focused on the entry of newcomers in work groups, and examined whether their *structural* role within the group (i.e. whether they have a temporary versus permanent position within the group) affects the initial expectations the group develops about their likely contributions, i.e., as a *diffuse* cue of their potential and value for the group. We examine how these expectations in turn influence the likelihood that temporary versus permanent newcomers offer unique input to the group and actually deviate from existing practices. In a second line of research, we examine whether *specific* status cues that characterise a newcomer (i.e. whether or not their expertise is made clear to the group) can overcome the adverse effects of more diffuse cues (i.e. their perceived lack of prototypicality within the group) on group acceptance and newcomer influence. Finally, in a third series of studies, we focus on existing group members and examine the influence of their fear for positional change on self-related concerns, the expression of dissent and displays of innovative behaviour.

Future Prospects of Newcomers

In this first line of research we examined the extent to which temporary versus permanent newcomers express their unique knowledge in the work groups they enter. Importantly, in these studies both the newcomers with a temporary status and the groups they entered were well aware that their position was fixed term (as in the case of interim managers in organisations, or employees hired through a temporary employment agency). We argued that, during the initial phases of socialisation, the future prospects of newcomers can serve as a diffuse cue on the basis of which old-timers develop expectations about the newcomers' behaviour in the group (Chen & Klimoski, 2003; Rink & Ellemers, 2009). When it is clear that a newcomer will obtain a long-term, core position in the group, he or she is expected to fit in with the group's culture and to act in the interest of the collective (Feldman, Doerpinghaus & Turnley, 1994). Yet, groups are less likely to expect temporary newcomers to adapt to the group or to behave in accordance with existing practices (Kraimer *et al.*, 2005).

We obtained initial support for this reasoning in a scenario study in which we asked participants to think of themselves as a member of a team that has been working together for quite a while. They were instructed to imagine that management has decided to hire an additional member (either permanently or temporarily) for the team to be able to deal with all the work that needed to be done. The results showed that participants taking the perspective of existing team members indeed developed expectations about the (dis-)similarity of the newcomer to the rest of the team, solely on the basis of the newcomer's future prospects. These expectations in turn caused them to like and accept permanent newcomers more than temporary newcomers.

We then conducted two further studies in which we examined real teams of interacting students where a newcomer entered after the other members had been working together for several rounds of tasks. The task that the groups had to perform together with the newcomer was set up in such a way that unique input from the newcomer was needed in order to reach the objectively best decision outcome (i.e., a so-called 'hidden profile' task, Stasser & Titus, 1985; see also Rink & Ellemers, 2009). We found that the future prospects of a newcomer again served as a diffuse cue for groups, determining the amount of influence that the newcomer was allowed within the group. Nevertheless, groups still preferred newcomers who represented the least disruption. That is, the temporary newcomers were given more space to provide unique ideas, and actually enhanced the level of innovation and task performance within the groups, compared to permanent newcomers. Yet they were evaluated relatively negatively by the existing group members. By comparison, permanent newcomers, who were expected to adapt to the group, were evaluated more positively while they in fact contributed sub-optimally to the group task. These findings clearly illustrate the tension between socialisation pressures and newcomers' desire to fit in on the one hand, and the group's ability to allow for dissent and innovation in order to perform optimally on the other. Whereas newcomers who have the prospect of becoming permanent group members are expected to fit in and are liked most, temporary newcomers actually are best able to voice the dissent that helps optimise the group's performance.

Expert Status

In our second line of research, we conducted an interactive group study to examine whether an explicitly task-specific status cue can overrule the effects of more diffuse newcomer characteristics on newcomer influence and newcomer acceptance. With this study we set out to examine whether the provision of concrete information about specific task-relevant features or behaviours of others can help suppress the effects of stereotypical beliefs about these others that are based on more general (dis-)similarity assumptions (Krueger & Rothbart, 1988; Rink & Ellemers, 2007). We argued that groups should respond in a more accurate and objective way towards changes introduced by a newcomer when such attempts to influence the group are to be expected on the basis of the newcomer's specific expert status.

Expert status is a strong source of social power and influence, and can provide a newcomer with one of the greatest resources available to a problem-solving group (McGrath, 1984). When a newcomer is identified as an expert, and clearly possesses unique skills, knowledge and abilities, groups are more likely to realise that this person can be valuable for the group's performance (Bass, 1960; Moreland, 1999; see also Stasser, Stewart & Wittenbaum, 1995; Stewart & Stasser, 1995). We therefore predicted that newcomers with a high level of task competence would be given more space to offer unique input and to participate in group decision-making processes than newcomers who are low in task competence, regardless of whether they possess more diffuse characteristics that signal their overall similarity versus diversity to the group (i.e. perceived level of similarity with existing group members). This type of process has been referred to as the *Galatea effect*, a term used to indicate a performance gain that is achieved by raising other peoples' expectations about one's competence in relation to the task (Eden, 1984).

We examined the validity of this reasoning with a study in which groups worked on several tasks before a newcomer entered. Together with the newcomer, groups had to perform a murder mystery task (Stasser & Titus, 1985). This task was designed so that the evidence suggested three possible suspects. In this hidden profile task, two of the suspects could be ruled out and the task could thus be accomplished successfully if all unique information available to individual group members were exchanged and pooled together. Importantly, the relevant information was distributed such that the newcomer always possessed the unique key information that was needed for the group to be able to solve the mystery. Prior to newcomer entry, groups learned that the newcomer was either highly similar to or different from them in terms of general personality features (for a similar manipulation see Jetten *et al.*, 2003). Additionally, existing group members were informed that the newcomer was either highly competent and an expert in solving these types of tasks, or that the newcomer – just like the other members of the group – had no previous experience with this specific type of task.

The results of this study show that – in the absence of more explicitly task-relevant information – diffuse features (i.e., overall similarity in personality features) affected the impact of the newcomer on the group's performance. That is, when no specific information about newcomers' expertise was available, newcomers with personality features similar to the group tended to be seen as prototypical group members. As a result, they were expected to fit in and hence were less likely to enhance the group's performance by contributing their unique information. Conversely, the group was more likely to allow newcomers to provide unique input and newcomers actually exerted more influence on the group's performance to the extent that they were more clearly different from other group members in terms of their personality features, and were seen as more peripheral to the group. Importantly, though, this effect of overall (dis-)similarity to the group was overruled when more specific task-relevant cues were made available. That is, when groups were explicitly made aware of the newcomer's level of expertise and experience on this type of task, newcomers were more frequently allowed to communicate their unique information and were more effective in influencing the group to reach the best joint decision, regardless of their overall similarity or dissimilarity to other group members in terms of general personality features.

In sum, this research on the one hand demonstrates that diffuse cues can play an important role in how groups respond to newcomers and change, and again shows that similarity expectations can prevent newcomers from expressing dissent and hence undermine the group's performance on tasks that require creative thinking. On the other hand, we have seen that this general tendency to avoid dissent can be overruled by providing unambiguous information about task-relevant aspects, such as the actual level of expertise of a newcomer. That is, clearly communicating the potential contribution the newcomer has to offer to the group can help overcome socialisation pressures and make groups more open to change, even when it is still uncertain how loyal or prototypical to the group these newcomers actually are.

Position (In)security and Task Performance

In the studies discussed so far, we examined the extent to which newcomers and the unique input they could provide to the group impacted on expressions of dissent and group innovation. In our final line of research, we focus on the perspective of existing group members to examine how they respond to compositional changes in the group. Taking into account how existing group members respond to the introduction of newcomers allows us to more fully comprehend the dynamics involved in compositional changes in work groups. Whereas the introduction of newcomers may directly benefit the group because of the unique information and novel input they can provide, such changes in the group's composition may also have a more indirect impact by influencing the behaviour and task contributions of existing group members. That is, to the extent that the introduction of newcomers to the group also causes existing group members to more freely express their dissent, compositional changes might represent a collective benefit that enhances group innovation and change in different ways. In our research we specifically focused on the extent to which changes in the group's composition undermine the position security of existing group members (as in the case of downsizes or mergers in organisations). We argue that for existing members too, future prospects about the (dis-)continuation of their current position in the group likely affect their interpersonal relations with others in the group as well as their willingness to develop their own potential and to engage in innovative behaviour (Rink & Ellemers, 2009).

As indicated above, previous research has shown that changes in one's status position within a group raise self-related concerns, but (at least initially) have limited effect on the importance that people attach to their group membership. When people notice that changes in the group increase their own level of position security or status, they report higher levels of self-esteem. However, when their position becomes insecure, their group-based self-esteem is under threat (Jetten *et al.*, 2003). As yet, relatively little is known about the way in which the self-related concerns thus raised in turn influence dissent and innovative behaviour in the group.

Results from field studies suggest that job insecurity may undermine collective task performance as these studies reveal negative correlations between job insecurity and displays of helping behaviours towards others. This negative relation between job insecurity and helping behaviour is particularly pronounced when examining the tendency to help newcomers, who are seen as likely competitors for future positions (Ashford, Lee & Bobko, 1989; Broschak & Davies-Blake, 2006; Kraimer *et al.*, 2005; Pearce, 1998). At the same time, however, experimental studies have shown that those who do not feel respected by fellow group members in fact tend to display more effort on collective tasks than highly respected group members. This has been explained by arguing that these efforts help individual group members bolster their feelings of self-worth (Sleebos *et al.*, 2006a, 2006b), even if they have little hope of improving their reputation in the eyes of other group members, or of enhancing their acceptance into the group. To the extent that these individual goals are achieved by displaying efforts that benefit the group as a whole, this may not seem overly problematic. Importantly, however, individual goals are not necessarily aligned with overarching group goals. This implies that the pursuit of such individual goals (i.e., improving feelings of self-worth) does not necessarily benefit the team as a whole, and may even undermine the team's collective performance (Ellemers, De Gilder & Haslam, 2004). Based on these previous findings, we argued that compositional changes that induce insecurity about one's own position in the group and the self-concerns thus raised may actually encourage existing group members to display deviance and dissent, while they are at the same time less likely to accept valuable input from newcomers that might contribute to group innovation.

These general predictions found support in two experimental studies in which we manipulated the security of existing group members about their own position in the group (for details see Rink & Ellemers, 2009). Those who were made insecure about the continuation of their own membership in the group indicated lower levels of self-esteem but reported equal levels of group commitment compared to members who were secure about their own position in the group – as was expected on the basis of prior findings. The increase in self-concerns raised by position insecurity fully explained the increase that we found on individual task efforts, as well as the higher levels of deviance that they displayed. At first sight, this would seem to suggest that emphasising position insecurity of existing group members may enhance individual effort and dissent and hence benefits the group's performance. Importantly, however, when existing members were insecure about their position, they also indicated that they felt more threatened by new members entering the group. This threat in turn caused them to reject innovative and objectively useful task contributions proposed by a newcomer. Thus, the downside of position insecurity and the self-concerns this raises among existing group members is that they are more critical of and less open to the influence of newcomers to the group. In other words, the primary effect of position insecurity is that it makes existing group members focus on their individual task contributions as they hope to establish their own position in the group. This type of effort may also backfire, however, in that it can easily jeopardise the team's potential for innovation when group members under threat fail to acknowledge and profit from valid newcomer contributions and in this way undermine the team's ability to perform well.

Implications and Conclusion

Research on the effects of compositional changes in work groups suggests that the desire for intragroup similarity may make work groups insufficiently open to the dissent and novel ideas that might benefit innovation and change. We therefore set out to identify conditions that increase pressures to adapt to existing practices, or enhance the group's ability to benefit from unique and novel contributions to the task offered by newcomers. The results of three recent strands of research reviewed here indicate some of the factors that are relevant in this respect, and yield information that may help balance these two opposing forces.

We have argued and shown, first, that group performance attributions and mutual expectations are important in this context. That is, the future prospects of a newcomer entering the team may determine the extent to which this newcomer is expected to adapt (i.e., when permanent placement in the group is in order), or when socialisation pressures are released, allowing for dissent and making the group more open to change (i.e., when the newcomer is added to the group on a temporary basis). Second, we have seen that diffuse similarity expectations (e.g., in terms of overall personality features) may activate socialisation pressures on newcomers that prevent them from offering different and unique contributions to the group. By contrast, when newcomers are expected to be different from existing group members in terms of diffuse personality features, the group is more likely to allow for the dissent that encourages newcomers to provide the input that can improve the group's performance and innovation potential. Third, we have shown that when more specific cues about the newcomer's likely contribution to the task are available (e.g., concerning task-relevant experience and expertise) the effects of more diffuse expectations can be overruled.

As a final way to examine the conditions under which compositional changes can either foster or impede the emergence of dissent as a way to achieve innovation in work groups, we have addressed the perspective of existing group members and the self-focused concerns they may have. The studies we carried out with this aim revealed that on the one hand, insecurity about one's own position in the group may elevate individual motivation and increase efforts of existing group members to contribute to the group. On the other hand, it turned out that these heightened self-concerns do not necessarily improve the group's potential for innovation and change. That is, due to the preoccupation with establishing their own position in the group, existing group members who were insecure about their continued membership in the group tended to see newcomers as a threat to themselves, rather than as a potential asset to the group. Accordingly, they were reluctant to acknowledge the value of the unique and novel contributions offered by newcomers in the group, making it less likely that the different insights proffered by newcomers benefit group performance.

The empirical results from our research programme contribute to theory development concerning the ways in which, and the reasons why, compositional changes in work groups can either enhance or undermine the group's potential for innovation and change. Due to the experimental nature of our studies, we also know which types of measures are likely to be effective and which boundary conditions have to be met for groups to be able to benefit from the unique insights that newcomers have to offer. Thus, the results carry very concrete implications that may help develop interventions to secure and enhance the added value of introducing newcomers to existing task groups. In concluding this chapter, we will therefore address the more practical implications of this research for the management of work teams in organisations.

The findings reviewed in this chapter suggest that it should be possible to design organisational structures, reward systems, activities and communications in such a way that they effectively manage the tension between socialisation pressures and the need to allow for dissent and change. These organisational tools should then be used to emphasise and enhance the development of a common work group identity as a way to provide security and feelings of inclusion to its members, while encouraging existing group members to be open to dissent and accepting of the unique input from newcomers that is relevant to the achievement of desired outcomes (Ashforth & Johnson, 2001; Spears, Ellemers & Doosje, 2005).

Importantly, this work reminds us that people who work together in groups are likely to experience a certain tension between the need for unity, acceptance and belongingness on the one hand, and the need for innovation and change on the other. One way to release newcomers into the group from concerns about the extent to which they can be accepted and fit into the group is to emphasise the temporary status of these new group members. Even if this implies that they are less likely to be valued and included at an interpersonal level, owing to their temporary presence in the group, this may not be experienced as an important drawback. At the same time, however, this should help the newcomers themselves as well as existing group members to focus on what they can contribute to the task, and enhances the likelihood that the group will benefit from their presence. Indeed, the results of our research suggest that for interim managers the explicitly temporary nature of their presence is likely to contribute to their success in completing tasks and realising change. However, if future prospects of newcomers are not explicitly addressed, both the newcomers and the groups they enter may implicitly assume that their introduction into the group constitutes a first step towards their continued and more permanent presence. At first sight this may not seem too problematic, and actually in the short term is likely to facilitate newcomer socialisation and mutual acceptance. Nevertheless, our results suggest that such conditions make newcomers inclined to suppress dissenting or novel views to avoid standing out from the group, forgoing the opportunity to draw the group in new and different directions. Thus, if the achievement of innovation and change are important group goals, our results suggest that there is added value in clearly articulating the future prospects of newcomers.

A second lesson is that we should be aware of and take into account people's expectations about the anticipated task contributions offered by newcomers. We have shown that relatively diffuse similarity cues may implicitly communicate expectations about likely task contributions. Even if these expectations are unwarranted initially, they may have a real and noticeable influence on newcomer behaviour and group performance, due to the Galatea effect. When the newcomer clearly differs from existing group members, this will help them anticipate dissent and increases the chances that the group acknowledges the unique contributions of these newcomers. Conversely, while the introduction of newcomers who seem similar to the group at a surface level (i.e., in terms of diffuse similarity cues), may seem less problematic or controversial, it is likely that these newcomers then experience more difficulty in having the group accept and value their dissenting views. Here too, it is important to be aware of the tradeoff between acceptance and inclusion versus contribution and change, and to guard against the temptation to add members to the group who are most likely to be accepted or who might most easily fit in. If the goal of adding new members to the group is to introduce novel insights and alternative views, then dissent should be anticipated and encouraged, for instance by explicitly seeking out newcomers who are different from existing group members, and emphasising these differences.

Complementing these insights on the effects of diffuse similarity expectations, we have seen that it is important not only to seek out individuals who possess specific expertise that is relevant to the task, but also to explicitly communicate this expertise to the group. If it is made clear that new members are introduced to the group for their specific knowledge, experience or expertise, this will make existing group members more open to and accepting of the contributions they offer, and make them focus less on the question of how they might fit in with or adapt to the group.

Finally, our data speak of approaches to human resource management that think of a flexible workforce as an organisational strength in a more general sense (e.g., Belous, 1989). While flexibility and compositional changes may seem an attractive solution to changing demands on the organisation, and may initially boost individual effort, our findings show that continued insecurity is likely to have long-term disadvantages. This is especially likely to be the case when innovation is required and when individual employees need to work together on collaborative tasks. Thus, the present research reminds us that even if employee mobility and position insecurity can increase individual efforts in the short term, this is likely to have adverse effects over time. That is, the preoccupation with securing one's own position in the group makes it less likely that existing group members acknowledge or benefit from contributions newcomers can make to the group. Additionally, if individuals have a long-term perspective that is chronically insecure, protracted efforts to prove themselves and secure their position may easily induce psychological and physical stress, which is likely to result in over-exertion and health complaints over time. Thus, despite the seeming attractiveness of work-force flexibility, organisations that can provide some long-term job security to their employees might be most effective in realising the performance advantages of compositional changes in work teams.

In conclusion, the research reviewed in this chapter helps understand the importance of dissent for innovation and change in work groups, and identifies a number of conditions that are conducive to the development of a group climate that allows for such dissent and its associated benefits. A key factor in our analysis is the tension between pressures towards socialisation and similarity on the one hand, and the need to value novel and unique task contributions on the other. This tension can be resolved either by addressing factors that make it less important for new group members to fit in, or by clarifying the reasons why different inputs to the task should be expected and welcomed. Additionally, some sense of security about one's own position is needed to draw away concerns about the establishment of individual worth and to enable individual group members to focus on the way in which their concerted efforts can complement each other or can be optimally combined to benefit the group as a whole.

Acknowledgements

The research reported in this chapter was made possible by a grant awarded to the authors by the Dutch National Science Foundation (NWO grant no. 472-04-044).

References

Ashford, S.J., Lee, C. & Bobko, P. (1989). Content, causes, and consequences of job insecurity: a theory-based measure and substantive test. *Academy of Management Journal*, *32*, 803–29.

Ashforth, B.E. & Johnson, S.A. (2001). Which hat to wear? The relative salience of multiple identities in organizational contexts. In M.A. Hogg & D.J. Terry (eds), *Social Identity Processes in Organizational Contexts* (pp. 31–48). Philadelphia: Psychology Press.

Bargh, J.A., Chaiken, S., Govender, R. & Pratto, F. (1992). The generality of the automatic attitude activation effect. *Journal of Personality and Social Psychology, 62*, 893–912.

Bass, B.M. (1960). *Leadership, Psychology, and Organizational Behavior*. New York: Harper.

Belous, R.S. (1989). *The Contingent Economy: The Growth of the Temporary, Part-Time, and Subcontracted Workforce*. Washington, DC: National Planning Association.

Berger, J. & Zelditch, M. (1998). *Status, Power, and Legitimacy: Strategies and Theory*. New Brunswick, NJ: Transaction.

Broschak, J.P. & Davis-Blake, A. (2006). Mixing standard work and nonstandard deals: the consequences of heterogeneity in employment arrangements. *Academy of Management Journal, 49*, 371–93.

Bunderson, J.S. (2003). Recognizing and utilizing expertise in work groups: a status characteristics perspective. *Administrative Science Quarterly, 48*, 557–91.

Chaiken, S. & Maheswaran, D. (1994). Heuristic processing can bias systematic processing – Effects of source credibility, argument ambiguity, and task importance on attitude judgment. *Journal of Personality and Social Psychology, 66*, 460–73.

Chen, G. & Klimoski, R.J. (2003). The impact of expectations on newcomer performance in teams as mediated by work characteristics, social exchanges, and empowerment. *Academy of Management Journal, 46*, 591–607.

Choi, H.-S. & Levine, J.M. (2004). Minority influence in work teams: the impact of newcomers. *Journal of Experimental Social Psychology, 40*, 273–80.

Cohen, B.P. & Zhou, X. (1991). Status processes in enduring work groups. *American Sociological Review, 56*, 179–88.

De Dreu, C.K.W. & West, M.A. (2001). Minority dissent and team innovation: the importance of participation in decision making. *Journal of Applied Psychology, 86*, 1191–201.

Eden, D. (1984). Self-fulfilling prophecy as a management tool: harnessing Pygmalion. *Academy of Management Review, 9*, 64–73.

Ellemers, N., De Gilder, D. & Haslam, S.A. (2004). Motivating individuals and groups at work: a social identity perspective on leadership and group performance. *Academy of Management Review, 29*, 459–78.

Ellemers, N., Kortekaas, P. & Ouwerkerk, J. W. (1999). Self-categorisation, commitment to the group and group self-esteem as related but distinct aspects of social identity. *European Journal of Social Psychology, 29*, 371–89.

Feldman, H.I., Doerpinghaus, W.H. & Turnley, W.H. (1994). Managing temporary workers: a permanent HRM challenge. *Organizational Dynamics*, *23*, 49–63.

Hornsey, M.J., Grice, T., Jetten, J., Paulsen, N. & Callan, V. (2007). Group-directed criticisms and recommendations to change: why newcomers arouse more resistance than old-timers. *Personality and Social Psychology Bulletin*, *33*, 1036–48.

Hornsey, M.J. & Imani, A. (2004). Criticizing groups from the inside and the outside: an identity perspective on the intergroup sensitivity effect. *Personality and Social Psychology Bulletin*, *30*, 365–83.

Hornsey, M.J., Trembath, M. & Gunthorpe, S. (2004). 'You can criticize because you care': identity attachment, constructiveness, and the intergroup sensitivity effect. *European Journal of Social Psychology*, *34*, 499–518.

Hornsey, M.J., Oppes, T. & Svensson, A. (2002). 'It's OK if we say it, but you can't': responses to intergroup and intragroup criticism. *European Journal of Social Psychology*, *32*, 293–307.

Jetten, J., Branscombe, N.R. & Spears, R. (2002). On being peripheral: effects of identity insecurity on personal and collective self-esteem. *European Journal of Social Psychology*, *32*, 105–23.

Jetten, J., Branscombe, N.R., Spears, R. & McKimmie, B.M. (2003). Predicting the paths of peripherals: the interaction of identification and future possibilities. *Personality and Social Psychology Bulletin*. *29*, 130–40.

Kane, A.A., Argote, L. & Levine, J.M. (2005). Knowledge transfer between groups via personnel rotation: effects of social identity and knowledge quality. *Organizational Behavior and Human Decision Processes*, *96*, 56–71.

Kane, A. & Rink, F. (2009). *Newcomers as Active Agents: How Different Types of Newcomer Influence Tactics Affect Team Innovation*. Unpublished research report.

Kraimer, M.L., Wayne, S.J., Liden, R.C. & Sparrowe, R.T. (2005). The role of job security in understanding the relationship between employees' perceptions of temporary workers and employees' performance. *Journal of Applied Psychology*, *90*, 389–98.

Krueger, J. & Rothbart, M. (1988). Use of categorical and individuating information in making inferences about personality. *Journal of Personality and Social Psychology*, *55*, 187–95.

Leary, M.R. & Forsyth, D.R. (1987). Attributions of responsibility for collective endeavors. *Review of Personality and Social Psychology*, *8*, 167–88.

McGrath, J.E. (1984). *Groups: Interaction and Performance*. Englewood Cliffs, NJ: Prentice Hall.

Moreland, R. (1999). Transactive memory and job performance: helping workers learn who knows what. In J. Levine, L. Thompson & D. Messick (eds), *Shared Cognitions in Organizations: The Management of Knowledge* (pp. 3–32). Mahwah, NJ: Lawrence Erlbaum.

Nemeth, C. & Owens, P. (1996). Making work groups more effective: the value of minority dissent. In M.A. West (ed.), *The Handbook of Workgroup Psychology* (pp. 125–41). Chichester: John Wiley & Sons.

Noel, J.G., Wann, D.L. & Branscombe, N.R. (1995). Peripheral ingroup membership status and public negativity toward outgroups. *Journal of Personality and Social Psychology, 68*, 127–37.

Pearce, J.L. (1998). Job insecurity is important, but not for the reasons you might think: the example of contingent workers. *Trends in Organizational Behavior, 5*, 31–46.

Phillips, K.W., Mannix, E.A., Neale, M.A. & Gruenfeld, D.H. (2004). Diverse groups and information sharing: the effects of congruent ties. *Journal of Experimental Social Psychology, 40*, 497–510.

Ridgeway, C.L. (2001). Social status and group structure. In M.A. Hogg & R.S. Tindale (eds), *Blackwell Handbook of Social Psychology* (pp. 352–75). Malden, MA: Blackwell.

Rink, F. & Ellemers, N. (2007). The role of expectancies in accepting task-related diversity: do disappointment and lack of commitment stem from actual differences or violated expectations? *Personality and Social Psychology Bulletin, 33*, 842–54.

Rink, F. & Ellemers, N. (2009). Temporary vs. permanent group membership: how the future prospects of newcomers affect newcomer acceptance and newcomer influence. *Personality and Social Psychology Bulletin, 35*, 764–76.

Sherman, D.K. & Kim, H.S. (2005). Is there an 'I' in 'Team'? The role of the self in group-serving judgments. *Journal of Personality and Social Psychology, 88*, 108–20.

Sleebos, E., Ellemers, N. & De Gilder, D. (2006a). The paradox of the disrespected: disrespected group members' engagement in group-serving effort. *Journal of Experimental Social Psychology, 42*, 413–27.

Sleebos, E., Ellemers, N. & De Gilder, D. (2006b). The carrot and the stick: affective commitment and acceptance anxiety as motives for discretionary group efforts by respected and disrespected group members. *Personality and Social Psychology Bulletin, 32*, 244–55.

Spears, R., Ellemers, N. & Doosje, B. (2005). Let me count the ways in which I respect thee: does competence compensate or compromise lack of liking from the group? *European Journal of Social Psychology, 35*, 263–79.

Stasser, G., Stewart, D.D. & Wittenbaum, G.M. (1995). Expert roles and information exchange during discussion: the importance of knowing who knows what. *Journal of Experimental Social Psychology, 31*, 244–65.

Stasser, G. & Titus, W. (1985). Pooling of unshared information in group decision-making – biased information sampling during discussion. *Journal of Personality and Social Psychology, 48*, 1467–78.

Stewart, D.D. & Stasser, G. (1995). Expert role assignment and information sampling during collective recall and decision making. *Journal of Personality and Social Psychology, 69*, 619–29.

Ziller, R.C. (1965). Toward a theory of open and closed groups. *Psychological Bulletin, 64*, 164–82.

5

Minority Influence in Interacting Groups

The Impact of Newcomers

John M. Levine and Hoon-Seok Choi

Groups are not static entities, but instead change in dynamic ways over time. Therefore, in order to understand group processes and outcomes, it is necessary to consider temporal aspects of group life (Arrow, McGrath & Berdahl, 2000). An important temporal event for most groups is membership change, defined as the entry of new members and/or the exit of current members (Thomas-Hunt & Phillips, 2003).[1] Although membership change is more common in some groups than others (Ziller, 1965), it is inevitable in all groups that exist for any period of time and can have both positive (e.g., Nemeth & Ormiston, 2007; Phillips, Liljenquist & Neale, 2009) and negative (e.g., Goodman & Leyden, 1991; Lewis *et al.*, 2007) effects on group performance. In the present chapter, we focus on when and how new members change the groups they enter.

New members' ability to exert influence is interesting in part because it sheds light on majority–minority relations in interacting groups. Although Moscovici's (1976) ground-breaking research on minority influence was motivated by an interest in group dynamics, most of the work on this topic has ignored the social dynamics of groups containing majority and minority factions in favour of the cognitive dynamics of isolated individuals responding to the views of putative minorities (for exceptions, see De Dreu, 2007, and Prislin, Davenport & Michalak, this volume). In addition to providing a new perspective on minority influence in interacting groups, research on new members' ability to introduce change also contributes to

Rebels in Groups: Dissent, Deviance, Difference and Defiance Jolanda Jetten and Matthew J. Hornsey

the burgeoning literature on group creativity (e.g., Paulus & Nijstad, 2003; Thompson & Choi, 2006).

Group Socialisation Theory

Group socialisation theory provides a useful framework for analysing how groups respond to new members (see Levine & Moreland, 1994; Moreland & Levine, 1982). The theory postulates that groups and individuals evaluate the past, present and anticipated future 'rewardingness' of their own and alternative relationships. These evaluations produce feelings of commitment in both parties, which can rise and fall over time. Commitment has implications for both the exercise of social influence and individuals' role transitions from one phase of group membership to another. The more commitment the group feels towards the individual, the easier it will be for him or her to exert influence. Similarly, the individual's commitment to the group determines his or her receptivity to influence attempts from it. Regarding role transitions, both the group and the individual have decision criteria (specific levels of commitment) that indicate when the person should move to a new phase of group membership. When the commitment levels of both parties reach their respective decision criteria, the person undergoes a role transition. The two parties' subsequent evaluations of one another produce further changes in commitment, which lead to additional role transitions when new decision criteria are reached. In this way, the individual can move through five phases of group membership (investigation, socialisation, maintenance, resocialisation and remembrance), separated by four role transitions (entry, acceptance, divergence and exit).

Of particular relevance to our present concerns is reciprocal influence between current and new members during the socialisation phase of group membership, which begins with the role transition of entry. During this phase current members attempt to influence new members, and, to the extent they are successful, new members undergo assimilation. In a parallel fashion, new members attempt to influence current members, and, to the extent they are successful, current members undergo accommodation. Although current members often are more successful in changing new members than vice versa, this is not always the case (Levine & Moreland, 1985). Under certain conditions (described below) new members can exert substantial influence. When, as typically occurs, new members are a numerical minority in the group they join, the influence they exert is a form of minority influence.

New Members as Influence Recipients

New members of groups and organisations are often the recipients of intensive socialisation efforts designed to alter their knowledge, skills and motivation in ways that will increase their contributions to collective goal attainment (Moreland & Levine, 2001). In many cases, new members are receptive to such efforts and exhibit a good deal of assimilation. An important source of this receptivity is the stress associated with being a new member, which derives from several sources, including lack of familiarity with other members, 'reality shock' associated with unrealistic expectations about group life, low status and power, uncertainty regarding role demands and performance anxiety (Moreland & Levine, 1989). An additional stressor for new members is negative treatment by current members (e.g., initiation ceremonies, hazing), which can range from mildly embarrassing to physically dangerous (Levine, Moreland & Hausmann, 2005).

The stress that new members experience elicits two motives. One is the epistemic goal of acquiring information that will increase one's success in the group. The other is the social goal of achieving acceptance and social integration in the group (Levine & Kerr, 2007). These two motives often make new members highly susceptible to influence attempts by current members (Levine & Moreland, 1991, 1999).

New Members as Influence Sources

Notwithstanding the evidence that new members are often relatively passive recipients of influence, they do not always behave this way. New members can produce two kinds of influence, both of which have consequences for group performance (Levine & Choi, 2010). The first involves general adaptations that groups make to the presence of new members (Levine, Moreland & Choi, 2001). The second, which we will focus on here, involves specific changes that new members produce in group task performance (Levine, Choi & Moreland, 2003).

New members may be a rich source of ideas for improving group performance, because they are not committed to the group's task strategy, bring fresh perspectives gained in other groups, and lack strong personal ties to other members that inhibit their willingness to challenge group orthodoxy (Nijstad & Levine, 2007). In order for new members to produce innovation, however, two conditions must be satisfied: (a) they must have the motivation and ability to produce ideas that might improve group performance and (b) current members must accept and implement these ideas (Levine *et al.*, 2003). Because of space considerations, we will restrict our attention to the latter condition.[2]

Assuming that new members suggest ideas that might enhance group performance, how likely are these ideas to find a receptive audience? In many (perhaps most) cases, the answer is 'not very likely'. Current members are typically reluctant to consider, much less accept, new members' ideas because they believe new members should assimilate to the group and 'know their place', which involves maintaining a low profile and not challenging group norms. In addition, current members are often comfortable with familiar task routines and resistant to new ways of doing things (cf. Gersick & Hackman, 1990). New members are also at a disadvantage in exerting influence because they are often numerical minorities. Such minorities typically have difficulty producing direct (public) influence (Wood *et al.*, 1994), and they are often disliked and rejected by majority members (Levine & Kerr, 2007). However, minority members can produce indirect (private) influence (Martin & Hewstone, 2001; Wood *et al.*, 1994), and they can stimulate majority members to engage in divergent thinking (Nemeth & Goncalo, this volume). Moreover, by using the right tactics, minorities that interact with majorities may be able to produce direct influence (Levine & Kaarbo, 2001).

Group socialisation theory, described above, suggests conditions under which new members might produce change (or innovation) in the groups they enter. According to the theory, current members' expectations about new members' future rewardingness should affect their commitment to these people and hence their willingness to consider new members' ideas. Stated differently, to the extent that they view new members' suggestions as opportunities (rather than threats) for future group performance, current members will be more receptive to these suggestions. This opportunity/threat analysis suggests a number of factors that should influence new members' success in gaining acceptance for their ideas. These factors can be classified into two broad categories: (a) characteristics and behaviours of new members and (b) characteristics of the groups they enter (Levine *et al.*, 2003; Levine & Choi, 2010). Because little explicit attention has been given to new members' ability to exert influence, the following discussion relies heavily on research regarding related phenomena, particularly minority influence and group productivity.

New members' characteristics and behaviours

To the extent current members are sensitive to the opportunities/threats posed by new members, they should be more receptive to suggestions from people who have high rather than low task expertise (cf. Allen, 1965; Eagly & Chaiken, 1993). Moreover, they should also be more receptive to new members who possess high rather than low status in the group. Such status may be influenced by several factors, including new members' reputation prior to entering the group, contributions to the group after they join and personal characteristics (e.g., race, sex) (Ridgeway, 2001). Compared to new members with low status, those with high status are likely to elicit more commitment from current members (Moreland & Levine, 1989) and higher performance expectations (cf. Milanovich *et al.*, 1998). For these reasons, new members with high status probably elicit less punishment for deviating from group norms (cf. Wiggins, Dill & Schwartz, 1965) and gain more acceptance for new ideas (cf. Torrance, 1955). In fact, when they occupy leadership positions, new members with high status may be expected to challenge group norms and produce innovation (cf. Abrams *et al.*, 2008; Suchner & Jackson, 1976).

An opportunity/threat calculation is also likely to influence how the size of the new members' faction affects their ability to produce influence (Levine & Kaarbo, 2001). Larger factions may be more effective than smaller ones (Tanford & Penrod, 1984) because they seem more correct (Nemeth, Wachtler & Endicott, 1977) and more likely to retaliate if their views are rejected. In contrast, smaller factions may be more effective than larger ones because they seem more confident and courageous (Nemeth *et al.*, 1977; see also Nemeth & Goncalo, this volume), more distinct and salient (Maass, West & Cialdini, 1987) and less threatening (Crano, 2001).

Moreover, it is probable that new members' similarity to current members affects their ability to exert influence because of its opportunity/threat value for the group. Current members are more motivated to integrate similar than dissimilar new members (Jackson, Stone & Alvarez, 1992), presumably because similar new members are perceived as more valuable. If so, similar new members should find it easier to produce innovation (Levine & Moreland, 1985). However, dissimilar new members who possess valuable characteristics, such as superior task-relevant ability, should also be effective influence agents. An important form of new member similarity is ingroup status based on shared social identity. Ingroup members are generally viewed more positively than outgroup members and are 'over-rewarded' in the distribution of resources (Brewer & Brown, 1998). In addition, ingroup members are generally more effective influence agents than are outgroup members (Crano, 2001; Mackie & Queller, 2000). Therefore, in most cases, new members who share a social identity with current members should be more influential (but see Phillips *et al.*, 2009).

The impact of new members' behavioural style (Moscovici, 1985) can also be explained in terms of its opportunity/threat implications for the group. For example, compared to new members who give inconsistent responses, those who give consistent responses may be more influential because they are perceived as more confident and hence correct (but see Wood *et al.*, 1994). A similar argument can be made for why assertive new members may be more effective than non-assertive ones (cf. Jentsch & Smith-Jentsch, 2001). In addition, new members who conform to group norms before trying to produce change should be more influential than those who offer suggestions immediately, because the former members are seen as more committed and trustworthy (cf. Hollander, 1960).

New members can use a variety of impression management tactics in trying to exert influence (Levine & Kaarbo, 2001), and the effectiveness of these tactics is likely to be influenced by their perceived opportunity/threat value. For example, new members may communicate that their views reflect careful analysis and are shared by knowledgeable outsiders and that they want to help the group rather than further their personal interests (cf. Hornsey *et al.*, 2007; Ridgeway, 1982). New members who can convince current members that they possess these valuable characteristics should find it easier to gain acceptance for their ideas.

Our analysis so far suggests that new members' success as change agents depends on their ability to convince current members that their ideas are valid. But, in some cases, new members may use punishment or reward tactics designed to create compliance rather than conversion (cf. Levine & Kaarbo, 2001), and the effectiveness of these tactics likely depends on the opportunities/threats they imply. For example, new members may threaten to undermine group performance or leave the group, or they may promise to work hard or remain in the group in spite of attractive alternatives. New members may also use tactics designed to maximise the size of their faction (e.g., by convincing current members to recruit people sympathetic to their views) or to control how the group makes decisions (e.g., by convincing current members to use the unanimity, rather than majority, rule – cf. Miller, 1989). These tactics are likely to be effective to the extent the group believes it will benefit from accepting them.

Group characteristics

Current members' assessments of the opportunity/threat posed by new members should also be affected by characteristics of the group. And these assessments should affect the likelihood that new members' ideas will be accepted.

Two potentially relevant group characteristics are openness to membership change and staffing level. 'Open' groups (which have high turnover and unstable memberships) work harder to minimise turnover-related problems and are more receptive to new ideas than are 'closed' groups (which have low turnover and stable memberships) (Ziller, 1965; Ziller, Behringer & Goodchilds, 1960). Therefore, compared to closed groups, open groups should view new ideas as opportunities rather than threats and hence should be more receptive to innovation on the part of new members (Ziller, Behringer & Jansen, 1961). Although openness to membership change has typically been defined as willingness to accept new members on a permanent basis, groups sometimes allow temporary visitors (Gruenfeld, Martorana & Fan, 2000). Because current members generally assume that temporary visitors will provide few benefits to the group, they should not be receptive to their views. However, this tendency may be mitigated by the fact that current members have little motivation to socialise temporary visitors (Rink & Ellemers, 2009). Staffing level is the relationship between the number of members the group has and the number it needs to perform satisfactorily (Barker, 1968). Compared to adequately staffed and overstaffed groups, understaffed groups should view new members as more valuable and hence allow them to exert more influence (Cini, Moreland & Levine, 1993).

Group development, defined as changes in group structure and dynamics over time (Moreland & Levine, 1988), may also affect new members' ability to produce influence. Because structural properties of groups (e.g., norms, roles) and interactions among members stabilise as time passes (Tuckman, 1965; Worchel, 1996), new members' ideas for changing the group may be perceived as more threatening in later than in earlier stages of group development. If so, new members who suggest changes during the early stages of group development should be more successful than those who do so later (Ford & Sullivan, 2004; Moreland & Levine, 1988; but see Worchel, Grossman & Coutant, 1994).

Group cohesion and climate are also likely to affect receptivity to new members' ideas. Cohesion, which tends to rise during group development, increases conformity to group norms (Festinger, Schachter & Back, 1950) and punishment of deviates (Schachter, 1951). Therefore, current members of high (as opposed to low) cohesive groups are more likely to view new members' influence attempts as threats rather than opportunities and hence to resist them (cf. Brawley, Carron & Widmeyer, 1988; Schachter, 1951). Regarding climate, evidence suggests that innovation is most likely in groups that have clear objectives, are committed to excellence and have norms favouring change (West, 1990; see also Moscovici & Lage, 1978). It is precisely these groups that should view new members' ideas as opportunities rather than threats.

In addition, group leaders may have an important impact on new members' ability to exert influence. Evidence suggests that, compared to autocratic leaders, democratic leaders are more receptive to innovation (Nyström, 1979) and more likely to demonstrate behaviours that encourage it, for example by giving subordinates a sense of empowerment (Burpitt & Bigoness, 1997) and providing them with emotional support (West & Wallace, 1991) and psychological safety (Edmondson, 2003). It is plausible, then, that democratic leaders will tend to view new members' ideas as opportunities rather than threats. To the extent this occurs, democratic leaders are likely to facilitate new members' ability to produce influence by protecting them from social pressure and encouraging other members to consider their views (cf. Maier & Solem, 1970).

Finally, an opportunity/threat analysis is helpful in explaining why a group's performance history and commitment to its current task strategy may influence its receptivity to new members' ideas. Because failing groups are more likely than succeeding groups to view new ideas as opportunities, the former groups should be more receptive to new members' influence attempts (Ziller & Behringer, 1960). Failure may not always have this consequence, however, because some groups refuse to abandon failing strategies (Gersick & Hackman, 1990) and instead execute them with increased vigour. Such 'entrapment' behaviour is especially common when groups have chosen (rather than been assigned) their strategy (cf. Kameda & Sugimori, 1993). In fact, groups that choose their task strategy, whether it fails *or* succeeds, may be more resistant to innovation efforts than groups that are assigned their strategy, because the former are more likely to view new ideas as threats. This effect would be consistent with research indicating that choice produces commitment and resistance to change (Staw, 1976).

Our Research

In the previous section, we presented a number of hypotheses about when new members influence the groups they enter. In this section, we summarise recent studies testing some of these hypotheses and also examining new members' impact on group performance.

Group's strategy choice and prior performance

In one experiment (Choi & Levine, 2004), we investigated how a group's receptivity to a new member's innovation attempt was influenced by the group's level of choice in determining its initial task strategy and performance prior to the new member's arrival. Based on reasoning presented above, we predicted that a new member's innovation attempt would be more readily accepted when the group: (a) was assigned rather than chose its strategy and (b) failed rather than succeeded when using this strategy.

A computerised air-surveillance task was used to test these hypotheses. Participants, in three-person teams, were randomly assigned to the role of either team leader (commander) or subordinate (specialists A and B). During task training, the specialists learned how to monitor several characteristics of planes flying through a simulated airspace (e.g., airspeed, altitude, weapons readiness), assign parameter values to these characteristics, and transmit these values to the commander using an email system. The commander learned how to integrate the parameter values in calculating a threat value for each plane and how to enter these values into his computer. Parameter values changed over time, making the task demanding for all participants, whose goal was to maximise the accuracy of the commander's threat assignments.

Teams either were allowed to choose one of two equally plausible strategies for apportioning specialists' monitoring responsibilities or were assigned a strategy. After completing Shift 1, teams learned that their score was either below or above a success criterion (75 out of 100). Prior to Shift 2, specialist B was replaced by a new member (a confederate) who had ostensibly completed individual training but not worked on a team before. During a get-acquainted emailing session, the new member suggested a plausible, but not demonstrably correct, new strategy for monitoring plane characteristics. The commander and specialist A used the email system to decide whether or not to accept this suggestion.

Consistent with hypotheses, the new member's suggestion was accepted more often by teams that had been assigned rather than chosen their strategy (73 per cent versus 36 per cent) and had failed rather than succeeded (77 per cent versus 32 per cent). The interaction was not significant. The overall amount of group acceptance was striking given that newcomers had low status on the team, did not advocate a clearly superior strategy and were imposed rather than selected by members.

New member's behavioural style and group's prior performance

In a second experiment (Hansen & Levine, 2009), which used a slightly modified version of the air-surveillance paradigm, we investigated how the new member's behavioural style in suggesting a new task strategy affected the team's receptivity to it. According to Moscovici (1976, 1985), behavioural style is *the* crucial factor underlying a minority's ability to influence a majority. Moreover, it has been suggested that behavioural style, particularly assertiveness, is an important determinant of influence in work teams (Jentsch & Smith-Jentsch, 2001; Milanovich, Driskell, Stout & Salas, 1998). In the present experiment, we varied whether the new member used an assertive or a non-assertive style in suggesting a change in specialists' strategy for looking up plane information. We predicted that new members' innovation attempts would be more successful in the former than in the latter condition.

We also extended Choi and Levine's (2004) study by providing a more sensitive test of the impact of prior team performance. In the present experiment, teams completed two shifts on the air-surveillance task prior to the new member's entry, and all teams failed in Shift 1. In Shift 2, teams improved either slightly, moderately or substantially, but in no case reached the success criterion. This manipulation allowed a test of whether performance improvement *without* final success is sufficient to affect group receptivity to a new member's influence attempt. And inclusion of three (rather than two) levels of improvement provided additional information about the relationship between the group's prior performance and the new member's ability to produce influence. We predicted that such influence would vary inversely with the group's level of improvement.

In addition, we expected that the new member's level of assertiveness would have less impact in the high and low improvement conditions than in the moderate condition. This prediction was based on the assumption that the former two conditions would produce clear performance expectations and hence little motivation to attend to the new member's behavioural style in deciding whether to accept or reject the proposed strategy change. In contrast, the moderate improvement condition would produce an ambiguous performance expectation and hence more motivation to attend to the new member's style.

As predicted, the new member's suggestion was accepted more often when it was presented in an assertive than a non-assertive manner (75 per cent versus 41 per cent). Moreover, acceptance varied inversely with the team's performance improvement prior to the new member's entry (low: 79 per cent; moderate: 63 per cent; high: 32 per cent). Although the interaction between the two independent variables was not significant, chi-square tests indicated that teams were more receptive to assertive than to non-assertive new members in the moderate improvement condition but not in the low or high improvement conditions. Moreover, with regard to teams' evaluation of the new member, the interaction was significant and in the predicted direction.

New member's task expertise and social identity

In a third experiment (Kane, Argote & Levine, 2005), we examined how new members' task expertise and shared social identity with other members affected their ability to exert influence. We predicted, based on reasoning presented earlier, that new members would be more influential when they had more expertise than other members and shared a social identity with them. In addition, we predicted an interaction between these variables, because people often analyse ingroup messages more thoroughly than outgroup messages and are more influenced by high-quality than low-quality arguments from ingroup, but not outgroup, members (Mackie & Queller, 2000; van Knippenberg, 1999). We expected that: (a) group members who shared a social identity with new members would adopt their task strategy when it was superior, but not inferior, to their own and (b) group members who did not share a social identity with new members would reject their strategy regardless of its quality.

In this study, groups of six participants learned that they would work as three-person teams to make origami sailboats. After manipulating the extent to which the two smaller groups shared an overarching social identity (e.g., by giving them the same versus different names and task materials, seating them in an integrated versus segregated fashion around a table), they were trained separately on the task. One group learned a superior (i.e., more efficient) routine, whereas the other learned an inferior routine. Each group then received a replacement (new) member, who had been trained in the other group and hence had more or less task expertise than the group he or she was entering. In addition, the new member either did or did not share a social identity with the recipient group.

As predicted, the new member's strategy was adopted more often in the shared than unshared identity condition (38 per cent versus 13 per cent) and in the superior than inferior expertise condition (46 per cent versus 4 per cent). Moreover, as expected, the new member's expertise had more impact on group adoption in the shared (67 per cent versus 8 per cent) than unshared (25 per cent versus 0 per cent) identity condition. Thus, groups in the shared identity condition were much more likely to adopt the new member's task routine when it was superior rather than inferior to their own, whereas groups in the unshared identity condition rarely adopted the new member's routine even when it was superior to their own. We also assessed how the entry of new members affected group performance on the origami task. When new members had a superior routine, performance improved much more in the shared than in the unshared identity condition. In contrast, when they had an inferior routine, performance was virtually identical in the two identity conditions.

New member's task expertise and social status

In a fourth experiment (Levine & Choi, 2004), we investigated the effects of new members' task expertise and social status on group performance. We predicted that new members with higher expertise would have a more positive impact on group performance than would those with lower expertise and that new members with higher status would have a greater impact (for better or worse) than those with lower status.

In this study, participants in three-person groups were trained on an earlier version of the air-surveillance task described above. Following practise, the groups performed four shifts, followed by veridical feedback regarding their performance. Approximately one week later, groups returned for a second session, in which they followed the same procedures as on Day 1, with one major exception. In the commander change and specialist change conditions, one group member was replaced by a person who previously played the same role in another group. In the no-change (control) condition, membership remained stable across Days 1 and 2.

We did not expect personnel turnover per se to substantially affect group performance on Day 2, because the group's task was highly structured and members received a good deal of practice in performing their specialised roles on Day 1. And in fact membership change did not influence group performance on Day 2. To test our hypotheses about the role of new members' task expertise and social status, we developed an index of new members' ability based on their task-relevant behaviours on Day 1 (e.g., how much specialists focused on more important, rather than less important, plane characteristics; how long commanders waited before assigning initial threat values to planes). Correlations between new members' ability and their receiving team's performance on Day 2 indicated, as expected, that: (a) new members with higher task expertise had a more positive effect on group performance than did those with lower expertise and (b) new members with higher status (commanders) had a greater impact than did those with lower status (specialists).

New member's influence on group creativity

Creativity is an important aspect of group performance. According to Nijstad and Levine (2007), new members can make unique contributions in each of three stages of group creativity – problem finding (identifying and defining the problem), idea finding (generating possible solutions to the problem) and solution finding (choosing the best solution and then developing and implementing it). In two final experiments (Choi & Thompson, 2005), we tested the hypothesis that the entry of new members would enhance a group's ability to generate creative ideas.

In the first study, participants were assigned to three-person groups that worked on a brainstorming task. Some groups then experienced membership change (one member was replaced by someone from another group), whereas others did not. Next, all groups worked on a second brainstorming task. We found, as expected, that groups with membership change displayed more creativity on the second task than did groups without such change. In the second study (which used similar experimental procedures), we investigated the contributions that both new and old members made to group creativity. As before, we found that membership change enhanced group creativity on the second task. In addition, we found that the more creative new members had been on the first task, the more creative the entire group was on the second task. Finally, we discovered that, although old-timers in both the membership change and membership stability conditions were more creative on the second task than on the first, they exhibited a greater increase in creativity in the former case, indicating that new members stimulated their creativity. Taken as a whole, these findings complement those reported by Levine and Choi (2004) in showing that new members' task expertise importantly affects group performance.

Conclusion

Substantial evidence indicates that groups often perceive dissent as dangerous and respond negatively to those who challenge the status quo (Levine & Kerr, 2007). Nonetheless, dissent is a ubiquitous feature of social life and often has productive consequences for the group in which it occurs as well as society at large (Moscovici, 1976). In this chapter, we discussed a neglected form of minority influence, namely new members' ability to change the groups they enter. We offered an opportunity/threat analysis, based on group socialisation theory, of the conditions that are likely to facilitate and inhibit such influence. We then summarised several studies showing that new members can indeed serve as agents of minority influence by changing the task strategies of the groups they enter (Choi & Levine, 2004; Hansen & Levine, 2009; Kane *et al.*, 2005) and, in some cases, the performance of these groups (Choi & Thompson, 2005; Kane *et al.*, 2005; Levine & Choi, 2004). Although these latter findings do not mean that groups always benefit from accepting new members' ideas, they sensitise us to the fact that people on the periphery of a group can, in some cases, be important sources of innovation and social change.

Notes

1. Entry is defined as new members joining an *existing* group to differentiate it from group formation. Exit is defined as a *subset* of current members leaving a group to differentiate it from group dissolution (Levine & Choi, 2004).
2. For a discussion of factors that influence new members' idea production, see Levine and Choi (2010).

References

Abrams, D., de Moura, G.R., Marques, J.M. & Hutchinson, P. (2008). Innovation credit: when can leaders oppose their group's norms? *Journal of Personality and Social Psychology, 95*, 662–78.

Allen, V.L. (1965). Situational factors in conformity. In L. Berkowitz (ed.), *Advances in Experimental Social Psychology* (Vol. 2, pp. 133–75). New York: Academic Press.

Arrow, H., McGrath, J.E. & Berdahl, J.L. (2000). *Small Groups as Complex Systems: Formation, Coordination, Development, and Adaptation.* Thousand Oaks, CA: Sage.

Barker, R.G. (1968). *Ecological Psychology.* Stanford, CA: Stanford University Press.

Brawley, L.R., Carron, A.V. & Widmeyer, W.N. (1988). Exploring the relationship between cohesion and group resistance to disruption. *Journal of Sport and Exercise Psychology, 10*, 199–213.

Brewer, M.B. & Brown, R.J. (1998). Intergroup relations. In D.T. Gilbert, S.T. Fiske & G. Lindzey (eds), *The Handbook of Social Psychology* (4th edition, Vol. 2, pp. 554–94). Boston, MA: McGraw-Hill.

Burpitt, W.J. & Bigoness, W.J. (1997). Leadership and innovation among teams: the impact of empowerment. *Small Group Research, 28*, 414–23.

Choi, H.-S. & Levine, J.M. (2004). Minority influence in work teams: the impact of newcomers. *Journal of Experimental Social Psychology, 40*, 273–80.

Choi, H.-S. & Thompson, L. (2005). Old wine in a new bottle: impact of membership change on group creativity. *Organizational Behavior and Human Decision Processes, 98*, 121–32.

Cini, M., Moreland, R.L. & Levine, J.M. (1993). Group staffing levels and responses to prospective and new members. *Journal of Personality and Social Psychology, 65*, 723–34.

Crano, W.D. (2001). Social influence, social identity, and ingroup leniency. In C.K. W. De Dreu & N.K. De Vries (eds), *Group Consensus and Minority Influence: Implications for Innovation* (pp. 122–43). Oxford: Blackwell.

De Dreu, C.K.W. (2007). Minority dissent, attitude change, and group performance. In A.R. Pratkanis (ed.), *The Science of Social Influence: Advances and Future Progress* (pp. 247–70). New York: Psychology Press.

Eagly, A.H. & Chaiken, S. (1993). *The Psychology of Attitudes.* Orlando, FL: Harcourt.

Edmondson, A.C. (2003). Speaking up in the operating room: how team leaders promote learning in interdisciplinary action teams. *Journal of Management Studies, 40*, 1419–52.

Festinger, L., Schachter, S. & Back, K. (1950). *Social Pressures in Informal Groups.* New York: Harper.

Ford, C. & Sullivan, D.M. (2004). A time for everything: how the timing of novel contributions influences project team outcomes. *Journal of Organizational Behavior, 25,* 279–92.

Gersick, C.J. & Hackman, J.R. (1990). Habitual routines in task-performing groups. *Organizational Behavior and Human Decision Processes, 47,* 65–97.

Goodman, P.S. & Leyden, D.P. (1991). Familiarity and group productivity. *Journal of Applied Psychology, 76,* 578–86.

Gruenfeld, D., Martorana, P.V. & Fan, E.T. (2000). What do groups learn from their worldliest members? Direct and indirect influence in dynamic teams. *Organizational Behavior and Human Decision Processes, 82,* 45–59.

Hansen, T. & Levine, J.M. (2009). Newcomers as change agents: effects of newcomers' behavioral style and teams' performance optimism. *Social Influence, 4,* 46–61.

Hollander, E.P. (1960). Competence and conformity in the acceptance of influence. *Journal of Abnormal and Social Psychology, 61,* 365–59.

Hornsey, M.J., Grice, T., Jetten, J., Paulsen, N. & Callan, V. (2007). Group-directed criticisms and recommendations for change: why newcomers arouse more resistance than old-timers. *Personality and Social Psychology Bulletin, 33,* 1036–48.

Jackson, S.E., Stone, V.K. & Alvarez, E.B. (1992). Socialization amidst diversity: the impact of demographics on work team oldtimers and newcomers. In L.L. Cummings & B.M. Staw (eds), *Research in Organizational Behavior* (Vol. 15, pp. 45–109). Greenwich, CT: JAI Press.

Jentsch, F. & Smith-Jentsch, K.A. (2001). Assertiveness and team performance: more than 'just say no'. In E. Salas, C.A. Bowers & E. Edens (eds), *Improving Teamwork in Organizations: Applications of Resource Management Training* (pp. 73–94). Mahwah, NJ: Lawrence Erlbaum.

Kameda, T. & Sugimori, S. (1993). Psychological entrapment in group decision making: an assigned decision rule and a groupthink phenomenon. *Journal of Personality and Social Psychology, 65,* 282–92.

Kane, A.A., Argote, L. & Levine, J.M. (2005). Knowledge transfer between groups via personnel rotation: effects of social identity and knowledge quality. *Organizational Behavior and Human Decision Processes, 96,* 56–71.

Levine, J.M. & Choi, H.-S. (2004). Impact of personnel turnover on team performance and cognition. In E. Salas & S.M. Fiore (eds), *Team Cognition: Understanding the Factors that Drive Process and Performance* (pp. 153–76). Washington, DC: American Psychological Association.

Levine, J.M. & Choi, H.-S. (2010). Newcomers as change agents: minority influence in task groups. In R. Martin & M. Hewstone (eds), *Minority Influence and Innovation: Antecedents, Processes, and Consequences* (pp. 229–62). New York: Psychology Press.

Levine, J.M., Choi, H.-S. & Moreland, R.L. (2003). Newcomer innovation in work teams. In P.B. Paulus & B.A. Nijstad (eds), *Group Creativity: Innovation through Collaboration* (pp. 202–24). Oxford: Oxford University Press.

Levine, J.M. & Kaarbo, J. (2001). Minority influence in political decision-making groups. In C.K.W. De Dreu & N.K. De Vries (eds), *Group Consensus and Minority Influence: Implications for Innovation* (pp. 229–57). Oxford: Blackwell.

Levine, J.M. & Kerr, N.L. (2007). Inclusion and exclusion: implications for group processes. In A.E. Kruglanski & E.T. Higgins (eds), *Social Psychology: Handbook of Basic Principles* (2nd edition, pp. 759–84). New York: Guilford.

Levine, J.M. & Moreland, R.L. (1985). Innovation and socialization in small groups. In S. Moscovici, G. Mugny & E. Van Avermaet (eds), *Perspectives on Minority Influence* (pp. 143–69). Cambridge: Cambridge University Press.

Levine, J.M. & Moreland, R.L. (1991). Culture and socialization in work groups. In L. Resnick, J. Levine & S. Teasley (eds), *Perspectives on Socially Shared Cognition* (pp. 257–79). Washington, DC: American Psychological Association.

Levine, J.M. & Moreland, R.L. (1994). Group socialization: theory and research. In W. Stroebe & M. Hewstone (eds), *The European Review of Social Psychology* (Vol. 5, pp. 305–36). Chichester: John Wiley & Sons.

Levine, J.M. & Moreland, R.L. (1999). Knowledge transmission in work groups: helping newcomers to succeed. In L.L. Thompson, J.M. Levine & D.M. Messick (eds), *Shared Cognition in Organizations: The Management of Knowledge* (pp. 267–296). Mahwah, NJ: Lawrence Erlbaum.

Levine, J.M., Moreland, R.L. & Choi, H.-S. (2001). Group socialization and newcomer innovation. In M.A. Hogg & R.S. Tindale (eds), *Blackwell Handbook of Social Psychology: Group Processes* (pp. 86–106). Oxford: Blackwell.

Levine, J.M., Moreland, R.L. & Hausmann, L.R.M. (2005). Managing group composition: inclusive and exclusive role transitions. In D. Abrams, M.A. Hogg & J.M. Marques (eds), *The Social Psychology of Inclusion and Exclusion* (pp. 139–60). New York: Psychology Press.

Lewis, K., Belliveau, M., Herndon, B. & Keller, J. (2007). Group cognition, membership change, and performance: investigating the benefits and detriments of collective knowledge. *Organizational Behavior and Human Decision Processes, 103*, 159–78.

Maass, A., West, S.G. & Cialdini, R.B. (1987). Minority influence and conversion. In C. Hendrick (ed.), *Review of Personality and Social Psychology* (Vol. 8, pp. 55–79). Newbury Park, CA: Sage.

Mackie, D.M. & Queller, S. (2000). The impact of group membership on persuasion: revisiting 'Who says what to whom with what effect?'. In D.J. Terry & M. A. Hogg (eds), *Attitudes, Behaviors, and Social Context: The Role of Norms and Group Membership* (pp. 135–55). Mahwah, NJ: Lawrence Erlbaum.

Maier, N.R.F. & Solem, A.R. (1970). The contribution of a discussion leader to the quality of group thinking: the effective use of minority opinions. *Human Relations, 5*, 277–88.

Martin, R. & Hewstone, M. (2001). Conformity and independence in groups: majorities and minorities. In M.A. Hogg & R.S. Tindale (eds), *Blackwell Handbook of Social Psychology: Group Processes* (pp. 209–34). Oxford: Blackwell.

Milanovich, D.M., Driskell, J.E., Stout, R.J. & Salas, E. (1998). Status and cockpit dynamics: a review and empirical study. *Group Dynamics: Theory, Research, and Practice, 2*, 155–67.

Miller, C.E. (1989). The social psychological effects of group decision rules. In P.B. Paulus (ed.), *Psychology of Group Influence* (2nd edition, pp. 327–55). Hillsdale, NJ: Lawrence Erlbaum.

Moreland, R.L. & Levine, J.M. (1982). Socialization in small groups: temporal changes in individual-group relations. In L. Berkowitz (ed.), *Advances in Experimental Social Psychology* (Vol. 15, pp. 137–92). New York: Academic Press.

Moreland, R.L. & Levine, J.M. (1988). Group dynamics over time: development and socialization in small groups. In J.E. McGrath (ed.), *The Social Psychology of Time: New Perspectives* (pp. 151–81). Newbury Park, CA: Sage.

Moreland, R.L. & Levine, J.M. (1989). Newcomers and oldtimers in small groups. In P.B. Paulus (ed.), *Psychology of Group Influence* (2nd edition, pp. 143–86). Hillsdale, NJ: Lawrence Erlbaum.

Moreland, R.L. & Levine, J.M. (2001). Socialization in organizations and work groups. In M.E. Turner (ed.), *Groups at Work: Theory and Research* (pp. 69–112). Mahwah, NJ: Lawrence Erlbaum.

Moscovici, S. (1976). *Social Influence and Social Change*. New York: Academic Press.

Moscovici, S. (1985). Social influence and conformity. In G. Lindzey & E. Aronson (eds), *Handbook of Social Psychology* (3rd edition, pp. 347–412). Reading, MA: Addison-Wesley.

Moscovici, S. & Lage, E. (1978). Studies in social influence IV: minority influence in a context of original judgments. *European Journal of Social Psychology, 8*, 349–65.

Nemeth, C.J. & Ormiston, M. (2007). Creative idea generation: harmony versus stimulation. *European Journal of Social Psychology, 37*, 524–35.

Nemeth, C.J., Wachtler, J. & Endicott, J. (1977). Increasing the size of the minority: some gains and some losses. *European Journal of Social Psychology, 7*, 15–27.

Nijstad, B.A. & Levine, J.M. (2007). Group creativity and the stages of creative group problem solving. In M. Hewstone, H.A.W. Schut, J.B.F. de Wit, K. van den Bos & M.S. Stroebe (eds), *The Scope of Social Psychology: Theory and Applications. Essays in Honour of Wolfgang Stroebe* (pp. 159–71). New York: Psychology Press.

Nyström, H. (1979). *Creativity and Innovation.* New York: John Wiley and Sons.

Paulus, P.B. & Nijstad, B.A. (eds) (2003). *Group Creativity: Innovation through Collaboration.* Oxford: Oxford University Press.

Phillips, K.W., Liljenquist, K.A. & Neale, M.A. (2009). Is the pain worth the gain? The advantages and liabilities of agreeing with socially distinct newcomers. *Personality and Social Psychology Bulletin, 35*, 336–50.

Ridgeway, C.L. (1982). Status in groups: the importance of motivation. *American Sociological Review, 47*, 76–88.

Ridgeway, C.L. (2001). Social status and group structure. In M.A. Hogg & R.S. Tindale (eds), *Blackwell Handbook of Social Psychology: Group Processes* (pp. 352–75). Oxford: Blackwell.

Rink, F.A. & Ellemers, N. (2009). Temporary versus permanent group membership: how the future prospects of newcomers affect newcomer acceptance and newcomer influence. *Personality and Social Psychology Bulletin, 35*, 764–76.

Schachter, S. (1951). Deviation, rejection, and communication. *Journal of Abnormal and Social Psychology, 46*, 190–207.

Staw, B.M. (1976). Knee-deep in the Big Muddy: a study of escalating commitment to a chosen course of action. *Organizational Behavior and Human Decision Processes, 16*, 27–44.

Suchner, R.W. & Jackson, D. (1976). Responsibility and status: a causal or only a spurious relationship? *Sociometry, 39*, 243–56.

Tanford, S. & Penrod, S. (1984). Social influence model: a formal integration of research on majority and minority influence processes. *Psychological Bulletin, 95*, 189–225.

Thomas-Hunt, M.C. & Phillips, K.W. (2003). Managing teams in the dynamic organization: the effects of revolving membership and changing task demands on expertise and status in groups. In R.S. Peterson & E.A. Mannix (eds), *Leading and Managing People in the Dynamic Organization* (pp. 115–33). Mahwah, NJ: Lawrence Erlbaum.

Thompson, L.L. & Choi, H.-S. (eds) (2006). *Creativity and Innovation in Organizational Teams.* Mahwah, NJ: Lawrence Erlbaum.

Torrance, E.P. (1955). Some consequences of power differences on decision making in permanent and temporary three-man groups. In A.P. Hare, E.F. Borgatta & R.F. Bales (eds), *Small Groups* (pp. 482–92). New York: Knopf.

Tuckman, B.W. (1965). Developmental sequence in small groups. *Psychological Bulletin, 63,* 384–99.

van Knippenberg, D. (1999). Social identity and persuasion: reconsidering the role of group membership. In D. Abrams & M.A. Hogg (eds), *Social Identity and Social Cognition* (pp. 315–31). Malden, MA: Blackwell.

West, M.A. (1990). The social psychology of innovation in groups. In M.A. West & J.L. Farr (eds), *Innovation and Creativity at Work: Psychological and Organizational Strategies* (pp. 309–333). Chichester: John Wiley and Sons.

West, M.A. & Wallace, M. (1991). Innovation in health care teams. *European Journal of Social Psychology, 21,* 303–15.

Wiggins, J.A., Dill, F. & Schwartz, R.D. (1965). On 'status-liability'. *Sociometry, 28,* 197–209.

Wood, W., Lundgren, S., Ouellette, J.A., Busceme, S. & Blackstone, T. (1994). Processes of minority influence: influence effectiveness and source perception. *Psychological Bulletin, 115,* 323–45.

Worchel, S. (1996). Emphasizing the social nature of groups in a developmental framework. In J.L. Nye & A.M. Brower (eds), *What's Social about Social Cognition? Research on Socially Shared Cognition in Small Groups* (pp. 261–82). Thousand Oaks, CA: Sage.

Worchel, S., Grossman, M. & Coutant, D. (1994). Minority influence in the group context: how group factors affect when the minority will be influential. In S. Moscovici, A. Mucchi-Faina & A. Maass (eds), *Minority Influence* (pp. 97–114). Chicago: Nelson-Hall.

Ziller, R.C. (1965). Toward a theory of open and closed groups. *Psychological Bulletin, 64,* 164–82.

Ziller, R.C. & Behringer, R.D. (1960). Assimilation of the knowledgeable newcomer under conditions of group success and failure. *Journal of Abnormal and Social Psychology, 60,* 288–92.

Ziller, R.C., Behringer, R.D. & Goodchilds, J.D. (1960). The minority newcomer in open and closed groups. *Journal of Psychology, 50,* 75–84.

Ziller, R.C., Behringer, R.D. & Jansen, M.J. (1961). The newcomer in open and closed groups. *Journal of Applied Psychology, 45,* 55–8.

Part II
Deviance in Groups

6

Questions about Leopards and Spots

Evaluating Deviance against a Backdrop of Threats to Collective Success

Thomas A. Morton

> *The Sicilians never want to improve for the simple reason that they think themselves perfect. Their vanity is stronger than their misery* (Don Fabrizio, head of the Salina family)
>
> *Unless we ourselves take a hand now, they'll foist a republic on us. If we want things to stay as they are, things will have to change. D'you understand?* (Tancredi, nephew of Don Fabrizio)

The above quotes are taken from the two central characters of Giuseppe Tomasi di Lampedusa's (1958) classic of Italian literature, *The Leopard*. The book details the slow decline of a fictional family of Sicilian aristocrats against the backdrop of the Risorgimento, the revolutionary movement that sought to unite separate states into a single Italy. At the beginning of the novel the arrival of revolutionaries on the island of Sicily triggers conflicting responses among the novel's main protagonists. On the one hand, there is a clear desire to hang on to old traditions and to maintain the status of the aristocracy within Sicilian society. On the other hand, there is recognition that change is inevitable, and that ultimately it might be wiser to take hold of change in order to further the interests of one's group, a sentiment clearly expressed by the character Tancredi. Interestingly, as the novel progresses, Don Fabrizio, perhaps the most prototypical instantiation of the aristocracy, does not attach himself firmly to either position. Instead he wavers ambivalently between the alternatives of stability versus change.

Rebels in Groups: Dissent, Deviance, Difference and Defiance Jolanda Jetten and Matthew J. Hornsey

In contrast to the conflicted feelings portrayed in *The Leopard*, much of social psychology has focused on the straightforward resistance that people display in the face of change. For example, research shows that continuity with the past is highly valued within groups (e.g., Sani *et al.*, 2007). When a group appears to be straying too far from its traditions, subgroups are likely to schism away from the whole in order to reassert their version of collective identity (e.g., Sani, 2005). Similar processes are evident in response to individuals who stray away from collective traditions and values. Individuals who contravene the norms of their group are typically met with hostility from their fellow group members. In extreme cases, these individuals will find themselves cut off from the rest of their group or cast out of it altogether (e.g., Schachter, 1951). In these ways, the social psychological literature tends to portray change as a negative and threatening experience, and those who signal and promote change as irritating deviants, rather than defiant rebels or inspiring revolutionaries.

Realistically, though, this can hardly reflect the whole story. If people always defended the traditions of their group, the social world would be a very static place. Although there often is remarkable stability within groups, history attests to the possibility of dynamic and radical change. Individuals sometimes do stand up and question the norms of their group. And sometimes they successfully lead their groups in new directions. Although change may be awkward to contemplate, it is not always shied away from. These observations raise two interesting questions for researchers interested in deviance. First, what might lead people to question the norms and practices of their group? And second, under what circumstances might others be open to hearing what they have to say, and to follow their lead? The present chapter presents some answers to this second question, touching along the way on themes relevant to the first as well (but see Packer, this volume, for a fuller discussion of this issue).

The Meaning of Deviance within Groups

The concept of deviance requires unpacking because it has multiple connotations. In contrast to how this word is used in popular language, in the social psychological literature deviance is typically defined in the context of group membership. Thus, deviance does not reflect some objective class of behaviour or some fixed property of the individual. Rather, what is considered to be deviant depends on the perceiver's point of view (i.e., their group membership) and the standards associated with that perspective (i.e., group norms). This account of deviance dates from early research on the 'black sheep effect' (Marques, Yzerbyt & Leyens, 1988) and has been expanded considerably in later work under the theoretical banner of 'subjective group dynamics' (see Abrams *et al.*, 2005, for an overview). Studies of this kind generally show that behaviour is perceived as (most) 'deviant', and thus evaluated (most) negatively, when it involves an ingroup member transgressing the core norms of one's group (Marques *et al.*, 1998). Outgroup members who transgress 'our' norms, or ingroup members who depart from more general social standards (e.g., Marques, Abrams & Serôdio, 2001), do not attract the same levels of negativity.

Having established this basic pattern, subsequent research has explored the conditions that accentuate or attenuate hostility towards ingroup deviants. This work shows that hostility towards norm-violating deviants is heightened when their behaviour is performed in intergroup settings rather than intragroup settings (Matheson, Cole & Majaka, 2002), when the group is experiencing some external threat to its value (Branscombe *et al.*, 1993), and when judgements are made by people who are highly identified with their group (Castano *et al.*, 2002; Marques *et al.*, 1998). These patterns support an identity-based interpretation of responses to deviance. Specifically, because the deviant represents a threat to ingroup identity, derogating these individuals and rejecting them from the group (psychologically or in actuality) allows group members to maintain a coherent image of the group as a whole (Castano *et al.*, 2002; Hutchison & Abrams, 2003) and to preserve the integrity of valued group norms (Abrams *et al.*, 2000; Marques, Paez & Abrams, 1998). Put simply, derogating ingroup deviants is a way of affirming ingroup identity.

Alternative Meanings of Deviance

Considerable evidence has amassed in support of this perspective. Highlighting the role of identity concerns in guiding responses to norm violation is an extremely important contribution of this body of work. However, having established this point, it may be time for social psychological research to take a broader perspective on deviance – and to connect the study of deviance within groups to broader issues of stability versus change within groups. Deviant group members do more within groups than simply serve as targets of criticism (e.g., Coser, 1962). In particular, deviance can play an underappreciated role in stimulating collective change. To understand this role, it seems important to consider alternative meanings of deviant behaviour, and how concerns beyond the simple reinforcement of existing ingroup norms might give rise to such alternative meanings.

Previous research has emphasised how commitment to groups determines how people attribute and react to deviance. This focus is fully consistent with the social identity approach (incorporating both social identity theory, Tajfel & Turner, 1979; and self-categorisation theory, Turner *et al.*, 1987; see Haslam, 2004, for a recent overview). Research from this perspective has shown that categorisation of the self as a group member precipitates a search for consensus within the group on identity-relevant attitudes, opinions and behaviours. Consensually agreed-upon elements become internalised as group norms. These group-based standards regulate behaviour when group membership is salient (Turner, 1991). Thus, norms are an undeniably important aspect of identity: they define what it means to be a member of a given group and adherence to them usually represents an expression of group-based identity (e.g., Terry & Hogg, 1996). However, identity is not always simply about constructing and defending norms. For example, the culture of a group will sometimes prescribe diversity and difference rather than conformity (e.g., Hornsey *et al.*, 2006). Moreover, additional factors may give rise to unique concerns that frame the ways in which identities are defined and enacted with respect to group norms. In particular, issues of *power* and *status* may place limits on the ways in which identities are expressed in the presence of specific others.

The idea that contextual factors – specifically those that relate to questions of power – might frame the expression of group normative behaviour is a key element of the subset of social identity theorising that has developed around the SIDE model. Although originally devised as an alternative account of classic deindividuation effects (i.e., the Social Identity model of Deindividuation Effects: Reicher, Spears & Postmes, 1995), some theorists in this area have developed a broader notion of SIDE as representing a model of Social Identity Definition and Enactment (e.g., Reicher, 2000; see also Klein, Spears & Reicher, 2007). Research from the latter perspective has particularly emphasised the strategic nature of group-based behaviour, and how people often tailor the representation of their group to others as a way of negotiating their relationship with these audiences and achieving particular goals in relation to them. Such goals can include displaying valued identity in the hope that it will be recognised and accepted (e.g., Barreto *et al.*, 2003). But these can also include more instrumental goals related to mobilising the support of audiences that are valuable to the ingroup's cause (e.g., Herrera & Reicher, 1998; Hopkins & Reicher, 1997; Reicher & Hopkins, 2001; Reicher, Hopkins & Condor, 1997; see also Scheepers *et al.*, 2002, 2003), or placating audiences that are potentially hostile and avoiding their disapproval (Klein & Licata, 2003; Klein *et al.*, 2003; see also Jetten, Hornsey & Adarves-Yorno, 2006, for a discussion of strategic conformity within groups). Of particular importance to the present chapter, the pursuit of instrumental goals can involve acting towards others in ways that are not entirely consistent with the norms of one's group.

For example, early work within this theoretical perspective showed that when participants were identifiable to a powerful outgroup audience, they tended to downplay public displays of intergroup bias (Reicher & Levine, 1994a) and ingroup normative behaviours that would likely be punished by their audience (Reicher & Levine, 1994b). Thus people will modify displays of group identity as a means of avoiding sanction by powerful others. More recent work also shows that people communicate varied representations of their group depending on the features of their audience and whether their goal is to mobilise these people towards or away from the ingroup position (e.g., Klein *et al.*, 2000; Sindic & Reicher, 2009). For example, group leaders involved in agitating for social change might communicate a passive image of their group to audiences who might otherwise stand in their way, while communicating a more angry and powerful image to ingroup members as a way of mobilising their group towards social change (e.g., Klein & Licata, 2003). Presumably, the 'authentic' or 'true' representation of the group and its norms is not what is being enacted in these different situations – despite the fact that social identity is likely to be equally salient. Instead, the representations that are being displayed are communicative tools designed to influence audiences in specific ways (e.g., Reicher *et al.*, 1997). We will return to this relationship between 'authentic' and 'strategic' representations later.

Taken together, the findings that have been produced within this framework alert us to the fact that although identity, norms and behaviour are often connected, there are situations within which they become disconnected – often intentionally – as group members pursue strategic objectives in relation to different audiences. One implication of this is that when individuals contravene ingroup norms, we cannot automatically assume that they are not committed to the group (see Packer, this volume). They may instead be operating as a highly committed group member, but with a particular understanding of the audience who is witness to their behaviour and the challenges or opportunities this audience represents to their ingroup. What might this possibility mean for the evaluation of deviants? Just as social psychologists should not automatically assume that anti-normative behaviour is 'deviant', group members themselves may sometimes recognise the strategic value in deviance when it contributes to the broader objectives of the group. From this perspective, the extent to which deviation away from group norms comes to be seen as negatively 'deviant' should depend on the features of the context within which deviations are performed, and on how deviation connects to the pursuit of group-based goals.

In the same way as they modify the enactment of identity *to* others, two key features that should moderate the evaluation of deviant acts performed *by* others are the extent to which outside perspectives are salient when deviance is considered, and the relationships of power that determine the value of these audiences to the ingroup's objectives. As part of our programme of research, my colleagues and I have explored how these kinds of considerations might frame responses to specific norm transgression within groups. Alongside this, we have also considered related questions of how strategic considerations might frame how group members represent their group as a whole (i.e., as diverse and encompassing of deviance versus more homogeneous and narrowly defined) and how group members think about broader issues of collective continuity versus change (i.e., deviations of the group itself from past traditions). In the following sections I briefly overview the key findings from this research, before turning to some of the new questions these findings raise and suggested directions for future research.

Evaluating Deviants: Strategic Considerations and Openness to Change

The implicit assumption of much previous social psychological research on deviance is that ingroups are the most relevant audience for deviant behaviour. Participants are typically presented with examples of norm-violating behaviour for which the participants themselves are the only meaningful source of evaluation. Rarely is any information provided about the alternative audiences to which norm violation is being performed, and who might also be evaluating behaviour. Where this type of information is provided (e.g., Matheson, Cole & Majaka, 2002), typically these audiences are members of a hostile outgroup. In the real world, though, relationships between groups are not always straightforwardly adversarial. In many cases, audiences have some material power to *facilitate* the ingroup's goals, rather than being empowered and motivated only to *impede* them. In such cases, the relationships among actor (e.g., the deviant), evaluator (i.e., the participant) and audience become overlaid with more complex concerns around power relations and the pursuit of ingroup goals.

The first question that arises from this perspective is: What happens when deviance is contemplated with external perspectives in mind? To examine whether taking an external perspective can be consequential for how individuals construe and express their identity, we (Morton & Postmes, 2005) conducted an online survey of supporters of the British Conservative Party. At the time this survey was conducted, the Conservative Party had been in a position of opposition for 8 years, had been trailing behind the Labour Party (who were in government) for at least 10 years, and consequently the fortunes of the party appeared to be in serious decline. Following their third successive electoral defeat, some within the Conservative Party were beginning to agitate for change – both in terms of the Party's leadership and in terms of its public image more generally. The sentiment behind this position was that change was necessary in order for the Party to regain the favour of the voting public and to maintain its position as a viable force within British politics. Indeed, some argued – much like Tancredi in *The Leopard* – that if the group did not change, it could risk disappearing from the political landscape altogether. Given this juncture in the group's history, and the existence of a debate about how to proceed into the future, we became interested in the factors that might be driving people towards or away from the notion of change.

Against this backdrop, we surveyed 27 Conservative Party supporters. Our participants were highly committed to the Party: the average level of identification was just above 5 on a 1-to-7 scale. We asked them about their perceptions of their group's historical continuity (following Sani *et al.*, 2007; e.g., 'The historical roots of the Conservative Party lay the foundations for the Conservative Party that exists today'), their desire for changes to their group and its image, and their estimations of the group's chances of future electoral success. Importantly, the questions about desire for change did not focus on only minor adjustments. Instead these included questions about support for fairly radical changes to the group, its image and the core values it represented. For example, we asked participants the extent to which they agreed with statements like:

> I would support moves to 're-brand' the Conservative Party (e.g., changing the party's logo or name).
>
> The Conservative Party should abandon traditional conservative values and develop a new identity.
>
> To continue to be a viable force in British politics, the Conservative Party needs to make fundamental changes to the core values of the group.

Into this survey, we embedded a manipulation designed to heighten the salience of external perspectives on their group. For a randomly selected half of the participants, two additional questions were inserted into the survey before they provided their responses to the questions about continuity, change and expected future success. Specifically, these participants were asked the extent to which they agreed (or disagreed) that the voting public did not have a clear image of their Party and what it stands for. Although these questions were fairly benign, and participants were free to express disagreement with their sentiments, our reasoning was that posing these questions forced participants to take the perspective of the electorate, rather than simply their ingroup, before they contemplated the issue of change. Importantly, in this context, the electorate is not isomorphic with the obvious outgroup (the Labour Party) but nonetheless is a relevant audience, with a meaningful relationship to the ingroup and some power to either facilitate *or* impede its broader objectives. The remaining participants were not asked these questions and, we reasoned, were therefore more likely to adopt the perspective of the ingroup rather than the electorate when giving their responses.

Consistent with our expectations, this manipulation had a significant effect on attitudes about change to the ingroup (see Figure 6.1). Those participants who were encouraged to consider the electorate's perspective were significantly *less* likely to draw connections between the party of the past and the party of the present (i.e., responded by de-emphasising historical continuity) and were significantly *more* enthusiastic about the idea of making radical changes to the group itself. Importantly, there was also some evidence that these effects were related to calculations about their group's chance of future success. Participants in the experimental condition were significantly *less* certain about their group's chances of winning the next election, and this perception was positively related to support for change and discontinuity with the past.

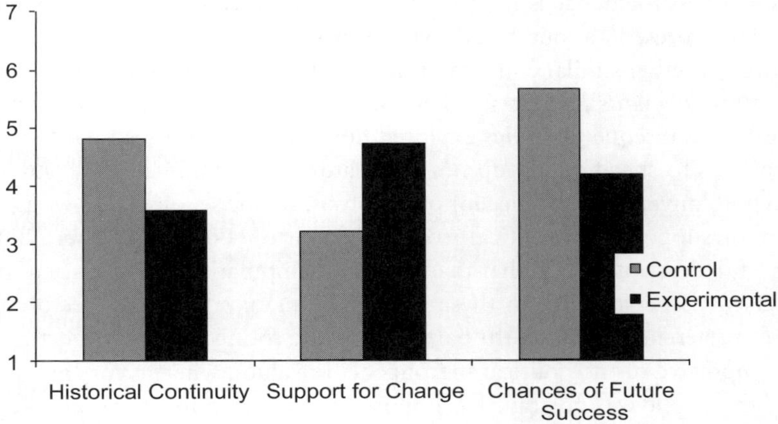

Figure 6.1 The effects of salient external perspectives on historical continuity, support for change and perceived future success

Although small, this study raises a number of interesting points. Even a highly identified group of participants did not shy away from the possibility of (radical) change. Instead, thinking about their group from the perspective of a relevant and meaningful audience raised concerns about the group's material position and this precipitated an increased willingness to entertain the possibility of collective change. This may be unsurprising given that the external perspective we activated was that of the voting public – a group that has the power to determine the ingroup's future outcomes in a very real way and who would likely respond positively to change within this group. Nonetheless, consistent research on the strategic aspects of group behaviour and identity expression demonstrates that external perspectives are important for how people consider their ingroup (see also Rabinovich & Morton, 2010; Vorauer, Main & O'Connell, 1998). More important, these findings also demonstrate that highly identified group members (cf., Castano *et al.*, 2002; Marques *et al.*, 1998) in the context of a very real threat (cf., Branscombe *et al.*, 1993) can be willing to tolerate, or even advocate, departures from their group's core values if doing so might be in the material interests of the group as a whole. Thus strategic concern might sometimes override more typical preferences for cohesion and continuity within groups.

Openness to change is not unrelated to questions of deviance – change, after all, represents a collective deviation. However, the above study does not address whether similar concerns influence the evaluation of specific norm-violating 'deviants', which is a key focus of this volume. To address this question, subsequent studies explored how similar processes might frame responses to specific ingroup norm violators. The results of these studies provide converging evidence for our analysis. In one set of studies we again drew on supporters of political groups (see Morton, Postmes & Jetten, 2007, for a full description). Rather than merely manipulating the salience of the electorate's perspective, in these studies we manipulated the electorate's likely preferences. For half the participants, the voting public was portrayed as supportive of the political ingroup's core values, whereas for the other half the public was portrayed as opposed to the ingroup's core values and more supportive of the political outgroup. After participants read this information about the context of public opinion, they were presented with a candidate from their ingroup who expressed opinions that were either normative or deviant for that group – for example, by arguing for a radical shift in the ingroup's image (Study 1) or expressing opinions that directly contradicted the defining norms of their groups (Study 2).

Again, our assumption was that a hostile voting public represents a clear threat to the ingroup. Our interest was in how participants would respond to the dilemma presented by this threat: that is, would they reassert ingroup identity in the face of a public likely to reject them (i.e., through continuing to give their support to a normative candidate), or would they put norms aside in the hope of appealing to the opinions of the public (e.g., through supporting the deviant)? A further interest of ours was who would follow each of these paths, high versus low identifiers. Based on previous research, it could be assumed that in the face of threat to the group, highly identified group members would prefer to uphold commitment to their group and its norms, for example by boosting support for normative group members. In contrast, however, we expected that high identifiers might actually be the group members who are most willing to modify their normal commitment to group norms in the interests of appealing to an audience who does not support the norm of this group.

Indeed, our results were consistent with the latter view. Across two studies, high identifiers preferred the normative candidate over the deviant only when public opinion was also supportive of the ingroup position. When the public opinion was instead against the group, this preference disappeared (Study 2) or even reversed (Study 1; see Figure 6.2). Interestingly, and reflective of the pattern observed in our online survey, there was evidence that high identifiers' differential support for normative and deviant candidates was related to strategic calculations. When the public was against their group, high identifiers were willing to support a deviant candidate because they saw this person as most likely to succeed (i.e., strategic calculations were significant mediators of candidate evaluation). Although this pattern may

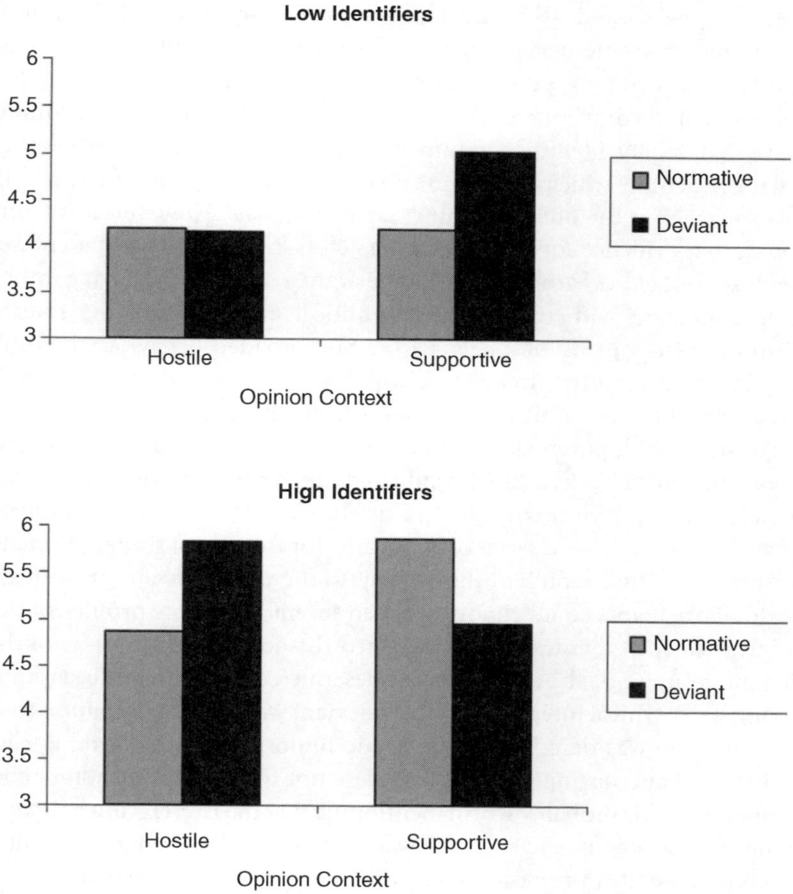

Figure 6.2 The effect of the interaction between identification and public opinion context on support for normative and deviant candidates *Source*: Morton, T.A., Postmes, T. & Jetten, J. (2007). Playing the game: when group success is more important than downgrading deviants. *European Journal of Social Psychology, 37*, 599–616, Study 1

seem 'rational', what is interesting is that such rational calculations were evident only among highly identified participants. Less identified participants did not seem so focused on strategic considerations and did not display the same systematic pattern of preference for normative and deviant candidates across conditions.

These effects suggest that the meaning of deviance can shift as a function of the strategic pressures that face the group. While deviance might ordinarily be viewed as an irritating departure from accepted wisdom, sometimes the same deviant acts can become meaningful by some other standard. Accordingly, people may be willing to put norms 'on hold' when doing so could contribute to the material goals of their group. Our studies show that highly identified group members are particularly attuned to situations within which desires for a coherent identity might need to be balanced against the pursuit of other collective goals. However, it is worth noting that evidence for this 'balancing act' is limited to highly identified members of *political* groups. It could be argued that playing such games is quite consistent with the norms of political groups – not the specific opinion-based norms of one's Party, but broader behavioural norms associated with politics. In a way, our participants' behaviour may simply reveal that they are intuitive politicians (Tetlock, 2002).

To counter this potential alternative interpretation of our prior work, we (Morton, Ford & Vargas, 2007) conducted a final study in which we stepped outside of the political context. In this study, Exeter University students were asked to evaluate a series of applicants for the role of student leader, a person who would represent their group to the university and the outside world. Participants could choose between several candidate profiles, which were varied such that they either reflected the demographic norms of this student group (e.g., the candidate was described as white, middle class and having stereotypical interests) or were a deviant within this population (e.g., the candidate was described as an ethnic minority, from a working-class background and having interests that were not typical of Exeter students). At this point, it is probably worth mentioning that the Exeter student body is highly homogeneous, and as such it was relatively easy to craft these profiles. Of course, we also pre-tested these profiles to determine that they were, indeed, perceived to be typical versus atypical for the group.

Before performing this leader selection task, in an earlier section of the study participants were asked for their opinions about a specific issue on campus – the issue of widening participation. Within the UK, widening participation refers to a set of government-supported policies to increase the diversity of groups represented on campus. Before asking for their opinions on this issue, we gave participants some background information. Half were told that the government had proposed financial incentives to encourage universities to increase student diversity, and that such money would flow to the university and be used to improve facilities directly used by students themselves. The other half were instead told that this money would be used primarily to improve services available to staff. Thus we framed the issue of increasing diversity as one that was either directly in the interests of the ingroup (students), or more directly in the interests of another group (staff). Following the logic from the previous studies, we were interested in how this manipulation would influence evaluations of normative versus deviant group members, and whether low or high identifiers would be most sensitive to such concerns.

Analyses revealed that when increasing campus diversity was presented as being in the interests of students, identification with the student ingroup was positively related to seeing widening participation policies as justified ($r = .28$, $p = .02$) and to representing the student group as actually more diverse ($r = 35$, $p = .002$). Conversely, when diversity was portrayed as being in the interests of staff but not students, identification was unrelated to support for widening participation policies ($r = .08$, $p = .52$) or to representations of ingroup diversity ($r = -.02$, $p = .90$). More interesting, these patterns were also evident in how the specific normative and deviant candidates were represented with respect to the rest of their group. As can be seen in Figure 6.3, when diversity was presented as being in the strategic interests of the student ingroup, highly identified group members portrayed the 'diversity candidate' as being equally typical for that group as the candidate who more closely reflected the group's actual demographic norm. Low identifiers under the same conditions rated the normative candidate as more typical than the deviant. When diversity was instead presented as being of little strategic value to the student ingroup (i.e., the financial benefits would flow to staff not students), both low and high identifiers rated the candidates in the same way: the normative candidate was rated more typical than the deviant (i.e., there was a significant three-way interaction between context, identification and candidate: $F_{(1, 140)} = 8.06$, $p = .005$, $\eta^2 = .05$).

These data, collected in a non-political context, again suggest that people sometimes forgo their preference for normative group members when doing so could further the material interests of their group. As before, this pattern of strategic thinking was most evident among highly identified group members. These findings imply that there is considerable flexibility in

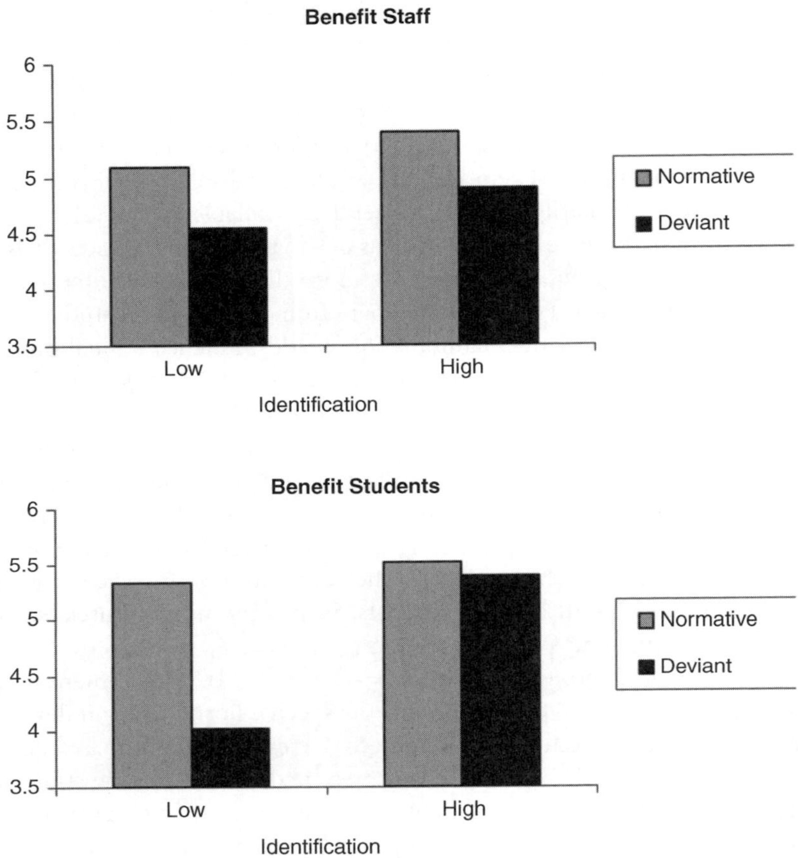

Figure 6.3 The interaction among identification, benefit context and candidate profile on evaluations of typicality *Source*: Morton, T.A., Ford, G. & Vargas, A. (2007). Unpublished data, University of Exeter

both high identifiers' evaluation of specific deviant ingroup members and also their representation of the group as a whole. In this study, high identifiers portrayed a 'strategic choice' as typical for their group, despite this person being factually deviant on more objective criteria. It remains unclear to what extent this representation of the deviant was sincere – that is, reflective of actual changes in high identifiers perceived as typical versus a purely strategic presentation of typicality limited to that moment. Notwithstanding this caveat, the pattern of enhanced perceptions of deviant typicality opens up the possibility that deviant individuals might sometimes find themselves in a position to redefine the meaning of the group and take it in new directions. In the final section of this chapter, I will try to draw out some of these broader implications.

Can a Leopard Change its Spots?

I began this chapter with the observation that much social psychological research tends to portray groups as highly resistant to change, and likewise resistant to individuals who might promote change by embodying departure from valued group norms. In contrast to this dominant view, however, I suggest that sometimes the pressures of a given situation will leave people needing to balance their desire to preserve collective traditions against a material reality in which it may be wiser for the group to rethink these practices in order to further the interests of the group. Striking a balance between continuity and change within groups is likely to be an awkward process. However, in our studies at least, high identifiers seem to resolve this balancing act relatively easily in favour of what is in the (broader) interests of their group, even if this means going against the collective grain (see also Packer, this volume). This process is evident in general thinking about change to the group, specific responses to norm-violating deviants, and representations of deviants within the group as a whole. These patterns extend the logic of previous research on strategic aspects of identity enactment, which has demonstrated that group members sometimes modify performances of identity in response to constraints imposed by a given setting. Along similar lines, our research shows that highly identified group members sometimes tolerate varied performances of identity by others when such performances might facilitate the achievement of important group goals. Although there are a number of issues that these findings might raise, we limit ourselves in the present discussion to just two: (a) the multiple meanings of deviance and (b) how strategic calculations might impact upon collective change.

One of the points we have tried to make through the present research is that deviant acts can attract multiple meanings. A single instance of deviant behaviour can be viewed as a meaningless distraction or an irritating violation of collective wisdom. Alternatively, the same behaviour could be seen as a brave act of individual self-expression or an interesting proposition for the rest of the group. Finally, people might simply find themselves confused by deviant behaviour and suspend their judgement until they know more. Interestingly, classic research (e.g., Schachter, 1951) suggests that the last of these alternatives might be the most typical response to encountering deviance. This research found that group members typically respond to deviance by first increasing their communication with the deviant individual. First and foremost, people wanted to understand the deviant. Only when the deviant did not subsequently respond to their group were they actually cut off. Although much contemporary theorising about deviance explicitly builds on the insights from these early interactive studies, in the transition from classic findings to contemporary theory the desire for people to make sense of deviants seems to have been lost (see Jetten, Iyer, Hutchison & Hornsey, this volume, for a similar point).

Through the research summarised here, we would like to suggest that sometimes deviance can be a meaningful act, and that when deviance is construed as meaningful it is not automatically rejected. Based on this research, it would seem that highly identified group members are the most motivated to resolve the meaning of deviant acts by ingroup members. This is because highly identified group members should be most concerned about the welfare of their group, and therefore most sensitive to the suggestion that collective welfare is at stake. Deviance, or more accurately dissent, is one source of such a suggestion. Thus in response to apparent deviance, highly identified group members might first seek to understand whether the individual is departing from group norms for their own personal reasons, or because they believe that the group as a whole needs to consider also taking such action. In the absence of direct communication with the deviant, highly identified group members may use contextual cues (e.g., the setting in which deviance is performed) as a way of decoding the meaning of such actions.

To capture this process of sense-making, it would seem important for future research on responses to deviance within groups to start to consider more fully the contexts within which deviance is performed, and how these contexts might represent different configurations of deviant action and collective interest. Beyond specific varied responses to deviant individuals, we believe that the study of deviance can also inform thinking about the processes of collective change. After all, collective change often results from some interplay between external pressure and internal dissent (see Hornsey *et al.*, 2006). Our studies suggest that external pressures can determine the extent to which highly identified group members police the norms of their group or relax these in the interests of the group. It would seem useful for future research to consider more fully the consequences of such flexibility for collective change.

The SIDE perspective, an important framework for this research, could be interpreted as suggesting that group members readily distinguish between the 'authentic' representation of their group and the representation that is performed to specific others. Thus it may be that norms are relaxed only within the specific context in which deviance is considered, and only for the deviant individual for whom external pressures are seen to be governing behaviour. However, the distinction between authentic and performative identities is unlikely to be quite so sharp (Klein *et al.*, 2007). Instead, the way in which identities are performed feeds back into how these are represented – identities are, in part, constituted and reconstituted through performance. If this is true, the pattern of strategic tolerance of deviance identified in this chapter raises an interesting question about the dynamism of responses to deviance more generally. Specifically, once the norms of one's group have been relaxed, because doing so might contribute positively to the goals of the group, do these norms then remain flexible? Or do they 'snap back' as soon as the context changes and strategic considerations recede? Or, indeed, might group members defend their new norms even more rigidly to avoid accusations of strategic posturing and inconsistency?

It seems likely that the answer to this question will depend on the extent to which deviant acts actually *do* lead to collective success – that is, the extent to which the strategy is realised. To the extent that a shifting away from accepted practices does reap dividends for the group, the once-deviant individual might find themselves now at the centre of the group and its (new) material reality. Thus deviant individuals who are initially accepted for strategic reasons may subsequently find themselves in a position of influence rather than just toleration. However, to the extent that strategically supported deviants are instead met with failure, it seems likely that they would run a particular risk of becoming a scapegoat for their group. In this sense, failure may lead flexible norms to 'snap back' and for evaluations of norm-violating deviants to become even more extremely negative. A similar concern has been raised in the literature on gender and leadership. Researchers in this area have shown that failing company fortunes often precede the appointment of atypical leaders (e.g., women, minorities), and that this situation represents both an opportunity to these individuals and a great risk if subsequent failure is attributed to them rather than to the conditions of their appointment (Ryan & Haslam, 2005, 2007). These divergent possibilities highlight the fact that the balance between the material realities of one's group and strategic positioning in response to this is often precarious, particularly for those individuals who find themselves acting at the intersection of these considerations.

Conclusion

Is vanity always stronger than misery? Or more precisely, will group members always (vainly) adhere to and enforce the norms of their group, even when doing so would consign their group to the misery of defeat? Standing behind the research that we have conducted is the assumption that groups can be responsive to the need for change and that sometimes they will act in ways that embrace change than resist it. On the one hand, our data suggest that the choice between vanity and misery is very easily resolved – at least among highly identified group members. If the interests of the group are at stake, then the norms must change. Thus, our data suggest that the sentiments of Tancredi might accurately capture the ways in which highly identified group members contemplate (necessary) changes to their group.

Despite the evidence we have presented in support of this position, we suspect that this dilemma is not always dealt with so easily. Any balance achieved between the demands of external realities and the needs or interests expressed within the group is likely to be a precarious one. Rather than being straightforwardly motivated by the goal of maximising the material success of their group, highly identified group members are perhaps most likely to be aware of the dilemmas faced by their group, and the opportunities as well as challenges represented by both continuity and change. Accordingly these group members should be most motivated to understand the actions of others that might signal the need for change (e.g., deviation by fellow group members) and to respond to such signals in ways that bring the group forward without pulling it apart. Thus, highly identified group members may, in fact, be more like Don Fabrizio as they contemplate both continuity and change with an equal awareness of the opportunities and pitfalls both these paths represent for their group.

References

Abrams, D., Marques, J. M., Bown, N. & Henson, M. (2000). Pro-norm and anti-norm deviance within and between groups. *Journal of Personality and Social Psychology, 78*, 906–12.

Abrams, D., Randsley de Moura, G., Hutchison, P. & Viki, G. T. (2005). When bad becomes good (and vice versa): why social exclusion is not based on difference. In D. Abrams, M. Hogg & J. Marques (eds), *The Social Psychology of Inclusion and Exclusion* (pp. 161–89). Hove: Psychology Press.

Barreto, M., Spears, R., Ellemers, N. & Shahinper, K. (2003). Who wants to know? The influence of audience on identity expression among minority group members. *British Journal of Social Psychology, 42,* 299–318.

Branscombe, N.R., Wann, D.L., Noel, J.G. & Coleman, J. (1993). Ingroup or outgroup extremity: importance of the threatened social identity. *Personality and Social Psychology Bulletin, 19,* 381–8.

Castano, E., Paladino, M., Coull, A. & Yzerbyt, V. (2002). Protecting the ingroup stereotype: ingroup identification and the management of deviant ingroup members. *British Journal of Social Psychology, 41,* 365–85.

Coser, L. (1962). Some functions of deviant behavior and normative flexibility. *American Journal of Sociology, 68,* 172–81.

Haslam, S.A. (2004). *Psychology in Organizations: The Social Identity Approach* (2nd edition). Thousand Oaks, CA: Sage.

Herrera, M. & Reicher, S.D. (1998). Making sides and taking sides: an analysis of salient images and category constructions for pro- and anti-Gulf war respondents. *European Journal of Social Psychology, 28,* 981–93.

Hopkins, N. & Reicher, S.D. (1997). The construction of social categories and processes of social change. In G. Breakwell & E. Lyons (eds), *Changing European Identities.* London: Butterworth.

Hornsey, M.J., Jetten, J., McAuliffe, B. & Hogg, M.A. (2006). The impact of individualist and collectivist group norms on evaluations of dissenting group members. *Journal of Experimental Social Psychology, 42,* 57–68.

Hutchison, P. & Abrams, D. (2003). Ingroup identification moderates stereotypes change in reaction to ingroup deviance. *European Journal of Social Psychology, 33,* 497–506.

Jetten, J., Hornsey, M.J. & Adarves-Yorno, I. (2006). When group members admit to being conformist: the role of relative intragroup status in conformity self-reports. *Personality and Social Psychology Bulletin, 32,* 162–73.

Klein, O., Azzi, A.E., Brito, R. & Berckmans, S. (2000). Nationalism and the strategic expression of identity. In T. Postmes, R. Spears, M. Lea & S. Reicher (eds), *SIDE Issues Centre Stage: Recent Developments in Studies of De-Individuation in Groups* (pp. 131–41). Amsterdam: Royal Netherlands Academy of Arts and Sciences.

Klein, O. & Licata, L. (2003). When group representations serve social change: the speeches of Patrice Lumumba during the decolonization of Congo. *British Journal of Social Psychology, 42,* 571–94.

Klein, O., Licata, L., Azzi, A.E. & Durala, I. (2003). 'How European am I?' Prejudice expression and the presentation of social identity. *Self & Identity, 2*, 251–64.

Klein, O., Spears, R. & Reicher, S.D. (2007). Identity performance: extending the strategic side of SIDE. *Personality and Social Psychology Review, 11*, 28–45.

Marques, J.M., Abrams, D., Paez, D. & Martinez-Toboada, C. (1998). The role of categorisation and in-group norms in judgments of groups and their members. *Journal of Personality and Social Psychology, 75*, 976–88.

Marques, J.M., Abrams, D. & Serôdio, R.G. (2001). Being better by being right: subjective group dynamics and derogation of ingroup deviants when generic norms are undermined. *Journal of Personality and Social Psychology, 81*, 436–77.

Marques, J.M., Paez, D. & Abrams, D. (1998). Social identity and intragroup differentiation as subjective social control. In S. Worchel, J. Morales, D. Paez & J.-C. Deschamps (eds), *Social Identity: International Perspectives* (pp. 124–41). New York: Sage.

Marques, J.M., Yzerbyt, V. & Leyens, J.-P. (1988). Extremity of judgments toward ingroup members as a function of ingroup identification. *European Journal of Social Psychology, 18*, 1–16.

Matheson, K., Cole, B. & Majaka, K. (2002). Dissidence from within: examining the effects of intergroup context on group members' reaction to attitudinal opposition. *Journal of Experimental Social Psychology, 39*, 161–9.

Morton, T.A., Ford, G. & Vargas, A. (2007). Unpublished data, University of Exeter.

Morton, T.A. & Postmes, T. (2005). Unpublished data, University of Exeter.

Morton, T.A., Postmes, T. & Jetten, J. (2007). Playing the game: when group success is more important than downgrading deviants. *European Journal of Social Psychology, 37*, 599–616.

Rabinovich, A. & Morton, T.A. (2010). Who says that we are bad people? The impact of criticism source and attributional content on responses to group-based criticism. *Personality and Social Psychology Bulletin, 36*, 524–36.

Reicher, S.D. (2000). Social identity definition and enactment: a broad SIDE against irrationalism and relativism. In T. Postmes, R. Spears, M. Lea & S. Reicher (eds), *SIDE Issues Centre Stage: Recent Developments in Studies of De-Individuation in Groups* (pp. 175–90). Amsterdam: Royal Netherlands Academy of Arts and Sciences.

Reicher, S.D. & Hopkins, N. (2001). *Self and Nation*. London: Sage.

Reicher, S.D., Hopkins, N. & Condor, S. (1997). Stereotype construction as a strategy of influence. In R. Spears, P. Oakes, S.A. Haslam & N. Ellemers (eds), *Stereotyping and Social Identity*. Oxford: Blackwell.

Reicher, S.D. & Levine, M. (1994a). Deindividuation, power relations between groups and the expression of social identity: the effect of visibility to the out-group. *British Journal of Social Psychology*, *33*, 145–63.

Reicher, S.D. & Levine, M. (1994b). On the consequences of deindividuation manipulations for the strategic communication of the self: identifiability and the presentation of social identity. *European Journal of Social Psychology*, *24*, 511–24.

Reicher, S.D., Spears, R. & Postmes, T. (1995). A social identity model of deindividuation phenomena. In W. Stroebe & M. Hewstone (eds), *European Review of Social Psychology* (pp. 161–98). Chichester: John Wiley & Sons, Ltd.

Ryan, M.K. & Haslam, S.A. (2005). The glass cliff: evidence that women are over-represented in precarious leadership positions. *British Journal of Management*, *16*, 81–90.

Ryan, M.K. & Haslam, S.A. (2007). The glass cliff: exploring the dynamics surrounding women's appointment to precarious leadership positions. *Academy of Management Review*, *32*, 549–72.

Sani, F. (2005). When subgroups secede: extending and refining the social psychological model of schisms in groups. *Personality and Social Psychology Bulletin*, *31*, 1074–86.

Sani, F., Bowe, M., Herrera, M., Manna, C., Cossa, T., Miao, X. & Zhou, Y. (2007). Perceived collective continuity: seeing groups as entities that move through time. *European Journal of Social Psychology*, *37*, 1118–34.

Schachter, S. (1951). Deviation, rejection and communication. *Journal of Abnormal and Social Psychology*, *46*, 190–207.

Scheepers, D., Spears, R., Doosje, B. & Manstead, A.S.R. (2002). Integrating identity and instrumental approaches to intergroup discrimination: different contexts, different motives. *Personality and Social Psychology Bulletin*, *28*, 1455–67.

Scheepers, D., Spears, R., Doosje, B. & Manstead, A.S.R. (2003). Two functions of verbal intergroup discrimination: identity and instrumental motives as a result of group identification and threat. *Personality and Social Psychology Bulletin*, *29*, 568–77.

Sindic, D. & Reicher, S.D. (2009). The instrumental use of group prototypicality judgments. *Journal of Experimental Social Psychology*, *44*, 1425–35.

Tajfel, H. & Turner, J. (1979). An integrative theory of intergroup conflict. In W. Austin & S. Worchel (eds), *The Social Psychology of Intergroup Relations* (pp. 33–47). Monterey, CA: Brooks/Cole.

Terry, D.J. & Hogg, M.A. (1996). Group norms and the attitude-behavior relationship. A role for group identification. *Personality and Social Psychology Bulletin*, *22*, 776–93.

Tetlock, P.E. (2002). Social functionalist frameworks for judgment and choice: intuitive politicians, theologians, and prosecutors. *Psychological Review, 109*, 451–71.

Tomasi di Lampedusa, G. (1958). *Il gattopardo* [The Leopard]. Milan: Feltrinelli.

Turner, J.C. (1991). *Social Influence.* Pacific Grove, CA: Brooks/Cole.

Turner, J.C., Hogg, M.A., Oakes, P.J., Reicher, S.D. & Wetherell, M.S. (1987). *Rediscovering the Social Group: A Self-Categorization Theory*. Blackwell: Oxford.

Vorauer, J.D., Main, K.J. & O'Connell, G.B. (1998). How do individuals expect to be viewed by members of lower status groups? Content and implications of meta-stereotypes. *Journal of Personality and Social Psychology, 75*, 917–37.

7

Debating Deviance

Responding to Those who Fall from Grace

Jolanda Jetten, Aarti Iyer, Paul Hutchison and Matthew J. Hornsey

Everyone makes mistakes. Even those who appear to be exemplary model citizens may at times go astray. Consider for instance the case of Nobel Prize winner Günter Grass, one of Germany's best and most renowned writers. For years Germans placed him on a moral pedestal, considering him to be the 'conscience of the nation'. Grass had always been open about the fact that, as a 17 year old, he was briefly in the German army at the end of World War II. Recently, however, he admitted that, in fact, he had joined the Waffen SS, and had done so voluntarily. The public responses to this revelation are perhaps more interesting than the question of why Grass had been silent about this for so many years.

Many people, such as the Polish politician Lech Walesa, felt that Grass had fallen from grace, and that the appropriate sanction would be the return of his Nobel Prize and other honours. Commentators wrote that Grass had committed 'moral suicide' – all his previous achievements had been reduced to ashes. People were particularly harsh on him because Grass was well known for demanding that all Germans should face up to their Nazi past: he had violated the high standard to which he had held others.

In contrast, there were also those who fiercely defended Grass, arguing that it is important to acknowledge the circumstances of his action. They reminded the world that Grass was very young at the time, and that he could not have known about the atrocities of the Waffen SS when he joined (because they mostly came to light after the war). Fellow author Salman Rushdie argued that Grass had not fired a shot while he was in the SS. Another author, John Irvin, emphasised the fact that these revelations did not diminish Grass' moral standing, but rather actually served to increase it.

Rebels in Groups: Dissent, Deviance, Difference and Defiance Jolanda Jetten and Matthew J. Hornsey

Specifically, Irvin commented that: 'Grass remains a hero to me, both as a writer and as a moral compass; his courage, both as a writer and as a citizen of Germany, is exemplary – a courage heightened, not lessened, by his most recent revelation' (Irvin, 2006).

Turning to the social psychological literature on responding to deviance, it is not the harsh punishment of Grass but the defence of him that – from our current theorising – we would have most difficulty explaining. Indeed, a scant reading of the literature would lead us to expect that fellow ingroup members would respond particularly harshly to those who have lied and damaged the reputation of the group with their deviant behaviour (e.g., Hornsey & Jetten, 2003; Marques & Paez, 1994; Marques, Abrams & Serôdio, 2001). It is argued that precisely because deviants undermine the integrity of our group, derogating such individuals and excluding them from the ingroup serves the important function of maintaining a positive and distinctive social identity (Hutchison & Abrams, 2003; Marques & Paez, 1994).

However, there are two aspects of the responses to Grass (and other deviants like him) that are typically not addressed in our theorising and these are the issues that we will focus on in this chapter. First, it appeared that it was those who were particularly close to Grass (e.g., ingroup members such as other writers or artists) who were most likely to argue that Grass' silence about his past was not deviant at all. And, even if they did classify his behaviour as an act of deviance, they did not necessarily endorse punishment. Indeed, as John Irvin's comment illustrates, Grass' deviance had, rather ironically, made him a better person in the eyes of those close to him. Second, even if ingroup members acknowledge that the group member engages in deviant behaviour, it may be just as common for ingroup members to turn a blind eye to transgressions as it may be to evaluate the deviant harshly. That is, despite the fact that Grass' deviant behaviour appeared clear and unambiguous, current theorising has difficulty explaining the reality that there was little consensus in the response to Grass' revelation: responses varied from strong condemnation to forgiveness. With our theorising geared at explaining ingroup condemnation, how can we account for more lenient responses by ingroup members to transgressions by other ingroup members?

In this chapter, we examine some of the factors that affect responses to two questions about a group member who appears to have committed a transgression. First, in the eyes of other ingroup members, should the behaviour of this individual be classified as deviant? As illustrated

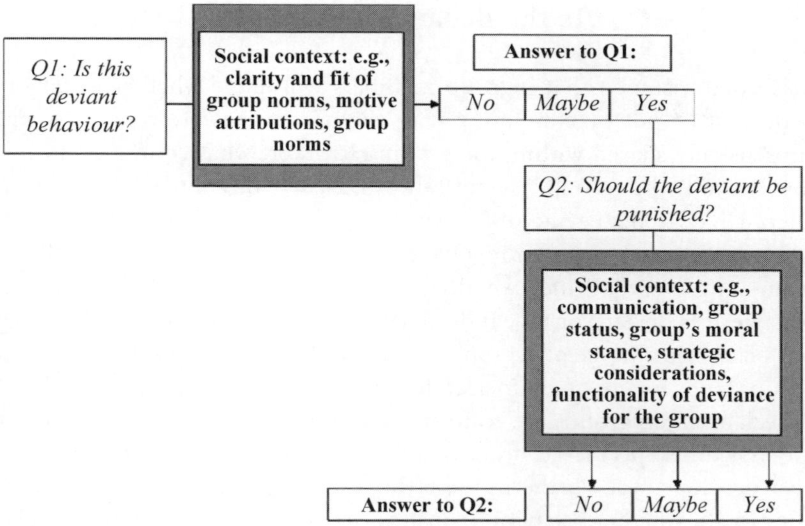

Figure 7.1 Responding to deviants

in Figure 7.1, we focus our analysis on the clarity of group norms, attributions about what motivated the individual to act as he or she did, and the content of group norms. In particular, we focus on how characteristics of the group, such as its endorsement of heterogeneity and individuality as a core group value or norm, can affect whether behaviour is labelled as deviance.

If the answer to the question of whether the behaviour should be appraised as deviance is 'yes', another question follows: Should the deviant be punished? The broader social context, including the position of the group in relation to other groups, is one important factor that will affect the answer to this question (see Figure 7.1). Our recent research provides some evidence that group members who have taken the moral high ground differ in their judgement of the extent to which deviant behaviour is damaging and should be punished, compared to groups that do not place themselves on a moral pedestal. Our reasoning is in line with other work that suggests that morality is a distinct dimension of comparison and that strong responses are evoked when morality is involved (Bandura *et al.*, 1996; Leach, Ellemers & Barreto, 2007). We also briefly discuss other factors such as the functionality of deviance for the group and strategic factors that may affect the extent to which group members endorse punishment of the deviant.

Is the Behaviour Deviant?

It is often assumed that ingroup members will judge whether behaviour is deviant or not by comparing it to the norms that are central to, and consensually shared within, the group. However, what counts as normative within the group is not always clear (Birchmeier, Joinson & Dietz-Uhler, 2005; Levine, 1989). In contrast to a typical laboratory setting where transgressions often involve clear rule violations or harmful behaviours, in everyday life, we do not always intuitively know whether behaviour is deviant or not. Indeed, labelling of behaviour as deviant may not occur for a range of reasons. For example, norms regarding what the group stands for are often unclear, implicit or perhaps not even articulated. Especially when groups are confronted with a particular transgression for the first time, specific group norms to judge the behaviour may not have been developed yet. Furthermore, as the case of Günter Grass illustrates, the question of whether behaviour constitutes deviance is often hotly debated.

Such discussions were observed in an online community where it was learned that one member had taken on a fake identity and had presented himself as someone else for an extended period of time (Birchmeier, Joinson & Dietz-Uhler, 2005). It appeared that, precisely because this type of deviance had not previously occurred in this community, there were no clear norms as to how to respond to the transgression. In the days that followed the revelation of fraud, communication within the group served the function of establishing whether the act should be appraised as deviance, what the norms of the group were, and what the most appropriate group response would be.

However, even if we agree with others that a person's behaviour is unambiguously deviant, there might still be considerable variability in others' appraisal of the behaviour and the individual. Birchmeier, Joinson & Dietz-Uhler (2005) show, for example, a range of responses to the deviant within the online community that they examined. Whereas some expressed strong hostility towards the deviant, others were more understanding of how the individual deviant could have gone astray. One of our own studies – which qualitatively examined how people respond to deviance in the context of serious deviant behaviour – provides additional evidence that there is typically no consensus within groups as to whether the behaviour should be labelled as deviant (Iyer & Jetten, 2009).

Our study was conducted in 2004, after allegations had emerged that American soldiers had abused Iraqi prisoners while stationed at the

Abu-Ghraib prison in Iraq. It then came to light that British troops had also abused Iraqi prisoners in separate incidents. In May 2004, the BBC website published an online bulletin board entitled 'Iraqi prisoner pictures: Your reaction'. Readers were invited to post their responses to photographs documenting abuse by British and American soldiers. Comments were posted from around the world, including Europe, Asia, North and Central America, Africa and the Middle East. The bulletin board thus provided an opportune real-world context for an exploratory analysis of ingroup members' (i.e., British and American citizens) and outgroup members' (i.e., citizens from other countries) responses to rule-breakers. In a content analysis of responses to British and American soldiers' abuse of Iraqi prisoners, we examined the extent to which ingroup members criticised the rule breaking or made attempts to excuse it.

Coding by two independent coders of the themes that emerged from the posts revealed a range of responses to rule breaking by fellow group members. We found that, like nearly all outgroup members, most British and American respondents had strong negative reactions to soldiers from their countries who had abused Iraqi prisoners. However, a quite sizeable minority also made statements excusing the soldiers' rule breaking and minimising the implications of the rule breaking. This study thus provides evidence for the key assumption in our argument: some ingroup members do attempt to excuse rule breaking or minimise its impact, regardless of the severe harm caused by these transgressions (e.g., psychological and physical harm to prisoners of war). Indeed, and consistent with our reasoning, there was more variability in ingroup members' responses to these transgressions than there was variability in outgroup members' responses.

Motive

In determining whether behaviour should be appraised as deviant, we also take into account people's attributions of what motivated the individual's transgression. Did he or she have a good reason to behave in this way, why did he or she not take an alternative course of action, and what were the specific circumstances? Research illustrates how important attributions of motive are in determining responses to ingroup members who have been critical of the group (Hornsey, 2006; Hornsey & Imani, 2004). It has been found that criticism is often tolerated, and even welcomed, by other ingroup members when the critic appears to be critical because s/he cares for the group. In such cases, pointing out potential problems appears to be a constructive attempt to improve the group, rather than a malicious attack to cause harm to the group. Arguably, then, questions about motive are also asked when an ingroup member engages in morally objectionable behaviour. Why did the person behave in this way? As the defenders of Grass highlighted, there were many circumstances that should be taken into account when making attributions about why Grass joined the SS. Indeed, it was argued that given the specific historical context, Grass did what everyone else would have done and that his decision to join the SS should therefore not reflect negatively on him personally.

In addition to attributions about what motivated the individual to engage in certain behaviours, we need to take into account the broader social context in order to understand whether the behaviour is labelled as deviant. In particular, the appraisal of deviance is contextually bound and determined by consensually held group norms that shape and determine appropriate conduct within groups. In his classic analysis of social influence, Moscovici (1976) already alluded to the importance of group norms when he proposed that in addition to objectivity norms (which enhance conformity to majority norms), group members may endorse preference norms (an absence of pressure to conform and tolerance for opinion diversity), and even originality norms (the pressure on individual group members to adopt unique positions).

Group Norms as Determinants of what is Deviant

Recently, researchers have systematically examined the moderating role of group norms in responding to deviance and dissent (e.g., Hornsey *et al.*, 2006; Postmes, Spears & Cihangir, 2001). For example, Hornsey and colleagues (2006) reported two studies showing that group norms moderated responses to dissenters in the group. In these studies, group norms were manipulated to prescribe either individualism or collectivism, and participants were asked to evaluate a group member expressing an attitude that either dissented from, or was in concordance with, the group. Not surprisingly, when norms prescribed collectivism, group members who held concordant attitudes were evaluated more positively than group members who held dissenting attitudes. However, in conditions where groups endorsed individualism, there was evidence in both studies that high identifiers in particular attenuated their preference for concordant over dissenting attitudes. It appeared that, in such conditions, being different and dissenting from others in the group became normative and was thus no longer appraised as deviant.

Groups can also endorse norms that encourage tolerance of differences (i.e., diversity norms). In such contexts, rather paradoxically, group members would show their loyalty to the group by supporting those who are different or even deviant within the group. We found some evidence for this in two studies where we manipulated the variability of the group and whether group members were typical or atypical (Hutchison, Jetten & Gutierrez, 2010). The first study revealed that evaluations of typical group members did not differ as a function of the perceived variability of the group. However, atypical ingroup members were evaluated more positively when the group was presented as heterogeneous than when it was presented as more homogeneous. A second study showed that this effect was moderated by group identification. Group identification was negatively associated with evaluations of the atypical group member when the ingroup was perceived as homogeneous, but was positively associated with target evaluations when the ingroup was perceived as heterogeneous. Thus, in particular those who were highly identified with the group responded favourably to those who were different when being different was an expression of group identity.

In sum, in everyday life (and in contrast to many laboratory situations) people are often presented with transgressions that may or may not be labelled as such. Some of these transgressions are serious and harmful, and others are less damaging. Regardless of how severe the transgression is, group members may answer the question of whether the behaviour is deviant with 'no', 'maybe' or 'yes' (see Figure 7.1). Ingroup members' response to this question depends on their perception of the broader social context and, in particular, their understanding of the normative context. However, even when group norms are available, group members may differ in the ways they interpret these norms, in whether they perceive the norms as applicable, and in the extent to which they agree that norms define the group. Norms are also tied to group membership: what is normative behaviour in one group may be considered to be deviant in another. Even if we make an attribution that the person was in the wrong by breaking important consensually endorsed group specific norms, we still appear to take into account why the person did what they did. Did they have a choice and was an alternative action possible? Indeed, the question of intentionality and motivation is one that is central to most legal systems (e.g., the difference between murder and manslaughter). Whether perceivers conclude that behaviour should be labelled as deviance or not is a question that needs to be answered before we can understand whether punishment is required.

Should the Deviant be Punished?

When rule breaking has been labelled as constituting a deviant act, previous research suggests that rejection and punishment appear to be the dominant responses. Indeed, researchers have emphasised the hostility and negativity expressed towards deviants and their exclusion from the group, either physically or psychologically (e.g., Festinger, Schachter & Back, 1950). However, it is also clear that group members are at times quite forgiving of other ingroup members' transgressions, even when they have been involved in extreme acts of deviance. Below, we outline a number of factors that have been shown to affect the extent to which a deviant can face forgiveness or harsh treatment.

Communicating with the deviant

Even if there is consensus within a group that the behaviour is deviant and despicable, immediate eviction from the group is often not possible (and is even less likely in laboratory settings). In such cases, it has been found that the nature of the responses to, and interactions with, the deviant change over time. A classic study by Schachter (1951) illustrates this point. In this study, three confederates took part in a group discussion where there was pressure for uniformity. The confederates either: (a) were extremely deviant throughout the whole discussion; (b) took a modal position throughout the discussion; or (c) started the discussion with an extremely deviant position, shifting over time to a more modal position (i.e., 'the slider').

Results showed that the deviant who remained deviant throughout the discussion attracted the most communication from other group members and that this communication was aimed at bringing the deviant back in line with the rest of the group. It was only at the end of the discussion that the amount of communication directed at the consistent deviant was reduced, presumably because group members had realised that their efforts to change the deviant's opinion were futile. Interestingly too, the slider, who was open to influence by the group, was increasingly accepted by the group over time. Communication with the slider also decreased once s/he had taken on a more modal position. It thus appears that the process of reinstating the dissenter or deviant can be quick, as long as the deviant is willing to adopt the majority view. The results also demonstrate that the deviant's history, as well as their response to the group's attempts to reform them, may influence other group members' willingness to punish them for their transgression. For example, whether the deviants show remorse for their actions, and whether this is their first offence (Gollwitzer & Keller, 2010), affects the extent to which punishment is likely.

Given these results, why is it that our current theorising suggests that automatic rejection of deviants is the norm? Perhaps one reason is that the methodology most often used to examine responses to deviant behaviour does not allow for the study of how responses develop over time, or how people communicate with the deviant. Indeed, the question of 'what should be done with the deviant' is difficult to examine using paper and pencil methods that preclude interaction with other members of the group. In addition, the research is often set up in such a way as to allow only a limited range of possible responses to the deviant, focusing primarily on acceptance versus rejection of the deviant (Santee & Maslach, 1982). Participants are typically not given the option of responding more actively, for example by being able to generate a number of different ways in which they would deal with the deviant (e.g., 'We would first try this strategy, and if it does not work, we would go on to try another one.'). In addition, in the typical social psychology experiment, only limited information about the deviant is provided to participants. The attempt to ensure experimental control typically results in nothing being said about whether there is a history of transgressions in the group, whether the deviant took a moral stance, or what the deviant's motivations may be (except of course if these variables are of central interest).

Although our procedures allow for a detailed examination of one particular response to deviance, they do not allow us to map out the diversity of the ways in which people may respond to deviance. Even more problematic is the fact that, because we do not allow for active and diverse responding, the focus of the theorising that we developed is by definition limited and does not capture the full spectrum of responses to deviance (see Haslam & McGarty, 2001, for a similar point).

Turning a blind eye

Even when there are clear norms about what is acceptable behaviour within a particular group, separating moral from immoral behaviour is not as straightforward as it might first appear. Rather paradoxically, precisely because the group emphasises a particular moral standard, it may more readily invite violations of that particular moral standard. This is because both the deviant and those who conform are bound by the same context and normative rules. Erikson (1966) makes the argument that conformity to important group norms and transgressions against those same norms are often closely related: 'The thief and his victim share a common respect for the value of property; the heretic and the inquisitor speak much the same language and are keyed to the same religious mysteries; the traitor and the patriot act in reference to the same political institutions, often use the same methods, and for that matter are sometimes the same person' (p. 20). Building on this argument, we propose that when groups take a moral stance, they are more likely to struggle in determining the appropriate response to those who break that norm. At times, the perfect past moral record and the high moral superiority of the group may make it harder for individuals to detect that wrongdoing has occurred. Moral superiority may confer an especially stable position of high status that is less immune to doubt or challenge.

We examined the idea that perceptions of a group's prior moral record should influence evaluations of rule breaking in studies where we directly manipulated moral superiority. In all studies, we also measured identification with the group to investigate its moderating influence on evaluations of rule breaking and its implications for the group (Iyer, Jetten & Haslam, 2010). In a first study among academics, we examined how high and low identifiers with a department evaluate an ingroup member who violated ethical principles in his research, comparing responses when the group had taken the high moral ground to those when it had not. Specifically, we were interested in participants' perceptions of the negative consequences of this rule breaking for the group, as well as their evaluations of the ingroup rule-breaker. Participants in the *control* condition read a simple description of the group context: 'As you know, we have an ethics committee in place at [the department] to ensure that all ethical issues are addressed in the research we carry out'. Participants in the *moral superiority* condition read a paragraph that emphasised the superior position of the department regarding ethics. This text sought to distinguish the department from others in terms of its high ethical and moral standards: 'As you know, we have an ethics committee in place at [the department] to ensure that all research carried out meets the highest ethical standards. We pride ourselves on our high ethical and moral standards, particularly when comparing our practices with those of many other institutions in Britain that don't always have the same rigorous procedures in place'.

Participants were next asked to imagine that Richard, a fictional lecturer/assistant professor in the department, had violated a number of ethics policies while conducting his empirical research. His studies focused on a topic of 'a sensitive nature', but had not been approved by the ethics committee. In addition, Richard did not have procedures in place to safeguard against ethical violations. The paragraph highlighted two negative consequences of this rule breaking: several students had sought counselling after participating in Richard's research; and the editor of a high-profile journal had submitted a written complaint to the department about the apparent non-compliance with professional ethical guidelines.

Results showed that the moral high ground appeared to provide ingroup members with room to manoeuvre in their appraisal of the severity of the offence. The results suggested that it is low identifiers, and not more highly committed group members, who were more likely to report the inconsistency between the rule-breaker's behaviour and the stance of the group. Compared to low identifiers, high identifiers perceived the rule breaking as less damaging for the group, and evaluated the rule-breaker more positively. Further, mediation analysis showed that perceptions of the implications of rule breaking for the group explained participants' evaluations of the rule-breakers. Participants who saw the rule breaking as damaging to the group were more likely to evaluate the rule-breaker negatively. This relationship mediated the experimental effects on negative evaluations of the rule-breaker.

This pattern of results was replicated in studies where we examined responses by British undergraduate students to British soldiers who violated rules of war when they abused prisoners of war in Iraq (Iyer, Jetten & Haslam, 2010, Study 2). In either a control condition or a moral superiority condition, high and low identifiers reported their evaluations of the rule-breakers; their perception that the rule breaking damaged the group; and the severity of the recommended punishment for the rule-breakers. Participants read a paragraph discussing the British military presence in Iraq, which randomly assigned them to one of two group position conditions. Participants in the *control condition* read a simple description of the group context: 'British troops have been stationed in Basra, Iraq, as part of the peace-keeping mission since the war ended in 2003. They have been working with the rest of the Coalition to help maintain the peace and rebuild the country'. Participants in the *moral superiority condition* read the same paragraph, as well as three additional sentences describing the 'superior moral conduct' of the British armed forces relative to other countries, because 'British soldiers are trained to treat people from other cultures with dignity and respect, and are required to follow the codes of the Geneva Convention when on active duty'. The last sentence stated that 'Other countries generally do not set such high standards for their armed forces'. After this, all participants next read four paragraphs describing the ongoing trial of three British soldiers charged with abusing Iraqi prisoners. The text described specific charges of abuse and assault, which were drawn from actual allegations reported in the media.

As in the study with academic researchers, results showed that when the ingroup was not presented as taking the moral high ground, high and low identifiers did not differ in their perceptions of the implications of severe rule breaking for the group, nor in their evaluations and punishment of the rule-breakers. In contrast, when the ingroup was in a position of moral superiority, high and low identifiers responded in markedly different ways to the rule breaking. Compared to high identifiers, low identifiers were more negative in their evaluations of the rule-breakers and perceived their behaviour to be more damaging to the group. These negative evaluations had important concrete implications as well: low identifiers recommended a harsher punishment for the rule-breakers than did the high identifiers. Taken together, the results suggested that high identifiers were more forgiving of rule breaking than were low identifiers when the group had taken the higher moral ground.

High identifiers appeared to see the rule-breakers as generally good individuals whose rule breaking constituted an isolated action, which suggests that the general reputation of the group was not undermined. Compared to low identifiers, high identifiers seemed to view the group's position of moral superiority as a protective buffer that could limit the negative impact of group members' rule breaking. Indeed, the moral record may have even blinded them to labelling deviant behaviour as such (Question 1, Figure 7.1). In this way, a moral reputation or record appeared to outweigh the negative consequences of individual rule-breakers' actions.

Functionality of deviance for the group

There are other reasons why ingroup members may be lenient in their punishment of the deviant, even if the behaviour is viewed as a transgression. Groups need deviance because transgressions are important for groups to understand and negotiate their identity. Acts of deviance lead groups to engage in some soul-searching to understand what the group is about. For instance, even though it appeared that there was no consensus about whether Grass engaged in deviant behaviour, or how to respond to it, the incident served the function of igniting a broad debate aimed at clarifying the identity of the group (i.e., Germany and its past).

The idea that deviance serves a function for broader society and may be beneficial to group life is an idea that has been extensively discussed by sociologists. For example, Erikson (1966) argues that deviant behaviour helps the system as a whole to define what is normative. Boundary transgressions by deviant individuals who are subsequently punished allow groups to make statements about what is normative within the group. This enhances norm clarity and helps to define the group's identity, which, in turn, increases stability and consistency for the group as a whole. Erikson goes one step further in arguing that 'deviant forms of conduct often seem to derive nourishment from the very agencies devised to inhibit them' (p. 14). Even though his point relates more to the idea that societies need criminals because they need to fill prisons and keep the police officers busy, the same can probably be said for psychological processes within groups: groups need deviants because deviants help to define the group and contribute in that way to the survival of the group. Consistent with this is Durkheim's (1958) reasoning. He makes the point that groups need deviance by speculating about a context entirely free of deviant acts:

> Imagine a society of saints, a perfect cloister of exemplary individuals. Crimes, properly so called, will there be unknown; but faults which appear venial to the layman will create there the same scandal that the ordinary defence does in ordinary consciousness. If, then, this society has the power to judge and punish, it will define these acts as criminal and will treat them as such (1958, pp. 68–9).

There are also examples of groups that may recognise deviant behaviour as an opportunity to define their identity. In an attempt to differentiate from the mainstream, groups may develop a rebel identity to set itself apart from the dominant group (Jetten & Branscombe, 2009; Jetten *et al.*, 2001). Even though behaviour by members of subcultures may be perceived as deviant, such behaviour may be rewarded rather than punished by other ingroup members because it serves the function of enhancing the formation of a rebel identity and helps the group distinguish itself from the mainstream. The more the mainstream labels these acts by minority members as deviant (and punishes them accordingly), the more identity-affirming these acts become in the eyes of the minority group (Emler & Reicher, 2005). This encourages a dynamic whereby the more ingroup members would appraise an act as deviant and harming the interests of the dominant group (Question 1, Figure 7.1), the less likely they would want to punish the transgressor (Question 2, Figure 7.1).

Strategic considerations that affect punishment of the deviant

There may be other reasons why group members will not endorse punishment of a deviant despite the recognition that s/he has committed a transgression. Particularly when transgressions are in the public eye, and when ingroup responses are carefully monitored, groups may be concerned about appearing to be inappropriately harsh or lenient (see also Matheson, Cole & Majka, 2002). Within groups, members may also differ in the extent to which they will endorse punishment of deviants. In a recent study of rugby players asked to evaluate members who break important rules in rugby, we found that status within the group (i.e., newcomer versus old-timer) affected the extent to which punishment of the transgression was endorsed (Jetten *et al.*, 2010). Results showed that old-timers' disapproval of rule-breakers was not affected by the status of the audience (high or low), the group membership of the rule-breaker (ingroup or outgroup member), or the form in which the punishment had to be delivered (mere disapproval or an intention to act and notify others of the transgression, i.e., whistle-blowing). In contrast, newcomers appeared much more strategic in responding to transgressions and they appeared to be more likely to engage in such acts when this would provide a strategic advantage (e.g., when the audience was high status, and when there was little risk of alienating other ingroup members). In fact, newcomers were just as disapproving of rule-breakers as old-timers when the status of the audience was high. However, newcomers were less likely to endorse punishment when an ingroup rule-breaker had to be openly corrected. Presumably the perceived costs of doing so exceeded the potential benefits of ingratiating oneself vis-à-vis a high status audience.

Other research suggests that deviance by way of betraying an ingroup norm is also tolerated when it is perceived as the only viable way to ensure the survival of the group. For example, Morton, Postmes and Jetten (2007; see also Morton, this volume) found that politicians who abandoned a previously endorsed position for strategic reasons (i.e., to win an election) were perceived as deviant by both ingroup and outgroup members (Question 1 in Figure 7.1). However, at times, this did not lead to disapproval among ingroup members. Instead, if ingroup members perceived that their party was losing support and that it was likely they would lose the next election, they tolerated and even applauded deviating from previously endorsed positions because this was perceived as advantageous to the group.

Concluding Remarks

We started this chapter with the observation that there are many factors that affect the extent to which acts are (a) labelled as deviance and (b) punished and condemned. Figure 7.1 was developed as an attempt to map out some of the factors that affect these judgements. Note that the factors and moderators discussed in this chapter are by no means exhaustive. It is also important to keep in mind that the model presented in Figure 7.1 is a simplification of the ways in which these processes may unfold. For example, Questions 1 and 2 cannot always be disentangled and may be part of intrinsically interwoven judgements. That is, we may not want to punish the deviant and as a result we may deny that the behaviour involved a deviant act in the first place.

Even though we can debate the details of the model and the way different processes interact and intertwine, the broader aim of this chapter was to map out the questions that have been addressed in previous research and the questions that have barely been alluded to. In particular, we aimed to show that labelling of deviance is not automatic or consensual within groups (i.e., that 'no' answers to Question 1 are just as likely as 'yes' answers), and that even when an act is labelled as deviant, that ingroup members may at times not endorse punishment of the deviant ('no' answers to Question 2). We discussed the role that the dominance of experimental laboratory studies may have in this, preventing us from addressing some questions and not others (Santee & Maslach, 1982).

However, and in addition, it could also be argued that our methodology reflects some deeper held implicit assumptions that have guided our thinking and theorising. These underlying assumptions were well articulated by Moscovici's (1976) discussion of research on conformity and responding to deviance. He notes that the final goal always appears to be 'the reclamation of deviants'. In particular, he argues that researchers in the field have focused on only one set of forces that drive group responses to deviance: 'making everybody alike, blurring the particularity and individuality of persons or subgroups. The further this process of identification and deindividuation is carried, the better each person's adaptation to others and to the environment' (Moscovici, 1976, p.17; see also Haslam & Reicher, this volume; Levine, 1989; Turner, 2006). Unfortunately, now, over 40 years later, these words still capture well our current theorising on responding to deviance.

The broader meta-theoretical framework in social psychology has focused on conformity instead of dissent, on stability rather than change, on uniformity instead of difference, and on passive responding rather than active behaviour by group members. One consequence is that research on responses to deviant behaviour has examined some processes, but not others (see Santee & Maslach, 1982, for a similar point). In that sense, Moscovici would probably agree with us that, so far, we have mostly focused on the eagerness of group members to label acts as deviant (Question 1) and examined that these behaviours should be punished (Question 2). What we have not studied in enough detail is when and why group members welcome deviance within groups (and will not label it as such), and when and why groups tolerate and invite deviance rather than punish it (Question 2). This one-sided analysis has resulted in a failure to understand the way groups and society more broadly change and, more specifically, how that change results from dissent within groups (Packer, 2008, see also Packer this volume), individual agency in groups (Postmes & Jetten, 2006), resistance (see Haslam & Reicher, this volume) and individual's creativity (Nemeth & Goncalo, this volume), just to name a few processes. It is the development of this research agenda that promises to be an important avenue for future work.

References

Bandura, A., Baranelli, C., Caprara, G.V. & Pastorelli, C. (1996). Mechanisms of moral disengagement in the exercise of moral agency. *Journal of Personality and Social Psychology, 71*, 364–74.

Birchmeier, Z., Joinson, A.N. & Dietz-Uhler, B. (2005). Storming and forming a normative response to a deception revealed online. *Social Science Computer Review, 23*, 108–21.

Durkheim, E. (1958). *Les Règles de la méthode sociologique* [The rules of sociological method]. Glencoe, IL: Free Press.

Emler, N. & Reicher, S. (2005). Delinquency: cause or consequence of social exclusion. In D. Abrams, M.A. Hogg & J.M. Marques (eds), *The Social Psychology of Inclusion and Exclusion* (pp. 211–42). New York: Psychology Press.

Erikson, K.T. (1966). *Wayward Puritans: A Study in the Sociology of Deviance.* New York: John Wiley and Sons.

Festinger, L., Schachter, S. & Back, K. (1950). *Social Pressures in Informal Groups.* New York: Harper.

Gollwitzer, M. & Keller, L. (2010). What you did only matters if you are one of us: offenders' group membership moderates the effect of criminal history on punishment severity. *Social Psychology, 41*, 20–6.

Haslam, S.A. & McGarty, C. (2001). A hundred years of certitude? Social psychology, the experimental method and the management of scientific uncertainty. *British Journal of Social Psychology, 40*, 1–21.

Hornsey, M.J. (2006). Ingroup critics and their influence on groups. In T. Postmes & J. Jetten (eds), *Individuality and the Group: Advances in Social Identity* (pp. 74–91). London: Sage.

Hornsey, M.J. & Imani, A. (2004). Criticizing groups from the inside and the outside: an identity perspective on the intergroup sensitivity effect. *Personality and Social Psychology Bulletin, 30*, 365–83.

Hornsey, M.J. & Jetten, J. (2003). Not being what you claim to be: impostors as sources of group threat. *European Journal of Social Psychology, 33*, 639–57.

Hornsey, M.J., Jetten, J., McAuliffe, B. & Hogg, M.A. (2006). The impact of individualist and collectivist group norms on evaluations of dissenting group members. *Journal of Experimental Social Psychology, 42*, 57–68.

Hutchison, P. & Abrams, D. (2003). Ingroup identification moderates stereotypes change in reaction to ingroup deviance. *European Journal of Social Psychology, 33*, 497–506.

Hutchison, P., Jetten, J. & Gutierrez, R. (2010). *Deviant but desirable: Perceived Group Variability and Judgements of Atypical Group Members.* Manuscript submitted for publication.

Irvin, J. (2006, August 19). Günter Grass is my hero, as a writer and a moral compass. *The Guardian.* Retrieved 21 April 2009 from www.guardian.co.uk/commentisfree/2006/aug/19/comment.germany.

Iyer, A. & Jetten, J. (2009). Unpublished data, University of Queensland, Australia.

Iyer, A., Jetten, J. & Haslam, S.A. (2010). *Sugaring o'er the Devil: Moral Superiority and Group Identification Help Individuals Downplay the Implications of Ingroup Rule-Breaking.* Manuscript submitted for publication.

Jetten, J. & Branscombe, N.R. (2009). Seeking minority group memberships: responses to discrimination when group membership is self-selected. In F. Butera & J. Levine (eds), *Coping with Minority Status: Responses to Exclusion and Inclusion* (pp. 155–76). New York: Cambridge University Press.

Jetten, J., Branscombe, N.R., Schmitt, M.T. & Spears, R. (2001). Rebels with a cause: group identification as a response to perceived discrimination from the mainstream. *Personality and Social Psychology Bulletin, 27*, 1204–13.

Jetten, J., Hornsey, M.J., Spears, R., Haslam, S.A. & Cowell, E. (2010). Rule transgressions in groups: the conditional nature of newcomers' willingness to confront deviance. *European Journal of Social Psychology, 40*, 338–48.

Leach, C.W., Ellemers, N. & Barreto, M. (2007). Group virtue: the importance of morality (vs. competence and sociability) in the positive evaluation of ingroups. *Journal of Personality and Social Psychology, 93*, 234–49.

Levine, J.M. (1989). Reactions to opinion deviance in small groups. In P.P. Paulus (ed.), *Psychology of Group Influence* (pp. 187–231). Hillsdale, NJ: Erlbaum.

Marques, J., Abrams, D. & Serôdio, R.G. (2001). Being better by being right: subjective group dynamics and derogation of in-group deviants when generic norms are undermined. *Journal of Personality and Social Psychology, 81*, 436–77.

Marques, J.M. & Paez, D. (1994). The black sheep effect: social categorization, rejection of ingroup deviates, and perception of group variability. In W. Stroebe & M. Hewstone (eds), *European Review of Social Psychology* (Vol. 5, pp. 37–68). New York: John Wiley & Sons.

Matheson, K., Cole, B. & Majaka, K. (2002). Dissidence from within: examining the effects of intergroup context on group members' reactions to attitudinal opposition. *Journal of Experimental Social Psychology, 39*, 161–9.

Morton, T.A., Postmes, T. & Jetten, J. (2007). Playing the game: strategic considerations and responses to normative and deviant group members. *European Journal of Social Psychology, 37*, 599–616.

Moscovici, S. (1976). *Social Influence and Social Change.* New York: Academic Press.

Packer, D.J. (2008). On being both with us and against us: a normative conflict model of dissent in social groups. *Personality and Social Psychology Review, 12*, 50–72.

Postmes, T. & Jetten, J. (eds) (2006). *Individuality and the Group: Advances in Social Identity.* London: Sage.

Postmes, T., Spears, R. & Cihangir, S. (2001). Quality of decision making and group norms. *Journal of Personality and Social Psychology, 80*, 918–30.

Santee, R.T. & Maslach, C. (1982). To agree or not to agree. Personal dissent amid social pressure to conform. *Journal of Personality and Social Psychology, 42*, 690–700.

Schachter, S. (1951). Deviation, rejection, and communication. *Journal of Abnormal and Social Psychology, 46*, 190–207.

Turner, J.C. (2006). Tyranny, freedom and social structure: escaping our theoretical prisons. *British Journal of Social Psychology, 45*, 41–6.

8

Children's Understanding of Deviance and Group Dynamics

The Development of Subjective Group Dynamics

Dominic Abrams and Adam Rutland

Rebellion is intrinsic to processes of social change and provides a focal point for relationships within and between groups to be forged and altered. An important question for psychologists is how people understand the relationship between rebels or deviants and the groups that surround them. Our research programme is framed by a developmental social psychological perspective (Durkin, 1995) that argues that developmental processes provide the frame and lens through which adults make sense of their social worlds (Abrams, 1989, 2004; Barrett, 2005; Bennett & Sani, 2004). We specifically focus on social inclusion and exclusion during childhood and investigate how children become aware of, and interpret, deviance in intergroup relationships. We set out a developmental model of subjective group dynamics (Abrams & Rutland, 2008; Abrams *et al.*, 2003), which holds that social perspective taking and social experience enable children to anticipate how people will respond to deviants in their own and other groups. As children get older they also become more responsive to prescriptive norms and cues that these norms are relevant in a particular situation. They use this understanding to reflect on how other ingroup members will respond to deviants. These assumptions about how others treat deviants then flow on to influence their own personal treatment of deviants.

Rebels in Groups: Dissent, Deviance, Difference and Defiance Jolanda Jetten and Matthew J. Hornsey

Overview

After introducing theories of small-group behaviour and the subjective group dynamics model as applied to adults (Marques, Páez & Abrams, 1998), we tour a programme of research examining, in middle childhood, the understanding and application of inclusion/exclusion within and between groups. We argue that the development of tacit understanding of the connection between intergroup and intragroup dynamics (that we label group nous – pronounced 'nowss') is a type of flexibly applied lay theory (Levy & Dweck, 1999). Group nous helps to explain why, rather than becoming less prejudiced with age as typically predicted by cognitive developmental theories in developmental psychology (see Abrams & Rutland, 2008; Nesdale, 2001), children become more systematic and strategic in their evaluations and judgements of ingroup and outgroup members. Our overall framework is shown in Figure 8.1, which distinguishes among three elements. On the left are the cognitive developmental and age-based inputs which are associated with perspective taking and classification skills. In the centre is the concept of group nous, which is children's understanding about how groups work; and on the right are the ways in which children apply and manifest this understanding in intergroup contexts, in particular by their judgements of normative and deviant group members. We will elaborate on the components of the model in the following sections.

The Value of Group Nous

We define group nous as the tacit understanding of the general ground rules of group membership (Abrams *et al.*, 2009). Group nous involves awareness that, in an intergroup context, a unified group is a good group in which all members may feel more comfortable, particularly if the group can find lower status outgroups with which to compare (Hogg, 1993).

Groups may demand rapid compliance so that they can function well and the high value groups place on consensus is well established (Schachter, 1951). Thus, an early lesson for children may be that groups value consensus.

Social psychology defines 'deviants' as people who deviate from prevailing group norms by expressing views or actions that oppose or do not comply with those norms (Abrams, 2010). Deviant or nonconforming members are liable to be excluded by other members in order to sustain group uniformity and locomotion. Being excluded by others can cause

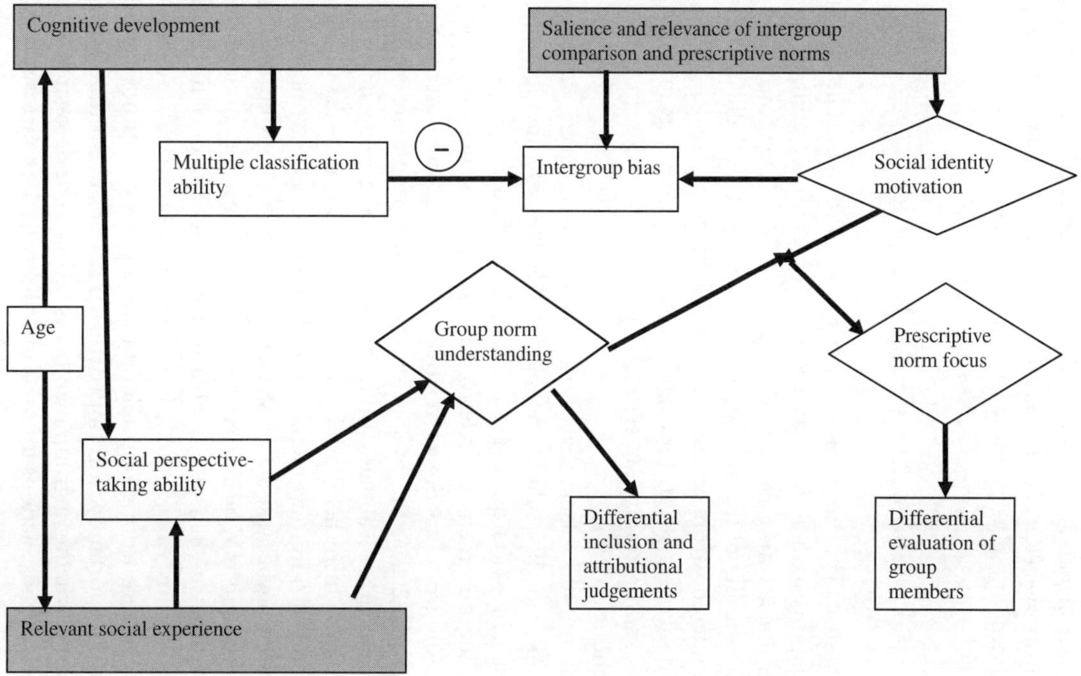

Figure 8.1 Developmental model of subjective group dynamics

anger, depression, withdrawal, self-handicapping, lowered self-esteem and impaired cognitive capacity (Williams, Forgas & von Hippel, 2005). We argue that if children are able to understand group dynamics, at least tacitly, they are in a stronger position, practically, materially, socially and ultimately in terms of survival (Kerr & Levine, 2008). This should help them to avoid being excluded, and also to know who to exclude or include.

Subjective Group Dynamics

Group consensus is as important (or perhaps more important) in intergroup situations as it is in small groups. For example, political parties depend on block voting to carry their policies. The intention is to demonstrate the validity of the position to the ingroup. This 'valid' position is actually rendered stronger and more valid by the knowledge that an outgroup disagrees with it. Similar dynamics may play out in children's peer networks, for example in terms of gender segregation in the school setting (Schofield, 1981).

Research on the 'black sheep effect' shows that, even when group membership is highly salient, people do not treat all members of the same group alike (Marques *et al.*, 1998). In particular, people derogate unlikeable ingroup members relative to likeable ones more than they do unlikeable outgroup members relative to likeable ones. According to Marques *et al.* (2001), the reason for this is that people are vigilant for evidence that either validates or undermines prescriptive norms. This evidence may be furnished both by the behaviour and attitudes of ingroup members and of outgroup members. A deviant ingroup member is especially threatening because he or she undermines the ingroup consensus. Outgroup deviants may be indirectly validating because they undermine the outgroup consensus. This is particularly likely when the deviance involves disloyalty (Abrams *et al.*, 2002), but it can also be true if the deviance involves departure from group-relevant stereotypes or attitudes (Abrams *et al.*, 2000). Importantly, it is not particular actions or attitude positions that determine whether a group member is favoured or derogated, it is the implications of those actions for ingroup validity in the context of a salient intergroup comparison (see also Randsley de Moura, Abrams, Marques & Hutchison, this volume).

Self-categorisation theory proposes that there is a 'functional antagonism' between differentiation between groups and differentiation within

(Turner *et al.*, 1987), such that greater differentiation between groups implies less differentiation within, and vice versa. However, the SGD model argues that there is sometimes functional complementarity between differentiation at the two levels. Specifically, that in order to actively define and defend important ingroup norms, and hence the positive distinctiveness of the group, people are likely to differentiate deviant members from others within a group. This focus on intragroup differences occurs in parallel with, rather than opposition to, intergroup differentiation since both processes are driven by a motivation to validate and defend group membership and group norms. Thus, SGD contends that individuals can shift their emphasis from cognitive differentiation between groups to a motivated psychological engagement with intragroup differences, but these are parallel and appropriate strategies for validating social identity as an ingroup member.

A Developmental Model of Subjective Group Dynamics

We can now draw these different theoretical strands together to set out the developmental subjective group dynamics (DSGD) model. Evidence for this model has been amassed working from the right-hand side of Figure 8.1 to the left and upper parts. We began by examining three propositions in the model that concern how relationships between intergroup and intragroup judgements might change as children get older. The fourth and fifth propositions concern children's developing focus on prescriptive group norms. The final proposition concerns the environmental and socio-cognitive inputs that may provide the developmental underpinnings of subjective group dynamics.

Cognitive developmental theory (CDT) (Aboud, 2008) holds that older children show less intergroup bias because they can see beyond an individual's social category membership (i.e. boy or girl), and focus instead on how individuals within groups differ in terms of multiple characteristics (e.g. friendliness, intelligence). This developmental juxtaposition of intergroup and intragroup differentiation is contrary to the proposition from the (adult) SGD model that people who show more intergroup bias *also* show more intragroup bias because they seek to distinguish among people who do and do not uphold prescriptive ingroup norms.

The DSGD account of the developmental progression of children's understanding of groups helps to explain the apparent disparity between CDT and adult patterns of prejudice and subjective group dynamics. The model focuses primarily on middle childhood, when the processes are most likely to be developing, but we are also aware that there will be additional aspects that will apply through later childhood and adolescence. The DSGD model proposes that younger children will tend to use intergroup and individual judgements independently. For example, when judging an individual they are prone to use the simple criterion of group membership (i.e. 'I like him because he is a boy') or moral reasoning about whether they are behaving in a good versus bad manner (i.e. 'I like him because he has done something good') (Killen *et al.*, 2002). In contrast, older children should, like adults, judge individual group members in terms of their adherence to prescriptive group norms. Thus, the first proposition of the DSGD model is that, *with age children's intergroup and intragroup judgements become related more systematically* (i.e. the more they show intergroup bias the more they will differentiate between normative and deviants members within groups).

The DSGD model proposes a socio-cognitive developmental progression that will be correlated with, but not causally tied to, age (Abrams, Rutland & Cameron, 2003). As children get older they are more likely to anticipate that *other* group members will selectively evaluate normative and deviant members of their own and other groups (e.g. that they will show a black sheep effect). We label this awareness of different inclusion preferences by ingroups and outgroups 'differential inclusion'. The model holds that older children will use awareness of differential inclusion to inform their own judgements of group members if and when the intergroup differences are important. Thus, the second proposition of the model is that, *as children get older, there will be a stronger link between their understanding that other group members will differentially include individuals from their own versus other groups, and the child's own evaluations of group members.*

The third proposition is that, among older children, *those who are more motivated to support their ingroup (i.e. those high in ingroup identification) will demonstrate a closer relationship between their understanding that groups will differentially include individuals and their own evaluations of normative and deviant group members.*

The General Paradigm

We constructed an experimental situation comparable to those used in previous research with adults. Specifically, we examined how children would evaluate ingroup and outgroup members who either showed 'normative' (loyal) behaviour or 'deviant' (disloyal) behaviour.

In the experiments children were first asked to rate how they felt towards the ingroup as a whole and the outgroup as a whole. Next, we described normative and deviant children who were either from an ingroup or an outgroup. In various studies the groups were either summer schools, schools, countries, or minimal groups and teams. Normative members made two positive statements about the group, such as 'I really like this group, it is a great group to belong to'. Deviants made one positive statement about the group but one positive statement about the other group (e.g., 'I really like this group, but the other group would also be great to belong to').

We also asked children about their expectations of the feelings that other members from the ingroup and from the outgroup would have towards the normative and deviant member. If subjective group dynamics are operating, evaluations of a group member will be more positive if, relative to other members, that member is more acceptable to the *ingroup*. Members who are relatively more accepted by an outgroup will be evaluated less positively.

The DSGD model focuses on differentiation between groups and among group members rather than the particular evaluations of one group or one member. Our predictions therefore centre on three measures of differentiation. The first is *intergroup bias* – evaluation of the ingroup as a whole minus evaluation of the outgroup as a whole. The second is *differential evaluation* of group members. This taps favourability towards individuals that provide *relatively* greater validation for the ingroup norm. For judgements of ingroup members we subtract evaluations of the deviant member from evaluations of the normative member because the latter should be favoured more strongly. For judgements of outgroup members we subtract evaluations of the normative member from evaluations of the deviant member, because theoretically it is the deviant who should be favoured more strongly. The third index is *differential inclusion.* This taps whether children perceive that each group would feel more favourable towards its own normative than deviant members.

The fact that the differential inclusion and differential evaluation indices are calculated differently is important. A positive relationship between them shows that children are more favourable towards the ingroup member they think is more popular among the ingroup but they are also more favourable towards the outgroup member they think is less popular within the outgroup. That is, a positive correlation between differential inclusion and evaluation would show that children favour those who provide relative support for the ingroup, and not just others who appear to be more popular per se.

Testing the Basic Predictions

Abrams *et al.* (2003) asked children, aged either 6–7 or 9–11 years, to evaluate their own summer school and an outgroup summer school. Children then judged normative and deviant individuals either from the ingroup summer school or the outgroup summer school. Older children significantly favoured the normative over the deviant member in the ingroup condition, and marginally significantly favoured the deviant over the normative member in the outgroup condition. In contrast, younger children did not evaluate these two members differently in either condition. In sum, only the older children showed significant differential evaluation. Moreover, consistent with the first proposition of our model, the relationship between intergroup bias and differential evaluation of group members was larger among older children, and only older children showed a significant relationship between differential evaluation and their anticipations of differential inclusion by others. In summary, this study showed that, with age, intergroup bias and selective bias in favour of specific group members are linked more strongly. Consistent with the third proposition in the model, children who expressed more intergroup bias also anticipated greater differential inclusion.

Abrams, Rutland and Cameron (2003) examined the motivational aspect of the model more directly. We asked nearly 500 English children, ranging in age from 5 to 12 to evaluate the ingroup and outgroup. They also were asked to evaluate members from either of these groups who were normative or deviant (i.e. loyal or disloyal to their group). The context was the 2002 Soccer World Cup and the normative and deviant members were either England or Germany supporters.

The main findings replicated those of Abrams *et al.* (2003). Intergroup bias and differential evaluation were positively related. Intergroup bias, differential inclusion and differential evaluation all increased with age. Differential inclusion mediated the effect of age on differential evaluation. Namely, with age, children showed a better understanding that groups will differentially include individuals who best validate group norms. Furthermore, the better children understood this, the more they themselves differentially evaluated individuals, favouring those that supported their ingroup norms. Importantly, this study showed that the relationship between differential inclusion and differential evaluation was moderated by both age and identification. Compared with low identifiers, those who identified more strongly with the ingroup also showed a significantly stronger relationship between differential inclusion and differential evaluation. As predicted, and as shown in Figure 8.2, this pattern was stronger among older children than younger children.

These results provided important convergent evidence for the DSGD model, supporting the propositions that older children use their greater tactical sophistication in support of their social identity. Those who did not identify strongly with England did not link their knowledge of differential inclusion to their judgements of the group members. Those who did identify strongly evaluated normative ingroup members and deviant outgroup members more positively than normative outgroup members and deviant ingroup members.

Underlying Processes

The next three studies focused on the component of the model that concerns prescriptive norm focus, which we see as the proximal determinant of evaluations of normative and deviant group members (see Figure 8.1). We tested two further propositions from the DSGD model. Proposition 4 is that *subjective group dynamics are likely to be domain specific.* Children should be capable of judging individuals differently based on many criteria (e.g., moral, stereotypical) (Killen *et al.*, 2002) but will link these judgements to group memberships more strongly if the behaviour is directly relevant to prescriptive norms, specifically, tapping into group loyalty.

Proposition 5 is that *children with greater social experience of groups should be more responsive to normative cues when opportunities arise to differentiate among group members.* These propositions are largely captured by the upper right grey box in Figure 8.1. This concerns the contextual relevance of social identity and group norms, which need to be high before children are likely to relate their intragroup judgements to their intergroup judgements.

For example, Abrams *et al.* (2008) set out to test whether children's subjective group dynamics would be manifested more powerfully when the norms were more clearly relevant to group membership (loyalty norms) than when they were less relevant (morality). We used the minimal group paradigm, assigning children by lottery either to a 'star' or 'diamond' team.

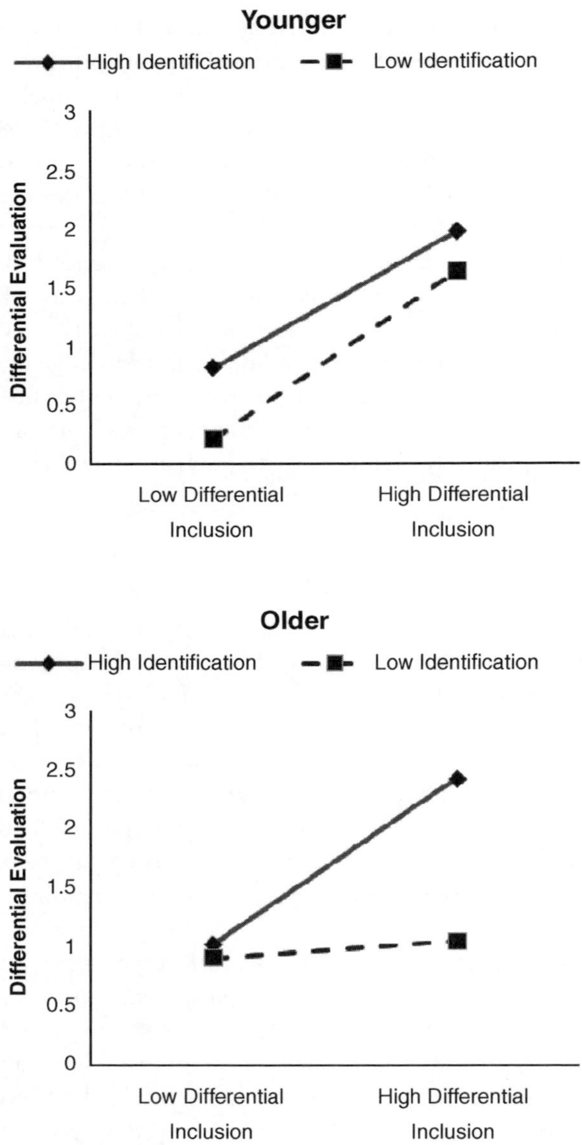

Figure 8.2 Older children who are high identifiers relate their differential evaluations of group members more strongly to their expectations about differential inclusion by other members

Source: Abrams, D., Rutland, A. & Cameron, L. (2003). The development of subjective group dynamics: children's judgements of normative and deviant ingroup and outgroup individuals. *Child Development, 74*, 1840–56

We asked them to judge both ingroup and outgroup members who were loyal and disloyal (Experiment 1) or behaved morally or immorally (Experiment 2).

Experiment 1 revealed the same pattern of findings as the two studies reported earlier, with preference for ingroup loyal over ingroup disloyal and preference for outgroup disloyal over outgroup loyal members. However, Experiment 2 revealed that children showed simple ingroup bias by preferring moral ingroup members over moral outgroup members but also immoral ingroup members over immoral outgroup members. That is, there was no preference of an outgroup immoral above an ingroup immoral member. Furthermore, there was no greater differentiation of moral versus immoral ingroup members as compared with moral versus immoral outgroup members. Taken together, these minimal group experiments demonstrate that subjective group dynamics affect children's judgements of group members (Experiment 1), but not when the norms are irrelevant to intergroup differences (Experiment 2).

The Role of Accountability Our model argues that one reason why older children show more pronounced subjective group dynamics is that they are better able to take different social perspectives. It follows that older children should also be more responsive to accountability cues that might focus their attention on prescriptive norms. Children are responsive to public accountability when they evaluate ingroups and outgroups (Rutland, 2004; Rutland *et al.*, 2005), and higher self-presentational concern moderates children's ingroup bias (Abrams & Brown, 1989). Indeed, if norms encourage bias, older children may express more bias (Rutland *et al.*, 2005).

Marques *et al.* (1998) established that, among adults, the black sheep effect is stronger when prescriptive norms are made more salient, either by explicitly telling participants what group members 'should do' (Experiment 2) or by telling participants that their answers would be viewed by other ingroup members (Experiment 3). Abrams *et al.* (2007) followed the latter experiment, using the summer school context to test the effects of accountability. As shown in Figure 8.3, we found that ingroup accountability increased both intergroup and intragroup differentiation, and more strongly among older children because older children's greater social experience with groups (Erwin, 1993) should give them a greater awareness of the obligations to comply with group norms when accountable.

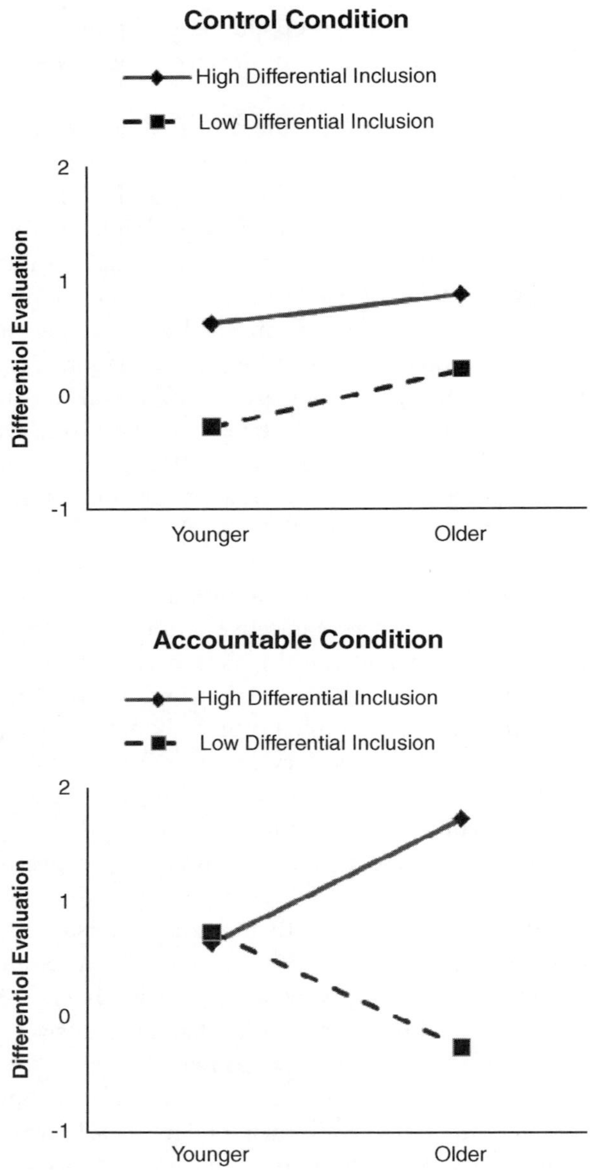

Figure 8.3 Older children relate their beliefs about differential inclusion to their own differential evaluation more strongly if they are accountable to ingroup members *Source*: Abrams, D., Rutland, A., Cameron, L. & Ferrell, J. (2007). Older but wilier: ingroup accountability and the development of subjective group dynamics. *Developmental Psychology, 43*, 134–48

Social Developmental Processes

The final proposition for the DSGD model concerns the role of cognitive and social development in these changes in subjective group dynamics. Specifically, proposition 6 is that *children's understanding of group inclusion processes should be related both to their social perspective taking and social experience, but not to their multiple classification ability.*

Figure 8.1 shows our reasoning about the likely social developmental processes in children's subjective group dynamics. Age contributes directly to cognitive maturation which facilitates both multiple classification ability and social perspective-taking ability. Age is also associated with wider and deeper relevant experiences (e.g., being a member of various types of group), which is likely to contribute both to perspective-taking ability and to children's general awareness of the implicit rules of being a group member (e.g., that one is expected to conform, agree, follow the group's direction etc.).

Social Perspective Taking To know how they should judge members of groups, children need some idea of the likely expectations of other group members. With age, children become more conscious that their own judgements of other group members should match the judgements made by other ingroup members (Abrams & Brown, 1989; Rutland, 2004; Rutland *et al.*, 2005). In a face-to-face group the pressure to conform may be explicit. But in the case of imagined groups (e.g., when other members are not present or they are anonymous category members) the child must infer the prescriptive norms as a guide to action. Moreover, in an intergroup context, the child must be able to distinguish ingroup from outgroup norms.

In our research we examine this issue by measuring *differential inclusion*, which requires children to consider that members of different groups will have different evaluations of the same targets. Previous research suggests that children below the age of eight years are relatively unskilled at coordinating first-, second- and third-person perspectives (Selman, 1971). Consequently, we might expect younger children to focus on either a person's group membership or the person's specific actions, but not have very much insight into the way the person will be perceived from the differing perspectives of ingroup and outgroup members (Spears Brown & Bigler, 2004).

The DSGD model holds that differential inclusion should relate to children's social perspective-taking abilities (Abrams *et al.*, 2005). We have tested this idea directly by examining performance on advanced false-belief tasks that have been used to study children's 'theory of mind'. Developmental research shows that beyond 7–8 years of age children show more advanced theory of mind (e.g., Baron-Cohen *et al.*, 1999). Consequently, it seems likely that older children would be better able to respond to higher order perspective-taking problems such as anticipating group members' perspectives on normative and deviant members from each group.

We developed a measure labelled 'Theory of Social Mind' (ToSM; Abrams *et al.*, 2009). The task we used was designed to be completely unconnected to the intergroup situations in the experiments so it does not simply measure knowledge of group norms. Instead the task measures whether children can distinguish between their own negative evaluation of a character who steals, and the evaluation held by someone who had no knowledge of the character's wrongdoing. Children with more advanced ToSM abilities should also show stronger evidence of differential inclusion – an understanding that groups will include and exclude members based on members' adherence to prescriptive norms. Although differential inclusion and differential evaluation should be related, especially among older children, ToSM should not directly affect evaluations of group members. Just because a child can understand that different perspectives exist, there is no reason why he or she should agree more with one perspective than another.

Social Experience A second developmental process underpinning subjective group dynamics must be social experience. Specifically, people have to learn the rules of group membership (Levine, Moreland & Hausmann, 2005). As children spend more time in their social world they are likely to learn about a wider variety of social categories (e.g. national, religion), gain specific group memberships (e.g. neighbourhood, school), discover more about the way groups can be created and dissolved (e.g. during classroom assignments), and learn more about the nature of relationships between different groups. This accrual of social experience should provide children with a better grasp of social conventions surrounding the inclusion and exclusion of group members. Indeed, research based on the socio-cognitive domain model shows that with age children increasingly explain peer exclusion using socio-conventional justifications such as 'group functioning' (i.e. 'the group won't work well with someone different in') (Killen *et al.*, 2002).

To examine these questions we followed the design of the England/Germany soccer study (Abrams, Rutland & Cameron, 2003) in the context of the 2004 European Soccer Championships (Abrams *et al.*, 2009, Study 1). An important variation from Abrams, Rutland and Cameron's (2003) design is that the outgroup was now France rather than Germany. Whereas England and Germany have a historically negative relationship (including of course two World Wars), England and France are familiar geographical neighbours, and children in the region of England in which the study was based have frequent contact with France via day trips across the English Channel. Previous research is consistent with the idea that British children are more positive towards France than Germany (Barrett, 2005). In addition, given that increased intergroup contact is associated with more positive attitudes (Pettigrew & Tropp, 2006) it seemed reasonable to expect the pattern of intergroup bias towards the French to decrease rather than increase with age.

Generally the results of this study consolidated our interpretation of the previous findings, though unlike the previous studies both intergroup bias and differential evaluation of members were negatively related to age. Moreover, consistent with the idea that differential inclusion involves a focus on prescriptive norms, new free response measures showed that children who anticipated greater differential inclusion also spontaneously explained peer judgements using attributions about loyalty and about group memberships (rather than attributions to the deviants' traits or personal characteristics).

As predicted, performance on the ToSM task improved significantly with age. More important was the finding that scores on this task were significantly related to differential inclusion, even when multiple classification skill was partialled out. ToSM performance was not related to either intergroup bias or differential evaluation. This makes good sense because the ability to understand different social perspectives should help with understanding that different groups will value different individuals, but should have no direct implication for one's own evaluation of the groups or the individuals.

Group Nous The relationships examined thus far were all established within the context of experiments in which the child was part of an intergroup comparison. Yet our model holds that children develop a more general understanding of group inclusion and prescriptive norms in intergroup situations. We labelled this tacit understanding 'group nous' (a common word in English, nous is defined as common sense or gumption in the *Pocket Oxford Dictionary*).

To examine group nous more directly we conducted a further study (Abrams *et al.*, 2009, Study 2) that only examined the socio-cognitive processes associated with understanding about group norms but that did not engage the children as members of the groups in question. We asked children ranging from 5–10 years of age to complete a series of multiple classification tasks, and also the ToSM task, and a generalised measure of group norm understanding. The aim of this last measure was to test whether children would anticipate group loyalty norms and would anticipate that groups favour ingroup members in general, and ingroup-supporting individuals in particular. Therefore this measure represents an analogue of the differential inclusion measure used in our previous studies but without the complication of the participant being a member of one of the groups and without the complication of using real groups. If, as we expect, some part of children's understanding of group dynamics is associated with social perspective taking we should find that performance on these two measures is related.

The group norm understanding measure described two teams (red and green) and showed two individuals (red and green) and first asked children which individual the red team would prefer. Children were then shown that both the red and green individuals expressed positive attitudes to both teams (analogous to the deviant in the previous experiments). We asked which individual the red team preferred. A generalised awareness of differential inclusion processes would lead children to select the green person (a partially disloyal member of an opposing group) rather than the red person (a similarly disloyal member of the same group).

We also established a simple index, other than the indirect measure via age, of relevant experience with groups. Therefore, after the other measures, we simply asked children to list all the groups to which they had ever belonged. While a little crude, this measure has the advantage that it taps cognitive accessibility of group memberships without requiring children to reflect on the details of any particular group.

The findings were highly consistent with the DSGD model. First, as expected, older children displayed better multiple classification skill, better ToSM performance and better group norm understanding. Moreover, as in the previous studies, multiple classification skill was unrelated to group norm understanding and number of group memberships. Useful statistically was that age and number of group memberships were unrelated to one another.

Second, consistent with the DSGD model, ToSM, group norm understanding and number of group memberships were all significantly positively interrelated. These findings showed that social perspective taking is related to generalised understanding about group loyalty norms. In addition, this understanding appears to increase if a child belongs to more groups, independently of the child's age. Taken together the results support the idea that social experience plays an important role in children's understanding of loyalty norms, whether by direct inference or because of its contribution to their perspective-taking abilities.

Multiple Classification Skill While testing these propositions we also explored the potential role of multiple classification ability because this is a central developmental variable associated with changes in intergroup bias according to cognitive developmental theory (Bigler & Liben, 2007). We considered that multiple classification skill might at most be a distal influence on subjective group dynamics (via its influence on intergroup bias), as shown in Figure 8.1.

We developed an asocial multiple classification task that detects children's propensity to use categories orthogonally to fit a data array parsimoniously (Abrams *et al.*, 2007).

Across all studies in which this task was included (Abrams *et al.*, 2007, 2008, 2009; Studies 1 and 2), multiple classification ability increased with age, consistent with expectations of CDT. In both of the 2008 studies and the 2009 intergroup study (Study 1) but not the 2007 study, multiple classification was negatively related to intergroup bias, again consistent with CDT.

However, CDT should predict that multiple classification ability would be associated with greater intragroup differentiation. We have found no support for this prediction across studies, and indeed in Abrams *et al.* (2009) we found that children who made more systematic use of orthogonal categories actually differentiated less among individual group members rather than more. Therefore, across four experiments we can now conclude that the distinct evaluation of members who diverge in adherence to prescriptive loyalty norms is not systematically related to multiple classification skill.

Conclusions – Rules, Inferences and Motives

The seven studies described in this chapter involved over 1000 children and four different intergroup contexts. The findings are highly consistent with the DSGD model shown in Figure 8.1, in which arrows represent causal pathways (negative where indicated), and intersecting arrows represent potential interactions. The variables can be divided into three elements. First there are cognitive developmental and age-based inputs, which contribute to social perspective taking and classification skills. Second is the development of 'group nous' – displayed through general group norm understanding such as the idea that people are likely to be biased towards ingroups, and to reject deviants from their ingroup. Third is the application of this knowledge in a specific situation. To the extent that intergroup comparisons and prescriptive norms are salient, applying group nous involves inferences about differential inclusion, and attributions about group members' behaviour. It involves relating these inferences to the child's own judgements of individual group members in the light of their adherence to prescriptive ingroup norms.

To put this in a developmental narrative, as children get older, they develop better multiple classification ability which can contribute to reduced intergroup bias in some contexts but does not appear to influence how deviant members are judged. More relevant is older children's better perspective-taking skills and greater social experience of groups. Both of these contribute to group nous, through children's expectations that ingroup and outgroup peers will want to include and exclude different individuals, and will react differently to deviants from each group (differential inclusion). Perspective taking and experience of groups also enables children to generalise their expectations of differential inclusion to novel intergroup situations and intergroup relationships of which they are not a part. Consequently, older children are likely to distinguish between different types of norms, paying greater attention to relevant prescriptive norms, for example when they feel accountable to other ingroup members. As a result of their greater group nous, older children are also more likely to reflect their identification with the ingroup by how strongly they link their own evaluations of individual group members with their expectations of differential inclusion. Thus, whereas younger children will tend simply to favour ingroup members over outgroup members, older children respond to normative and deviant members more strategically depending on how much it matters to support the ingroup.

The development of subjective group dynamics has implications for a range of aspects of social exclusion. One application is in the area of bullying (Rutland, Abrams & Cameron, 2007). Peer rejection often seems to be based on physical or behavioural lack of fit, and research often focuses on the psychological or social abnormality of either victims or bullies (e.g. Craig, 1998). Yet the DSGD model highlights the potential role of group norms in bullying and social rejection. Whether an individual is included or excluded from peer relationships may depend on whether particular intergroup comparisons become relevant in that setting, because this comparison affects which prescriptive norms are relevant and therefore which individuals are perceived to be deviant. We expect that victimisation may be directed at those who challenge the validity of an ingroup (e.g. by working 'too hard' compared with other members). In schools, teachers with greater awareness of intergroup dynamics in the classroom may be better equipped to address school-based bullying by working with group boundaries and norms rather than focusing only on the bully or the victim.

A more general implication for social psychology is that intergroup prejudice can often be disguised by more sophisticated forms of bias. Just as we have shown a developmental continuum from simplistic ingroup favouritism to sophisticated targeting of preferences for particular individuals, adults also may express their ingroup biases in a variety of ways depending on the context and the audience. For example, it may be quite consistent with ingroup bias to favour an outgroup member who has sacrificed some level of loyalty to his or her own group.

We are aware that many avenues remain to be explored. To what extent do children seek out information about prescriptive norms? How do they react when norms emphasise shared identity with outgroup members rather than ingroup loyalty? To what extent can prescriptive norms such as loyalty override or interact with others such as stereotypical fit to a group prototype? If multiple classification skill is not directly implicated in children's subjective group dynamics, are there other cognitive processes or implicit biases that are involved? Are there other aspects of social perspective-taking ability that might converge to contribute to children's application of differential inclusion? To what extent do children's expectations in a new intergroup context reflect inferences based on specific salient past experiences of exclusion and inclusion in groups?

Finally, we wish to emphasise the value of combining social and developmental psychological research. Although we have not dwelt on later developmental changes, it is likely that social experience through adolescence continues to enable further refinement and specificity in the development of group nous. For example there may be more awareness that different types of groups might have different types of normative structure or expectations. That is, the domain specificity of different types of norms may be understood better. Moreover, we might reverse the questions and ask whether and how social perspective taking and understanding about group norms is involved in adult's subjective group dynamics. The issue is not so much to chart development as to understand variation – to pinpoint the moderators that make adult responses to rebels more like those of younger or older children, and by inference reflect similar types of processes. As pointed out by Durkin (1995) and others (Abrams, 2004; Barrett, 2005; Bennett & Sani, 2004) there is much to be gained by understanding the developmental processes that frame social behaviour, just as there is much to be gained by asking what social psychological processes must be at work to enable children to engage in complex social phenomena that are commonplace among adults.

Acknowledgements

As well as the contribution of direct collaborators Lindsey Cameron, Joseph Pelletier, Jennifer Ferrell and Jose Marques, this programme of research has benefited from discussions with members of the Center for the Study of Group Processes including Melanie Killen, Norb Kerr and John Levine, as well as with Drew Nesdale and John B. Nezlek. The work has been supported by research grants from the British Academy and the Economic and Social Research Council (R000230401).

References

Aboud, F.E. (2008). A social-cognitive developmental theory of prejudice. In S.M. Quintana & C. McKown (eds), *Handbook of Race, Racism, and the Developing Child* (pp. 55–71). Hoboken, NJ: John Wiley & Sons Inc.

Abrams, D. (1989). Differential association: social developments in gender identification during adolescence. In S. Skevington & D. Baker (eds), *The Social Identity of Women* (pp. 59–83). London: Sage.

Abrams, D. (2004). The development of social identity: what develops? In M. Bennett & F. Sani (eds), *The Development of the Social Self* (pp. 291–312). New York: Psychology Press.

Abrams, D. (2010). Deviance. In J. Levine & M. Hogg (eds), *Encyclopedia of Group Processes and Intergroup Relations* (pp. 206–11). Thousand Oaks, CA: Sage.

Abrams, D. & Brown, R.J. (1989). Self-consciousness and social identity: self-regulation as a group member. *Social Psychology Quarterly*, *52*, 311–18.

Abrams, D., Marques, J.M., Bown, N. & Dougill, M. (2002). Anti-norm and pro-norm deviance in the bank and on the campus: two experiments on subjective group dynamics. *Group Processes and Intergroup Relations, 5,* 163–82.

Abrams, D., Marques, J.M., Bown, N.J. & Henson, M. (2000). Pro-norm and anti-norm deviance within ingroups and outgroups. *Journal of Personality and Social Psychology, 78,* 906–12.

Abrams, D., Randsley de Moura, G., Hutchison, P. & Viki, G. T. (2005). When bad becomes good (and vice versa): why social exclusion is not based on difference. In D. Abrams, M.A. Hogg & J.M. Marques (eds), *The Social Psychology of Inclusion and Exclusion* (pp. 161–90). New York: Psychology Press.

Abrams, D. & Rutland, A. (2008). The development of subjective group dynamics. In S.R. Levy & M. Killen (eds), *Intergroup Attitudes and Relations in Childhood through Adulthood* (pp. 47–65). Oxford: Oxford University Press.

Abrams, D., Rutland, A. & Cameron, L. (2003). The development of subjective group dynamics: children's judgements of normative and deviant ingroup and outgroup individuals. *Child Development, 74,* 1840–56.

Abrams, D., Rutland, A., Cameron, L. & Ferrell, J. (2007). Older but wilier: ingroup accountability and the development of subjective group dynamics. *Developmental Psychology, 43,* 134–48.

Abrams, D., Rutland, A., Cameron, L. & Marques, J.M. (2003). The development of subjective group dynamics: when ingroup bias gets specific. *British Journal of Developmental Psychology, 21,* 155.

Abrams, D., Rutland, A., Ferrell, J.M. & Pelletier, J. (2008). Children's judgements of disloyal and immoral peer behavior: subjective group dynamics in minimal intergroup contexts. *Child Development, 79,* 444–61.

Abrams, D., Rutland, A., Pelletier, J. & Ferrell, J.M. (2009). Group nous and social exclusion: the role of theory of social mind, multiple classification skill and social experience of peer relations within groups. *Child Development, 80,* 224–43.

Baron-Cohen, S., O'Riordan, M., Stone, V., Jones, R. & Plaisted, K. (1999). Recognition of faux pas by normally developing children and children with Asperger syndrome or high-functioning autism. *Journal of Autism & Developmental Disorders, 29,* 407–18.

Barrett, M. (2005). Children's understanding of, and feelings about, countries and national groups. In M. Barrett & E. Buchana-Barrow (eds), *Children's Understanding of Society* (pp. 251–86). New York: Psychology Press.

Bennett, M. & Sani, F. (eds) (2004). *The Development of the Social Self.* Philadelphia: Psychology Press.

Bigler, R.S. & Liben, L.S. (2007). Developmental intergroup theory: explaining and reducing children's social stereotyping and prejudice. *Current Directions in Psychological Science, 16,* 162–6.

Craig, W.M. (1998). The relationship among bullying, victimization, depression, anxiety, and aggression in elementary school children. *Personality and Individual Differences, 24,* 123–30.

Durkin, K.D. (1995). *Developmental Social Psychology: From Infancy to Old Age.* Oxford: Blackwell.

Erwin, P. (1993). *Friendship and Peer Relations in Children.* Chichester: John Wiley & Sons.

Hogg, M.A. (1993). *The Social Psychology of Group Cohesiveness.* Hemel Hempstead: Harvester Wheatsheaf.

Kerr, N.L. & Levine, J.M. (2008). The detection of social exclusion: evolution and beyond. *Group Dynamics, 12,* 39–52.

Killen, M., Lee-Kim, J., McGlothlin, H. & Stangor, C. (2002). How children and adolescents evaluate gender and racial exclusion. *Monographs of the Society for Research in Child Development, 67.*

Levine, J.M., Moreland, R.L. & Hausmann, L.R.M. (2005). Managing group composition: inclusive and exclusive role transitions. In D. Abrams & M.A. Hogg (eds), *The Social Psychology of Inclusion and Exclusion* (pp. 137–60). New York: Psychology Press.

Levy, S.R. & Dweck, C.S. (1999). The impact of children's static vs. dynamic conceptions of people on stereotype formation. *Child Development, 70,* 1163–80.

Marques, J.M., Abrams, D., Páez, D. & Hogg, M.A. (2001). Social categorization, social identification, and rejection of deviant group members. In M.A. Hogg & R.S. Tindale (eds), *Blackwell Handbook of Social Psychology: Group Processes* (Vol. 3, pp. 400–24). Oxford: Blackwell.

Marques, J.M., Abrams, D., Páez, D. & Martinez-Taboada, C.M. (1998). The role of categorisation and ingroup norms in judgements of groups and their members. *Journal of Personality and Social Psychology, 75,* 976–88.

Marques, J.M., Páez, D. & Abrams, D. (1998). Social identity and intragroup differentiation as subjective social control. In J.F. Morales, D. Páez, J.C. Deschamps & S. Worchel (eds), *Current Perspectives on Social Identity and Social Categorization* (pp. 124–42). New York: Sage.

Nesdale, D. (2001). Development of prejudice in children. In M. Augoustinos & K.J. Reynolds (eds), *Understanding Prejudice, Racism and Social Conflict.* London: Sage.

Pettigrew, T.F. & Tropp, L.R. (2006). A meta-analytic test of intergroup contact theory. *Journal of Personality and Social Psychology, 90,* 751–83.

Rutland, A. (2004). The development and self-regulation of intergroup attitudes in children. In M. Bennett & F. Sani (eds), *The Development of the Social Self* (pp. 247–65). New York: Psychology Press.

Rutland, A., Abrams, D. & Cameron, L. (2007). Children's attitudes towards non-conformists: intergroup relations and social exclusion in middle childhood. *International Journal of School Disaffection, 4*, 45–52.

Rutland, A., Cameron, L., Milne, A. & McGeorge, P. (2005). Social norms and self-presentation: children's implicit and explicit intergroup attitudes. *Child Development, 76*, 451–66.

Schachter, S. (1951). Deviation, rejection, and communication. *Journal of Abnormal and Social Psychology, 46*, 190–208.

Schofield, J.W. (1981). Complementary and conflicting identities: images and interaction in an interracial school. In S.R. Asher & J.M. Gottman (eds), *The Development of Children's Friendships* (pp. 53–90). New York: Cambridge University Press.

Selman, R.L. (1971). Taking another's perspective: role-taking development in early childhood. *Child Development, 42*, 1721–34.

Spears Brown, C. & Bigler, R.S. (2004). Children's perceptions of gender discrimination. *Developmental Psychology, 40*, 714–26.

Turner, J.C., Hogg, M.A., Oakes, P.J., Reicher, S.D. & Wetherell, M.S. (eds) (1987). *Rediscovering the Social Group: A Self-Categorisation Theory.* Oxford: Blackwell.

Williams, K.D., Forgas, J.P. & von Hippel, W. (eds) (2005). *The Social Outcast: Ostracism, Social Exclusion, Rejection, and Bullying.* New York: Psychology Press.

9

Impostors within Groups

The Psychology of Claiming to be Something You Are Not

Matthew J. Hornsey and Jolanda Jetten

One of us once met a man who had become weary of dinner parties. He confessed that sometimes, to combat his boredom, he would pretend to be someone he was not. So for example he might pretend to the stranger next to him that he was a communist or an ambassador, or a part-time rodeo clown, and he would maintain the ruse as long as he could. The story was mildly funny until he mentioned that one night he had spent hours masquerading as an academic. Suddenly the story seemed considerably less funny. The conversation was effectively over.

What was hard to work out afterwards was why so many negative emotions were aroused about what was ultimately a private joke. Why the disproportionate anger, and why only when it was the academic identity he was laying claim to? In reflecting on this, it occurred to us that echoes of this annoyance permeate adult life. Frequently criticisms are levelled against people who, in our view, lay claim to being something that they are not: people who masquerade as members of the Left, for example, when we 'know' them to hold conservative attitudes; or people who 'try on' a subcultural identity at social events but return to their mainstream lives during the week; or people who claim to be vegetarians even though they eat chicken and fish. Conversations we have had and heard are crossed with references to 'poseurs', 'frauds', 'rent-a-crowds', 'chardonnay socialists', 'wannabes' and (most damningly) 'impostors'. There appears to be considerable vigilance about authenticity in group membership, but it is not completely clear what is driving this vigilance. In short, why should it matter if people pretend to be something they are not?

Rebels in Groups: Dissent, Deviance, Difference and Defiance Jolanda Jetten and Matthew J. Hornsey

In this chapter we try to answer these questions, with reference to a handful of experiments and a dash of intuition. Before doing so, however, we first need to mark out what we mean by 'impostor', and how it differs from some of the other types of deviance discussed in this book. Specifically, we are often asked how an impostor might differ from a 'black sheep' (Marques & Páez, 1994; Marques, Yzerbyt & Leyens, 1988). We define 'impostorism' in our experiments as people who make a public claim for group membership while disguising their failure to fulfil key criteria for group membership (Hornsey & Jetten, 2003). For black sheep, the deviance is wrapped up in their behaviour; they are dislikeable, incompetent, non-normative or disloyal (Coull *et al.*, 2001; Hutchison & Abrams, 2003). For impostors the problem is not their behaviour per se, but rather the gulf between their claims for identity and their claims for behaviour. Black sheep are themselves, whereas impostors are masquerading, engaging in some deliberate misrepresentation. Furthermore, one cannot necessarily question the right of black sheep to self-categorise as a member of a group. No matter how annoying or incompetent an academic might be, he or she is still an academic. For impostors, however, what is at stake is their right to call themselves group members at all. In other words, black sheep are still sheep; impostors are wolves in sheep's clothing (Hornsey & Jetten, 2003).

In this chapter, we first present a taxonomy of impostors, a concession to the fact that impostorism can take many forms and that some structure is needed to make sense of this complexity. We first review examples of what we call 'objective impostors' – people whose impostorism is undeniable and a matter of fact because these individuals fail to meet key criteria of group membership. These categories of impostors are illustrated with reference to historical examples; people who are remembered by history precisely because they pretended to belong to groups they could not legitimately claim membership in. We then move into the murkier world of 'eye-of-the-beholder impostors'; people who face allegations of impostorism. Their impostorism is typically unprovable, ambiguous and contested.

Before beginning, a quick disclaimer: we will not be talking about examples of impostorism whereby individuals substitute themselves for another individual's identity. Suffice to say that history is full of extraordinary examples of fake husbands being received by unsuspecting wives, strangers passing as long-lost children, and rogues passing as generals (films such as *The Return of Martin Guerre* and *Six Degrees of Separation* provide entrees to two of the more famous stories of identity theft; see Goffman, 1963, for more examples). Neither will we discuss the tradition of the celebrity anthropologist – popular in the late nineteenth century and disturbingly prevalent today – where people fake or embellish personal tales of adventure in remote lands. Rather, our focus will be on people who fake group or collective identities, and the implications of this for genuine group members.

Objective Impostors

We distinguish five types of 'objective' impostor: shape shifters, corner cutters, Trojan horses, closet dwellers and history thieves. What all these impostors have in common is that they cross group boundaries and lay claim to group membership without meeting key criteria for group membership. Sometimes these boundaries might be ostensibly impermeable (in the case of shape shifters); at other times group boundaries are perceived as more permeable (in the case of corner cutters). The last three categories of objective impostors differ in the specific motivation for their impostorism. They are either motivated to pass as a member of the outgroup in order to cause it damage (Trojan horses), to avoid prejudice and persecution (closet dwellers) or to reinvent their past (history thieves). Below, we discuss these types of real impostors in turn.

The Shape Shifters

Shape shifters are those who, in laying claim to a group membership to which they do not belong, find themselves crossing what are thought to be impermeable boundaries (e.g., of sex, nobility or race). Of all the types of impostors, these are the ones who are most often remembered and mythologised, presumably because the transgression is so bold.

There are many reasons why someone might take the rather risky step of shape shifting. Historically, this has often been a result of a daring play for social mobility in a stratified and inequitable society. Until relatively recently in human history, a woman, for example, could not realistically become a doctor, and a pauper could not realistically attain wealth and social standing. In such a world, individuals may take the step of faking their identities in a desperate ploy for status, social standing or personal wish fulfilment.

Two of the best-known impostors in history fit this profile. James Barry was a nineteenth-century English woman who became a well-respected doctor, credited with performing the first successful emergency caesarean in the UK. This impressive feat was only made possible by pretending to be a man, an implausible secret that she somehow managed to take to her grave. The same year that James Barry started her medical career, a woman was found in England apparently disoriented and babbling in a strange language. After she was given refuge by some aristocrats, her remarkable story emerged. The strange lady was revealed as Princess Caraboo from an island called Javasu. On an ocean voyage her ship had run aground, and she was quickly embraced and feted as an exotic relic of a mysterious and undiscovered kingdom. This fantasy was sustained for months until 'Princess Caraboo' was finally exposed as Mary Baker, a cobbler's daughter from a neighbouring village.

It is hard not to admire the bravado of the types of James Barry and Princess Caraboo, and tempting to read something heroic in the way they circumvented (and highlighted) the prejudices of a stifling, static society. But not all shape shifters are motivated for these reasons. There are many examples of working-class people who have faked nobility merely as a way of defrauding people of money or as a way of seducing women. Similarly, there are examples of shape shifters who are motivated for no identifiable reason at all. Billy Tipton, for example, was a female jazz trumpeter who managed to pass her adult life as a man (and married five times). Unlike James Barry, however, it is unclear whether Tipton would need to do this in order to progress in her career, and certainly unclear whether the payoffs to her career would be sufficient to compensate for the rather extraordinary lengths she went to in order to disguise her anatomical reality from her unsuspecting wives.

Another subcategory of the shape shifter is the person who fakes his or her race. Chief Buffalo Child Long Lance, for example, endeared himself to white America with his apparently redemptive life story as a Native American and his compelling insights into the erosion of Native American culture. After his suicide at 41, it emerged that Chief Buffalo Child Long Lance was in fact Sylvester Long, a child of mixed racial descent who in the South would have most likely been categorised at the time as a Negro. The most famous Native American of his generation turned out to have few genuine Native American ties, and most of his life story was fabricated.

Two similar stories emerge from Australia. In the late 1970s, B.Wongar wrote a celebrated series of short stories drawing on his experiences as an Aboriginal Australian and highlighting the destructive effects of colonisation on indigenous Australians. Rather like Chief Buffalo Child Long Lance, B.Wongar was one of the best recognised ambassadors for his people, and considered a voice of authentic aboriginality. It was three years before he was exposed as Stretan Bozic, a Yugoslavian immigrant. The second example is Helen Demidenko. Demidenko's debut novel – supposedly based on stories that Demidenko's uncle had told her about World War II – won Australia's most prestigious literary prize in 1995. Demidenko made a great deal of her Ukranian history, dressing in traditional dress, singing traditional songs and speaking passionately about the racism she was subjected to at her high school. After two years, the headmaster of this allegedly racist school lost patience and exposed her as Helen Darville, the Australian daughter of British immigrants.

Two themes emerge from these stories of ethnic shape shifting. First, the impostors were extremely successful at breaking through into the consciousness of the ethnic majority, a feat that was elusive for genuine members of the ethnic minority. Impostors appear to be well equipped to present a portrait of minority culture that is acceptable to the majority, and majorities arguably prefer being fed this version of minority life when it comes from one of their own. An interesting illustration of this is the popularity of the sub-genre of ethnic perspective taking, where members of the dominant group use makeup to pass as members of a minority culture, and then write about their subsequent experiences (e.g., John Howard Griffin's *Black Like Me* or Günter Wallraff who exposed mistreatment of guest workers by taking on a Turkish guest-worker identity).

The second lesson is that shape shifters, presumably because the public does not consider it to be possible to cross certain group boundaries, seem to be able to fool the population for an extraordinarily long period of time. There would have been hundreds of Australians who knew Helen Darville, who met her parents and who were subsequently surprised to see her feted on the front pages of newspapers as the Ukranian Demidenko. Yet it was two years before the whistle was blown. This paradox was spectacularly exemplified by James Barry who was once stripped to the waist and flogged as punishment for getting drunk on a naval ship. The captain, in his log, noted 'breast-like shapes' on Barry's chest, yet still did not suspect Barry's secret. The fact that a woman could not only fake a life as a man but also go on to be a leading surgeon presumably lay so far outside the realm of the captain's imagination that Barry's impostorism went undetected even in the face of hard evidence.

Corner Cutters

The corner cutter differs from the shape shifter in that the latter crosses impermeable boundaries, whereas the former crosses boundaries that are permeable. In other words, the corner cutter could feasibly gain legitimate entry into a certain group, but for whatever reason is not prepared to make the commitments that are necessary to do so. Whereas shape shifters invest an enormous amount of effort in sustaining one gigantic lie, corner cutters strive to achieve entry into groups with minimal effort. They are the people who would prefer to fake a degree than to earn one; would prefer to dress like a soldier than to train as one; would prefer to affect the language and appearance of a socialist than to live like one; and would prefer to call themselves a Christian than to act like one.

The most famous example of the corner cutter is Frank Abagnale Jr, made famous as the protagonist of the film *Catch Me If You Can.* Abagnale spent decades faking qualifications, licences and CVs to gain entry into various professions. His best-known escapade was to dress as an airline pilot, a simple ruse that he was able to leverage into free international travel and a million-dollar lifestyle. But he was also able to effectively pass as a doctor, an attorney, and for six months as a sociology lecturer at the Brigham Young University (where he was apparently well respected by his students). Abagnale was clearly a brilliant man who could have achieved almost anything if he had put his mind to it. But rather than work towards a single goal, he lived the life of the compulsive chameleon, trying on new hats (sometimes literally) every few months.

The deeper cultural significance of Frank Abagnale Jr – like James Barry before him – is that he highlights how impressionable people can be in the face of external signs of status. As an ordinary person, Frank Abagnale Jr was largely invisible. But dressed as an airline pilot, he found himself overwhelmed with romantic attention, and respected so unquestioningly that he was able to cash millions of dollars in fraudulent cheques. A romanticist, then, might see the corner cutters as saboteurs of a ridiculous world that prioritises pedigree and spin over substance, skill and character.

Another lesson is that, even now, it is surprisingly easy to migrate across professional boundaries. In the Middle Ages, without electronic identification processes, serious legal penalties were applied to people who dressed in other people's costumes, because costumes and uniforms *were* people's identification. Although we now live in a world of formal electronic identification processes, how often do we really investigate people's CVs, for example, or inspect their licences, or interrogate their claims about their past? We still live in a world that trusts that people are who they say they are, a trust that can be exploited by those who are willing to con their way through life, whether it be for money, status or social acceptability. For Frank Abagnale Jr, the fraud carried legal risk (and ultimately he was caught and jailed). But for many social identities one does not need to wear uniforms or fake documentation, because many identities do not have objective entry criteria. There is no objective way, for example, of assessing whether someone is truly a Christian, or an animal-lover, or a Republican voter. We have little choice than to take people's word for it, leaving enormous opportunity for budding impostors. That said, we predict that once these corner cutters are caught, genuine group members may punish them harshly because they jeopardise the existing status hierarchy and because their impostorism undermines the group's status (Stapel, Koomen & Spears, 1999).

Trojan Horses

In his poem *The Aeneid*, Virgil tells the tale of how the Greeks finally conquered the city of Troy after a 10-year siege. After appearing to withdraw from battle, the Greeks stowed a handful of soldiers in the belly of a giant wooden horse, which they left outside the Trojans' city gates. Mistaking it for a victory trophy, the Trojans pulled the horse inside the gates, from which the soldiers emerged and precipitated a devastating battle that decided the war. The metaphor of the Trojan horse can be used to describe a certain type of impostor, who passes as a member of the outgroup in order to cause it damage.

Sometimes the motivation of such an impostor might be to achieve personal gain. The individual who dresses as a policeman in order to commit a theft, or the person who fakes employee status in order to hack into a computer system and steal money can be considered a type of impostor. Other Trojan horses will be motivated purely out of a desire to cause mischief and/or destruction within an outgroup. Examples include 'trolls', a term invented to apply specifically to online impostors. Of course one of the attractions of online worlds is that identity migration – whether it be personal or social – is so effortless. In a world where everyone is ultimately anonymous, the potential for impostorism is virtually endless. In this environment, trolls distinguish themselves because their motives are to infiltrate a community from the outside in order to cause them damage, perhaps by creating division, planting counter-arguments or even hacking into the site. Trolls may be operating as agents of a rival group, or may simply be acting out a personal malice towards a group.

In the 'offline' world, such a person might be more commonly called a spy or a mole. The history of spying – whereby people fake a group allegiance in order to steal sensitive information – is almost as long as the history of intergroup conflict. Famous examples include Robert Philip Hanssen, the FBI counter-intelligence agent who sold secrets to the Soviets for over 20 years; Donnie Brasco, an FBI agent who infiltrated and betrayed the Bonanno crime family in the USA; and Stetson Kennedy, who in collaboration with John Brown was able to infiltrate and weaken the Ku Klux Klan. In these cases, impostorism is an organised, strategic and highly risky form of intergroup combat. At times, of course, the Trojan horse may overlap with the shape shifter. Consider, for example, the strange case of Song Liling, a Chinese opera diva whose passing as a woman was so effective that he developed an intimate relationship with a male French ambassador, from whom he was able to gather sensitive information for the Chinese government.

Closet dwellers

The metaphor of the closet dweller – the person who conceals their stigmatised identity from others – emerged from observers of gay identity negotiation, but can equally apply to a range of identities. Closet dwellers distinguish themselves from other impostors in that their motivation is to avoid prejudice and persecution; rather than trying to gain something positive, the closet dweller is trying to avoid something negative (Warner, Hornsey & Jetten, 2007). In some cases, little active concealment is required because the stigma is not visible. For example, there are no reliable visible 'markers' of homosexuality. Members of the mainstream are likely to presume, by default, that others are also members of the mainstream, and so impostorism can be as much a matter of failing to reveal one's true identity as of actively concealing it. For others, though, the markers of minority status are biological and so closet dwellers may need to resort to shape shifting (for example those who work in 'youth-worshipping' industries and so resort to plastic surgery and lying about their age in order to stay employable; see Schoemann & Branscombe, in press).

The benefits of closet dwelling are obvious: for the Jew in World War II, denying ethnicity could be a matter of life or death. For the gay man, denying sexuality might be the only way to avoid ostracism or physical assault. But there are considerable costs as well. This was illustrated by Frable, Platt and Hoey (1998), who tracked six groups in college: half of whom possessed a visible stigma, and half of whom possessed a non-visible stigma. Somewhat counter-intuitively, those with visible stigma fared better – they had lower levels of depression and higher levels of self-esteem than their counterparts. Frable and colleagues showed that it was the visibility of their stigma that, ironically, was their saving grace. Although the visibility could attract persecution and prejudice, the visibility also allowed them to find other people who shared the same stigma. It was this social support that then buffered their self-esteem and protected their mental health.

In a related programme of research, Molero *et al.* (in press) found that those who are HIV-positive and were hiding their stigma faced less discrimination directed at them personally and this, in turn, positively affected well-being. However, this also prevented them from becoming identified with the minority group that would allow them to collectively tackle group-based discrimination (Stürmer and Simon, 2004). That is, it was those who were more open about being HIV-positive who were able to become more identified with the minority group and this enhanced collective action intentions and protected well-being from the negative consequences of group-based discrimination (see also Jetten *et al.*, 2001).

Intuitively aware of this 'damned if you do, damned if you don't' dilemma, many people with non-visible stigma invent creative ways of advertising their identity to insiders at the same time as disguising it from members of the mainstream. The fish symbol – used to indicate Christianity – was originally used as a code to find like-minded people while escaping persecution at the hands of the Ancient Romans. Similarly, members of the Ku Klux Klan relied on intricate passwords and riddles to identify sympathisers. More recently, gay culture has developed an intricate, localised and shifting set of visual markers that can act as a way of coming out to people 'in the know', while remaining closeted to the heterosexual mainstream.

History thieves

For some, the identity deception is wrapped up not in who they are in the present, but rather who they have claimed to be in the past. History thieves are those who misrepresent their past in order to position themselves in a community defined by history. Much history theft surrounds major military conflicts, presumably because these conflicts are generation-defining events that are arenas of courage, heroism, brutality and slaughter, where society's sense of right and wrong, good and evil, are open to contest (see Reicher & Hopkins, 2001). It is understandable that, once the dust has settled, people are tempted to forge histories to make sure that they remain on the socially acceptable line of this shifting standard of morality. Prominent examples of history thieves include those who deny membership of the Nazi Party post-World War II, and those who fraudulently claim to be members of the anti-Nazi Resistance.

Like most of the examples described above, the motives for history theft are complex and multi-dimensional. Some may be escaping imprisonment or execution, as in the case of those who deny membership of a vanquished enemy in the aftermath of a war. Others may be motivated to avoid shameful histories or to claim glorious ones. Some may be motivated for public attention and financial reward. For example, there have been several examples in which people have profited from their stories of being a Holocaust survivor, or a September 11 survivor, only to be exposed subsequently as impostors. For others, the motivation might be a sense of community and togetherness. For example, in Australia and the USA, there has been a growing phenomenon of non-soldiers masquerading as Vietnam veterans. The standard profile of the fake Vietnam veteran tends to be the lonely outsider, who relishes the solidarity that their veteran status offers. These people are not looking for social status, but rather the kind of cohesiveness that is forged in the crucible of shared trauma, shared grief and collective memory. In the absence of a community of their own, these impostors plunder history to manufacture a community to which they have no legitimate claim. Because history is a fuzzy, murky and slippery reality, it provides considerable opportunity for the potential impostor to hide undetected.

Eye-of-the-Beholder Impostors

Until now, we have reserved our attention for people who are, by some objective criteria, impostors. In each case, the impostor has been a masquerader, publicly misrepresenting their identities at the same time as keeping secret their failure to fulfil key criteria for group membership. In this section we examine examples of those who might attract the accusations of impostorism, but do not conform to the strict definition of being an impostor. For these people, accusations of impostorism are not objectively verifiable, but rather represent a value judgement, a suspicion, a political weapon or a hunch. Genuine group members may accuse individuals of impostorism to psychologically remove them from the group which justifies treating them as an outgroup member. We identify four types of accusations of impostorism: those who lie on the margins of a group; those being accused of being a traitor; a 'Clayton's' group member; or a parasite.

Marginals

When illustrating groups in schematic form, there is a tendency for social psychologists to represent a group as a circle, with the members of the group as crosses within that circle. It is also traditional that the crosses closest to the centre represent the prototypical, defining exemplars of the group, whereas the crosses towards the outer of the circle represent the fringe dwellers, the marginal members who embody far fewer of the defining characteristics of the group. In reality, of course, the 'circle' is a dynamic and shifting set of fuzzy properties that define true group membership (Oakes, Haslam & Turner, 1999). Not only do these fuzzy properties shift depending on context, they also shift as a function of the perceiver. For some people, the circle is broad and inclusive, encompassing anyone who meets the minimal criteria for group membership. For others, the circle of genuine group membership is small and restrictive, and the criteria for true group membership are narrow and exclusive.

This state of affairs means that marginals – who self-define as members of the group but do not share all the defining features of the group – are in a vulnerable position. Depending on how tightly perceivers draw the circle of group membership, these peripherals can be seen as respected members of the 'broad church' or as fraudulent impostors who have no legitimate claim to group membership. This tension is present in all groups, although probably no more obviously than among those who are members of crossed categories; that is, those who straddle multiple group memberships. Examples include bisexuals and people of mixed ethnic descent (e.g., one white and one black parent). Although these people may feel they have genuine claims over the labels of being 'gay' or 'black', respectively, others may dispute that right (Jetten & Branscombe, 2009).

But even for people who do not straddle two worlds, questions of purity remain. Can people describe themselves as Christian if they do not go to church? Can a person be a vegetarian if they eat seafood, or if they lapse and eat meat once a year? There are typically no objective answers to these questions, and the debate is often wrapped in emotion and politics. In this debate, the accusation of impostorism might be a shot fired in a battle to define the non-negotiable norms of the group. Identification of 'impostors' might be a way that group members define the group in their (or their subgroup's) image.

Traitors

What we refer to here as traitors are people who publicly represent themselves as members of the group, but endorse attitudes or behaviours that the perceiver believes are hostile to the group's genuine values or goals. These people may be accused of impostorism because their actions or attitudes disqualify them from legitimate group membership in the eyes of some. Their superficial claims for group identity might be incontestable, but their deeper values are seen to be so anti-group that it justifies the word 'impostor', often synonymous with the word 'traitor'.

Examples of this type of impostor are usually found in politics, and often among politicians who carry minority status. A cursory review of history reveals pioneering female politicians who are accused of being anti-women, black politicians who are accused of being anti-black or 'not black enough', and gay politicians who support parties with policies that are perceived as anti-gay. But mainstream politicians can also face this accusation: Tony Blair in the UK was often criticised for not being a 'true Labour man' among some members of the Left, and some members of the Right in the USA saw John McCain as a traitor to the Republican cause.

Like the marginals described earlier, traitors exist in the eye of the beholder, and accusations of traitorousness are likely to be used as a manifestation of a broader ideological struggle to define what the group stands for. But in the case of traitors, the debate has a bitter edge to it. The accusation is not just that the individual fails to embody the defining features of the group, but that the individual is actively doing damage to the group while simultaneously claiming to represent it. One particularly clear example of the difference might be the case of Muslims who engage in anti-Western terrorism. From a literal perspective these people are indisputably Muslim, and presumably see themselves as particularly prototypical exemplars of that category. But for moderate Muslims, these people may be seen as embodying such a grotesque version of Islam, and of doing so much damage to the Islamic cause that they have revoked the right to the label at all. Depending on one's understanding of what the group represents, the very same behaviour can be seen as either heroic or traitorous; group-defining or impostorish.

Claytons

'Claytons' was a drink – marketed most heavily in Australia and New Zealand – that was packaged as though it was whisky even though it was non-alcoholic. Although the product is long forgotten, the term 'claytons' is still used in Australia and New Zealand as an adjective to describe something that superficially represents something else of substance but is essentially empty. In the context of this chapter, we use the term 'claytons' to refer to a person who superficially possesses the characteristics of a group, but on a deeper level is perceived to have little in common with other group members. Their claim for group membership might be difficult to dispute (as opposed to marginals) and their values might not be seen to be explicitly hostile to the interests of the group (as opposed to the traitors). But their claims for group membership might be seen to be skin-deep, with the suspicion that their deeper cultural values have more in common with relevant outgroups.

Popular culture has invented a number of terms used to describe those who are perceived to have the superficial characteristics of one race and the deeper cultural characteristics of another race: 'Oreo' or 'coconut' (black on the outside, white on the inside), 'banana' or 'Twinkie' (Asian on the outside, white on the inside), 'egg' (white on the outside, Asian on the inside), 'apple' (Native American on the outside, white on the inside), and 'whitewashed' (non-white on the outside, white on the inside). These terms are sometimes used neutrally or affectionately, but more frequently are meant to be derogatory – accusations that someone is trying to be something that they are not, and in so doing is rejecting or diluting something distinctively 'ethnic'. The term is also applied flexibly according to the perceiver's understandings of what the group represents: an accusation of being a coconut, for example, could be precipitated by anything from listening to classical music to wearing a suit to merely being liked and embraced by the white community. The accusation of impostorism can be an enforcement of what the speaker believes to be the core values of the group, an instrument of control over individuals who pursue cultural cosmopolitanism, or even a way of punishing ingroup members who are embraced by a despised outgroup. History provides one rather ironic example of this process – the African American turned Native American Chief Buffalo Child Long Lance. One of the sadder aspects of his short life was that, although he was embraced internationally as an ambassador for his people, many members of the Native American community rejected him as being 'too much of a white boy'.

Parasites

Finally, we use the term 'parasites' to refer to people who express all the attitudes and behaviours that one might expect of a group, but the perceiver suspects that they have selfish and individualistic motives for doing so. Like the parasite, who finds sustenance and survival by living off a host, these individuals are seen to be exploiting the collective in order to pursue their personal interests. An example might be the politician who is seen to adjust his ideology for reasons of career expediency, the celebrity who is keen to publicly embrace a football team to shore up local popularity, or the media figure who is seen to be exploiting her ethnicity for reasons of self-promotion.

Of course one can never get 'smoking gun' evidence of what people's motives are, and so there is no objective way of gauging whether someone is a genuine group member or a parasite. But suspicions of impostorism might persist, possibly because the perceiver is extrapolating from the person's previous behaviour, possibly out of a hunch, or possibly out of a malicious effort to damage a rival. As with the other accusations of (eye-of-the-beholder) impostorism, defining someone as a parasite is difficult to objectively verify but equally difficult to disprove, making it a slippery and dangerous rhetorical weapon.

What Does Social Psychology have to Say About Impostors?

The short answer to this question is: not a lot. But this situation is starting to change, and it is fair to say that the foundations for looking at impostorism have been well laid. Indeed, Goffman's (1959) dramaturgical metaphor for social interaction is perfectly positioned to account for impostorism. According to this model, the world is a stage, and individuals are actors who engage in performances designed to appeal to certain audiences. These actors try on different roles, complete with masks and costumes, and obey socially constrained 'scripts'. The performance element of life is a given in this model; the skill is to make sure that performances are seen by the audience to be authentic. If one's group membership is inconvenient or inappropriate for an audience, then the actor has the option of disguising or changing their performance – to 'pass' – and the success of this strategy rests on the extent to which the performance is convincing to the audience. According to this model, group membership is not so much what you are as what you *claim to be.*

While there is considerable research on the 'impostor phenomenon' or 'impostor syndrome' (examining the tendency for some people to fret that their reputation in the workplace exceeds their 'true' abilities; see Clance & Imes, 1978) there has been much less research on people who, quite objectively, are engaging in impostorism, and the consequences of this for group identity. In the last few years we have tried to respond to this empirical vacuum and we review this literature below. To do research on 'objective' impostorism, one needs to find a group identity for which there are relatively clear and non-negotiable criteria for entry. One example of such a group is vegetarianism. Although this term means different things to different people, it is more or less consensually understood that a true vegetarian would not eat meat. In a series of studies (Hornsey & Jetten, 2003; Jetten *et al.*, 2005), we asked vegetarians to evaluate a target (Matthew Grey) who claimed to be a vegetarian. After gathering personality evaluations of the target, we then revealed Matthew Grey to either be an authentic vegetarian (someone who never ate meat) or somebody who gave in to meat cravings about once a fortnight (for the sake of convenience, this target is referred to here as the impostor). Not surprisingly, the impostor was derogated quite heavily whereas evaluations of the authentic target were relatively stable. In other words, our vegetarian participants assumed authenticity, and then derogated the target quite heavily when the assumption was violated. The derogation of the impostor was alleviated significantly if: (a) the target made private rather than public claims for vegetarian identity; and (b) the target openly admitted their meat eating. In other words it is the gulf between claims for identity and claims for behaviour that is most influential in determining whether or not someone is judged as an impostor. If the claims for identity are public, and/or the violation of norms kept secret, then the impostorism is most pronounced and most condemned.

One may argue that this is an unsurprising and theoretically sterile manifestation of the fact that impostors are liars, and that people do not like liars. Why see this as an identity issue at all? In response to this, three findings are noteworthy. First, the effects emerged even after covarying out ratings of how deceptive the target was seen to be. In other words, something was driving the derogation over and above the acknowledgement that in the impostor condition Matthew Grey was a liar. Second, the derogation was almost exclusively found among those participants who identified strongly as vegetarians. Weakly identified vegetarians were relatively relaxed in their evaluations of the impostor, and non-vegetarians did not seem to mind the impostor at all (indeed, there was some evidence that the revelation of impostorism was mildly amusing to them). It should be noted that this same trend has been found in recent studies examining targets who try to pass as younger than they really are; such targets are evaluated quite negatively, but this effect is most pronounced among those who identify strongly with their 'youth' identity (Schoemann & Branscombe, in press). Third, the effects emerged not just on how likeable the target was seen to be, but also the extent to which they were seen to be doing damage to the group. Together, these findings suggest that derogation of an impostor is not a manifestation of an interpersonal process whereby people condemn liars; it seems also to be driven by identity considerations.

The obvious question would then be: why should group members care whether someone in their ranks is authentic or not? Note that, in the examples above, the impostor is engaging in what is ostensibly a victimless crime. If a self-proclaimed vegetarian sneaks some meat, or if a middle-aged person tries to pass as young, the group is not actively damaged or hurt (note that we chose impostorism where the group was not directly harmed; this is different from some of the impostors described above such as the Trojan horses or the traitors). So why the concern, and what can explain this subjective sense of 'damage'?

One answer to these questions might be that the impostor is threatening the distinctiveness of the group relative to relevant outgroups. From a social identity perspective, it is argued that group members strive for a *coherent* sense of self. A prerequisite for self-definition – and in many ways a prerequisite for collective self-esteem – is that one's group identity is seen to be unique or distinct. As a result, group members often engage in efforts to ensure that the group remains significantly differentiated from the mainstream (or from relevant outgroups). With their apparent disrespect for group boundaries, impostors make a mockery of this process. Impostors blur what it means to be vegetarian (or young, or gay) and it is in this sense that they are seen to be 'damaging'.

To examine this, we exposed gay participants to information about a target who claimed to be either straight or gay (Warner, Hornsey & Jetten, 2007). After gathering impressions of the target, we then revealed the target to be either authentic in their claims for sexuality or inauthentic. In the inauthentic conditions, the target predominantly (Study 1) or exclusively (Study 2) had relationships with people that contradicted their claimed sexuality. The authentic targets, on the other hand, made claims for sexuality that were backed up by their behaviour. This meant that we had two authentic targets (one straight, one gay) and two impostors (a straight person trying to pass as gay, and a gay person trying to pass as straight). Note that we again controlled for deception: even the authentic targets were revealed as having kept aspects of their love life (but not their sexuality) secret.

Interestingly, the gay target who tried to pass as straight was not seen as less likeable than the authentic gay target (presumably our gay participants sympathised with the closeted target) but she was seen to be doing damage to the standing and reputation of the group. These perceptions of damage were driven by the fact that, by attempting to pass as a member of the mainstream, the target was expressing shame about her sexuality. This might be seen as a relatively unsurprising response to the news that people are not 'owning' their group membership. But what about the straight person who tries to pass as gay? Far from signifying stigma, to have a member of the majority group try to pass as a minority group member might be seen as flattering, or an endorsement of social status.

Not for our participants though: compared to the authentically straight target, the straight person who pretended to be gay was rated as being both less likeable and more damaging to the group. The effects on damage were mediated by perceptions of distinctiveness threat. By trying to pass as an ingroup member, the impostor was seen to be blurring or ambiguating the boundaries between the ingroup and the outgroup, boundaries that are important in terms of nourishing self-definition. The impostor in this case is like adding water to a solution, something that adds volume but dilutes essence.

The earliest experimental examination of impostorism (at least to our knowledge) suggests that impostors themselves intuitively understand this psychological dynamic. Breakwell (1979) showed that women who had been given illegitimate entry into a group engaged in heightened discrimination against the outgroup. This effect emerged on all dimensions of differentiation – not just those relevant to the original groupings – suggesting that the impostors were compensating for their illegitimate entry by enhancing intergroup differentiation and, by extension, distinctiveness.

Although there is no systematic data to this effect, there are at least two reasons to argue that themes of distinctiveness and authenticity are more important for minority than majority groups. First, there is evidence that minority group members use group solidarity as a buffer against stigma (Branscombe, Schmitt & Harvey, 1999; Jetten *et al.*, 2001). It is the group's support and solidarity that reinforces self-esteem in the face of rejection from the mainstream, and elements that threaten the distinctiveness of the group also jeopardise the potential of the group to protect the self against discrimination. For this reason, minority groups might be more vigilant in the face of impostors than majority groups. Second, distinctiveness can provide the psychological launching pad for changing the status quo and restoring the group's prestige. As pointed out by Moscovici and others, minorities are able to precipitate societal change to the extent that they are consistent and well defined in the eyes of the majority (Moscovici, Mucchi & Maass, 1994). By blurring intergroup boundaries, impostors risk muddying what the minority group represents to the majority.

This emphasis on distinctiveness among minorities might help explain why our vegetarians seemed so concerned about impostorism when the meat-eating sample was relatively relaxed. It might also help explain the phenomenon of 'horizontal hostility', the tendency for groups to reserve the greatest antipathy towards groups that are most similar to them, but just a little bit more mainstream (White & Langer, 1999; White, Schmitt & Langer, 2006). For those on the fringes, a more mainstream group threatens to dilute what the group represents, both in the eyes of others and in the eyes of the self. From this perspective, whole groups might be seen as impostors who are betraying a broader ideal (e.g., vegans who see vegetarians as compromisers of the broader cause).

Summary

The first goal of this chapter was to present a taxonomy of impostorism, with a view to creating some structure or order to what is clearly a complex psychological phenomenon. Like any taxonomies, one could argue that the list is incomplete or the categories insufficiently discrete. Consider, for example, the term 'mockney', which in the UK is used to refer to when people affect or exaggerate a Cockney accent in order to disguise a privileged education and to endear themselves to a working-class audience. Whether mockney-speakers are parasites, marginal group members or closet-dwellers could well depend on their individual circumstance, their private motivations and other indefinable elements of the context. Our taxonomy should be interpreted as the beginning of a conversation about the dimensions of impostorism, rather than a full stop.

The second goal of the chapter was to summarise the empirical work that has already been conducted on impostors in groups. It will be clear already to the reader that the body of empirical knowledge is very thin, and this reveals the true goal of the taxonomy; not to be exhaustive, but to act as a preliminary framework that can guide future theorising and empirical work on the topic. Already, it is clear that there is more empirical work on 'objective' impostorism than on 'eye-of-the-beholder' impostorism, but even within the rubric of objective impostorism there are whole domains on which the literature is virtually silent (e.g., Trojan horses). It is also clear that the two broad dimensions of impostorism are intertwined in complex and as-yet unexplored ways.

Finally, it is clear that the emphasis has been exclusively on the negative side of impostorism, which is unsurprising given the potential for impostors to cause psychological and material damage to the group. But some of the historical examples reviewed above reveal a more complex picture. For all their failings, it is undeniable that, by virtue of their impostorism, individuals such as James Barry and Chief Buffalo Child Long Lance did important work and left the world a better place than they found it. Others (such as Princess Caraboo and Frank Abagnale Jr) left a different legacy, highlighting the foolishness of a society that finds it easier to judge people on the basis of their pedigree or their uniform than on the quality of their character. It is in this spirit that comedians such as Sacha Baron Cohen continue to flush out people's hidden prejudices, pretensions and vanities, holding a mirror to society by pretending to be something they are not. Impostors might be threatening, devious, selfish or destructive, but ultimately they all remind us that life is a performance, with all the excitement, anarchy and possibility that this implies.

References

Branscombe, N.R., Schmitt, M.T. & Harvey, R.D. (1999). Perceiving pervasive discrimination among African Americans: implications for group identification and well -being. *Journal of Personality and Social Psychology, 77*, 135–49.

Breakwell, G.M. (1979). Illegitimate group membership and intergroup differentiation. *British Journal of Social and Clinical Psychology, 18*, 141–9.

Clance, P. & Imes, S. (1978). The impostor phenomenon in high achieving women: dynamics and therapeutic intervention. *Psychotherapy: Theory, Research & Practice, 15*, 241–7.

Coull, A., Yzerbyt, V.Y., Castano, E., Paladino, M.-P. & Leemans, V. (2001). Protecting the ingroup: motivated allocation of cognitive resources in the presence of threatening ingroup members. *Group Processes and Intergroup Relations, 4*, 327–39.

Frable, D.E.S., Platt, L. & Hoey, S. (1998). Concealable stigmas and positive self-perceptions: feeling better around similar others. *Journal of Personality and Social Psychology, 74*, 909–22.

Goffman, E. (1959). *The Presentation of Self in Everyday Life*. New York: Doubleday Anchor.

Goffman, E. (1963). *Stigma: Notes on the Management of Spoiled Identity*. London: Penguin.

Griffin, J.H. (1977). *Black Like Me*. Boston: Houghton Mifflin.

Hornsey, M.J. & Jetten, J. (2003). Not being what you claim to be: impostors as sources of group threat. *European Journal of Social Psychology, 33*, 639–57.

Hutchison, P. & Abrams, D. (2003). Ingroup identification moderates stereotypic change in reaction to ingroup deviance. *European Journal of Social Psychology, 33*, 497–506.

Jetten, J. & Branscombe, N.R. (2009). Seeking minority group memberships: responses to discrimination when group membership is self-selected. In F. Butera & J. Levine (eds), *Coping with Minority Status: Responses to Exclusion and Inclusion* (pp. 155–76). New York: Cambridge University Press.

Jetten, J., Branscombe, N.R., Schmitt, M.T. & Spears, R. (2001). Rebels with a cause: group identification as a response to perceived discrimination from the mainstream. *Personality and Social Psychology Bulletin, 27*, 1204–13.

Jetten, J., Summerville, N., Hornsey, M.J. & Mewse, A.J. (2005). When differences matter: intergroup distinctiveness and the evaluation of impostors. *European Journal of Social Psychology, 35*, 609–20.

Marques, J.M. & Páez, D. (1994). The 'black sheep effect': social categorization, rejection of ingroup deviates, and perception of group variability. In W. Stroebe & M. Hewstone (eds), *European Review of Social Psychology* (Vol. 5, pp. 41–68). New York: John Wiley and Sons.

Marques, J.M., Yzerbyt, V.Y. & Leyens, J.-P. (1988). The 'black sheep effect': extremity of judgment towards ingroup members as a function of group identification. *European Journal of Social Psychology, 18*, 1–16.

Molero, F., Fuster, M.J., Jetten, J. & Moriano, J.A. (in press). Living with HIV/AIDS: a psychosocial perspective on coping with prejudice and discrimination. *Journal of Applied Social Psychology.*

Moscovici, S., Mucchi, S.A. & Maass, A. (eds) (1994). *Minority Influence.* Chicago: Nelson-Hall.

Oakes, P.J., Haslam, S.A. & Turner, J.C. (1999). The role of prototypicality in group influence and cohesion: contextual variation in the graded structure of social categories. In. S. Worchel, J.F. Morales, D. Paez & J.-C. Deschamps (eds), *Social Identity: International Perspectives* (pp. 75–92). London: Sage.

Reicher, S. & Hopkins, N. (2001). *Self and Nation.* London: Sage.

Schoemann, A.M. & Branscombe, N.R. (in press). Looking young for your age: perceptions of anti-aging actions. *European Journal of Social Psychology.*

Stapel, D.A., Koomen, W. & Spears, R. (1999). Framed and misfortuned: identity salience and the whiff of scandal. *European Journal of Social Psychology, 29*, 397–402.

Stürmer, S. & Simon, B. (2004). The role of collective identification in social movement participation: a panel study in the context of the German Gay Movement. *Personality and Social Psychology Bulletin, 30*, 263–77.

Warner, R., Hornsey, M.J. & Jetten, J. (2007). Why minority members resent impostors. *European Journal of Social Psychology, 37*, 1–18.

White, J.B. & Langer, E.J. (1999). Horizontal hostility: relations between similar minority groups. *Journal of Social Issues, 55*, 537–59.

White, J.B., Schmitt, M.T. & Langer, E.J. (2006). Horizontal hostility: multiple minority groups and differentiation from the mainstream. *Group Processes & Intergroup Relations, 9*, 339–58.

Part III

Difference in Groups

10

Groups in Transition

Differences in the Context of Social Change

Radmila Prislin, Cory Davenport and John Michalak

Being different within a group comes with a price tag. The costs of being different on group-important characteristics are many and range from marginalisation (Brewer & Pickett, 1990; Festinger, 1950; Blackstone & Scherbaum, 1990) and social stigmatisation (Crocker, Major & Steele, 1998; Moscovici, 1994), to prosecution and extermination (Moscovici, 1976). Those who are different bear a larger share of social disadvantages (Evers & van der Flier, 1998), and receive a smaller share of social benefits (Sidanius & Veniegas, 2000). Not surprisingly, they are motivated to change this unfavourable payoff matrix. They typically do so by trying to transform themselves from different to normative. To achieve this goal, they must change the group's position on difference-defining characteristics. Negotiation of differences, therefore, is at the heart of group dynamics with those deemed different trying to influence those deemed normative and vice versa.

Social change occurs when a group changes its position on what is normative. Specifically, groups can either reverse initially normative and anti-normative positions or incorporate an initially anti-normative position into the realm of what is normative. In this chapter, we will examine the meaning of differences within a group in the context of social change. The basic premise of the research programme presented here is that differences in opinions on group-important issues are interpreted and evaluated in the context of one's position within a group (e.g., Tata *et al.*, 1996). Thus, as members' position within a group changes, so do their interpretations and evaluations of group issues. In this chapter, we will examine how those who initially hold (anti-)normative positions within a group evaluate differences

Rebels in Groups: Dissent, Deviance, Difference and Defiance Jolanda Jetten and Matthew J. Hornsey

within the group. Typically, those who hold normative position (majority) dominate the group both numerically and in terms of status and power. In contrast, those who hold anti-normative position (minority) are inferior in terms of their size but also status and power (Prislin, 2010). We will explore how evaluations of differences change as group members move from being normative (majority) to being anti-normative (minority) and vice versa. We will examine the implications of these dynamic construals of differences on the relations between normative and anti-normative factions within a group. We will conclude by discussing the motivational underpinnings of these effects and how they may translate into different strategies used in pursuit of social change.

Evaluating Differences Within a Group: The Majority Perspective

Groups in which opinions on group-important issues are bimodal and asymmetrical typically consider opinions held by most group members (majority) as normative and opinions espoused by fewer group members (minority) as anti-normative. This designation reflects the tendency for people to use opinions held by the majority as a reference against which all other opinions are judged. As a result, those who espouse anti-normative positions are thought of as being different within a group. That is, although the majority is different from the minority and vice versa, it is the minority who is considered different within a group by members of the majority. This designation of who is different has important implications for understanding reactions to differences within a group. The well-documented negative reactions to opinion differences within a group are exclusively reactions of those in the majority within a group (Levine, 1989; Levine & Moreland, 1990; Schachter, 1951).[1] To the extent that they perceive different others as threatening their construction of social reality (Festinger, 1950; Hardin & Higgins, 1996), their social action (Festinger, 1950) or both, they reject different others, labelling them as deviant (Levine, 1989; Levine & Moreland, 1990).

Particularly informative about the majority's reactions to differences is research in the tradition of social identity theory (Tajfel, 1981) and self-categorisation theory (Turner, 1987). This research has revealed that majorities, who consider the group a reflection of their own position and themselves as representative of the group (Marques, Abrams & Serôdio,

2001; Prislin & Christensen, 2005a), are likely to reject those who oppose their view. Furthermore, they do so more strongly when opponents come from the ranks of their own group ('black sheep') than when they are outgroup members (Marques & Páez, 1994). This rejection of ingroup members who challenge the prevailing view within the group is particularly strong among those who identify highly with the group (Hutchison & Abrams, 2003); especially when their prototypicality or representativeness of the group is questioned (Schmitt & Branscombe, 2001). In short, from the perspective of majority members who identify highly with the group and consider themselves and the group as interchangeable categories, being different is being deviant. This view is functional in preserving the majority's position within the group, indicating that reactions to differences are affected by self-interest (Jones & DeCharmes, 1957; Levine & Moreland, 1990; Miller & Anderson, 1979; Schachter, 1951; Sherif & Sherif, 1979).

Evaluating Differences Within a Group: The Minority Perspective

In contrast to the majorities who are studied as arbitrators of differences on group-relevant characteristics, minorities are examined almost exclusively as targets of verdicts issued by the majorities.[2] Because minorities have been 'pigeonholed, pathologized, deprecated, stigmatized, and dismissed in countless ways' (Moscovici, 1994, p. 239), being different is associated with being disadvantaged within a group (for review, see Prislin & Christensen, 2005a). Not surprisingly, these marginalised, peripheral members of the group develop quite a different perspective of the group than their majority counterparts. They are less likely to define themselves in group terms (Jetten, Spears & Manstead, 1997) and they tend to emphasise their personal identity, especially when they face the prospect of further marginalisation (Jetten, Branscombe & Spears, 2002). Because judgemental reactions about the group are closely related to perceived similarity to the group (Clement & Krueger, 1998; Simon, Pantaleo & Mummendey, 1995), these dissimilar, marginal members are unlikely to evaluate the group positively (Prislin, Limbert & Bauer, 2000), unless they secure a reliable improvement in their position (Prislin & Christensen, 2005b; Prislin, Levine & Christensen, 2006).

How do minorities evaluate differences within a group? The ingroup projection model is a useful framework for analysing how structural positions within a group affect evaluation of differences (Mummendey & Wenzel, 1999). According to the model, differences are evaluated against the background of a shared group membership. That is, differences in opinions held by majority and minority will be considered and evaluated only if both factions are included in a shared, superordinate category (Waldzus & Mummendy, 2004). Inclusion in the superordinate category, however, does not imply that both factions will share the same representation of the category. Their representations may differ with respect to their prototypes of the inclusive category or understanding of what is normative for the category. To the extent that one faction claims that its own characteristics better represent the category and therefore are normative, it will evaluate deviations from the claimed prototype as negative. Because of their numerical supremacy within the inclusive category, majorities are particularly likely to engage in ingroup projection, claiming that their own characteristics generalise to the inclusive category. In doing so, they increase the value of their characteristics and decrease the value of different, minority characteristics. Indeed, research about the majority perspective on anti-normative opinions within a group supports this line of reasoning (e.g., Levine, 1989).

In contrast to majorities, minorities are less likely to engage in ingroup projection. Their numerical inferiority within a superordinate category imposes an 'objective', physical constraint to the claim that their characteristics are exclusively prototypical of the category. This, however, does not imply that minorities are destined to be non-prototypical and therefore less valued. Although they cannot claim that they exclusively represent what is normative, they can claim to be part of what is normative (Prislin & Filson, 2009). This claim can be accommodated when the prototype of the superordinate category is construed broadly and encompasses a variety of characteristics, including minority characteristics. Research on multiculturalism supports this line of reasoning. This research has documented that cultural minorities, in comparison to cultural majorities, endorse more strongly the norm of diversity. Specifically, they prefer a conglomeration of cultures as a societal prototype to a prototype reduced to the majority culture (Verkuyten, 2005).

The presumed inclusion of multiple factions in the minority (preferred) prototype of the superordinate group is functional. It enables minorities to preserve the value of their own characteristics within the group where their characteristics are shared by few. Importantly, such a prototype has implications for the evaluation of differences within the group. If differences themselves are part of the preferred prototype, then any characteristic different from one's own is more likely to be evaluated more positively, or at least less negatively, than when one's own characteristics are considered normative (Waldzus *et al.*, 2003). Thus, other things being equal, minorities should evaluate differences more positively than majorities when both factions are included in a shared superordinate group.

Some suggestive evidence in support of this hypothesis comes from a study in which we used the method that serves as a paradigm for much of the research we consider in this chapter. The basic procedure involves one participant and up to seven trained confederates exchanging opinions on important social issues ostensibly as part of a study of 'group communication' or 'political campaign'. Each group member first completes a questionnaire assessing whether they support or oppose the issue under consideration (e.g., legalisation of marijuana). Next, the group members state their (dis)agreement with the issue by answering a series of questions pertaining to the issue (e.g., should marijuana be used as a legally available pain killer, would legalisation of marijuana lead to an increase in drug addiction). The experimenter structures the exchange so that the participant always speaks first, followed by each of the confederates. Having the participant state his or her (dis)agreement with the issue first allows the confederates to adjust their statements so that the participant is placed in the intended numerical position. For example, if a participant agrees with the issue (e.g., that marijuana should be legalised), most of the confederates would also agree with the issue and therefore with the participant. This pattern of responses places the participant in the majority position within a group. Conversely, if a participant agrees with the issue, most of the confederates would disagree with the issue and therefore with the participant. This pattern of responses places the participant in the minority position within a group. An important aspect of this methodological approach is that it allows participants to experience actively their social positions within interacting groups. This stands in contrast to the prevailing methodological approach in which social positions are reduced to information presented to participants (Levine & Kaarbo, 2001; Prislin & Wood, 2005).

Using the procedure described above, participants and confederates in the Prislin, Brewer and Wilson (2002, Stable group condition) study exchanged opinions on a series of socially important issues. The alleged purpose of the study was to establish whether there was any truth in a common criticism that opinions expressed in the laboratory did not reflect those expressed in real life. In each session, a participant and confederates were placed in a group whose task was to form opinions on a series of socially relevant issues. The group opinions were allegedly to be compared to those established in a survey on a representative national sample. Group opinion on each issue was decided by majority rule. Following opinion exchange that established their 'group position', participants were invited to list thoughts that they had during the exchange. Participants were free to list thoughts about any aspect of their experience they considered worth mentioning. These thoughts were later coded for common themes. Importantly, many of these spontaneously generated reflections on the experience pertained to differences in opinions within the group. Two independent coders categorised participants' comments about differences within a group as either negative or positive. The former cast differences as deviance (e.g., 'My opponents had extremely closed minds'; 'There were some weird people in my group'). The latter cast differences as diversity (e.g., 'We disagreed but everyone is entitled to their opinion'; 'It was interesting to hear how differently people can think about the same thing'). An index of the valence of thoughts about differences in opinions was created by dividing the difference between the number of positive thoughts (differences-as-diversity) and the number of negative thoughts (difference-as-deviance) by the sum of the two types of thoughts. Analyses on this index revealed that participants evaluated differences in opinions very differently depending on their own position within the group. Whereas those in the minority evaluated opinion differences slightly positively, those in the majority evaluated them clearly negatively. This differential evaluation of divergent opinions within a group was accompanied by differential evaluation of the group. In contrast to somewhat negative evaluations among participants in the minority, evaluations among participants in the majority were clearly positive. This pattern of results suggests that group prototype defined solely by the majority opinion will make the group attractive to the majority but not to the minority. Moreover, it suggests that minorities prefer diversity as a group prototype. Presumably, because such a prototype would incorporate their own opinion among the group-defining characteristics and reflect their appreciation for differences, it would make the group more attractive to the minority.

On Becoming Normative Within a Group

Whereas the majority's self-serving construction of differences as negative may be temporarily functional, in the long run, it plants the seed of social change. When evaluated negatively and excluded from the realm of normative within a group, minorities are especially likely to seek social change that will alter social structure within a group. Such a change could be effected by convincing a sufficient number of group members to reverse their standing on what is normative within the group (Moscovici, 1976; Prislin & Christensen, 2009). Although a daunting goal that can be reached only under a highly circumscribed set of circumstances, it nonetheless can be achieved (for a review see Butera & Levine, 2009; Hewstone & Martin, 2009; see also Nemeth & Goncalo, this volume).

When minorities convert numerous group members to their position, they transform their status to a majority. Importantly, this form of social change still preserves the notion of a single position as normative within the group. However different the new norm may be from the old one in what it prescribes, it remains the same in its exclusion of opposing positions. Thus, upon becoming a majority, former minorities are likely to embrace the same idea that initially placed them in a disadvantaged position and inspired their fight for change – the idea about superiority of a dominant faction within a group. This implies that social change should alter not only minorities' position within a group but also how they approach differences within the group. Upon becoming new majorities, former minorities should embrace fewer diverging positions as acceptable and they should evaluate differences within a group less positively than they did when they were in the minority. The hypothesised decrease in the scope of acceptable divergences and their evaluation should reflect the dynamic nature of cognitive interpretations of differences within a group. These differences should be interpreted based on one's own position within the group and relation to the group norm.

The hypothesis about narrowing the scope of acceptable differences among new majorities received support in a study in which participants with very positive attitudes towards preservation of the environment discussed the issue with confederates who took the opposite position (Prislin, Limbert & Bauer, 2000; Initial minority condition). For half of the participants, this initial minority position remained stable throughout the entire interaction. For the other half, initial minority position was converted to majority when, halfway through the interaction, most of the confederates who opposed the participants switched alliances to side with the participants. At the end of the interaction, the participants indicated which of the seven positions on preservation of the environment, which ranged from extremely positive to extremely negative, they found unacceptable. They also indicated how important the issue of preservation of the environment was to them as well as the extent to which they identified with the discussion group.

In line with the hypothesis, the results revealed that minorities' successful conversion of others' minds closed their own. Upon becoming majorities, former minorities significantly narrowed the scope of different opinions about preservation of the environment that they found acceptable. On average, they rejected all but the three most positive attitudinal positions that closely matched their own. Noteworthy, not only did they reject all the positions opposing preservation of the environment, but most rejected as unacceptable a position that was only mildly in favour of preservation. That is, they rejected not only all anti-preservation opinions but also a mild pro-preservation opinion. It is possible that the latter was not perceived as (sufficiently) supportive of the issue (Sherif, Taub & Hovland, 1958). Interestingly, new majorities' (former minorities') narrow definition of what is normative was significantly different even from that observed among stable majorities (participants who received consistent support from the confederates throughout the interaction). Apparently, new majorities took a purist approach when it comes to what is acceptable within a group. These findings demonstrate that cognitive interpretations of differences in opinions are dynamic and vary according to the degree of support provided by ingroup members (Turner *et al.*, 1994).

Two additional findings were of interest in understanding group dynamics in the aftermath of social change. Along with narrowing the scope of acceptable differences within a group, new majorities attached more weight to those differences. In comparison to minorities whose position within a group remained unchanged, those who rose to become majorities considered the issue of preservation of the environment significantly more important. Yet, they did not change their disposition towards the group that elevated them to the majority by converting to their position. New majorities' (former minorities') identification with the group remained as low as it was in stable minorities. It is only after they are reassured about their newly acquired position either by spending a prolonged time in it (Prislin & Christensen, 2002) or by securing reliable supporters (Prislin, Levine & Christensen, 2006) that new majorities (former minorities) increase their identification with the superordinate category that encompasses both themselves and new minorities (former majorities).

Taken together, these findings suggest volatility in the group in the immediate aftermath of social change: new majorities' decreased tolerance for different positions, on issues of increasing importance, may make new majorities discriminatory, if not openly hostile, towards new minorities. This possibility was empirically documented in a study in which participants underwent change in their position within a group from minority to majority or, alternatively, remained in the minority throughout the entire interaction with other group members (confederates). In anticipation of the alleged second part of the study in which new majorities and new minorities would engage in a trading game, participants expressed their preferences for rules that would regulate their trading. Participants who acquired a majority position after initially being in the minority (new majorities) endorsed majority-favouring rules (e.g., only majority members have the right to decide when a trade must occur) significantly more strongly than stable minorities, suggesting that what minorities profess when in a disadvantageous position, may change when they become majorities. This tendency for new majorities to discriminate against minorities was especially strong when new majorities felt insecure about their newly acquired position. Given that social change often is accompanied by uncertainty, groups may be well advised to put in place mechanisms that would prevent this apparent tendency for new majorities to discriminate against new minorities (Prislin, Williams & Sawicki, 2009).

On Becoming Different Within a Group

When minorities convert a sufficient number of group members to their position to become majorities, they *ipso facto* transform former majorities to new minorities. New minorities' loss of the normative position within a group severely limits their ability to claim that their characteristics are exclusively prototypical of the group that they occupy along with former minorities (new majorities). Stripped of their 'right' to ingroup projection, which enables stable majorities to justify their tendency to evaluate differences within a group negatively (Mummendey & Wenzel, 1999), former majorities (new minorities) are forced to redefine their approach to differences.

It would be too naive to expect new minorities to become advocates for differences in the aftermath of social change. Full appreciation of differences would contradict their devaluation of differences while in the majority, thus aggravating loss with inconsistency. In the quandary, new minorities must approach differences creatively to reconcile their newly designated anti-normative position within the group with their previous normative position within the group. They may do so by tolerating differences rather than appreciating them outright.

Appreciation and tolerance are two different responses to differences. Our use of these terms echoes Allport's (1958) distinction between 'warmer grade of tolerance' found in a person who 'makes no distinction of race, color, or creed' (Allport, 1958: p. 398) and tolerance as endurance in spite of disapproval and disliking. Appreciation imputes value to differences; tolerance indicates willingness to sacrifice and put up with differences in spite of disliking them. According to Chong (1994), these two responses reflect qualitatively different types of adjustments to differences. Appreciation requires change in the notion of what is good for the group and the construal of differences as socially desirable. Because appreciation represents normative change, it does not require exercise of self-control. In contrast, tolerance requires self-restraint. Because it represents an attempt to maintain the existing norm that casts differences as socially undesirable, tolerance requires exercise of self-control to temper negative reactions to differences (Chong, 1994).

According to Mummendey and Wenzel (1999), differences are tolerated when they are perceived to be so fundamental that they preclude inclusion of different groups into a superordinate category. In the absence of a common superordinate category, neither group has the need to project its own attributes as normative of the entire superordinate category or to construe different characteristics as negative in order to boost its sense of self-worth. Thus, groups may tolerate each other by enduring each other's differences when they perceive their differences as so irreconcilable that they preclude a shared normative standard. In contrast, a shared standard of worth is a prerequisite for appreciation. Groups may appreciate each other's differences when their prototype of a superordinate category to which they belong is vague enough to allow for multiple inclusions. Alternatively, they may appreciate each other's differences when the prototype explicitly includes different attributes (Waldzus *et al.*, 2003). The power of group norms in regulating reaction to differences was nicely documented in a series of studies showing greater appreciation of dissenting group members in groups that espoused individuality rather than conformity as normative (Hornsey *et al.*, 2006; see also Hutchison *et al.*, 2006).

An important implication of this reasoning is that the existence of a shared superordinate category should moderate types of positive reactions to differences. That is, groups will appreciate each other's differences when they share a prototypically vague and explicitly diverse superordinate category but they will tolerate each other's differences in the absence of a shared category. Thus, to understand how new minorities (former majorities) may react toward different others, it is important to assess their representation of the category in which they lost their majority status. Previous research has amply documented that new minorities (former majorities) strongly dis-identify from the group in which they lose their normative position (for meta-analytical review, see Prislin, 2009). This disidentification suggests new minorities' refusal to share the same superordinate category with members newly in the majority. Indeed, research directly examining new minorities' representation of their interaction with new majorities revealed that they conceptualise their interaction at the level of two separate groups rather than an inclusive, single group (Prislin, Christensen & Jacobs, 2005). This self-exclusion from a superodinate, inclusive category and the resultant absence of a shared standard of evaluation implies that new minorities are unlikely to increase their acceptance of social differences upon loss of their majority position. However, the same absence of a shared standard may increase their tolerance for apparently irreconcilable differences.

Prislin *et al.* (2009) examined these predictions in a study in which participants, interacting with confederates in six-member groups, were initially placed in the majority. This initial majority position was either kept stable throughout the entire interaction or it was changed to minority halfway through the interaction. Upon completing their interaction with others, participants responded to a questionnaire assessing their acceptance of differences with the group (e.g., 'Dissenting opinions enhance this group') and their tolerance for differences (e.g., 'When it comes to dissenting opinions within this group, my motto is "live and let live"'). Measures of these two constructs, developed within an independent study, proved to be only moderately positively correlated (Filson, 2005).

In support of the predictions, participants who lost their majority position to become a new minority, in comparison to those who remained in the majority throughout the entire interaction, increased significantly their tolerance for differences. That is, they became increasingly willing to coexist with different others as long as that coexistence did not imply relatedness. This form of social disengagement however, is hardly a prescription for peaceful coexistence. Ignoring each other may allow new minorities and new majorities to avoid conflict but precludes finding a solution when conflict does occur. Moreover, if it leads to mutual avoidance, tolerance may preclude factions from capitalising on their complementary strengths. This possibility is further suggested by the finding that new minorities (former majorities) maintained the same low level of appreciation for differences as stable majorities. Lack of appreciation for differences, coupled with an increased willingness to coexist with different others without being related, suggest that becoming minority within a group leads to social withdrawal.

Social Change through Advocacy for Diversity

Inherent in all attempts at social change that seek to replace one group with another in the position of dominance, privilege or prototypicality is the idea that different others are inferior others. In the immediate aftermath of social change that perpetuates this idea, intergroup relations are tenuous at best. Whatever little in common groups had before social change appears lost in the aftermath of social change. As our review has shown, those elevated to the dominant position become increasingly intolerant of different others. Those relegated to the position of inferiority seek to sever social ties with different others. Both new majorities and new minorities reject membership in a common, superordinate category. In concert, these reactions set the stage for disengagement between the groups (Prislin & Christensen, 2005b). Alternatively, if disengagement is not possible because groups remain mutually dependent, these reactions fuel social conflict (Prislin, Williams & Sawicki, 2009).

Yet, social change need not perpetuate the idea about inferiority of different others. An alternative form of social change occurs through advocacy for their equality. That is, agents of change may advocate for equality of different characteristics rather than for superiority of one characteristic. For some minorities pursuing social change, advocacy for equality of their characteristics may be more desirable or more feasible than advocacy for superiority of their characteristics. When they convince a sufficient number of those not sharing their characteristics to accept them as equal, they effectively change the superordinate category prototype from exclusive and defined by the majority group's characteristics to inclusive and defined by both majority and minority groups' characteristics (Mummendey & Wenzel, 1999).

This type of social change makes diversity normative rather than deviant. Diversity as a norm has important implications for regulation of differences. Rather than being contested, differences should be regulated through mutual accommodation and respect. Thus, even those who lose their exclusively normative position due to social change should feel included in the newly established diversity norm, or at least, they should not feel excluded from it. This should stand in contrast to regulation of differences among groups who compete for superiority of their characteristics over different ones. Their differences should be regulated through conflict. Social change may even exacerbate this type of regulation.

The hypothesis about a more conciliatory approach to differences in the aftermath of social change that establishes diversity as a group norm rather than replaces one normative attribute with another was obtained in a study that manipulated type of minority advocacy (Prislin & Filson, 2009; Study 2). Participants in the study who were initially placed in opinion-based minority advocated either for acceptance of different positions on a socially relevant issue (diversity) or for adoption of a single position on the issue and rejection of others (uniformity). Half of the participants were led to believe that they were successful in their advocacy as some of the confederates in their group who initially disagreed with their advocacy started agreeing with it. Another half was led to believe that they were unsuccessful as they were consistently opposed by most of the confederates in their group. Upon interaction, participants indicated the extent to which they expected that disagreements within their group would be resolved constructively versus leading to social conflict. The results revealed significantly different expectancies for regulation of differences depending on the type of advocacy. Minorities who successfully advocated for diversity had significantly stronger expectations for conciliatory regulation of differences than those who successfully advocated for uniformity (i.e., superiority of their own characteristics over characteristics of the majority within a group). Importantly, majorities who lost their dominant position due to minorities' successful advocacy for diversity had lower social conflict expectations than those who lost their dominant position due to minorities' successful advocacy for uniformity. This pattern of reactions suggests that social change that elevates the value of diversity may result in more constructive relations among different groups than social change that replaces one group's dominance with another.

In spite of the apparent beneficial effects of advocacy for diversity, it is unlikely that promotion of diversity could be adopted as a universal or even dominant mode of social change. Minorities seek social change for a number of reasons, only some of which are served by advocacy for diversity. Among the needs that are likely met by increased acceptance of diversity is the need to belong (Baumeister & Leary, 1995). Traditionally, it has been assumed that those who are different within a group (minorities) would satisfy their need to belong by yielding to the norm (majorities) (Deutsch & Gerard, 1955; Prislin & Wood, 2005). Yielding, however, may be more efficient in satisfying need for affiliation than need for belonging. Thus, rather than yielding, minorities may seek acceptance of diversity in order to satisfy their need to belong. Indeed, racial minorities prefer multiculturalism, which respects cultural differences, to assimilation, which requires them to yield to the dominant culture (Verkuyten, 2005). They also feel more accepted by racial majorities when their distinct perspectives are recognised as valuable (Mendoza-Denton *et al.*, 2002). Thus, need to belong may motivate efforts at conciliatory relations among different segments of the group and lead to advocacy for diversity.

Other needs, however, may be better served by advocacy for uniformity. For example, instrumentally motivated minorities are likely to advocate for superiority of their own over different attributes when access to tangible benefits is limited to those with a specific characteristic. For example, minority parties in majoritarian political systems advocate for superiority of their positions and inferiority of different positions in order to gain political power (Levine & Kaarbo, 2001). Whereas they may support diversity in characteristics (seemingly) unrelated to power, they must insist on their superiority in the characteristic leading to power (i.e., political orientation) if they are to survive in the political arena.

Another motive that may inspire advocacy for superiority is social validation (Festinger, 1954). Social validation confers a sense of correctness to a minority position. Although minorities may draw their initial sense of correctness from non-social or only remotely social factors, to survive, minorities motivated to maintain their sense of correctness must convince others to join their ranks and forgo others (Moscovici, 1976). In doing so, they transform their subjective sense of correctness to widely shared and therefore 'objective' reality (Hardin & Higgins, 1996). Thus, somewhat paradoxically, minorities seeking to validate their difference must invalidate others.

Conclusion

Differences within groups are ubiquitous, even on group-defining issues. No amount of social pressure towards uniformity can erase bastions of difference, giving rise to minorities within groups (Latané & Nowak, 1997). Thus, understanding how groups manage differences is essential to understanding group dynamics. Researchers have traditionally approached this issue adopting a static perspective that reflects majority view. That is, differences within a group have been traditionally examined from the perspective of stable majorities reacting to stable minorities. This research has revealed that majorities, who consider their attributes representative of the group and the group a reflection of who they are, reject differences. Much less is known about how stable minorities approach differences. Existing evidence suggests that stable minorities may have a more nuanced approach to differences, possibly adjusting their specific reactions to the level to which their own attributes are included in the group prototype. Excluded minorities may tolerate different others as a way of detached coexistence with them. In contrast, minorities whose attributes are included in the group prototype may genuinely appreciate differences within the group.

Minority and majority, however, are not static categories. When active minorities successfully challenge the status quo, they effect social change. They may do so by either reversing the existing (anti)-normative positions or expanding the existing normative position to include previously rejected differences. The former mode of social change transforms minority into majority and vice versa. This reversal of positions has important implications for regulation of differences within a group. New majorities (former minorities) appear particularly likely to regulate differences through social conflict, rejecting them even more strongly than stable majorities. Their strong rejection may make it difficult for new minorities (former majorities) to remain tolerant as a way of coexisting with disliked others. Without an existing conciliatory mechanism in place, differences are likely to be hotly contested in the immediate aftermath of social change that reverses the (anti)-normative position. When social change expands what is normative, rather than reversing what is normative, differences within the group are likely to be regulated through conciliatory (versus antagonistic) mechanisms. Though apparently less disruptive, this mode of social change may be of greater interest to minorities motivated to be accepted by the group than to those seeking social validation or tangible benefits within the group. Thus, efforts to reduce the costs of being different by making differences normative are likely to be limited.

Notes

1. These negative evaluations have been documented in reactions to anti-normative differences. However, group members may also hold different but pro-normative opinions when they espouse positions that are evaluatively consistent with the norm but more extreme than the norm (Blanton & Cristie, 2003). Not only are these pro-normative differences perceived as less atypical than anti-normative differences, they are also evaluated more positively (Abrams *et al.*, 2000; Hornsey & Jetten, 2004; Packer, 2008).
2. An exception to this rule is research on minority influence (for review see Butera & Levine, 2009; Hewstone & Martin, 2009). It could be argued, however, that minorities become agents of influence in reponse to negative reactions that they received from majorities (Moscovici, 1994).

References

Abrams, D., Marques, J.M., Bown, N. & Henson, M. (2000). Pro-norm and anti-norm deviance within and between groups. *Journal of Personality and Social Psychology, 78*, 906–12.

Allport, G. (1958). *The Nature of Prejudice.* Garden City: Anchor Books.

Baumeister, R.F. & Leary, M.R. (1995). The need to belong: Desire for interpersonal attachments as a fundamental human motivation. *Psychological Bulletin, 117*, 497–529.

Brewer, M.B. & Pickett, C.L. (1999). Distinctiveness motives as a source of the social self. In T.R. Tyler, R.M. Kramer & O.P. John (eds), *The Psychology of the Social Self* (pp. 71–87). Mahwah, NJ: Erlbaum.

Blanton, H. & Christie, C. (2003). Deviance regulation: a theory of action and identity. *Review of General Psychology, 7*, 115–49.

Butera, F. & Levine, J. (2009). *Coping with Minority Status: Responses to Exclusion and Inclusion.* Cambridge: Cambridge University Press.

Chong, D. (1994). Tolerance and social adjustment to new norms and practices. *Political Behavior, 16*, 21–53.

Clement, R. & Krueger, J. (1998). Liking persons versus liking groups: a dual-process hypothesis. *European Journal of Psychology, 28*, 457–69.

Crocker, J., Major, B. & Steele, C. (1998). Social stigma. In D.T. Gilbert, S.T. Fiske & G. Lindzey (eds), *The Handbook of Social Psychology* (pp. 504–95). Boston, MA: McGraw-Hill.

Deutsch, M. & Gerard, H.B. (1955). A study of normative and informational influences upon individual judgment. *Journal of Abnormal and Social Psychology, 51*, 629–36.

Evers, A. & van der Flier, A. (1998). Ethnic minorities on the labor market. In P.J.D. Drenth, T. Henk & C.J. de Wolf (eds), *Handbook of Work and Organizational Psychology* (Vol. 2, pp. 229–59). Hove: Psychology Press.

Festinger, L. (1950). Informal social communication. *Psychological Review, 57*, 271–82.

Festinger, L. (1954). A theory of social comparison processes. *Human Relations, 7*, 117–40.

Filson, J. (2005). *Social Creation of Differences: The Creation of a Scale.* Unpublished master's thesis. San Diego State University.

Frable, D.E.S., Blackstone, T. & Scherbaum, C. (1990). Marginal and mindful: deviants in social interactions. *Journal of Personality and Social Psychology, 59*, 140–9.

Hardin, C.D. & Higgins, E.T. (1996). Shared reality: how social verification makes the subjective objective. In R.M. Sorentino & E.T. Higgins (eds), *Handbook of Motivation and Cognition* (Vol. 3, pp. 28–84). New York: Guilford.

Hewstone, M. & Martin, R. (2009). *Minority Influence and Innovation: Antecedents, Processes and Consequences.* Hove: Psychology Press.

Hornsey, M.J. & Jetten, J. (2004). The individual within a group: balancing the need to belong and the need to be different. *Personality and Social Psychology Review, 8*, 248–64.

Hornsey, M.J., Jetten, J., McAuliffe, B.J. & Hogg, M.A. (2006). The impact of individualist and collectivist group norms on evaluations of dissenting group members. *Journal of Experimental Social Psychology, 42*, 57–68.

Hutchison, P. & Abrams, D. (2003). Ingroup identification moderates stereotype change in reaction to ingroup deviance. *European Journal of Social Psychology, 33*, 497–506.

Hutchison, P., Jetten, J., Christian, J. & Haycraft, E. (2006). Protecting threatened identity: sticking with the group by emphasizing ingroup heterogeneity. *Personality and Social Psychology Bulletin, 32*, 1620–32.

Jetten, J., Branscombe, N.R. & Spears, R. (2002). On being peripheral: effects of identity insecurity on personal and collective self-esteem. *European Journal of Social Psychology, 32*, 105–23.

Jetten, J., Spears, R. & Manstead, A.S.R. (1997). Distinctiveness threat and prototypicality: combined effects on intergroup discrimination and collective self-esteem. *European Journal of Social Psychology, 27*, 636–57.

Jones, E.E. & DeCharms, R. (1957). Changes in social perception as a function of the personal relevance of behavior. *Sociometry, 20,* 175–85.

Latané, B. & Nowak, A. (1997). Self-organizing social systems: necessary and sufficient conditions for the emergence of consolidation, clustering, and continuing diversity. *Progress in Communication Science, 13,* 43–74.

Levine, J.M. (1989). Reactions to opinion deviance in small groups. In P.P. Paulus (ed.), *Psychology of Group Influence* (pp. 187–231). Hillsdale, NJ: Erlbaum.

Levine, J.M. & Kaarbo, J. (2001). Minority influence in political decision-making. In C.K.W. De Dreu & N.K. De Vries (eds), *Group Consensus and Minority Influence: Implications for Innovation* (pp. 229–57). Oxford: Blackwell.

Levine, J.M. & Moreland, R.L. (1990). Progress in small groups research. *Annual Review of Psychology, 41,* 585–634.

Marques, J.M., Abrams, D. & Serôdio, R.G. (2001). Being better by being right: subjective group dynamics and derogation of in-group deviants when generic norms are undermined. *Journal of Personality and Social Psychology, 81,* 456–7.

Marques, J.M. & Pàez, D. (1994). The black sheep effect: social categorization, rejection of ingroup deviates, and perception of group variability. In W. Stroebe & M. Hewstone (eds), *European Review of Social Psychology* (Vol. 5, pp. 37–68). New York: Wiley.

Mendoza-Denton, R., Downey, G., Purdie, V.J., Davis, A. & Pietrzak, J. (2002). Sensitivity to status-based rejection: Implications for African American students' college experience. *Journal of Personality and Social Psychology, 83,* 896–918.

Miller, C.E. & Anderson, P.D. (1979). Group decision rules and the rejection of deviates. *Social Psychology Quarterly, 42,* 354–63.

Moscovici, S. (1976). *Social Influence and Social Change.* New York: Academic Press.

Moscovici, S. (1994). Three concepts: minority, conflict, and behavioral style. In S. Moscovici, A. Mucchi-Faina & A. Maas (eds), *Minority Influence* (pp. 233–51). Chicago, IL: Nelson-Hall.

Mummendey, A. & Wenzel, M. (1999). Social discrimination and tolerance in intergroup relations: reactions to intergroup difference. *Personality and Social Psychology Review, 3,* 158–74.

Packer, D.J. (2008). On being both with us and against us: a normative conflict model of dissent in social groups. *Personality and Social Psychology Review, 12,* 50–72.

Prislin, R. (2009). Dynamics of change: minority influence makes the world go around. In M. Hewstone & R. Martin (eds), *Minority Influence and Innovation: Antecedents, Processes, and Consequences.* Hove: Psychology Press.

Prislin, R. (2010). Minority groups in society. In J.M. Levine & M.A. Hogg (eds), *Encyclopedia of Group Processes and Intergroup Relations* (vol. 2, pp. 562–6). Thousand Oaks, CA: Sage.

Prislin, R., Brewer, M. & Wilson, D.J. (2002). Changing majority and minority positions within a group vs. an aggregate. *Personality and Social Psychology Bulletin, 28*, 640–7.

Prislin, R. & Christensen, P.N. (2002). Group conversion versus group expansion as modes of change in majority and minority positions: all losses hurt but only some gains gratify. *Journal of Personality and Social Psychology, 83*, 1095–102.

Prislin, R. & Christensen, P.N. (2005a). Social change in the aftermath of successful minority influence. *European Review of Social Psychology, 16*, 75–111.

Prislin, R. & Christensen, P.N. (2005b). The effects of social change within a group on membership preferences: to leave or not to leave? *Personality and Social Psychology Bulletin, 31*, 595–609.

Prislin, R. & Christensen, P.N. (2009). Influence and its aftermath: motives for agreement among minorities and majorities. In F. Butera & J.M. Levine (eds), *Coping with Minority Status: Responses to Exclusion and Inclusion* (pp. 333–53). Cambridge: Cambridge University Press.

Prislin, R., Christensen, P.N. & Jacobs, E. (2005). Group size, power allocation, and change: effects on conceptual representations of group interaction. *Review of Psychology, 12*, 81–9.

Prislin, R., Davenport, C., Michalak, J. & Xu, Y. (2009). Tolerating vs. appreciating differences in a group. Unpublished data.

Prislin, R. & Filson, J. (2009). Seeking conversion versus advocating tolerance in the pursuit of social change. *Journal of Personality and Social Psychology, 97*, 811–22.

Prislin, R., Levine, J.M. & Christensen, P.N. (2006). When reasons matter: quality of support affects reactions to increasing and consistent agreement. *Journal of Experimental Social Psychology, 42*, 593–601.

Prislin, R., Limbert, W.M. & Bauer, E. (2000). From majority to minority and vice versa: the asymmetrical effects of losing and gaining majority position within a group. *Journal of Personality and Social Psychology, 79*, 385–97.

Prislin, R., Williams, K. & Sawicki, W. (2009). *New Majorities' Abuse of Power: Effects of Perceived Control and Social Support.* Manuscript under review.

Prislin, R. & Wood, W. (2005). Social influence: the role of consensus in attitudes and attitude change. In D. Albarracín, B.T. Johnson & M.P. Zanna (eds), *The Handbook of Attitudes and Attitude Change* (pp. 671–706). Mahwah, NJ: Erlbaum.

Schachter, S. (1951). Deviation, rejection, and communication. *Journal of Abnormal and Social Psychology, 46*, 190–217.

Schmitt, M.T. & Branscombe, N.R. (2001). The good, the bad, and the manly: threats to one's prototypicality and evaluations of fellow in-group members. *Journal of Experimental Social Psychology, 37*, 510–17.

Sherif, M. & Sherif, C. (1979). Research on intergroup relation. In W.G. Austin & S. Worchel (eds), *The Social Psychology of Intergroup Relations*. Monterey, CA: Brooks/Cole.

Sherif, M., Taub, D. & Hovland, C.I. (1958). Assimilation and contrast effects of anchoring stimuli of judgments. *Journal of Experimental Social Psychology, 55*, 150–5.

Sidanius, J. & Veniegas, R.C. (2000). Gender and race discrimination: The interactive nature of disadvantage. In S. Oskamp (ed.), *Reducing Prejudice and Discrimination. The Claremont Symposium on Applied Social Psychology* (pp. 47–69). Mahwah, NJ: Erlbaum.

Simon, B., Pantaleo, G. & Mummendey, A. (1995). Unique individual or interchangeable group member? The accentuation of intragroup differences versus similarities as an indicator of the individual self versus the collective self. *Journal of Personality and Social Psychology, 69*, 106–19.

Tajfel, H. (1981). *Human Groups and Social Categories: Studies in Social Psychology*. Cambridge: Cambridge University Press.

Tata, J., Anthony, T., Lin, H., Newman, B., Tang, S., Millson, M. & Sivakumar, K. (1996). Proportionate group size and rejection of the deviate: a meta-analytical integration. *Journal of Social Behavior and Personality, 11*, 739–52.

Turner, J.C. (1987). A self-categorization theory. In J.C. Turner, M.A. Hogg, P.J. Oakes, S.D. Reicher & M.S. Wetherell (eds), *Rediscovering the Social Group: A Self-Categorization Theory* (pp. 42–67). Oxford: Blackwell.

Turner, J.C., Oakes, P.J., Haslam, S.A. & McGarty, C. (1994). Self and collective: cognition and social context. *Personality and Social Psychology Bulletin, 20*, 454–63.

Verkuyten, M. (2005). Ethnic group identification and group evaluation among minority and majority groups: Testing the multiculturalism hypothesis. *Journal of Personality and Social Psychology, 88*, 121–38.

Waldzus, S. & Mummendy, A. (2004). Inclusion in a superordinate category, in-group prototypicality, and attitudes towards out-groups. *Journal of Experimental Social Psychology, 40*, 466–77.

Waldzus, S., Mummendey, A., Wenzel, M. & Weber, U. (2003). Towards tolerance: representations of superordinate categories and perceived ingroup prototypicality. *Personality and Social Psychology Bulletin, 39*, 31–47.

11

The Independence Paradox

Jessica Salvatore and Deborah A. Prentice

In the 1960s, Ayn Rand convened an intellectual salon that she called 'The Collective'. Coming from the founder and articulator of Objectivism, a philosophy of radical individualism, this was a deliberately provocative, tongue-in-cheek name. Yet it captured an important truth about Rand's followers: they were truly followers. They were influenced by her philosophy, her vision, and wanted to share their views with like-minded others. True, those views espoused the intellectual and moral primacy of the individual – the 'virtue of selfishness', as Rand and Branden (1964) termed it – but the intellectual movement that grew up around those ideas was formed and sustained by group processes. The Collective spawned numerous institutes, think-tanks and newsletters designed to draw in new members; there were struggles for status within the group; and Rand herself became an extremely powerful figure, surrounded and protected by a fiercely loyal inner circle. Indeed, a number of commentators have likened the Objectivist movement to a cult (e.g., Shermer, 1993; Walker, 1999).

The Collective provides an excellent illustration of what we refer to as the *independence paradox*. In groups that value individuality, ranging in scale from Rand's Collective to North American societies, acts of independence have a paradoxical status: they both challenge the group's power and conform to its norms. These acts signify personal freedom and, at the same time, collective identification (see also Hornsey & Jetten, 2004; Jetten, Postmes & McAuliffe, 2002). The prototypical members of individualistic groups are mavericks, iconoclasts and deviates who, by rejecting their embeddedness in groups, embody the values of these groups. The peripheral members of these groups are conformists, followers and team players who, by recognising and even embracing their embeddedness, reinforce their

Rebels in Groups: Dissent, Deviance, Difference and Defiance Jolanda Jetten and Matthew J. Hornsey

marginality. In this chapter, we aim to conceptualise the paradoxical interplay of conformity and independence in the psychology of people at both ends of this spectrum. The latter part of the chapter is devoted to describing our model of the self-regulatory dynamics that characterise acts of (non)independence within cultures that value independence, and the experimental evidence that supports the model. We begin, however, with an overview of research on a construct that we believe holds the key to understanding the independence paradox: the independent self-construal.

The Independent Self-Construal

The story of the independent self-construal begins with the cognitive revolution of the mid-1970s, when social cognition researchers showed a burgeoning interest in social representations. Markus (1977) contributed to this approach by conceptualising the self as a knowledge structure, analogous to the knowledge structures that organise information about other people, social groups and both social and non-social categories. Markus introduced the concept of a *self-schema* – a cognitive generalisation about the self that serves to organise self-knowledge and facilitate social information processing. She maintained that individuals vary in the contents of their self-schemas, and, in her empirical research, examined differences between individuals who had self-schemas in a particular content domain and those who did not. She defined *schematics* as people who considered themselves relatively extreme on a given dimension of self-assessment and also considered that dimension to be highly self-relevant; and *aschematics* as those who did not consider the dimension to be particularly self-relevant.

Markus' research interest was not in schematicity per se, but rather in its profound functional consequences for the processing of self-related information. As she put it: 'Once established, these schemata function as selective mechanisms which determine whether information is attended to, how it is structured, how much importance is attached to it, and what happens to it subsequently' (Markus, 1977, p. 64). Markus demonstrated that schematic self-knowledge was stable across time and was linked to memories of past behaviour as well as expectations for future behaviour. Interestingly, her early studies focused on the dimension of independence–dependence, exploring differences between individuals who were *independent–schematic*, *dependent–schematic* or *aschematic*. This choice was somewhat arbitrary;

Markus used the independence–dependence dimension solely because her research participants varied on that dimension in an empirically useful way. Nevertheless, this research provided an early empirical investigation of independence, conceptualised as a stable self-knowledge structure.

A more deliberate focus on independence was a central aspect of Markus' later work, which introduced another way of thinking about self-schemas: as self-knowledge structures shaped profoundly by cultural values. In this view, independence was not just an available self-schema that gave rise to differences between individuals; it was a cultural product, the psychological vehicle through which cultural values are expressed in individual behaviour. This reconceptualisation of the independent self-schema (now termed the independent self-construal) owed much to the ascendant cultural psychology tradition of the late 1980s. After long assuming that the processes they studied were invariant across cultures, psychologists awoke to the fact of cultural differences in even the most basic cognitive and perceptual processes (see Markus, Kitayama, & Heiman, 1996, for a review). To study these differences, they needed a way of identifying and conceptualising one or a small number of dimensions along which the world's cultures predictably varied. Fortunately, prominent anthropologists had, nearly a half-century before, advanced the idea that certain fundamental differences existed between East Asian and North American cultures (see, e.g., Benedict, 1946). Drawing on this work and a growing body of empirical evidence of their own, cultural psychologists converged on the dimension of *individualism–collectivism* as one that captured the primary differences between East Asian and Western cultures (see Triandis, 1990).

The question then was how to conceptualise the psychological mechanism through which a culture's location on the individualism–collectivism dimension was expressed in the thoughts, feelings and behaviours of that culture's members. Markus and Kitayama (1991) proposed that, within any given culture, these dominant ideas would be manifested in how culture members came to perceive themselves with respect to others. In other words, culture-level ideas would shape the structure of the self. Although the original focus in this literature was on broad differences in cultural emphases, over time social psychologists and cultural psychologists together became interested in how those broad differences produced two quite distinct ideas about the self: one in which the self is perceived as bound to others (interdependent self-construal) versus another in which the self is perceived as distinct from others (independent self-construal).

Measurement of the independent self-construal

The changing role of the independent self-construal, from individual difference variable to cultural product and mediator of cultural differences, required a change in measurement strategy. Markus's (1977) original measure of the independent self-schema was individualised and labour-intensive to use; it was therefore not well suited to the conduct of cross-cultural research. A much simpler, standardised measure of independent and interdependent self-construals was developed by Singelis (1994), and it very quickly gained popularity. Indeed, in the decade and a half since the article describing this measure was published, it has been cited over 500 times.

The Singelis scale has informed a substantial amount of published research and has been administered to samples around the globe. However, the ongoing accretion of data has yielded decidedly mixed evidence for the ideas on which the scale was based. In some cases, the results have reaffirmed the notion that the cultures of North America and Western Europe tend to be more individualistic than East Asian and South Asian cultures, but in other cases, that distinction has not held up well (Oyserman, Coon & Kemmelmeier, 2002; see also Church *et al.*, 2003, Study 3).

There are at least two ways to interpret these mixed results. One traces the problem to the scale and its psychometric properties. Although Singelis (1994) demonstrated the scale's construct validity in early samples (see also Singelis & Sharkey, 1995), more recent investigations have been much less supportive (see, e.g., Bresnahan *et al.*, 2005; Levine *et al.*, 2003). In addition, the scale has been plagued by unsatisfactory reliabilities, prompting researchers to reassess Singelis's claim for a two-factor structure (see, e.g., Grace & Cramer, 2003; Hardin, 2006). These challenges to the validity and reliability of the Singelis scale may explain why the original article's citation rate appears to have dropped off slightly in recent years.

An alternative interpretation is that the problem lies in the theory, not the measure. That is, the Singelis scale may offer a psychometrically adequate measure of the independent self-construal, but the field's understanding of how culture, self-construal and behaviour interrelate may be lacking. One indication that theory, rather than measurement, may be the problem is the failure of existing models to account for within-culture variability, the magnitude of which often swamps between-culture variability (Matsumoto, 2006; Suh, Diener & Updegraff, 2008). We ourselves have acquired scores on the independent self-construal subscale from over 600

American college students and observe that although the distribution's mean is shifted above the midpoint of the scale ($M = 4.62$ on a scale from 1 to 7), scores are not very tightly clustered around that mean (see Salvatore, 2007).

We find the spread of this distribution particularly interesting. In a culture that values independence (Kim & Markus, 1999), what does it mean to be a high scorer (whom we will term a *high independent*) or a low scorer (a *low independent*)? What does it mean to believe strongly in one's own independence? Consider two possibilities, both suggested by previous research on the independent self-construal: one, this belief may reflect an accurate assessment of one's own behaviour, past and present. High scorers may be those individuals who march to the beat of their own drum, those who act consistently on their own attitudes and dispositions. Alternatively, this belief may reflect a high value placed on being independent, an aspiration for the self, a standard for self-regulation. High scorers may be those individuals who most strongly identify with the cultural value placed on independence, those who are most inclined to conform to the norms of the group. Similar logic applies to the question of what it means to believe strongly that one is *not* independent: dependent individuals make take their cues from those around them and blow with the prevailing wind, or they may be bold and self-determined enough to go against the individualistic norms of their culture. Note that these interpretations are not mutually exclusive and that both are broadly consistent with the way independence has been conceptualised and studied. Indeed, scores on the Singelis scale crystallise the tension between the formal semantic meaning of independence and the concept's master status as a pervasive, culturally sanctioned guide for behaviour. The question then becomes: What do individual differences in independent self-construal scores reflect – conformity to cultural norms or deviation from them? Some clues may be found in previous research on correlates of the independent self-construal. We turn now to a consideration of this research.

Correlates of the independent self-construal

Over the past two decades, a variety of scholarly literatures have accumulated evidence about the psychology of high and low independents, though it is worth noting that virtually all of these studies have focused on individuals raised and socialised within individualistic cultures. A number of differences between high and low scorers have emerged, starting at the level of basic perception and cognition. In general, independents tend to be more 'context-blind' in their information processing; for example, Kuhnen, Hannover and Schubert (2001) provided participants with embedded figures and found that independents were insensitive to the context in which they occurred.

High and low independents also differ in their motivational orientations: high independents are more promotion focused (see, e.g., Elliot *et al.*, 2001; Lee, Aaker & Gardner, 2000). Our own correlational data corroborate and extend this robust effect. High independence scores are associated with chronic promotion focus, but not with chronic prevention focus. As a manifestation of this general approach orientation, high scorers are absorbed with independence as a 'life task' (Zirkel & Cantor, 1990): they report higher levels of engagement with the goal of 'being my own person, independent of others', and see that task as both more important and more rewarding (Salvatore, 2007). Importantly, independents may be more preoccupied with this personal project, but they see it in *positive* terms (staying resolute, focused on the self) rather than in *negative* terms (avoiding conformity, worrying about how they look to others). Like others' findings, ours converge upon a coherent, holistic picture of high scorers: instead of relating anxiously to others (as potential influencers to be feared and avoided), they experience themselves as easily, organically independent.

Their promotion focus has both positive and negative consequences for high independents. On the one hand, they sometimes fail to self-regulate appropriately. For example, high independents engage in more compulsive consumption than low independents do (Zhang & Shrum, 2009). More generally, though, it appears that (at least in a North American context) independence facilitates a highly functional way of being. Independents tend to score high on measures of self-esteem and well-being (Kim, Kasser & Lee, 2003) and low on measures of social anxiety and distress (Okazaki, 1997). Consistent with their general promotion focus, high independents are interpersonally proactive, at least when it comes to giving voice to relationship dissatisfactions (Sinclair & Fehr, 2005).

Acting Independently

The foregoing review suggests that individual differences in the independent self-construal relate meaningfully and predictably to various aspects of individual and social functioning; it does not, however, demonstrate that high independents act more independently. That is, high independents see themselves as separate, bounded units, focus on themselves, promote themselves and benefit psychologically from being self-focused. But does their belief in their own independence insulate them from social influence? Do high independents behave more independently? Surprisingly few investigations have addressed this question directly (Suh, Diener & Updegraff, 2008), and the existing literature is equivocal. Some findings, especially from the interpersonal domain, suggest that high independents may be less interpersonally sensitive and connected than low independents. In addition, on the basis of a meta-analysis of responses to the Asch (e.g., 1956) line-matching paradigm, Bond and Smith (1996) concluded that participants from collectivistic (East Asian) countries conformed more than those from individualistic (Western) countries. There is every reason to think that self-construal might mediate this effect, just as it mediates so many other culture-level mean differences.

However, other lines of evidence suggest that high scorers may be just as socially embedded, if not more socially embedded, than low scorers. For example, our own data showed that independence scores were negatively associated with seeing oneself as lonesome and positively associated with seeing oneself as amiable, agreeable and likeable. These correlations suggest that high independents may hold their own sociability in higher regard than do low independents. What accounts for this somewhat surprising result? One possibility is that high independents are measuring themselves against lower standards for sociability than are low independents. However, it is also possible that their perceptions are accurate – that high independents are more central members of their social groups than low independents, and therefore are more amiable, agreeable, likeable and socially connected.

In addition, the literature contains a few, albeit scattered, examples of links between independent self-construals and forms of social influence. First, a consistent finding in the consumer persuasion literature is that people have better memory for (Aaker & Lee, 2001) and are more persuaded by (Chang, 2009) appeals that are based on a regulatory focus congruent with their self-construal. Thus, people with an independent self-construal *can be* persuaded, so long as the appeal is promotion-focused and thus resonates with their pre-existing sense of self. Second, Zhang, Feick and Price (2006) showed that high independents' overall tendency to evaluate angular shapes more positively than rounded ones is more pronounced when they believe they are being evaluated by an ingroup member. Again, then, people with an independent self-construal *can be* sensitive to social evaluation. Like the first finding, this one underscores the point that people with independent self-construals are subject to social influence, especially when that influence reflects their sense of their own independence and is endowed with relevance and meaning by a source that reflects their connection to a group (for a similar point, see Hornsey & Jetten, 2004).

Taken together, these findings suggest that the belief in one's own independence might translate poorly into the enactment of independence (see also Prentice, 2006). Of course, such a disjunction between self-belief and behaviour has ample precedent in the literature: countless investigations have shown that people's behaviours often belie their most cherished self-beliefs (Armor, 1998; Pronin, Lin & Ross, 2002). Disjunctions between self-beliefs and behaviours arise most commonly for qualities high in social desirability: objectivity, fairness, freedom from bias. Presumably, the desire to have these highly valued qualities, to be exemplary members of society, leads people to overlook or reinterpret any actions that counter-indicate them. We have good reason to expect self-beliefs about independence to be similarly insulated from behavioural disconfirmation. Indeed, in one particularly relevant demonstration, Pronin, Berger and Molouki (2007) showed that people have a blindspot when it comes to their own conformity – actions they see as conformist in others are interpreted as preference-driven in the self.

This analysis, if correct, complicates predictions about the relationship between scores on the independent self-construal scale (Singelis, 1994) and independent behaviour in cultures where independence is strongly valued (i.e., in North American and European societies). Despite the substantial within-culture variability in independent self-construals, cultural values still function as strong prescriptive norms in these cultures. Thus, people who see themselves as high in independence are seeing themselves in socially valued terms; indeed, as we noted at the beginning of the chapter, they are an individualistic culture's prototypical members. As such, they may be much more tightly engaged with the collective and with its project of promoting independence than they realise or acknowledge. Their high scores on the independent self-construal scale reflect their commitment to being independent, to be sure, but these scores also reflect a self-definition that is culturally prescribed. Low independents, on the other hand, may be explicitly open to influence, and yet these individuals are out of step with cultural norms in the way they define themselves. In short, there may be two self-definitional processes working in opposition here: an explicit process that reflects chronic self-understanding and an implicit process that reflects prepotent sociality, or a chronic norm responsiveness. Both of these processes may be reflected by scores on the Singelis scale, and both may influence behaviour. Although this possibility is broadly consistent with a great deal of theory and empirical evidence, it has not been formalised or tested empirically. In the next section, we describe a dual-process model of the self-regulation of independence and present some initial empirical support for the model.

The Self-Regulation of Independence

Our model draws on recent conceptualisations of self-regulation as an effortful process. Numerous studies have shown that regulating behaviour – bringing behaviour into line with self-beliefs, for example – consumes a global, yet limited, resource (Baumeister *et al.*, 1998). When that resource is available – that is, when people have *self-regulatory capacity* – they use their self-beliefs to guide their behaviour. However, when self-regulatory capacity is impaired, people are unable to override prepotent thoughts, feelings and behaviours, those that are triggered by the dispositional and situational cues that are salient in the moment. They are unable to act like the people they want (and, here, believe themselves) to be. Thus, when in a state of *ego depletion*, people do not show correspondence between their self-beliefs and their behaviours. Researchers have used a muscle metaphor (Muraven & Baumeister, 2000) to emphasise the speed with which self-regulatory capacity can be exhausted in the short term but also its ability to grow in strength with repeated exercise (Muraven, Baumeister & Tice, 1999).

Two processes of independence regulation

We maintain that the independent self-construal functions as a self-regulatory standard: it serves as a goal to which behaviour is directed. The significance of that goal, its power to channel behaviour, depends on two factors. The first is the strength of the independent self-construal, the importance an individual attaches to the goal of being independent. This factor is captured by scores on the Singelis measure. The second is regulatory capacity, the resources an individual has available to control his or her behaviour. These two factors interact, such that when regulatory capacity is high – when people have mental energy available – those with a strong independent self-construal seek to avoid social influence whereas those with a weak independent self-construal do not. When regulatory capacity is low – when mental energy is depleted – self-construals do not control behaviour. Instead, people are guided by whatever responses are prepotent.

Thus far, our model offers a standard self-regulatory analysis of independent behaviour. The twist comes when we consider the prepotent responses that guide behaviour when regulatory capacity is impaired. What might these responses be? One sensible and well-supported proposition is that, with impaired self-regulatory capacity, people are reflexively social: they look to others for cues about appropriate behaviour. The literature is replete with evidence for people's reflexive sociality, and for their failure to appreciate it fully (e.g., Pronin, Berger & Molouki, 2007; Sinclair *et al.*, 2005; Vorauer & Miller, 1997). If this is the case, everybody should show a high level of conformity when regulatory capacity is depleted, and individual differences should emerge only when regulatory capacity is intact.

There is, however, an additional observation to incorporate into the framework: people vary in their reflexive sociality. Some people are more attuned, and therefore more inclined to conform, to their social surroundings than others. How can we capture this variation in the implicit inclination to conform? Ironically, the independent self-construal scale (Singelis, 1994) may serve admirably in this role. As we noted earlier, scores on the independent self-construal scale are valid indicators of not one but two underlying constructs: the belief in one's independence and the congruence of self-beliefs with cultural norms. This latter construct may serve as an excellent proxy for the inclination to conform without being aware of it.

Thus, our model posits that independence is regulated by two processes that work in opposition to each other. One process is implicit conformity – that is, the reflexive attunement to social norms. This process is implicit and automatic, and produces a negative relationship between independent self-beliefs and independent behaviours. The second process is self-regulation – that is, the conscious attempt to act in accordance with the self-concept. This process is explicit and effortful, and produces a positive relationship between independent self-beliefs and behaviours. When regulatory capacity is intact, both of these processes operate simultaneously, leading to an overall null relationship between independent self-beliefs and behaviours. When regulatory capacity is depleted, self-regulation is compromised; thus, behaviour is a function of implicit conformity alone, leading to a negative relationship between independent self-beliefs and behaviours.

Empirical evidence

This model inspired our own empirical research on how people regulate the alignment between independent self-beliefs and behaviours (Salvatore, 2007; Salvatore & Prentice, 2010). Preliminary evidence in support of the model came from correlations we observed in our initial studies: self-construal scores were associated with systematic patterns of trait endorsement. Although all of our participants tended to rate socially desirable traits as more self-descriptive, this correlation varied as a function of scores on the independent self-construal scale: the higher the independence score, the stronger the correlation. This finding suggests that high independents see themselves as being very much in step with societal norms for appropriate behaviour. In addition, independent self-construal scores were associated with a tendency to rate *ambiguously* desirable traits as *less* self-descriptive. In other words, high independents rejected as bases for self-definition traits whose social desirability was unclear, flexible or contingent.

We also obtained correlational evidence in support of the idea that individuals who score high on the independent self-construal scale are those who take independence to be an important self-regulatory standard. Specifically, we found that self-construal scores were strong predictors of anticipated social behaviour (e.g., high scorers believed they would behave more independently during the course of a group discussion than did low scorers). Interestingly, they were not reliable predictors of *past* social behaviour (e.g., high scorers did not name more examples of independent behaviours they enacted in the past than did low scorers). This pattern of results supports the idea that the beliefs expressed by scores on the independent self-construal scale are more akin to values for the self than observations of the self.

Armed with correlational support for our model's assumptions, we next sought direct evidence for its main predictions in two laboratory experiments. In both of these experiments, we manipulated the self-regulatory capacity of individuals representing the full range of scores on the independent self-construal scale. Specifically, half of the participants began the experiment with a task designed to deplete their regulatory capacity, whereas the other half completed a control task. All participants then read a brief description of an obscure policy topic and expressed their support for the proposed policy. For a random subset of the participants in each regulatory-capacity condition, the description included information about their peers' opinions for the policy, in the form of poll data that were congruent with the facts presented. (That is, the facts suggested that one should support the policy, and the poll data indicated that the majority of people did support it.) These participants thus had an opportunity to conform to or remain independent from their peers' opinions. The remaining participants received no information about their peers' opinions.

In the first study, we simply measured participants' opinions after they had read about the policy topic and observed that, when regulatory capacity was depleted, those participants with the strongest beliefs in their own independence showed the strongest tendency to conform. That is, among participants who received information about their peers' opinions, we observed a positive correlation between their own independence scores and endorsement of the position supposedly favoured by the majority of their peers. There was no relationship between independence scores and opinions for participants who did not receive the poll data and similarly no relationship for those whose regulatory capacity was intact (regardless of whether they received the poll data). These results supported the predictions of our theoretical model.

In a second study, we included a pre-measure of opinions in our design and operationalised independence as the strength of the correlation between this pre-measure and the post-measure of opinions (taken after the manipulations of regulatory capacity and peer information were introduced). The higher the pre–post correlation, the more independent participants were remaining from the information they had received in between. This correlation was very strong for participants who did not receive information about their peers' opinions ($r = .74$), as we expected. It was also strong for participants in a new condition we added to this study, in which the information about peers' opinions *conflicted with* the background information they received about the topic ($r = .55$). This result suggests that people are sensitive to the reasonableness of the social information they receive, and are not prepared to conform to majority views that seem unreasonable. The correlation was much weaker for participants who received congruent (i.e., apparently reasonable) information about their peers' opinions ($r = .31$). Moreover, the strength of the correlation in this condition varied as a function of independence scores and regulatory capacity: when capacity was intact, the pre–post relationship was positive for high independents and zero for low independents; when capacity was depleted, the pre–post relationship was positive for low independents and zero for high independents. These results were entirely consistent with the model's predictions.

In sum, the results of our research illustrate how people navigate the independence paradox. In a group or society with strongly individualistic norms, people are faced with a choice: they can conform by deviating or deviate by conforming. We believe they make this choice without realising it was a choice at all, and experience little tension around their resulting self-beliefs. Nevertheless, when stripped of their capacity to self-regulate, an ironic pattern of behaviour emerges: high independents conform to and low independents deviate from the prevailing social norms. Of course, because they cannot closely monitor their behaviour in an ego-depleted state, they are unlikely to notice the irony and even less likely to revise their self-views accordingly. Thus, their phenomenological experience encompasses only one side of the paradox, and it does not feel like a paradox at all.

Implications

The dual-process model and the evidence we have accumulated in support of it have implications for a number of key issues in the study of self-regulation and cultural differences. First, consider the implications for the perennial debate about the accuracy of self-knowledge. We have shown that high independents' strong and consistent beliefs about themselves do not always match up well with their behaviour, and that they seem to be insensitive to disconfirming evidence about themselves. One might see them as illustrating the naivety of the motivated social thinker, whose self-knowledge is deeply imperfect (see also Vazire & Mehl, 2008). This interpretation gains additional support from the recent finding that collectivists predict their future behaviour (especially in socially desirable domains) with greater accuracy than do individualists (Balcetis, Dunning & Miller, 2008). Thus, we might take high independents as poster children for the lack of insight that comes with considering oneself in isolation from other people and from the social context.

A contrasting characterisation would focus not on all behaviour, but only on truly self-directed behaviour, behaviour that is brought into line with self-knowledge. If one adopts this view, the best measure of accuracy might be the ability to realise the desired congruence between self-beliefs and behaviour when resources are intact, compared to when they are depleted. By this measure, high independents are accurate indeed. The difference between these views lies in the definition of self, the former relying on a trait-like, backward-looking definition and the latter on a motivational, forward-looking one. By the former definition, high independents are largely inaccurate about themselves; by the latter definition, they are largely accurate.

Our results also speak to the meaningfulness of scores on the Singelis independent self-construal scale and to their utility for predicting behaviour. Our experimental evidence, in particular, suggests that what the field needs is not a different measure of the independent self-construal, but rather a different model of how culture and personality combine to produce individual differences in self-beliefs and behaviours. Scores on the independent self-construal scale do not measure what people do; they measure what people value and believe about themselves, and these beliefs bear a much more complex relationship to behaviour than previous research has acknowledged. Our research represents just the beginnings of an attempt to specify formally and disentangle empirically the psychological processes that connect the two.

If our findings complicate the interpretation of self-construal scores in the United States, they complicate the interpretation of scores across cultures to an even great extent and thereby call into question the meaning of the mean-level differences so often observed in cross-cultural research. Earlier in the chapter, we reviewed evidence pertaining to the correlates of the independent self-construal, noting that the preponderance of this evidence comes from individualistic cultures. What might self-construal scores signify among people raised and socialised within collectivistic cultures, where independence is not idealised and collectively valued? We have no evidence with which to answer this question, as our own data come exclusively from the population of North American college students. However, our theoretical model suggests that independence may not have the same paradoxical qualities in collectivistic cultures as it does in individualistic ones. In any culture, some people are more reflexively attuned to their social surroundings than others. In keeping with other universal tendencies that take different forms in different cultures (e.g., self-enhancement; Heine *et al.*, 1999), culture likely shapes the specific manifestations of this temperament. In individualistic cultures, more socially attuned members become high scorers on the independence subscale of the Singelis (1994) self-construal measure, and expend effort trying to be less influenced by others. In line with the data we have already collected, we would expect considerable variability in the behaviour of these individuals, as a function of the availability of regulatory resources, and would expect self-regulation to be highly effortful for them. In collectivistic cultures, more socially attuned members may instead become high scorers on the *inter*dependence subscale, and expend effort trying to be even more attuned to others. Because their temperament and self-regulatory efforts would pull in the same direction, these individuals should expend, and need to expend, less effort on self-regulation. The important point here is that culture interacts with temperament to produce very different patterns of self-experience and behaviour. More specifically, this analysis makes clear that culture determines the meaning of the self-construal scale, and that two people with the same score but different cultural backgrounds cannot be counted on to respond similarly to social influence.

Concluding Remarks

Although The Collective broke apart in the 1970s and Ayn Rand herself died in 1982, Rand's novels and ideas remain popular. Recently, *The New Yorker* covered the monthly meeting of 'a group of Ayn Rand enthusiasts'. Apparently, the inclination of objectivists to collectivise remains strong. The members of this group are presumably people who see themselves as iconoclasts like Howard Roark and John Galt, the heroes of Rand's two major works of fiction, and disdain collectivism in all forms. And yet, in a remarkable echo of the past, one current enthusiast suggested that Rand's disciples should 'organize an Objectivist gang', to be called the Galts: a collective dedicated to promoting and enacting individualism. Although it is tempting to present this suggestion in all its ironic and paradoxical splendour, we wish to present it instead as anecdotal evidence in support of our central argument. Independence is clearly an ideal around which many groups and societies rally. For members of these independence-loving groups, the pursuit of autonomy is both an individual and a collective project.

References

Aaker, J.L. & Lee, A.Y. (2001). 'I' seek pleasures and 'we' avoid pains: the role of self-regulatory goals in information processing and persuasion. *Journal of Consumer Research*, *28*, 33–49.

Armor, D.A. (1999). The illusion of objectivity: a bias in the perception of freedom from bias. Unpublished dissertation, University of California, Los Angeles.

Asch, S.E. (1956). Studies of independence and conformity: I. A minority of one against a unanimous majority. *Psychological Monographs, 70*, 70.

Balcetis, E., Dunning, D. & Miller, R.L. (2008). Do collectivists know themselves better than individualists? Cross-cultural studies of the holier-than-thou phenomenon. *Journal of Personality and Social Psychology, 74*, 1252–67.

Baumeister, R.F., Bratslavsky, E., Muraven, M. & Tice, D.M. (1998). Ego depletion: is the active self a limited resource? *Journal of Personality and Social Psychology, 74*, 1252–65.

Benedict, R. (1946). *The Chrysanthemum and the Sword: Patterns of Japanese Culture.* Oxford: Houghton & Mifflin.

Bond, R. & Smith, P.B. (1996). Culture and conformity: a meta-analysis of studies using Asch's (1952b, 1956) line judgment task. *Psychological Bulletin, 119*, 111–37.

Bresnahan, M.J., Levine, T.R., Shearman, S.M., Lee, S.Y., Park, C.-Y. & Kiyomiya, T. (2005). A multimethod multitrait validity assessment of self-construal in Japan, Korea, and the United States. *Human Communication Research, 31*, 33–59.

Chang, C. (2009). Enhancing the effectiveness of antismoking messages via self-congruent appeals. *Health Communication, 24*, 33–40.

Church, A.T., Ortiz, F.A., Katigbak, M.S., Avdeyeva, T.V., Emerson, A.M., Vargas Flores, J. de J. *et al.* (2003). Measuring individual and cultural differences in implicit trait theories. *Journal of Personality and Social Psychology, 85*, 332–47.

Elliot, A.J., Chirkov, V.I., Kim, Y. & Sheldon, K.M. (2001). A cross-cultural analysis of avoidance (relative to approach) personal goals. *Psychological Science, 12*, 505–10.

Grace, S.L. & Cramer, K.L. (2003). The elusive nature of self-measurement: the self-construal scale versus the twenty statements test. *Journal of Social Psychology, 143*, 649–68.

Hardin, E.E. (2006). Convergent evidence for the multidimensionality of self-construal. *Journal of Cross-Cultural Psychology, 37*, 516–21.

Heine, S.J., Lehman, D.R., Markus, H.R. & Kitayama, S. (1999). Is there a universal need for positive self-regard? *Psychological Review, 106*, 766–94.

Hornsey, M.J. & Jetten, J. (2004). The individual within the group: balancing the need to belong with the need to be different. *Personality and Social Psychology Review, 8*, 248–64.

Jetten, J., Postmes, T. & McAuliffe, B.J. (2002). 'We're all individuals': group norms of individualism and collectivism, levels of identification and identity threat. *European Journal of Social Psychology, 32*, 189–207.

Kim, H. & Markus, H.R. (1999). Deviance or uniqueness, harmony or conformity? A cultural analysis. *Journal of Personality and Social Psychology, 77*, 785–800.

Kim, Y., Kasser, T. & Lee, H. (2003). Self-concept, aspirations, and well-being in South Korea and the United States. *Journal of Social Psychology, 143*, 277–90.

Kuhnen, U., Hannover, B. & Schubert, B. (2001). The semantic-procedural interface model of the self: the role of self-knowledge for context-dependent versus context-independent modes of thinking. *Journal of Personality and Social Psychology, 80*, 397–409.

Lee, A.Y., Aaker, J.L. & Gardner, W.L. (2000). The pleasures and pains of distinct self-construals: the role of interdependence in regulatory focus. *Journal of Personality and Social Psychology, 78*, 1122–34.

Levine, T.R., Bresnahan, M.J., Park, H.S., Lapinski, M.K., Wittenbaum, G.M., Shearman, S.M. *et al.* (2003). Self-construal scales lack validity. *Human Communication Research, 29*, 210–52.

Markus, H. (1977). Self-schemata and processing information about the self. *Journal of Personality and Social Psychology, 35*, 63–78.

Markus, H.R. & Kitayama, S. (1991). Culture and the self: implications for cognition, emotion, and motivation. *Psychological Review, 98*, 224–53.

Markus, H.R., Kitayama, S. & Heiman, R. (1996). Culture and 'basic' psychological principles. In E.T. Higgins & A.W. Kruglanski (eds), *Social Psychology: Handbook of Basic Principles* (pp. 857–913). New York: Guilford.

Matsumoto, D. (2006). Culture and cultural worldviews: do verbal descriptions about culture reflect anything other than verbal descriptions of culture? *Culture and Psychology, 12*, 33–62.

Muraven, M. & Baumeister, R.F. (2000). Self-regulation and depletion of limited resources: does self-control resemble a muscle? *Psychological Bulletin, 126*, 247–59.

Muraven, M., Baumeister, R.F. & Tice, D.M. (1999). Longitudinal improvement of self-regulation through practice: building self-control strength through repeated exercise. *Journal of Social Psychology, 139*, 446–57.

Okazaki, S. (1997). Sources of ethnic differences between Asian American and White American college students on measures of depression and social anxiety. *Journal of Abnormal Psychology, 106*, 62–70.

Oyserman, D., Coon, H.M. & Kemmelmeier, M. (2002). Rethinking individualism and collectivism: evaluation of theoretical assumptions and meta-analyses. *Psychological Bulletin, 128*, 3–72.

Prentice, D.A. (2006). Acting like an individual versus feeling like an individual. In T. Postmes & J. Jetten (eds), *Individuality and the Group: Advances in Social Identity*. Thousand Oaks, CA: Sage.

Pronin, E., Berger, J. & Molouki, S. (2007). Alone in a crowd of sheep: asymmetric perceptions of conformity and their roots in an introspection illusion. *Journal of Personality and Social Psychology, 92*, 585–95.

Pronin, E., Lin, D.Y. & Ross, L. (2002). The bias blind spot: perceptions of bias in self versus others. *Personality and Social Psychology Bulletin, 28*, 369–81.

Rand, A. & Branden, N. (1964). *The Virtue of Selfishness: A New Concept of Egoism.* New York: Signet.

Salvatore, J.A.S. (2007). The regulation of normative behavior. Unpublished dissertation, Princeton University.

Salvatore, J. & Prentice, D.A. (2010). Yielding to independence: self-regulatory consequences of individual differences in norm responsiveness. Manuscript under review.

Shermer, M. (1993). The unlikeliest cult in history. *Skeptic, 2*, 74–81.

Sinclair, L. & Fehr, B. (2005). Voice versus loyalty: self-construals and responses to dissatisfaction in romantic relationships. *Journal of Experimental Social Psychology, 41*, 298–304.

Sinclair, S., Lowery, B.S., Hardin, C.D. & Colangelo, A. (2005). Social tuning of automatic racial attitudes: the role of affiliative motivation. *Journal of Personality and Social Psychology, 89*, 583–92.

Singelis, T.M. (1994). The measurement of independent and interdependent self-construals. *Personality and Social Psychology Bulletin, 20*, 580–91.

Singelis, T.M. & Sharkey, W.F. (1995). Culture, self-construal, and embarrassability. *Journal of Cross-Cultural Psychology, 26*, 622–44.

Suh, E.M., Diener, E. & Updegraff, J.A. (2008). From culture to priming conditions: self-construal influences on life satisfaction judgments. *Journal of Cross-Cultural Psychology, 39*, 3–15.

Triandis, H.C. (1990). Cross-cultural studies of individualism and collectivism. In J.J. Berman (ed), *Nebraska Symposium on Motivation, 1989: Cross-Cultural Perspectives.* Lincoln, NE: University of Nebraska Press.

Vazire, S. & Mehl, M.R. (2008). Knowing me, knowing you: the accuracy and unique predictive validity of self-ratings and other-ratings of daily behavior. *Journal of Personality and Social Psychology, 95*, 1202–16.

Vorauer, J.D. & Miller, D.T. (1997). Failure to recognize the effect of implicit social influence on the presentation of self. *Journal of Personality and Social Psychology, 73*, 281–95.

Walker, J. (1999). *The Ayn Rand Cult.* La Salle, IL: Open Court Publishing.

Zhang, Y. & Shrum, L.J. (2009). The influence of self-construal on impulsive consumption. *Journal of Consumer Research, 35*, 838–50.

Zhang, Y., Feick, L. & Price, L.J. (2006). The impact of self-construal on aesthetic preference for angular versus rounded shapes. *Personality and Social Psychology Bulletin, 32*, 794–805.

Zirkel, S. & Cantor, N. (1990). Personal construal of life tasks: those who struggle for independence. *Journal of Personality and Social Psychology, 58*, 172–85.

12

Explaining Differences in Opinion Expression

Direction Matters

Kimberly Rios Morrison and Dale T. Miller

For many, expressing minority opinions is a difficult task. Even in individualistic societies like the United States and Western Europe, where people strive to be unique and independent (Markus & Kitayama, 1991; Triandis, 1995), learning that others disagree with oneself can lead to discomfort (Matz & Wood, 2005; Priester & Petty, 2001) and reduced self-esteem (Pool, Wood & Leck, 1998). As a result, people are often reluctant to voice opinions that they believe are different from those of the majority. In a classic demonstration of this phenomenon, Asch (1956) found that participants publicly agreed with confederates' judgements of the length of several lines, despite their knowledge that these judgements were incorrect. Indeed, not only do people withhold their minority opinions, but under some circumstances they may even falsify these opinions by pretending to side with the majority (see also Hewlin, 2003; Kuran, 1995).

According to spiral of silence theory (Noelle-Neumann, 1974, 1993), individuals' reticence to express minority viewpoints stems primarily from a fear of social isolation. Supporting this idea, a meta-analysis of spiral of silence research revealed a small but statistically significant relationship between perceived support for opinion and self-reported willingness to speak out (Glynn, Hayes & Shanahan, 1997). A more recent set of experiments by Bassili (2003) demonstrated that the impact of perceived minority status can extend to behavioural measures of opinion expression, such as response latency. Specifically, majority opinion holders are faster to state their opinions in a telephone survey than minority opinion holders. As the presumed percentage of majority (relative to minority) opinion holders

Rebels in Groups: Dissent, Deviance, Difference and Defiance Jolanda Jetten and Matthew J. Hornsey

increases in the population, so does the magnitude of this effect (Bassili, 2003). Minorities' concerns about expressing their opinions are justifiable, given the wealth of empirical evidence indicating that they face derogation, ostracism and punishment by other group members (Levine, 1989; Marques and Pàez, 1994; Schachter, 1951).

Some minorities are willing to make their opinions known in spite of the potential ramifications involved. Noelle-Neumann (1974, 1993) posited that there exists a 'hard core' of individuals who constitute an exception to the spiral of silence. Members of the hard core, due to the conviction with which they hold their opinions, will speak out regardless of whether they believe their opinions are shared (see also Moscovici, 1991). For them, the need to be correct overrides the need to be accepted by others (Lasorsa, 1991). Supporting this idea, minorities whose opinions have a strong moral basis tend to be more vocal than those whose opinions have a weak moral basis (Hornsey *et al.*, 2003), and minorities who are highly certain of their opinions tend to be more vocal than those who are less certain of their opinions (Matthes, Morrison & Schemer, in press).

The studies reviewed above advance our understanding of the characteristics of minority opinion holders that lead them to speak out versus fall prey to the spiral of silence. In the present chapter we identify another characteristic of minority opinion holders that, along with the magnitude of their deviation from the majority (Bassili, 2003; Glynn, Hayes & Shanahan, 1997) and the strength with which they hold their opinions (Hornsey *et al.*, 2003; Matthes, Morrison & Schemer, in press), influence their willingness to speak out: the direction of their deviation from the majority. The goals of this chapter are threefold. First, we introduce a model that distinguishes those minorities who deviate in a direction consistent with the group prototype ('descriptive norm deviants') from those who deviate in a direction inconsistent with the group prototype ('prescriptive norm deviants'). Second, we review recent studies elucidating why descriptive norm deviants are more willing to express their opinions than both prescriptive norm deviants and non-deviants. Third, we propose several directions for future research in this area.

Group Norms and Opinion Expression

Descriptive and prescriptive norm deviance

Conceptualising deviance in terms of the direction of difference from the majority acknowledges the existence of two types of group norms.

Descriptive norms refer to the attitudes and behaviours that most group members actually adopt (Cialdini, Reno & Kallgren, 1990; Prentice & Miller, 1996). To the extent that the distribution of group members' attitudes and behaviours is not skewed in a particular direction, the descriptive group norm can be thought of as the group average (Morrison & Miller, 2008). By contrast, prescriptive (or injunctive) norms refer to the attitudes and behaviours that group members believe they *should* adopt in order to fit in with their peers (Cialdini, Reno & Kallgren, 1990; Prentice & Miller, 1996). From a social identity perspective, prescriptive group norms can be thought of as markers of the group prototype – in other words, the attitudes and behaviours that best distinguish the ingroup from relevant outgroups (Hogg & Reid, 2006).

Under some circumstances, the descriptive and prescriptive group norms will be highly overlapping. In a study of binge-eating behaviours among college sorority members, Crandall (1988) found that moderate bingers in one sorority tended to be more popular than either frequent bingers or infrequent bingers. In this context, the descriptive norm (i.e., the amount that most sorority members binged in reality) appeared to correspond to the prescriptive norm (i.e., the amount that sorority members ought to binge in order to gain popularity). Under other circumstances, however, the descriptive and prescriptive group norms will diverge. In a different sorority in the Crandall (1988) study, there was a strong positive correlation between binge eating and popularity. That is, the more a sorority member engaged in binge eating, the more popular she tended to be, even though most members did not binge on a regular basis.

The distinction between descriptive and prescriptive group norms implies that deviant group members can be separated into two categories. The first category deviates from the descriptive norm in a direction consistent with the prescriptive norm. Because these group members deviate from the descriptive (but not prescriptive) norm, we will refer to them as 'descriptive norm deviants'. The second category also deviates from the descriptive norm, but in a direction inconsistent with the prescriptive norm. Because these group members deviate away from both the prescriptive and descriptive norms, we will refer to them as 'prescriptive norm deviants'. Thus, even though both descriptive and prescriptive deviants are discrepant from the statistical group average, the former are more prototypical than the latter. As a concrete example, consider again the sorority in which members were more popular the more often they binged (Crandall, 1988). Within that sorority, the frequent binge eaters (whose behaviour differed from that of the average group member but corresponded to how group members *should* behave) could be classified as descriptive norm deviants, whereas the infrequent binge eaters (whose behaviour differed from that of the average group member and reflected how group members *should not* behave) could be classified as prescriptive norm deviants.

Social norms apply to opinions and attitudes, not just behaviours (Glynn, 1997). As such, it is possible to link the concepts of descriptive and prescriptive norm deviants to different attitudes in a population. Consider the distribution of political attitudes at Stanford University, where we conducted the research we report in this chapter. At Stanford, most students tend to be somewhat politically liberal. Many of these students join campus organisations such as College Democrats, whose political views are considered mainstream. Other students join presumed 'radical' organisations such as the Stanford Labor Action Coalition (SLAC), and still others join conservative organisations such as College Republicans. Given that the descriptive norm at Stanford is somewhat liberal, members of SLAC, College Democrats, and College Republicans can be categorised as descriptive norm deviants, non-deviants and prescriptive norm deviants, respectively (see Figure 12.1 for a visual depiction of this distribution).

The above examples of descriptive and prescriptive norm deviance can be explained in terms of self-categorisation theory's meta-contrast principle (Turner *et al.*, 1987). This principle states that groups seek to establish their identities by differentiating themselves from one another. As a result, the group prototype will eventually shift away from the mean or midpoint of the ingroup, in a direction opposite to the prototypical behaviours and attitudes of relevant outgroups (i.e., other sororities in the case of the binge-eating study, conservatives or College Republicans in the case of the liberal university campus).

Opinion expression among descriptive and prescriptive norm deviants

Some studies suggest that descriptive norm deviants are judged more positively than prescriptive norm deviants. For instance, British college students whose attitudes towards asylum seekers are deviant in a direction consistent with the group prototype (i.e., who advocate stricter procedures) are better liked by their peers than those whose attitudes are deviant in a direction inconsistent with the group prototype (i.e., who advocate more lenient procedures) (Abrams *et al.*, 2000, Study 2). Similarly, in a work

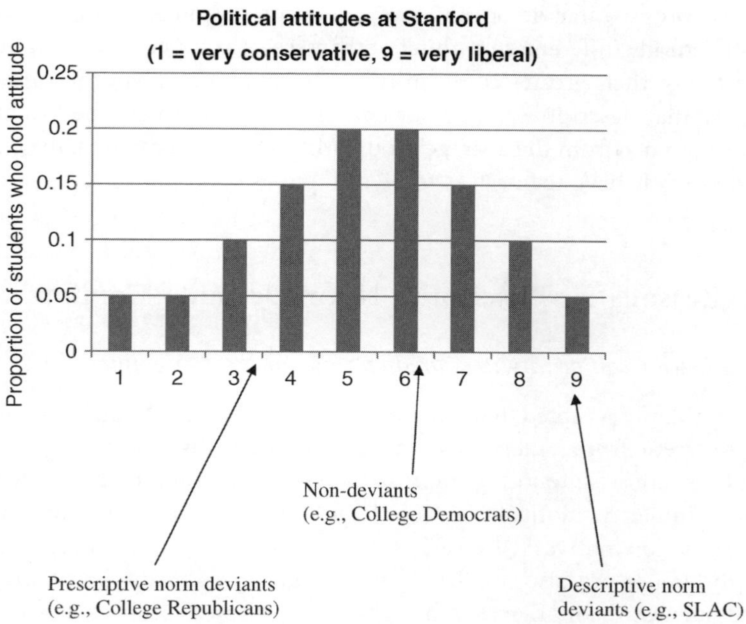

Figure 12.1 Political attitudes at Stanford

organisation where the norm is to have a moderate work ethic, extremely conscientious employees (relative to their lackadaisical counterparts) are better liked by their colleagues (Abrams *et al.*, 2002, Study 1). In further support of the relationship between descriptive norm deviance and (reduced) perceptions of marginality, deviant group members whose attitudes are extremely prototypical (i.e., radical feminists in a mildly feminist group of students) tend to exert more influence within their peer groups than do those whose attitudes are non-prototypical (i.e., anti-feminists in the same group) (Paicheler, 1976).

A logical extension of the research reported above is that descriptive norm deviants, in addition to being perceived as less marginal than prescriptive norm deviants, will actually *feel* less marginal and more like 'good' group members. As a result, the former may be more willing to express their opinions on controversial social issues than the latter, even though both types of deviants are equally discrepant from the average group opinion. But why might descriptive norm deviants not feel deviant? In this section, we examine two possibilities and present empirical evidence in support of each.

First, we propose that descriptive norm deviants, despite knowing that they are statistically different, may think of themselves as superior to their peers by virtue of their greater conformity to the group prototype. Second, we propose that descriptive norm deviants may underestimate the extent of their difference from the average group attitude. In other words, they may erroneously believe themselves to be in the majority.

Reasons for Descriptive Norm Deviants' Comfort

Superior conformity as a predictor of comfort: an empirical test

It is commonly accepted that individuals are motivated to be both similar to and different from others. According to optimal distinctiveness theory, people do not wish to join groups that are too small (and therefore do not satisfy similarity motives) or too large (and therefore do not satisfy differentiation motives) (Brewer, 1991). The competing drives for similarity and difference are also applicable to intragroup contexts. For example, as uniqueness theory demonstrates, individuals resist feedback suggesting that they are either extremely similar to or extremely different from other members of their group (Snyder & Fromkin, 1980).

One way that group members might fulfil their simultaneous needs for similarity and difference is through adhering more closely to group norms than their peers, a phenomenon referred to as *superior conformity* (Codol, 1975; see also Hornsey & Jetten, 2004). Indeed, some research has shown that individuals strive to outdo their peers by shifting their attitudes away from the group average and towards the group prototype (Myers, 1978). In other words, they would prefer to 'stand out' from their group in good ways, as opposed to 'stick out' from their group in bad ways (see Blanton & Christie, 2003). To the extent that this is true, descriptive norm deviants should be more willing to express their opinions than prescriptive norm deviants because of their awareness that they differ from other group members in a prototypical direction.

In an initial test of this hypothesis (Morrison & Miller, 2008, Study 1), we administered a short vignette study to Stanford University undergraduates. Specifically, we had participants imagine that they had been assigned to give a speech promoting a descriptive norm deviant position (e.g., strongly in favour of affirmative action), a non-deviant position (e.g., somewhat in favour of affirmative action), or a prescriptive norm deviant position (e.g., strongly opposed to affirmative action). Then we asked them how comfortable they would feel delivering the speech to another Stanford student.

Consistent with our hypothesis, participants in the descriptive norm deviant condition reported feeling more comfortable than participants in both the prescriptive norm deviant and non-deviant conditions. Importantly, the relationship between position and comfort was mediated by descriptive norm deviants' perception that their assigned positions made them seem 'different from [their] peers in a "good" way', but not by their perception that their assigned positions rendered them similar to their peers. These results indicate that descriptive norm deviants' knowledge of their difference from (or rather, their superiority to) the average group member was precisely what made them more willing to publicise their opinions.

Next, we tested the role of superior conformity using a behavioural measure of opinion expression (Morrison & Miller, 2008, Study 2). Participants, all Stanford undergraduates, were actually videotaped delivering a descriptive norm deviant, non-deviant or prescriptive norm deviant speech on affirmative action. Those who had been assigned to deliver the descriptive norm deviant speech reported higher levels of pride-related emotions than did those who had been assigned to deliver either the non-deviant or prescriptive norm deviant speech. They were also coded by an independent judge as appearing more proud in the videotape, and were more likely to give the experimenter permission to use their videotape in future research.

A pretest conducted prior to these studies confirmed that participants were accurate in their estimates of the average Stanford student's attitude towards affirmative action. In other words, their estimates did not differ significantly from the actual group average. Descriptive norm deviants, despite knowing that they were statistically different, were especially proud of and willing to publicise their opinions, apparently because they saw themselves as differing from the group average in the 'right' direction.

In a third study (Morrison & Miller, 2008, Study 3), we extended our investigation of deviance, superior conformity and opinion expression to a field setting. Shortly after the 2004 US Presidential election, we visited the parking lots of several locations of a large department store in two different geographical areas – a 'blue' (moderately Democratic) county and a 'red' (moderately Republican) county – and counted the numbers of liberal and conservative political bumper stickers on vehicles. We then compared the proportions of Democratic and Republican stickers to the proportions of

Democratic and Republican registered voters within each county, the assumption being that putting a bumper sticker on one's car is a sufficiently extreme act to qualify oneself as a deviant.

Consistent with the results of the laboratory experiments, the proportion of Democratic (relative to Republican) stickers in the 'blue' county (93 per cent) significantly exceeded the proportion of Democratic voters (63 per cent), whereas the proportion of Republican (relative to Democratic) stickers in the 'red' county (73 per cent) significantly exceeded the proportion of Republican voters (57 per cent). These findings indicate that the descriptive norm deviant opinion (i.e., extremely liberal [conservative] in the 'blue' ['red'] county) was overrepresented, and the prescriptive norm deviant position (i.e., extremely conservative [liberal] in the 'blue' ['red'] county) underrepresented, in each population. Moreover, the results of a survey – which we asked bumper sticker holders to complete and return to us by mail – indicated that descriptive norm deviants knew their opinions were extreme. Specifically, they rated their attitudes towards the Presidential candidate from their own party as more positive, and their attitudes towards the candidate from the opposing party as more negative, than they rated the attitudes of the typical resident of their county. Again, descriptive norm deviants' awareness of their superior conformity rendered them more willing to publicise their opinions by displaying a political bumper sticker.

Perceived majority status as a predictor of comfort: an empirical test

In the previously described studies, descriptive norm deviants were found to be more willing to express their opinions despite recognising that their attitudes differed from that of the average group member. The reason, we argued, is that they saw their deviance as a sign of their moral superiority. An exaggerated perception of the commonness of their opinions may not be necessary for descriptive norm deviants to feel comfortable expressing their opinions, but it is still possible that this bias is sufficient to produce the effect in some circumstances. Although people are often accurate in their assessments of the distribution of public opinion (Nisbett & Kunda, 1985; see also Noelle-Neumann, 1974), there are many instances where they do misperceive the group norm. This misperception can result in group members who are non-deviant actually assuming that they are deviant: a phenomenon known as pluralistic ignorance (Miller & McFarland, 1987). For example, college students tend to believe that their classmates are more comfortable with campus drinking practices than they are (Prentice & Miller, 1993) and that they are less fearful of appearing deviant than they are (Miller & McFarland, 1987; Van Boven, Loewenstein & Dunning, 2005). Norm misperception can also lead group members who actually are deviant to assume that they are non-deviant.

We propose that when the distribution of group members' attitudes is inaccurately perceived, one reason that descriptive norm deviants may be more willing to express their opinions is because they mistakenly believe they are in the majority. We tested this idea using attitudes towards campus drinking practices as the context, because college students generally overestimate their peers' comfort with alcohol usage (see Prentice & Miller, 1993). In one study (Miller & Morrison, 2009, Study 1), we asked Stanford University undergraduates to indicate: (i) their attitude towards the administration's alcohol policies (on a scale from 'policies are much too lenient' to 'policies are much too strict'); (ii) the percentage of other students that they thought shared their attitude; and (iii) the extent to which they would feel comfortable expressing their attitude to another student. Participants were classified as descriptive [prescriptive] norm deviants if their attitude towards the alcohol policies was at least one standard deviation above [below] the sample mean (i.e., if they held extremely liberal [conservative] attitudes towards alcohol) and as non-deviants if their attitude was within one standard deviation of the mean.

As predicted, descriptive norm deviants reported being more comfortable expressing their attitude, and estimated that a higher proportion of their classmates shared their attitude, than did either non-deviants or prescriptive deviants. Importantly, the relationship between deviance direction and comfort was partially mediated by perceived commonness of opinion, suggesting that descriptive norm deviants' erroneous belief that they were in the statistical majority caused them to be more vocal.

In a follow-up study (Miller & Morrison, 2009, Study 2), we experimentally manipulated participants' perceptions of the average group attitude. Our reasoning was that if perceived commonness of opinion does in fact explain descriptive norm deviants' comfort, then informing descriptive norm deviants of their minority status should reduce their willingness to voice their opinions. Participants in this study, after reporting their own attitude toward the Stanford administration's alcohol policies, were presented with one of two purportedly actual distributions of student opinion. One distribution depicted an extremely pro-alcohol campus (where the average group attitude was similar to that of a descriptive norm deviant), and the other distribution depicted an extremely anti-alcohol campus (where the average group attitude was similar to that of a prescriptive norm deviant).

Participants then read that the researchers were seeking volunteers for a separate study on focus group discussions and wanted to gauge students' interest in discussing a variety of topics. They were given a list of three issues, including alcohol usage on campus, and were asked to indicate the issue they would most want to discuss in the focus group. Consistent with the findings reported above, descriptive norm deviants were more likely than either non-deviants or prescriptive norm deviants to select alcohol usage as their top choice issue. However, this effect was only present among participants who had read that the average student attitude was extremely pro-alcohol. Among those who had read that the average student attitude was extremely anti-alcohol, there was no relationship between deviance direction and desire to discuss alcohol in the focus group. Thus, descriptive norm deviants were only more comfortable than their peers to the extent that they had an exaggerated perception of the commonness of their opinion.

Superior conformity versus perceived majority status

To date, our research has shown that descriptive norm deviants are more willing to express their opinions than non-deviants or prescriptive norm deviants for one of two reasons. First, they may know that their opinions differ from that of the average group member in the 'right' (i.e., prototypical) direction, hence believing themselves to be superior conformists. Second, they may mistakenly think that they hold the average group opinion. Although we have provided evidence supporting each of these two mechanisms, an important question still remains: Under what conditions is superior conformity a better explanation for descriptive norm deviants' comfort than perceived majority status, and vice versa?

Based on our current data, one potential answer involves the nature of the issue at hand. On average, participants in the superior conformity studies (Morrison & Miller, 2008) were accurate in their perceptions of where the typical group member stood on political issues such as affirmative action and the Presidential election. By contrast, participants in the norm misperception studies (Miller & Morrison, 2009) believed that their peers held much more liberal attitudes towards alcohol than they did in reality. Issues such as alcohol consumption, on which people's private attitudes are often inferred from their public behaviours (see Miller, Monin & Prentice, 2000; Prentice & Miller, 1993), may be more likely to breed norm misperception than other types of issues, which are less directly tied to public action. For example, a college student who is seen drinking at a party can be assumed to hold a permissive attitude towards alcohol, but a college student who supports affirmative action would not necessarily exhibit specific behaviours tied to his/her attitude. On the latter (non-behavioural) types of issues, individuals' desire to 'one-up' other group members and be superior conformists could rival or even outweigh their desire to fit in with the group and be average.

Another possible determinant of descriptive norm deviants' greater willingness to express their opinions may have to do with the psychological motives that are salient at the time. As noted earlier, individuals have simultaneous, sometimes competing needs to be both similar to and distinct from others (Hornsey & Jetten, 2004). However, these needs may not always be equally pronounced. For instance, being part of a large and amorphous group (e.g., pop music fans) could heighten uniqueness needs, whereas being part of a small and unusual group (e.g., punk rock fans) could heighten similarity needs (Brewer, 1991; Pickett, Silver & Brewer, 2002). When the need for uniqueness is salient, descriptive norm deviants may be more motivated to voice their opinions to the extent that they believe they are superior conformists. By contrast, when the need for similarity is salient, descriptive norm deviants may be more motivated to voice their opinions to the extent that they think they are in the majority.

Individualism and collectivism could also play a role explaining descriptive deviants' comfort. Generally speaking, in individualistic societies such as the United States and Western Europe, people seek to be different and independent from others; but in collectivistic societies such as East Asia, people seek to belong to and be accepted by their groups (Markus & Kitayama, 1991; Triandis, 1995). As a result, uniqueness has more of a positive connotation in individualistic than collectivistic cultures, whereas conformity is more positively regarded in collectivistic than individualistic cultures (Kim & Markus, 1999). Indeed, some research has shown that both classic conformity effects (i.e., in the Asch line judgement paradigm) and the spiral of silence phenomenon (i.e., the relationship between perceived support for opinion and willingness to express that opinion) are more pronounced among collectivists than individualists (Bond & Smith, 1996; Huang, 2005). Given collectivists' greater emphasis on fitting in with others, descriptive norm deviants in these societies may be particularly likely to voice their opinions when they misperceive the group norm. Conversely, given individualists' greater emphasis on distinguishing themselves from others, descriptive norm deviants in these societies may be emboldened by virtue of their belief that they are 'different but good'. In a similar vein, perhaps descriptive norm deviants who are primed to adopt an interdependent self-construal derive their comfort from norm misperception, whereas descriptive norm deviants who are primed to adopt an independent self-construal derive their comfort from perceptions of their superior conformity (see Brewer & Gardner, 1996).

Implications and Future Directions

Potential additional mechanisms for asymmetries in opinion expression

Superior conformity and norm misperception may not be the only two determinants of deviant opinion expression. Both of these mechanisms are proposed to occur at the intragroup level, but moving forward, it may be worthwhile to explore intergroup explanations as well. According to Abrams and colleagues, group members who deviate in a prototypical direction are better liked than those who deviate in a non-prototypical direction because the former reinforce intergroup differences (Abrams *et al.*, 2000, 2002). Like our model of descriptive and prescriptive norm deviance, this work is largely based on the meta-contrast principle of self-categorisation theory, which postulates that the group prototype will eventually shift in a direction that best distinguishes the ingroup from outgroups (Turner *et al.*, 1987). For example, at a college football game, an overly enthusiastic fan will be more positively evaluated by his/her peers than an un-enthralled spectator. Even though both are equally deviant from the group norm, the enthusiastic fan serves to differentiate his or her team from its rivals, whereas the un-enthralled spectator does not. Under some circumstances, a similar process could be responsible for descriptive norm deviants' greater willingness to express their opinions. When an intergroup context is made salient (e.g., when college students' attitudes towards alcohol are explicitly contrasted with those of the presumably more conservative school administration), the position–comfort relationship may be mediated by the extent to which group members see their opinion as different from that of the outgroup.

Notably, the need for group distinctiveness might have been at least partially responsible for the results of the political bumper sticker study discussed earlier, in which descriptive norm deviants in both liberal and conservative counties were more willing than other group members to display stickers on their vehicles. Political parties (e.g., Democrats and Republicans), like other types of groups, often define themselves in opposition to one another in an attempt to establish a meaningful identity (Tajfel, 1978; Turner *et al.*, 1987). These intergroup distinctions could have made the prototypical group members – Democratic sticker holders in the 'blue' county and Republican sticker holders in the 'red' county – especially inclined to publicise their opinions, as these opinions were most distant from those of the outgroup political party. However, such an explanation is speculative at this point and awaits further investigation.

It is also possible that the characteristics of descriptive and prescriptive norm deviants' attitudes themselves, in addition to these deviants' perceptions of their standing relative to other group members, could contribute to the observed differences in comfort. For instance, descriptive norm deviants might be more vocal than prescriptive norm deviants because they hold their attitudes with greater certainty. Previous research has demonstrated that minorities are more willing to express their opinions the more certain they are of their attitudes (Matthes, Morrison & Schemer, in press) and the more closely their attitudes are linked to their moral values (Hornsey *et al.*, 2003). Furthermore, one indicator of attitude certainty is an individual's belief that his or her opinion is correct (Lasorsa, 1991; Petrocelli, Tormala & Rucker, 2007). By virtue of their greater prototypicality – specifically, the fact that their attitudes, more so than those of other group members, serve to distinguish the ingroup from outgroups (see Turner *et al.*, 1987) – descriptive norm deviants may be more likely than non-deviants and prescriptive norm deviants to be certain that they hold the 'correct' opinion. Given that people who are certain of their opinions are more willing to express them, it may be that attitude certainty mediates the position–comfort relationship.

The moderating role of group identification

In addition to specifying the reasons underlying descriptive and prescriptive norm deviants' patterns of opinion expression, it will be important to determine how deviant group members' social identities influence their willingness to speak out. In particular, to what extent might group identification increase (or decrease) comfort in opinion expression? According to social identity theory (Tajfel & Turner, 1986), individuals generally derive a sense of self-worth by affiliating with social groups. However, they can vary in how important or central a particular group membership is to their self-concept (e.g., Luhtanen & Crocker, 1992). High group identifiers tend to conform more to group norms than do low group identifiers (Terry & Hogg, 1996), which may result in the former being less inclined to express deviant opinions within their group. Consistent with this notion, Hornsey and colleagues found that group members whose attitudes towards controversial issues had a strong moral basis were actually more likely to voice minority than majority opinions, but only if they were low identifiers. High identifiers were too concerned about upholding their reputation within the group to express their minority opinions in public (Hornsey *et al.*, 2003).

Highly identified group members may not always refrain from voicing minority opinions, though. In fact, sometimes they are *more* inclined to deviate from the majority sentiment. Recent research by Packer (2008, 2009) has shown that when people identify strongly with a group, they will express dissent to the extent that they believe the group norm is potentially harmful to the group's well-being. To these group members, the need to change group norms for the better is of utmost importance. Less identified group members, by contrast, will either keep silent or disengage from the group altogether.

Our model of descriptive and prescriptive norm deviance has possible implications for how to reconcile these two sets of findings – one pointing to greater expression among low identifiers (Hornsey *et al.*, 2003; Terry & Hogg, 1996) and another pointing to greater expression among high identifiers (Packer, 2008, 2009). Specifically, whether group identification increases or decreases minority opinion expression may depend on the direction in which the opinion deviates from the majority. When the opinion deviates in a direction consistent with the group prototype (i.e., when the opinion holder is a descriptive norm deviant), high identifiers may be especially likely to express their opinions. The reason is that these individuals, due to the fact that they feel less marginal than other group members, may think that speaking out will benefit their group. However, when the opinion deviates in a direction away from the group prototype (i.e., when the opinion holder is a prescriptive norm deviant), low identifiers may be especially likely to express their opinions. The reason is that these individuals do not care whether their opinions are in line with group norms, and so they will speak out regardless of their standing in the group.

In a preliminary investigation of this possibility (Miller & Morrison, 2009, Study 3), we gave false information to Stanford undergraduates about their peers' attitudes towards alcohol after measuring their own attitudes. Half of the participants were told that the majority of their peers were very pro-alcohol, and the other half were told that the majority of their peers were very anti-alcohol. Participants also responded to several items assessing their level of identification with Stanford (e.g., 'How similar are you to other Stanford students?' 'How important is Stanford to you?'). Consistent with our other norm misperception studies reviewed earlier (Miller & Morrison, 2009), we found that participants who identified themselves as pro-alcohol (descriptive norm deviants) were more comfortable than their anti-alcohol counterparts (prescriptive norm deviants) discussing alcohol with their peers, especially when they perceived the group norm as very pro-alcohol. Importantly, this result was more pronounced among high than low identifiers, such that only those descriptive norm deviants who identified with Stanford became more [less] comfortable upon learning of their majority [minority] status. These findings suggest that highly identified group members are willing to express descriptive norm deviant (prototypical) positions, but are reluctant to express prescriptive norm deviant (non-prototypical) positions.

Conclusion

The notion that group members who deviate from the average attitude in one direction (descriptive norm deviants) will be more comfortable expressing their opinions than those who deviate in the other direction (prescriptive norm deviants) has potential long-term implications for the development and maintenance of group norms. If descriptive norm deviants regularly speak out with greater ease, this could lead the descriptive group norm (i.e., the average group attitude) to become more extreme, and closer to the prototypical group attitude, over time. One way that this might occur is through descriptive norm deviants' greater capacity than prescriptive norm deviants to exert social influence within their group (see Paicheler, 1976).

Even if the actual descriptive norm does not change, however, group members' *perceptions* of the descriptive norm may shift because of the overrepresentation of descriptive norm deviant voices in the population. Such perceptions could increase the discrepancy between the comfort levels of descriptive and prescriptive norm deviants, with the latter believing themselves to be even further from the majority than they were before.

To the extent that the prototype is harmful to the group or its individual members (e.g., binge eating, excessive alcohol consumption), these changes in perceptions of group norms would come at a perilous price. But when the prototype involves a positive, pro-social attitude or behaviour (e.g., creativity in an organisation, tolerance of different racial and ethnic groups), an eventual shift in that direction would likely benefit the group as a whole.

References

Abrams, D., Marques, J., Bown, N. & Dougill, M. (2002). Anti-norm and pro-norm deviance in the bank and on the campus: two experiments on subjective group dynamics. *Group Processes & Intergroup Relations, 5*, 163–82.

Abrams, D., Marques, J., Bown, N. & Henson, M. (2000). Pro-norm and anti-norm deviance within and between groups. *Journal of Personality and Social Psychology, 78*, 906–12.

Asch, S.E. (1956). Studies of independence and conformity: a minority of one against a unanimous majority. *Psychological Monographs, 70*(9).

Bassili, J.N. (2003). The minority slowness effect: subtle inhibitions in the expression of views not shared by others. *Journal of Personality and Social Psychology, 84*, 261–76.

Blanton, H. & Christie, C. (2003). Deviance regulation: a theory of action and identity. *Review of General Psychology, 7*, 115–49.

Bond, R. & Smith, P.B. (1996). Culture and conformity: a meta-analysis of studies using Asch's (1952, 1956b) line judgment task. *Psychological Bulletin, 119*, 111–37.

Brewer, M.B. (1991). The social self: on being the same and different at the same time. *Personality and Social Psychology Bulletin, 17*, 475–82.

Brewer, M.B. & Gardner, W. (1996). Who is this we? Levels of collective identity and self-representations. *Journal of Personality and Social Psychology, 71*, 83–93.

Cialdini, R.B., Reno, R.R. & Kallgren, C.A. (1990). A focus theory of normative conduct: recycling the concept of norms to reduce littering in public places. *Journal of Personality and Social Psychology, 58*, 1015–26.

Codol, J.P. (1975). On the so-called 'superior conformity of the self' behavior: twenty experimental investigations. *European Journal of Social Psychology, 5*, 457–501.

Crandall, C. (1988). Social contagion of binge eating. *Journal of Personality and Social Psychology, 62*, 658–68.

Glynn, C.J. (1997). Public opinion as a normative opinion process. *Communication Yearbook, 20,* 157–83.

Glynn, C.J., Hayes, A.F. & Shanahan, J. (1997). Perceived support for one's opinions and willingness to speak out: a meta-analysis of survey studies on the 'spiral of silence'. *Public Opinion Quarterly, 51,* 452–63.

Hewlin, P.F. (2003). And the award for best actor goes to. . .: facades of conformity in organizational settings. *Academy of Management Review, 28,* 633–42.

Hogg, M.A. & Reid, S.A. (2006). Social identity, self-categorization, and the communication of group norms. *Communication Theory, 16,* 7–30.

Hornsey, M.J. & Jetten, J. (2004). The individual within the group: Balancing the need to belong with the need to be different. *Personality and Social Psychology Review, 8,* 248–64.

Hornsey, M.J., Majkut, L., Terry, D.J. & McKimmie, B.M. (2003). On being loud and proud: non-conformity and counter-conformity to group norms. *British Journal of Social Psychology, 42,* 319–35.

Huang, H. (2005). A cross-cultural test of the spiral of silence. *International Journal of Public Opinion Research, 17,* 324–45.

Kim, H. & Markus, H.R. (1999). Deviance or uniqueness, harmony or conformity? A cultural analysis. *Journal of Personality and Social Psychology, 77,* 785–800.

Kuran, T. (1995). *Private Truths, Public Lies.* Cambridge, MA: Harvard University Press.

Lasorsa, D.L. (1991). Political outspokenness: factors working against the spiral of silence. *Journalism Quarterly, 68,* 131–40.

Levine, J.M. (1989). Reactions to opinion deviance in small groups. In P. Paulus (ed.), *Psychology of Group Influence* (pp. 375–427). Hillsdale, NJ: Erlbaum.

Luhtanen, R. & Crocker, J. (1992). A collective self-esteem scale: self-evaluation of one's social identity. *Personality and Social Psychology Bulletin, 18,* 302–18.

Markus, H.R. & Kitayama, S. (1991). Culture and the self: implications for cognition, emotion, and motivation. *Psychological Review, 98,* 234–53.

Marques, J.M. & Pàez, D. (1994). The black sheep effect: social categorization, rejection of ingroup deviates, and perception of group variability. In W. Stroebe & M. Hewstone (eds), *European Review of Social Psychology* (Vol. 5, pp. 37–68). New York: Wiley.

Matthes, J., Morrison, K.R. & Schemer, C. (in press). *A Spiral of Silence for Some: Attitude Certainty and the Expression of Political Minority Opinions.* Manuscript submitted for publication.

Matz, D.C. & Wood, W. (2005). Cognitive dissonance in groups: the consequences of disagreement. *Journal of Personality and Social Psychology, 88,* 22–37.

Miller, D.T. & McFarland, C. (1987). Pluralistic ignorance: when similarity is interpreted as dissimilarity. *Journal of Personality and Social Psychology, 53,* 298–305.

Miller, D.T., Monin, B. & Prentice, D.A. (2000). Pluralistic ignorance and inconsistency between private attitudes and public behaviors. In D.J. Terry & M.A. Hogg (eds), *Attitudes, Behavior, and Social Context* (pp. 95–117). Mahwah, NJ: Erlbaum.

Miller, D.T. & Morrison, K.R. (2009). Expressing deviant opinions: believing you are in the majority helps. *Journal of Experimental Social Psychology, 45,* 740–7.

Morrison, K.R. & Miller, D.T. (2008). Distinguishing between silent and vocal minorities: not all deviants feel marginal. *Journal of Personality and Social Psychology, 94,* 871–82.

Moscovici, S. (1991). Silent majorities and loud minorities. *Communication Yearbook, 14,* 298–308.

Myers, D.G. (1978). Polarizing effects of social comparison. *Journal of Experimental Social Psychology, 14,* 554–63.

Nisbett, R.E. & Kunda, Z. (1985). Perception of social distributions. *Journal of Personality and Social Psychology, 48,* 297–311.

Noelle-Neumann, E. (1974). The spiral of silence: a theory of public opinion. *Journal of Communication, 24,* 43–51.

Noelle-Neumann, E. (1993). *The Spiral of Silence.* Chicago: University of Chicago Press.

Packer, D.J. (2008). On being both with us and against us: a normative conflict model of dissent in social groups. *Personality and Social Psychology Review, 12,* 50–72.

Packer, D.J. (2009). Avoiding groupthink: whereas weak identifiers remain silent, strong identifiers dissent about collective problems. *Psychological Science, 20,* 546–8.

Paicheler, G. (1976). Norms and attitude change I: polarization and styles of behavior. *European Journal of Social Psychology, 6,* 405–27.

Petrocelli, J.V., Tormala, Z.L. & Rucker, D.D. (2007). Unpacking attitude certainty: attitude clarity and attitude correctness. *Journal of Personality and Social Psychology, 92,* 30–41.

Pickett, C.L., Silver, M.D. & Brewer, M.B. (2002). The impact of assimilation and differentiation needs on perceived group importance and judgments of ingroup size. *Personality and Social Psychology Bulletin, 28,* 546–58.

Pool, G.J., Wood, W. & Leck, K. (1998). The self-esteem motive in social influence: agreement with valued majorities and disagreement with derogated minorities. *Journal of Personality and Social Psychology, 75,* 967–75.

Prentice, D.A. & Miller, D.T. (1993). Pluralistic ignorance and alcohol use on campus: some consequences of misperceiving the social norm. *Journal of Personality and Social Psychology, 64*, 243–56.

Prentice, D.A. & Miller, D.T. (1996). Pluralistic ignorance and the perpetuation of social norms by unwitting actors. In M. Zanna (ed.), *Advances in Experimental Social Psychology* (Vol. 28, pp. 161–209). San Diego: Academic Press.

Priester, J.R. & Petty, R.E. (2001). Extending the basis of subjective attitudinal ambivalence: interpersonal and intrapersonal antecedents of evaluative tension. *Journal of Personality and Social Psychology, 80*, 19–34.

Schachter, S. (1951). Deviation, rejection, and communication. *Journal of Abnormal and Social Psychology, 46*, 190–207.

Snyder, C.R. & Fromkin, H.L. (1980). *Uniqueness: The Human Pursuit of Difference.* New York: Plenum Press.

Tajfel, H.C. (1978). *Differentiation between Social Groups: Studies in the Social Psychology of Intergroup Relations.* Oxford: Academic Press.

Tajfel, H.C. & Turner, J.C. (1986). The social identity theory of intergroup behavior. In S. Worchel & W.G. Austin (eds), *Psychology of Intergroup Relations* (pp. 7–24). Chicago: Nelson-Hall.

Terry, D.J. & Hogg, M.A. (1996). Group norms and the attitude-behavior relationship: A role for group identification. *Personality and Social Psychology Bulletin, 22*, 776–93.

Triandis, H.C. (1995). *Individualism and Collectivism.* Boulder, CO: Westview.

Turner, J.C., Hogg, M., Oakes, P., Reicher, S. & Wetherell, M. (1987). *Rediscovering the Social Group: A Self-Categorization Theory.* Oxford: Blackwell.

Van Boven, L., Loewenstein, G. & Dunning, D. (2005). The illusion of courage in social predictions. Underestimating the impact of fear of embarrassment on other people. *Organizational Behavior and Human Decision Processes, 96*, 130–41.

13

Innovation Credit

When and Why do Group Members Give their Leaders License to Deviate from Group Norms?

Georgina Randsley de Moura, Dominic Abrams, José M. Marques and Paul Hutchison

Leaders of organisations, teams and groups are often required to change the group's direction or forge an innovative path. Examples can be seen in political and organisational arenas on a daily basis. The USA has seen the appointment of a new President, Barack Obama, who won the election with the slogan: 'Change we can believe in'. Organisations also often face the challenge of change by bringing in a new leader or CEO. For example, the UK broadcaster Channel 4 has recently appointed a new CEO, David Abraham, who has been quoted as saying he will manage a period of uncertainty in the organisation through 'the biggest creative transformation' (Burrell, 2010). When and why do groups allow leaders to innovate? Why are new leaders often associated with changes in direction? This chapter will explore these issues and examine what happens when leaders resist the tide of opinion within their groups.

Traditional as well as more recent research shows that groups like consensus and that, in certain circumstances, deviant group members are liable to be rejected or encouraged to conform (e.g. Marques, Paez & Abrams, 1998; Marques, Abrams & Serodio, 2001; Pinto, Marques, Levine & Abrams, 2010). However, group leaders are in a unique position within groups as they are often required to diverge from the group's traditions or actions and to take the group in a new direction (e.g. Hogg, 2005; Yukl, 2002). In fact, Fielding and Hogg (1997) state that part of leadership

Rebels in Groups: Dissent, Deviance, Difference and Defiance Jolanda Jetten and Matthew J. Hornsey

is '. . .the power to be innovative and constructively deviant' (p. 41). This leads to interesting questions as to how, when and why leader deviance is tolerated and license to innovate is granted by other members. Our chapter explores some of these questions. We begin by outlining the subjective group dynamics (SGD) model which offers an explanatory account of how ingroup and outgroup deviants are evaluated. We then discuss social identity theory research into leadership deviance and provide an overview of our own research findings. Finally, we offer some theoretically driven reasons why reactions to deviant leaders might not always match reactions to deviant members and why incoming leaders who are deviant may be given license to take the group in new directions.

Subjective Group Dynamics

Although leaders may embody the typical characteristics of a group (e.g. Hains, Hogg & Duck, 2006), it is also true that effective leaders are often different from other group members and, to some extent, can be conceived of as positive deviates (Abrams, Randsley de Moura, Marques & Hutchison, 2008). Our leadership research, informed by the SGD model (e.g. Marques, Páez & Abrams, 1998; see also Abrams & Rutland, this volume), examines how and why, in an intergroup context, group members engage in *intra*group differentiation and what the potential consequences of this differentiation might be.

Research has shown that people's overall preference for ingroup members over outgroup members (differentiation between groups) may, at times, be qualified. For example, the 'black sheep effect' (Marques, Yzerbyt & Leyens, 1988; Marques & Páez, 1994) captures the tendency for group members to evaluate likeable ingroup members more positively than likeable outgroup members, but unlikeable ingroup members are evaluated more negatively than unlikeable outgroup members, thus reversing the usual pattern of ingroup bias. This effect raises a fundamental question for group processes research. Given that people generally favour ingroups over outgroups, why should they sometimes prefer an outgroup deviant engaging in a similar type of behaviour? According to the SGD model, a deviant ingroup member presents a threat by undermining the subjective validity of people's beliefs about the relative superiority of the ingroup over the outgroup as a whole (e.g. Marques *et al.*, 1998). By the same token, an outgroup deviant may help to sustain the ingroup's validity while undermining that of the outgroup. Importantly, this suggests that it is not a particular action or attitude position that determines whether a group member is favoured or derogated. Rather, evaluations are motivated by the implications of those actions for the subjective validity of the ingroup's norms in the context of a salient intergroup comparison. Since different group memberships are made salient by different intergroup comparisons, a person who is viewed as deviant in one context could be viewed as normative in another. Furthermore, if an ingroup/outgroup distinction is relevant or important, members are likely to attach importance to sustaining prescriptive ingroup norms (i.e., the norms prescribing to members what they should be doing). Therefore, in those circumstances where people show stronger *inter*group bias, they are also likely to show stronger *intra*group bias whereby they should make a sharper contrast when evaluating normative and deviant members within groups. This process should be most pronounced among high identifiers (Marques *et al.*, 1998).

In sum, whereas it may feel gratifying to learn of a rebel within an outgroup, it is likely to be alarming to discover a rebel within one's own. How then can groups embrace change or move in a different direction? We contend that there may be circumstances in which deviance emerging is perceived as functional for generating positive ingroup distinctiveness. In such circumstances, instead of jeopardising other members' subjective validity, deviants may be viewed as a potential source of reinforcement of such validity. These members may therefore adopt (and be endowed by the group) a leadership role (see Levine, 1989). Our application of the SGD model to leadership processes has investigated whether reactions to deviants vary depending on the deviant's role within the group. Specifically, we have focused on how the leadership role might impact on intragroup differentiation. We compared responses to deviant group leaders and deviant group members who are not leaders and examined whether responses differed.

Social Identity, Leadership and Deviance

The social identity approach – consisting of social identity theory (Tajfel & Turner, 1979) and self-categorisation theory (Turner *et al.*, 1987) – has been applied to leadership by emphasising the role of group members' prototypicality. Prototypicality is defined by *meta-contrast* whereby the prototypical position represents the position that maximises intergroup differences and minimises intragroup differences. The social identity perspective on leadership (e.g. Haslam, 2001; Hogg, 2001a, 2001b; Hogg & van Knippenberg, 2003) proposes that a primary feature of leadership is the extent to which the leader embodies the group prototype. It suggests that group members are likely to emerge as a leader if they best represent the group's identity and best reflect the subjective perception of the group's consensual or prototypical attitudes or goals (Turner, 1991).

This raises an interesting set of questions. Firstly, to what extent is the most prototypical person the 'natural leader' in a group? Secondly, to what extent can a leader deviate from group norms and still retain the support of members? And finally, is it possible for a leader to shift the group prototype towards their own position and preferences (Coser, 1962; Hollander, 1958; Homans, 1974; Reicher & Hopkins, 2003)?

In response to some of these questions, Hogg (2001a, 2001b; Hogg & van Knippenberg, 2003) theorises that three processes — prototypicality, social attraction and attribution — need to be taken into account to explain how active leadership emerges. The group prototype is used as a standard against which group members evaluate and define the extent to which the self and other group members match the defining ingroup's attitudes, beliefs and behaviours (Hogg, 1996, 2001b; Schmitt & Branscombe, 2001). When group salience increases, sensitivity to prototypicality also increases (e.g. Turner, 1991; Turner *et al.*, 1987) and this enhances the importance of the extent to which group members match the group prototype (e.g. Haslam *et al.*, 1995).

This leads to the prediction that the longer a group member has been prototypical in the group the more likely it is that the member is able to exert social influence and leadership (Hogg, 2001a). Importantly too, because of their fit to the prototype, the most prototypical group member is also the most socially attractive. This further enhances that individual's ability to exercise social influence and leadership (e.g. Hogg, 1992, 1993). Hogg (2001a) further argues that the most prototypical member attracts the most attention, as they are most informative about group norms and how group members should behave. A likely consequence of increased attention on the most prototypical member is that their perceived influence will be attributed to internal factors. This may explain why leaders are often perceived as charismatic (see Haslam *et al.*, 2001; Hollander & Julian, 1970).

There is some evidence that the most prototypical member is most likely to emerge as a leader. For example, in a study examining the selection of leaders, Hogg, Hains and Mason (1998) found that chosen leaders were considered to be more prototypical for the group than other group members. Moreover, the more intergroup comparisons are salient encouraging members to judge one another in terms of a depersonalised prototype, the more social attraction, internal attribution and depersonalisation will co-occur (Abrams & Hogg, 1990; Hogg, 1992, 1993; Turner, 1991). For example, Hains, Hogg and Duck (1997) found that participants who identified highly with their ingroup rated a leader as more effective if they had been informed that the leader was prototypical of the ingroup. In sum, social identity theory's analysis of leadership is consistent with the idea that perceived entitlement to take on a leadership role *accrues* from prototypicality. The question of whether the leader subsequently has the mandate to define and further refine the group norm has also been examined from a social identity perspective. For example, Fielding and Hogg (1997) suggested that leadership positions might be used as a normative anchor for the group. This echoes Hollander's (1958) classic research which showed that group members who are loyal to the group gain, over time, 'idiosyncrasy credits' which allow leeway to change the direction of the group. More recently, Reicher and Hopkins (2003, p. 201) have extended these ideas and coined the concept of leaders as 'entrepreneurs of identity'. They suggested that leaders need to maintain their prototypical position and may do this by changing the comparative context and thereby changing the group prototype.

Previous Research on Leader Deviance

There is a growing body of research which suggests that perceived prototypicality of the leader is a key determinant of the extent to which the leader is effective and influential. For example, Haslam and Platow (2001) demonstrated the importance for leaders to act in accordance with normative group expectations and to affirm ingroup identity. In their research, they asked participants to view a video-recording of an ingroup student leader discussing a decision to nominate union board members for a prize. This leader was either 'identity affirming' (ingroup favouring), even-handed, or 'identity negating' (outgroup favouring) in their nominations. The leader was judged to be fairest when even-handed, but attracted most support when he showed ingroup favouritism. Interestingly, only when the leader had shown ingroup favouritism did participants express willingness to generate arguments to support his new project for a campus billboard. In another study, Platow and van Knippenberg (2001) varied the prototypicality and behaviour of ingroup leaders. Participants viewed information that showed two distinct but overlapping distributions of traits for an ingroup and outgroup (cf. Jetten, Spears & Manstead, 1997). They were then informed about a leader who was depicted as having traits that were ingroup normative or were in the tails of the ingroup distribution, either towards the outgroup norm ('outgroup bordering') or away from the outgroup norm (an 'outlier'). The leader allocated a mix of enjoyable (positive) and boring (negative) tasks to an anonymous ingroup member and an anonymous outgroup member. Results confirmed that the leader who veered away from the outgroup norm (the 'outlier') was endorsed less than prototypical leaders, regardless of how the leaders distributed the tasks. Endorsement of the outgroup bordering leader remained high when that leader showed ingroup favouritism but was lowered significantly when the leader showed outgroup favouritism. This demonstrates that prototypicality was important when predicting leader endorsement, but that behaving in a way that benefited the ingroup could make up for a prototypicality deficit.

Haslam *et al.* (2001) provided further evidence that leadership perceptions and endorsement are contingent on whether the leader acts in an identity-affirming way. A study where the organisation was presented either as in decline or as positively turning a crisis around shows that the leader was seen as more charismatic when prior behaviour had been identity affirming or even-handed rather than identity negating. These findings draw attention to the difficult and vulnerable position that outgroup bordering non-prototypical leaders find themselves in. These leaders may perceive conflict between their own preferences or opinions and group norms and may come under attack as soon as their behaviour can be interpreted as contrary to the ingroup's interests (Platow & van Knippenberg, 2001).

What remains to be investigated is whether evaluations of leaders resulted from their prototypicality *per se* or from occupancy of the leader role in combination with prototypicality. We argue that it is important to examine the potentially separate effects of occupancy of the leader role and prototypicality in order to be clear about how groups respond to leaders specifically and not just members who differ in prototypicality. So far, there has been no systematic comparison of leaders versus non-leaders who share the same levels of prototypicality. Our research has redressed this by comparing responses to non-prototypical leaders versus non-prototypical non-leaders (e.g. Abrams *et al.*, 2008).

Leadership Phase

We also examined whether responses depend on whether the leader is a leader of the past (i.e., ex-leader), a current leader or a group member who is likely to take on a leadership role in the future (labelled as a future leader; Abrams *et al.*, 2008; Abrams *et al.*, 2005; Randsley de Moura & Abrams, 2002; Randsley de Moura, Abrams & Marques, 2008). We examine leadership phase because this captures an important aspect of group dynamics: it reflects the reality that groups do change over time and that group members' positions within the group change (e.g. Levine & Moreland, 1994). For example, many organisations will have different members occupying roles that reflect phase or tenure such as President-Elect, President or Vice-President.

It seems likely, then, that group members might attach different meanings to ex-leadership, future leadership, current leadership or ordinary membership. Furthermore, leaders in these different phases of leadership will, because of differences in group members' expectations, differ in their scope for influence within the group. For example, ex-leaders may once have been esteemed and valued members of the group but no longer have explicit authority. Unlike ex-leaders, current leaders may have authority, but they are also more dependent on group members' current support in order to sustain their role. In contrast, incoming or future leaders are in a privileged position within the group as they have a guaranteed position of authority. This might go some way in explaining why future leaders are given scope to make radical changes and will often enjoy a 'honeymoon period' in which to do so. For example, when Tony Blair was fighting the UK election campaign in 1997 it was against the backdrop of major changes to the Labour Party's core, so much so that the Party became known as 'New Labour' and commentators spoke of the 'Blair Revolution' (Mandelson & Liddle, 1996). The many everyday examples of incoming leaders in politics and new leaders in organisations who proclaim they differ from the past highlight why the role of incoming leaders poses a particularly interesting problem for the social identity approach to leadership and for the SGD model.

We contend that people employ two distinct criteria for evaluating leaders: the 'accrual' criterion which is based on a leader's demonstrable adherence to the group prototype and the 'conferral' criterion which is based on the inference that mere occupancy of the leadership role accords greater latitude to determine the group's norms. We also propose, as highlighted above, that the phase of leadership (ex, current, future) should affect the weight members attach to the accrual and conferral criteria (Abrams *et al.*, 2008). Before outlining studies testing our predictions, we first develop the way accrual and conferral criteria interact with phase of leadership.

Accrual and Conferral

The social identity perspective to leadership posits that leadership *accrues* from prototypicality (e.g. Haslam, 2001; Hogg, 2001a, 2001b, 2005; Hogg & van Knippenberg, 2003). That is, prototypicality affords influence and the group member perceived as most prototypical is predicted to emerge as the leader within the group. The accrual process is fairly mechanical and suggests that all anti-norm group members should be derogated due to their non-prototypicality regardless of whether they occupy a leadership role or not. In addition, there is also some evidence to suggest that the leadership role may *confer* prototypicality. For example, Fielding and Hogg (1997) found that the longer the leadership position was held, the more prototypical the leader was perceived to be. Put differently, the longer leaders have been in their role, the more they are given scope to innovate or deviate from group norms and to redefine the prescriptive norm, goals or values of the group (see Hollander, 1958).

There are several reasons why conferral might occur. For example, leaders can be assumed to have greater expertise or commitment to the group than ordinary members and this could translate into influence (e.g. Lord, Brown & Harvey, 2001). Furthermore, it might not always be easy for group members to assess the prototypicality of their group leader. In these contexts the leadership role could be used as a heuristic whereby group members might assume the leader is a good representation of the prescriptive norm. In line with this argument, Hogg (2001c) proposes that stereotypical qualities of 'good' leaders are likely to be attributed to people who already hold the leadership role. From this, we would predict that anti-norm leaders would be evaluated more positively than equivalent anti-norm members.

We contend that the processes of leadership accrual and prototypicality conferral are not contradictory but complementary when considering leadership evaluations (Abrams *et al.*, 2008). Some initial evidence for this was obtained in a study where we measured how important participants rated a series of items tapping leader normativeness (e.g. 'a good leader's attitudes and values should match those of the group') and distinctiveness (e.g. 'really good leaders stand out from the group'). Our results showed that *both* normativeness and distinctiveness were perceived as important features of leadership. We also found preliminary evidence that phase of leadership might affect expectations of leader behaviour (Abrams *et al.*, 2008). We asked participants whether new or ex-leaders should be able to disagree with the group's past positions. Participants believed that new leaders should be able to disagree significantly more than ex-leaders.

The Phase Effect

Our preliminary evidence provided support for our assumptions that leadership accrual, prototypicality conferral and phase are relevant concepts in the consideration of judgements about group leaders. Therefore, we conducted a series of five experimental studies to further test our ideas (Abrams *et al.*, 2008). This series of leadership studies used a paradigm similar to Abrams *et al.* (2000). Specifically, we informed participants about the different norms of their ingroup (psychologists) and a fictional outgroup (customs and immigration officers). The issue was about asylum seeking and the numbers granted asylum in Britain. Participants were told that psychologists generally thought the current numbers were about right (0 percent change in numbers granted asylum). For the fictional outgroup the information stated that customs officers would like a 30 percent reduction in the numbers granted asylum. We then presented participants with information about a set of six ingroup members including one pro-norm, four normative and one anti-norm. The pro-norm deviant target held an opinion that there should be a 15 percent increase in the numbers granted asylum. This opinion was divergent from the custom officers' norm and more extreme than the psychologists' norm too. The anti-norm deviant target opinion diverged towards the customs officers' norm and away from the psychologists' norm, advocating a 15 percent reduction in the numbers granted asylum. The normative members' opinion was to maintain the status quo and varied between −5, 0, +5 percent change in numbers granted asylum. The pro-norm and anti-norm positions are illustrated in Figure 13.1. We also manipulated leadership. In Studies 1 to 4 the anti-norm deviant was either identified as the leader or it was not specified which target was the leader. Study 5 compared an anti-norm past leader, an anti-norm future leader and a no leadership control condition.

As expected all studies showed support for the accrual hypothesis in that the normative targets were preferred and non-leader anti-norm targets were derogated. Furthermore, there was a clear phase effect. Derogation was highest when the anti-norm target was an established or a past leader. In contrast, when the anti-norm target was a future leader the target was evaluated more positively than an anti-norm non-leader (see Study 3 shown

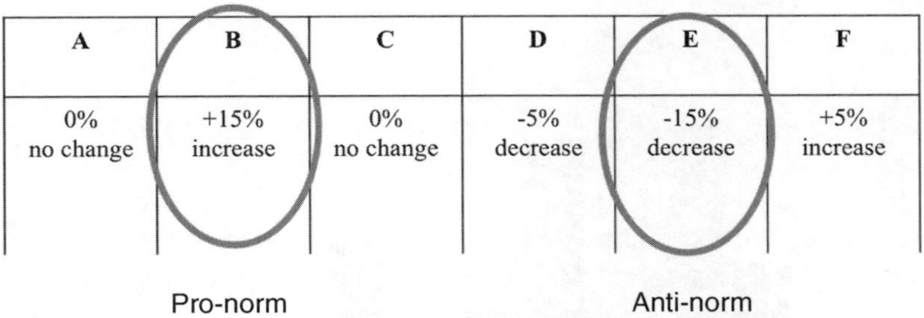

Figure 13.1 Target group member positions on asylum seeking – percent change in number that should be given approval (ingroup norm = 0 percent; outgroup norm = −30 percent)

in Figure 13.2) and was given greater innovation credit revealing a prototypicality conferral effect (see Study 5 shown in Figure 13.3). At first sight, this might seem contrary to Hollander's (1958) idiosyncrasy credit findings. However, it is worth considering that Hollander did not have a future leader condition *per se*. It might be the case that idiosyncrasy credits are more related to the accrual effects that we also found support for.

Our research to date demonstrates that judgements of *non*-leader anti-norm group members are consistently negative. We also show that occupancy of the leadership role *does* affect evaluations of anti-norm targets, but leadership phase further affects this. In line with previous research (e.g. Haslam & Platow, 2001; Platow & van Knippenberg, 2001) and the accrual hypothesis, group members generally were less favourable towards anti-norm members than other members. However, in line with the conferral and the phase hypotheses, anti-norm *future* (incoming) leaders were treated more favourably than anti-norm members or anti-norm ex-leaders. Furthermore, our findings suggest that people may be willing to entrust future leaders with freedom to be innovative or to hold different positions from established group norms and thereby to be constructively deviant (cf. Coser, 1962; Fielding & Hogg, 1997; also see Hornsey, 2006). Ultimately, our findings are in line with the SGD model and show that group members are motivated to defend the image of the ingroup. Allowing deviant leaders to innovate might be one way in which this defence is achieved. Indeed, our results suggest that deviance, or consensus breaching in the group *per se*, is not the crucial determinant of the way group members react to deviants. As proposed by SGD, the real issue for group members seems to be the

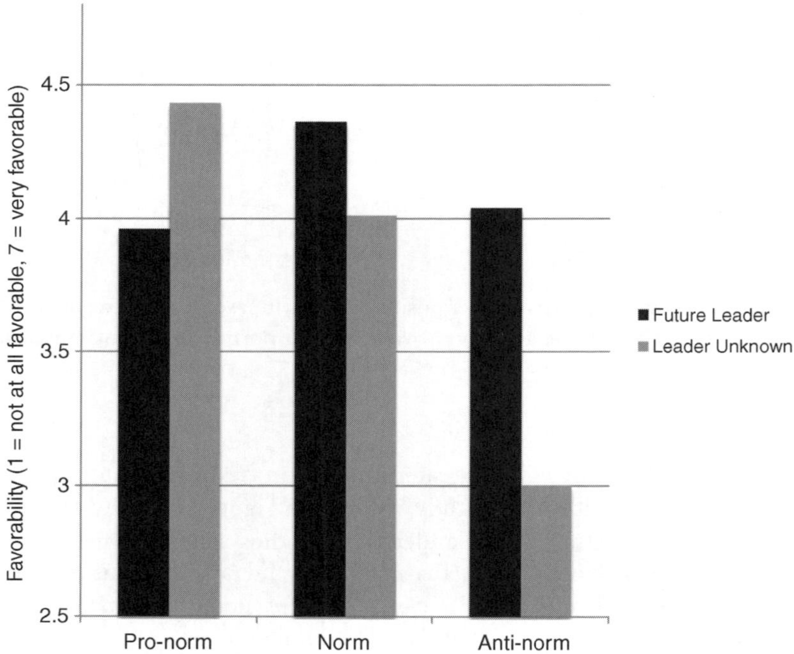

Figure 13.2 Favourability judgements of targets as a function of leadership phase
Source: based on Abrams, D., Randsley de Moura, G., Marques, J.M. & Hutchison, P. (2008). Innovation credit: when can leaders oppose their group's norm? *Journal of Personality and Social Psychology, 95*, 662–78, Study 3

implications of such deviance for the ultimate goal of securing a positive social identity. Where deviance offers the possibility of achievement of this goal, it may be praised and even followed by the group.

This theoretical account of leadership phase effects provides a novel perspective on leader effectiveness, but it also raises key questions as to *why* incoming anti-norm leaders are granted innovation credit and are perceived more favourably than anti-norm past leaders or non-leaders. For example, we need to know whether normative future leaders are also given this innovation credit or whether incoming leaders are actively expected to invoke changes in norms. In other words, might people sometimes *prefer* deviant over normative incoming leaders? It is also possible that the phase effect is moderated by identity strength and social context, whereby social identification is likely to act as an anchor to the group triggering cost-benefit

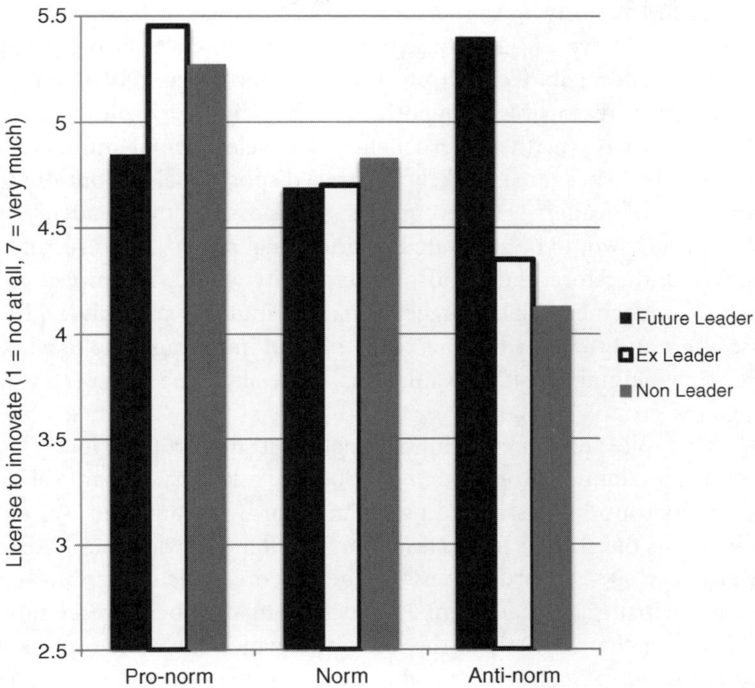

Figure 13.3 License to innovate judgements of targets as a function of leadership phase

Source: based on Abrams, D., Randsley de Moura, G., Marques, J.M. & Hutchison, P. (2008). Innovation credit: when can leaders oppose their group's norm? *Journal of Personality and Social Psychology, 95*, 662–78, Study 5

driven behaviours (Randsley de Moura *et al.*, 2009, see also Packer, 2008, this volume).

Leadership and Attribution

Part of the reason why prototypical group members are influential is because they attract favourable attributions about their attitudes, motives and behaviours and this further strengthens their leadership position (Turner, 1991). Specifically, it has been argued that the process of attributing causes to dispositional rather than situational factors (the fundamental attribution error, Ross, 1977) is more likely to occur for individuals whose group identity is salient to observers (Hogg, 2001a). Given the salience of prototypical group members, their influence on the group is more likely to be attributed to dispositional factors (Hogg, 2001b). Based on these ideas it is reasonable to hypothesise that non-prototypical incoming leaders (who have neither the benefits of developmental influence nor prototypical salience) are less likely to attract dispositional attributions than other types of leaders. However, it is also possible that leaders' non-prototypicality would be attributed to situational rather than dispositional factors and, therefore, their non-prototypicality would not impact group members' judgements. This suggests that attributions may underpin the phase effect and that attributions could play an important role in whether leaders can maintain positive evaluations, especially if the leader is trying to change the group's direction.

We have collected some preliminary data that support these ideas. Using the same paradigm as Abrams *et al.* (2008) we asked participants about a range of ingroup targets including an anti-norm deviant who was either designated as the group's future leader or not (Randsley de Moura, Abrams & Marques, 2008). In order to assess the potential role of attribution we asked participants 'to what extent does each group member have a vision for the future' (a characteristic of the individual which therefore represents a *dispositional attribution*) and 'to what extent do the circumstances require each group member to have vision' (related to external circumstance which therefore represents a *situational attribution*). We found that attributions were affected by whether the deviant was a future leader or not (in our analyses, we included attributions about the other members as covariates, as in Abrams *et al.*, 2008). As expected and shown in Figure 13.4, the vision of the anti-norm future leader was attributed to the situation more than the vision of the anti-norm non-leader. Furthermore, the future leader's vision was attributed significantly more to situational than dispositional causes. For the anti-norm non-leader target there was no difference in the vision for situational or dispositional attribution. In this study, participants rated non-prototypical future leaders as having vision for the future *based on the circumstances* more than they rated them as simply having vision (a disposition) and more than compared to non-leaders. This supports our idea that the phase effect might be partially explained by attribution processes. Specifically, if people believe that there are situational pressures on new leaders to be innovative then this might explain why they are more accepting of anti-normative new leaders than of anti-norm members, current leaders and ex-leaders.

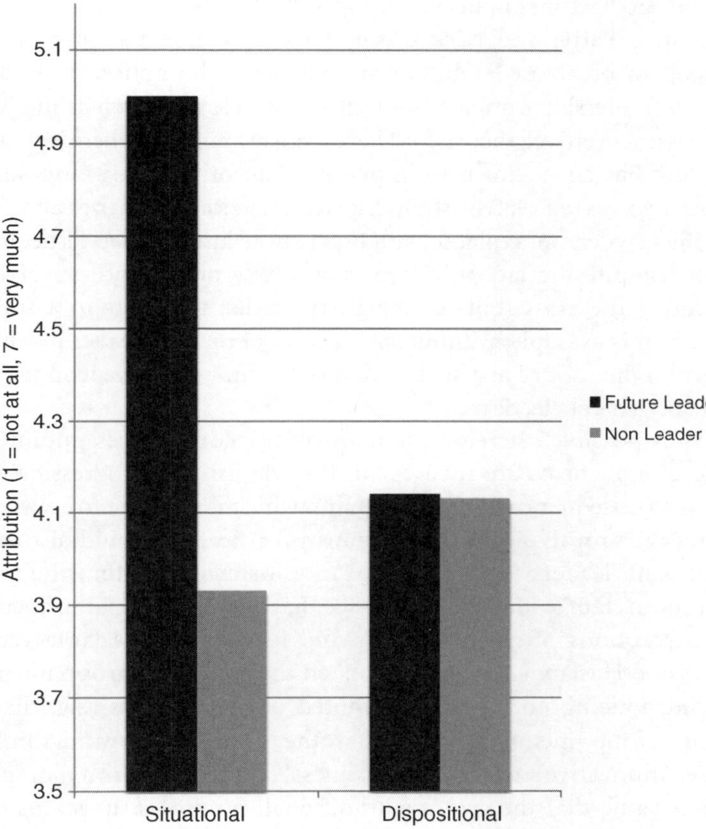

Figure 13.4 Level of situational and dispositional attribution as a function of the leadership role

The Role of Group Norms

We propose that a second key variable that may moderate the phase effect is whether innovation norms are present or not. Societal or specific group norms may dictate that future leaders have a 'right' to innovate and take the group in a new direction. For example, in current UK politics all the leaders of the main parties stated that they wished to change direction when first appointed. The then Prime Minister Gordon Brown (Labour Party) spoke of an agenda for 'change'; David Cameron (Conservative Party) stated the word 'change' 15 times in his victory speech when he became leader of the Conservative Party; and Nick Clegg (Liberal Democrats) proposed his leadership to be about 'ambition and change'. The notion of a change agenda for leadership campaigns is well known. However, when and why it works has not been well theorised. There are also examples where installing a new leader has been shown to improve group outcomes. A well-known example involves the 1983 Australian general election, when the Labor Party leader Bill Hayden was replaced with Bob Hawke just a few weeks before the election. Despite the fact that Bob Hawke was not always perceived as representing the grass roots of the Party, he led the Party to a surprise victory. In this example, without the election of the new leader just before the election the Labor Party would almost certainly not have won the 1983 Australian general election.

It seems possible, therefore, that when new leaders are appointed or emerge group norms are focused on innovation and progression. This could be a consequence of new leadership which is separate from whether the leader is prototypical of group norms or not, but could also afford new 'deviant' leaders further opportunity for change within the group. Recent research provides some evidence that norms prescribing creativity affect perceptions of group outputs and its members. Adarves-Yorno, Postmes and Haslam (2007) manipulated the content of group norms by either introducing norms that promoted progressiveness (e.g. the majority of group members value that the group is forward-thinking, creative, innovative) or conservativeness (e.g. the majority of group members value that the group is traditional, promotes the status quo). When group membership was highly salient, a conservative group norm led participants to rate non-novel work as more creative. These results highlight the possibility that whether group norms emphasise progressiveness or conservativeness is likely to affect perceptions of deviants within groups. It seems reasonable to assume that groups with a progressive norm would value innovation (e.g. deviance) more, whereas groups with a conservative norm would not. Furthermore, it is possible that this would interact with phase of leadership, whereby ex anti-norm leaders would be tolerated relatively more when norms are conservative (maintaining status quo) and incoming anti-norm leaders tolerated more when norms are progressive. These effects should be further moderated by group outcomes such as success or failure (see Morton, Postmes & Jetten, 2007; see also Morton, this volume). Future research should examine these hypotheses.

Summary and Conclusion

This chapter started with an outline of the SGD model and applied some of this model's reasoning to deviant leaders. Given SGD theorising that groups like consensus and that rebellion within outgroups is looked upon more favourably than rebellion within ingroups, the question arises how can we explain that groups change over time? In addition, we asked to what extent, how and when are leaders pivotal in facilitating that change? In the chapter we have shown that incoming deviant leaders are afforded greater innovation credit than deviant ex-leaders or deviant non-leaders (a phase effect). We also discussed potential psychological processes that might moderate the leadership phase effect and focused on whether leader deviance affects dispositional and/or situational attributions and on whether group norms encourage innovation. We argue that applying the SGD model to leadership opens up new theoretical avenues and stimulates new questions about the conditions under which leadership is perceived as deviant or innovative. Our finding that leaders can be influential even when they are not prototypical represents a new avenue for theory development both for the social identity approach to leadership and the SGD model more generally. This will have implications for social psychological theories of group and intergroup processes and, more practically, the processes through which leaders may galvanise social and political change.

Acknowledgements

With thanks to Louise Ainslie for her contribution to the attribution study reported in this chapter and Tim Hopthrow for comments on an earlier draft.

References

Abrams, D. & Hogg, M.A. (1990). Social identification, self categorisation and social influence. In W. Stroebe & M. Hewstone (eds), *European Review of Social Psychology*, (Vol. 1, pp. 195–228). Chichester: John Wiley & Sons.

Abrams, D., Marques, J.M., Brown, N. & Henson, M. (2000). Pro-norm and anti-norm deviance within and between groups. *Journal of Personality and Social Psychology, 78*, 906–12.

Abrams, D., Randsley de Moura, G., Hutchison, P. & Viki, G.T. (2005). When bad becomes good (and vice versa): why social exclusion is not based on difference. In D. Abrams, M.A. Hogg & J.M. Marques (eds), *The Social Psychology of Inclusion and Exclusion* (pp. 161–90). New York: Psychology Press.

Abrams, D., Randsley de Moura, G., Marques, J.M. & Hutchison, P. (2008). Innovation credit: when can leaders oppose their group's norm? *Journal of Personality and Social Psychology*, *95*, 662–78.

Adarves-Yorno, I., Postmes, T. & Haslam, S.A. (2007). Creative innovation or crazy irrelevance? The contribution of group norms and social identity to creative behavior. *Journal of Experimental Social Psychology*, *43*, 410–16.

Burrell, I. (2010). Channel 4 appoints 'bloke called Dave' as new CEO. *The Independent*. Retrieved Februrary 2, 2010, from www.independent.co.uk/.

Coser, L. A. (1962). Some functions of deviant behavior and normative flexibility. *American Journal of Sociology*, *68*, 172–81.

Fielding, K.S. & Hogg, M.A. (1997). Social identity, self-categorisation and leadership: a field study of small interactive groups. *Group Dynamics: Theory, Research and Practice*, *1*, 39–51.

Hains, S.C., Hogg, M.A. & Duck, J.M. (1997). Self-categorization and leadership: effects of group prototypicality and leader stereotypicality. *Personality and Social Psychology Bulletin*, *23*, 1087–100.

Hains, S.C., Hogg, M.A. & Duck, J.M. (2006). Self-categorization and leadership: effects of group prototypicality and leader stereotypicality. In J.M. Levine (ed.), *Small Groups: Key Groups* (pp. 383–400). New York: Psychology Press.

Haslam, S.A. (2001). *Psychology in Organizations: The Social Identity Approach*. London: Sage.

Haslam, S.A. & Platow, M.J. (2001). The link between leadership and followership: how affirming social identity translates vision into action. *Personality and Social Psychology Bulletin*, *27*, 1469–79.

Haslam, S.A., Oakes, P.J., McGarty, C., Turner, J.C. & Onorato, R.S. (1995). Contextual changes in prototypicality or extreme and moderate outgroup members. *European Journal of Social Psychology*, *25*, 509–30.

Haslam, S.A., Platow, M.J., Turner, J.C., Reynolds, K.J., McGarty, C., Oakes, P.J. *et al.* (2001). Social identity and the romance of leadership, the importance of being seen to be 'doing it for us'. *Group Processes and Intergroup Relations*, *4*, 191–205.

Hogg, M.A. (1992). *The Social Psychology of Group Cohesiveness: From Attraction to Social Identity*. Hemel Hempstead: Harvester Wheatsheaf.

Hogg, M.A. (1993). Group cohesiveness: a critical review and some new directions. *European Review of Social Psychology*, *4*, 85–111.

Hogg, M.A. (1996). Intergroup processes, group structure and group identity. In M.A. Hogg & R.S. Tindale (eds), *Blackwell Handbook of Social Psychology: Group Processes* (Vol. 3) Oxford: Blackwell.

Hogg, M.A. (2001a). Social categorization, depersonalization and group behavior. In M.A. Hogg & R.S. Tindale (eds), *Blackwell Handbook of Social Psychology: Group Processes* (pp. 56–85) Oxford: Blackwell.

Hogg, M.A. (2001b). A social identity theory of leadership. *Personality and Social Psychology Review, 5*, 184–200.

Hogg, M.A. (2001c). Social identification, group prototypicality and emergent leadership. In M.A. Hogg & D.J. Terry (eds), *Social Identity Processes in Organizational Contexts* (pp. 197–212). Philadelphia: Psychology Press.

Hogg, M.A. (2005). The social identity perspective. In S.A. Wheelan (ed.), *The Handbook of Group Research and Practice* (pp. 133–58). London: Sage.

Hogg, M.A. & van Knippenberg, D. (2003). Social identity and leadership processes in groups. In M.P. Zanna (ed.), *Advances in Experimental Social Psychology* (Vol. 35, pp. 2–55). London: Academic Press.

Hogg, M.A., Hains, S.C. & Mason, I. (1998). Identification and leadership in small groups: salience, frame of reference and leader stereotypicality effects on leader evaluations. *Journal of Personality and Social Psychology, 75*, 1248–63.

Hollander, E.P. (1958). Conformity, status and idiosyncrasy credit. *Psychological Review, 65*, 117–27.

Hollander, E.P. & Julian, J.W. (1970). Studies in leader legitimacy, influence and innovation. In L. Berkowitz (ed.), *Advances in Experimental Social Psychology* (Vol. 2, pp. 485–537). New York: Random House.

Homans, G.C. (1974). *Social Behavior: Its Elementary Forms.* New York: Harcourt.

Hornsey, M.J. (2006). Ingroup critics and their influence on groups. In T. Postmes & J. Jetten (eds), *Individuality and the Group: Advances in Social Identity* (pp. 74–91). London: Sage.

Jetten, J., Spears, R. & Manstead, A.S.R. (1997). Distinctiveness threat and prototypicality: combined effects on intergroup discrimination and collective self-esteem. *European Journal of Social Psychology, 27*, 635–57.

Levine, J.M. (1989). Reactions to opinion deviance. In B.P. Paulus (ed.), *Psychology of Group Influence* (pp. 187–231). Hillsdale, NJ: Erlbaum.

Levine, J.M. & Moreland, R.L. (1994). Group socialization: theory and research. In W. Stroebe & M. Hewstone (eds), *European Review of Social Psychology* (Vol. 5, pp. 305–36). Chichester: John Wiley & Sons.

Lord, R.G., Brown, D.J. & Harvey, J.L. (2001). System constraints on leadership perceptions, behavior and influence: an example of connectionist level processes. In M.A. Hogg & R.S. Tindale (eds), *Blackwell Handbook of Social Psychology: Group Processes* (pp. 283–310). Oxford: Blackwell.

Mandelson, P. & Liddle, R. (1996). *The Blair Revolution: Can New Labour Deliver?* London: Faber & Faber.

Marques, J.M., Abrams, D., Páez, D. & Martinez-Taboada, C. (1998). The role of categorisation and ingroup norms in judgments of groups and their members. *Journal of Personality and Social Psychology, 75*, 976–88.

Marques, J., Abrams, D. & Serôdio, R. G. (2001). Being better by being right: subjective group dynamics and derogation of ingroup deviants when generic norms are undermined. *Journal of Personality and Social Psychology, 81*, 436–47.

Marques, J.M. & Paez, D. (1994). The 'black sheep effect': social categorization, rejection of ingroup deviates and perception of group variability. In W. Stroebe & M. Hewstone (eds), *European Review of Social Psychology* (Vol. 5, pp. 38–68). Chichester: John Wiley & Sons.

Marques, J.M., Páez, D. & Abrams, D. (1998). Social identity and intragroup differentiation as subjective social control. In S. Worchel, J.F. Morales, D. Páez & J.-C. Deschamps (eds), *Social Identity: International Perspectives* (pp. 124–41). New York: Sage.

Marques, J., Yzerbyt, V. & Leyens, J.-Ph. (1988). The 'Black Sheep Effect': extremity of judgments toward ingroup members as a function of group identification. *European Journal of Social Psychology, 18*, 1–16.

Morton, T.A., Postmes, T. & Jetten, J. (2007). Playing the game: when group success is more important than downgrading deviants. *European Journal of Social Psychology, 37*, 599–616.

Packer, D.J. (2008). On being with us and against us: a normative conflict model of dissent in social groups. *Personality and Social Psychology Review, 12*, 50–72.

Pinto, I., Marques, J. Levine, J.M. & Abrams, D. (2010). Member status and subjective group dynamics: who triggers the black sheep effect? *Journal of Personality and Social Psychology, 99*, 107–19.

Platow, M.J. & van Knippenberg, D. (2001). A social identity analysis of leadership endorsement: the effects of leader ingroup prototypicality and distributive intergroup fairness. *Personality and Social Psychology Bulletin, 27*, 1508–19.

Randsley de Moura, G. & Abrams, D. (2002, June). *Does Leadership Role Alone Enhance Trust in a Non-Prototypical Group Member?* Paper presented at the 13th General Meeting of the European Association of Experimental Social Psychology, San Sebastian, Spain.

Randsley de Moura, G., Abrams, D. & Marques, J.M. (2008, June). *Innovation Credit: When Can Leaders Oppose their Group Norms?* Paper presented at the

15th General Meeting of the European Association of Experimental Social Psychology, Opatija, Croatia.

Randsley de Moura, G., Abrams, D., Retter, C., Gunnarsdottir, S. *et al.* (2008). Identification as an organizational anchor: how identification and job satisfaction combine to predict turnover intention. *European Journal of Social Psychology*, early view published online, DOI: 10.1002/ejsp.553.

Reicher, S. & Hopkins, N. (2003). On the science and art of leadership. In D. van Knippenberg & M.A. Hogg (eds), *Leadership and Power: Identity Processes in Groups and Organizations* (pp. 197–209). Oxford: Blackwell.

Ross, L. (1977). The intuitive psychologist and his shortcomings. In L. Berkowitz (ed.), *Advances in Experimental Social Psychology* (Vol. 10, pp. 173–220). San Diego, CA: Academic Press.

Schmitt, M.T. & Branscombe, N.R. (2001). The good, the bad and the manly: threats to one's prototypicality and evaluations of fellow in-group members. *Journal of Experimental Social Psychology, 37*, 510–17.

Tajfel, H. & Turner, J. (1979). An integrative theory of intergroup conflict. In W.G. Austin & S. Worchel (eds), *The Social Psychology of Intergroup Relations* (pp. 33–47). Monterey: Brooks-Cole.

Turner, J.C. (1991). *Social Influence.* Buckingham: Open University Press.

Turner, J.C., Hogg, M.A., Oakes, P.J., Reicher, S.D. & Wetherell, M.S. (1987). *Rediscovering the Social Group: A Self-Categorisation Theory.* Oxford: Blackwell.

Yukl, G.A. (2002). *Leadership in Organizations* (3rd edition). New Jersey: Prentice Hall.

Part IV

Defiance in Groups

14

Reactions to Defiant Deviants

Deliverance or Defensiveness?

Benoît Monin and Kieran O'Connor

In this chapter, we propose a social psychological analysis of reactions to defiance. Deviants are often presented in social sciences as the passive victims of oppressive social orders for which they play a crucial function. We distinguish various classes of deviance, singling out the special case of *defiance*, where individuals are fully aware of the normative demands of an authority figure, group, society or culture, yet choose to flaunt them openly as inappropriate, and are often disliked as a result. Next, we review classic work in social psychology, where defiant confederates offer deliverance from conformity or obedience, and are often liked as a result. Finally, we propose to solve this apparent inconsistency by suggesting that defensiveness moderates whether defiant rebels elicit positive or negative reactions, and we present our own data supporting this claim.

When Deviance Becomes Defiance

The social construction of deviance

One recurrent claim of 20th-century social sciences has been that deviance says more about a society than about the deviants themselves. When cultural anthropologist G. Bateson writes that 'a character structure which is normal among us may be deviant among the Kwakiutl' (1944), he is using the term in its most common acceptation, to describe a statistical relationship to a norm, a position in a distribution. Social scientists have studied at length the social construction of deviance (see Kelly & Clarke, 2003), and cast light on the potential group benefits of defining some individuals as deviants, to

Rebels in Groups: Dissent, Deviance, Difference and Defiance Jolanda Jetten and Matthew J. Hornsey

understand why groups would sacrifice resources to identify, label, stigmatise, harass, reject, medicate or incarcerate deviants. One great value of this work has been to expose that categories reified as intrinsically worthy of stigma (e.g., mentally ill, see Jodelet, 1989; Szasz, 1974; criminal, see Foucault, 1975/1995; drug addict, see Lidz & Walker, 1980) are socially constructed, and that their treatment therefore merits re-examination. This subversive social criticism goes beyond pointing out the arbitrariness of deviance, by showing that the act of stigmatising a group plays a functional role (Erikson, 1966, 2003), reinforcing the cohesion of the ingroup, clarifying norms and group boundaries, or exorcising a threat by projecting it on a deviant that can then be cast out or eliminated.

This approach often takes a humanistic tone, depicting deviants as passive victims typecast by others in a role they did not choose, sacrificial lambs who serve the greater need of the group. When not given such a noble role, deviants are presented as mere inconveniences that individuals or groups in power are able to dominate to further their own self-serving agendas. Marxist models suggest that groups dominating society define deviance to cement the legitimacy of their own power, and wield the tools of oppression against those individuals who would otherwise question their authority or the distribution of labour and wealth.

Somewhere between these societal approaches and the psychological approach described below, the microsociological work of Erving Goffman on stigma (1963) shifts the perspective of enquiry from explaining the construction of deviance in society to understanding the predicament of those labelled deviants. The subtitle of the book, *Notes on the Management of Spoiled Identity*, makes clear that the focus is on the actor's perspective of the social world, and the strategies deployed to navigate it. But as in much classic deviance work, the emphasis is on the impact of stigmatisation on the person (the 'spoiling'), with less attention to the impact of these deviants on the rest of society.

Psychological analyses of the deviant predicament

This shift to the individual perspective was completed by psychologists focusing on the deviant predicament, while still portraying deviants as the victims of an oppressive majority. Schachter (1951) created 'deviates' by instructing confederates to take positions at odds with the small group they participated in, and studied interpersonal reactions, focusing particularly on patterns of communication addressed to deviants. Deviants were the targets of much initial communication, most likely persuasion attempts, but with time the groups gave up and reduced communication. Eventually, deviants were relegated to the worst position in what participants thought were real student organisations. Social exclusion, though seemingly innocuous compared to more violent repression, is extremely aversive for individuals (Williams, Cheung & Choi, 2000) and therefore often used to bring deviants back into the fold. Thus, unfortunate deviants often find themselves rejected by groups, relegated to outskirts and low status positions, with lasting impact on their well-being and self-esteem (Leary, 2004). Moscovici (1985) writes of the 'social death' that befalls deviants when the group gives up on bringing them back into the fold. This work suggests that the external costs endured by deviants may be accompanied by more hidden psychological costs. Surprisingly, investigators have only recently started to document systematically the discomfort associated with being at odds with one's group: when participants in Matz and Wood (2005) received false feedback that their opinion drastically differed from the rest of their group, they reported experiencing the type of psychological discomfort typically denoting cognitive dissonance. This discomfort was reduced when deviants conformed with the majority, persuaded others to agree with them, or joined a more congenial group.

This psychological approach departs from the sociological approach described above by focusing on the deviant's predicament, and showing that the benefits afforded to the group by pressures towards uniformity have significant costs at the individual level, both external (e.g., Schachter, 1951) and internal (e.g., Matz & Wood, 2005). However, both approaches depict deviance as a predicament with little attention to the deviant's motivations.

A topological descriptor, but a psychological question mark

The two perspectives evoked so far share their description of deviance as victimhood, as a situation relative to a group or norm, and look at its social and psychological consequences. These perspectives, however, do not address the diversity of psychological motivations and biographical narratives which can lead to this predicament, and which are being ignored by the blanket 'deviance' label. In this sense, the concept is really a *topological* one, denoting the position of an individual in a field of forces (Lewin, 1936), but remains a psychological question mark. Less work documents why deviants end up in this situation in the first place. For sociologists, deviance is a social fact resulting from forces outside the individual, and the upstream psychological make-up of the deviant is of little import. For psychologists, the emphasis on engineering deviance, by instructing for example confederates to act as deviants (e.g., Schachter, 1951), or by manipulating feedback so that naive participants believe that their opinions are at odds with their group's (e.g., Matz and Wood, 2005), has left little room for studying the upstream characteristics and motivations of real individuals cast in the role of deviants.

And yet it only takes bringing to mind a few cases of real-life deviance to realise the rich heterogeneity of the categories that are lumped under this heading. Just as Chekhov famously claimed that all happy families resemble each other, but that each unhappy family is unhappy in its own unique way, conformists may all have similar motivations, but deviants come in all kinds and sizes. Labelling someone a deviant thus raises more psychological questions than it answers. Table 14.1 illustrates how ambiguous deviance can be. A woman deemed eccentric by society might suffer pressures against her deviant style of dress – but that does not tell us whether she dresses that way because she is oblivious to fashion (ignorance), because she has a desire to stand out (desire for originality), because she is a fashion designer who is rewarded for cultivating this image (self-interest), because she knows it is inappropriate dress but cannot help herself (compulsion), because she cannot afford to wear anything else due to meagre finances (inability), or (this last type being the focus of this chapter) because she finds current fashion styles deeply objectionable to her sense of style or offensive to her sense of modesty (principled disagreement). The deviant label is a psychological question mark.

A noteworthy feature of the example narratives in Table 14.1 is that some psychological explanations for deviance imply more intention than others. The ignorant deviant is simply unaware of the norm. Others know the norm but lack the means or the ability to conform. In that sense, unintentional deviants are very much like those presented in the sociological literature, victims of a social order that they may not even fully comprehend. The psychological motivation of the second group of deviants, which we call intentional deviants in the bottom half of Table 14.1, is quite different, because they are fully aware of the norm but decide to flaunt it anyway.

Table 14.1 A (non-exhaustive) sampler of deviances

Unintentional	
Tail of the distribution	Random variation placing one just beyond the threshold of what is acceptable (e.g., a co-worker is 'weird' for liking a popular TV show just a little too much)
Norm shifting	Not realising that norms have changed, making one a deviant for abiding to obsolete norms, or joining a new group where one's old norm-abiding behaviour no longer has currency
Ignorance	Not perceiving or understanding the norm
Inability	Not having the resources or ability to follow the norm (e.g., mental illness, low financial resources)
Duress	Being forced by external circumstances to break the norm (e.g., losing one's job)
Compulsion	Not being able to help oneself, feeling compelled to break the norm
Intentional	
Principled disagreement	Refusing to follow a norm that one deems wrong
Disdain	Feeling that one is above the norm, not beholden to it
Spite	Wanting to upset the mainstream, or a powerful minority
Desire for originality	Wanting to be at odds with a norm, non-conformist
Self-interest	Breaking the norm is rewarded so it is considered worth it despite potential social costs (e.g., crime)

Deviance versus defiance

This chapter focuses on reactions to intentional deviants, with a special emphasis on reactions to principled disagreement. These rebels have a special significance to observers because their choices can be taken as a statement and therefore influence others. Furthermore, social observers give particular significance to gestures performed in the face of strong countervailing pressures (Jones, 1972), thus intentional resistance to known social pressures should appear especially meaningful. We propose to use the term *defiance* to refer to knowingly and overtly flaunting a norm when one had the means and ability to conform, as opposed to the more general case of simply finding oneself at odds with a group's norm or demands. In contrast to deviance, which connotes a plight befalling an actor, defiance is a psychological descriptor; whereas deviance captures a status, defiance captures a stance. Defiance is thus a special case of deviance, but one worth circumscribing because we propose that defiant deviants (whether they are truly defiant or construed as such by observers) play a special part in social psychology. In contrast to the passive victim model of deviance reviewed above, the study of defiance in social psychology has put more emphasis on the impact of defiant individuals on others. Whereas deviants are studied as victims, defiers are studied in much classic social psychology for their ability to deliver others from the pressures of conformity or obedience. In contrast to the negative treatment of deviants reviewed in this section, the next section thus reviews the liberating impact of defiant rebels, and the positive reactions that they elicit.

Defiance and Deliverance from Social Pressures

We propose to focus in the rest of this chapter on the special case of deviance which we have called defiance, the knowing and willing refusal of an authority's, a group's or society's demands. We now turn to examples in classic social psychology where defiance promises to deliver individuals from powerful group pressures. In a field that often depicts the evils of conformity and obedience, defiance offers the hope that a handful of rebels can stand up for decency and sway an otherwise sheepishly obedient majority.

Defiance delivers from conformity

A classic demonstration of the liberating power of defiance is the 'partner effect' demonstrated in Asch's conformity paradigm, in which naive participants indicated which of three lines matched a template. Participants famously went from fewer than 1 per cent errors when tested alone to over 36 per cent when misled by a majority instructed by the experimenter to give a wrong answer (Asch, 1955, 1956). When provided with a partner who gave the truthful answer in the face of a misleading majority, participants conformed much less (Asch, 1955), in some reports as rarely as 5.5 per cent of the time (Asch, 1951). Did this liberating effect come from the deviant giving the right answer, or simply from disturbing the group's apparent unanimity? The latter possibility brings up the intriguing prediction that a deviant should liberate participants even if they know he is wrong. Indeed, Asch (1955) reports that even when an 'extreme dissenter' was instructed to choose a response that was further from the truth than the misleading majority's, conformity by naive participants dropped to 9 per cent. Even when a deviant chose the right visual stimulus while wearing thick eyeglasses and pretending to have poor eyesight (Allen & Levine, 1971), this significantly reduced conformity. In other words, defiance *per se*, the explicit flaunting of a majority's claim for truth, significantly reduces the grip of conformity on observers, even when the form of defiance appears misguided.

These misguided 'extreme dissenters' seem most effective when there is an objectively correct answer to be provided, as with perceptual questions such as the length of a line in Asch's paradigm, or with informational questions, such as providing the capital of Tanzania. In these cases what matters to reduce conformity is reducing the pressure of unanimity, and the dissenter, even wrong, helps to do this. With more subjective opinions, when there is no objective, ascertainable correct response, and no physical reality other than the social reality created by the responses of other individuals (Festinger, 1954), variance of opinions is to be expected. This makes the misguided extreme dissenter less surprising, and less effective at dispelling the power of the majority. When Allen and Levine (1968, 1969) tested the partner effect varying the type of information that they asked about, extreme dissenters reduced conformity only on perceptual (e.g., number of dots on a slide) and informational items (e.g., distance from LA to New York), but did not significantly affect responses to opinion items (e.g., most young people receive too much education). In the case of opinions, breaking the group's consensus without supporting the participant directly was not enough to significantly reduce conformity to group norms. On the other hand, a supportive partner who gave a defiant response in agreement with the naive participant's was effective in liberating individuals to reject the group's majority, even for opinion items. So with opinion items, principled deviants can only liberate likeminded individuals from the shackles of conformity, whereas with perceptual and informative items, they can even liberate those whose minority view differs from their own.

Do principled deviants weaken the grip of the majority because naive participants know of their defiance, or because naive participants know that *the majority knows* of the rebel's defiance, making naive participants feel less conspicuous in their own dissent? Both possibilities make sense, but at least one study suggests that the effect is of the more private kind: in Bragg and Allen (1972), when participants were supported by an agreeing partner without the majority knowing it (by simulating the malfunction of the experimental apparatus), they resisted the majority just as much (if anything, slightly more) as when everyone knew about the partner's dissent. This suggests that defiance weakens unanimity in the eyes of the prospective dissenter, rather than changing the meaning of the dissent in the eyes of the majority.

At a broader level, principled deviants have been shown to influence the majority even when a consensus is already established, provided that the deviants act consistently and appear autonomous and objective: indeed, Moscovici (1985) even suggests that this type of minority influence can in some regards be more powerful than conformity to the majority, because the latter encourages surface compliance, whereas minority influence, when it works, brings about deeper conversion and lasting attitude change.

Defiance delivers from obedience

Principled deviants are also given the most flattering role in another canonical demonstration of the pressures on individual integrity, Milgram's studies of destructive obedience (1963). Milgram looked directly at the power of authority figures, and famously reported that 65 per cent of his teacher-participants agreed to shock a learner-confederate to the full 450 volts. Less often cited is the finding (Milgram, 1965) that when working with two confederates who refused to go all the way, only 10 per cent of participants showed the full destructive obedience. Just as in the case of group pressure, principled deviants are thus suggested as a potential antidote to the perverting power that authorities hold over individuals. Rosenhan (1969) showed a similar liberating effect of defiers in a Milgram-type obedience paradigm. Whereas 85 per cent of base-rate participants fully obeyed, and 88 per cent did so when they first witnessed an obedient model, rates dropped to 58 per cent after seeing a 'humane' model (who courteously refused to go beyond 210 volts), and to 53 per cent after seeing a 'de-legitimising' model (who questioned the credentials of the experimenter 'with indignation', and finally stomped out of the room 'in evident outrage'). Note that whereas the rebels in Milgram (1965) were partnered with the naive participants to inflict the shocks together, Rosenhan's participants waited their turn while they watched the model perform their whole scripted sequence, which may explain the difference in liberation between the two studies.

Meeus and Raaijmakers (1986) showed similar liberating effect of principled deviants in an administrative obedience paradigm, where participants were instructed to utter 15 negative remarks to upset a confederate while he was taking an oral test that would allegedly determine if he was selected for a job. For example, some of the statements read 'Up to now, your test score is totally insufficient' and 'This job is much too difficult for you according to the test' (p. 13). Participants could see the applicant-confederate getting upset through physiological readings reportedly coming from electrodes on his skin, and they were told that he could be rejected for the job if he made too many errors as a result of stress. Yet 92 per cent of control participants uttered all 15 stress-inducing remarks nonetheless. Principled deviants, however, once more saved the day: when two confederates posing as participants refused to continue after the eighth of the 15 stress remarks, only 16 per cent of naive participants went all the way.

One explanation for the liberating power of principled deviance is that they demonstrate the absence of negative external consequences following rebellion. Another is that they demonstrate positive internal consequences for the rebel. In an ingenious experiment, Powers and Geen (1972) once more tested aggressive obedience in a shock-giving paradigm after witnessing obedient or rebellious models, but they varied (through non-verbal behaviour and bogus oscilloscope readings) the apparent arousal of the model before and after the rebellion. They found that the most liberating models were the rebels who appeared calm after the rebellion, whether or not they appeared nervous beforehand. Rebels who appeared nervous throughout or became nervous after rebellion did reduce obedience, but to a lesser extent than rebels who appeared relieved from having done the right thing.

Ironic effects of liberation

The liberating power of defiance can backfire in unexpected ways. When participants were paired in a new task with their fellow dissenter from a previous conformity paradigm, who now made systematic mistakes, they were more likely to conform to his erroneous pronouncements than they were with a member of the previous majority or with a novel participant (Darley *et al.*, 1974). Thus the partnership established in the 'partner effect' initiates bonds of its own, and the liberator became, so to speak, the new master.

Another counterintuitive finding is that principled deviants can spare others from the need to express their own rebellion, and thus lead to more conformity than if they had not rebelled. In Worchel and Brehm (1971), naive participants were instructed to choose to work on one of two similar tasks, which were equally attractive to control participants. When a bully confederate snapped that it was obvious which task they should work on and that there was 'really no question about it', participants in one study reacted by choosing the opposite task 83 per cent of the time. But when a second confederate stood up to the bully by asserting that he had not made up his mind yet, now paradoxically 83 per cent of participants went along with the bully, as if the rebel, by restoring his own freedom, vicariously restored the participant's, making it then acceptable to follow the bully's suggestion. Defiance can thus in some cases indirectly facilitate conformity.

Despite these occasional ironic effects, the research reviewed so far suggests that principled deviants have the power to free individuals from the pressure of groups and authority figures. Instead of the passive victims that we encountered in the first section, these deviants are therefore proactive liberators with noble roles to play. In our effort to document the reactions to principled deviants more generally, we turn now from the effect they have on other actors to the way they are perceived by observers.

Perception of defiance

The research so far suggests that defiant rebels can liberate other actors from the pressure of conformity or obedience. This says much about their power, but little yet about how they are perceived by others. In contrast to the rejection of deviants documented in the first section, we find that they are often liked, and ascribed positive attributes. A frequent ancillary finding in the studies reviewed above is that rebels did not just liberate others, they were also liked more. In Asch (1955), they inspired warmth, closeness and confidence; in Darley *et al.* (1974), participants reported liking them more and feeling closer to them than to members of the majority; in Worchel and Brehm (1971), they were liked and chosen as future work partners, rated as more capable and as better leaders; in Allen and Levine (1969), socially supportive dissenters were seen as highly likeable, intelligent, sincere and well-adjusted.

Morris, Miller and Spangenberg (1977) varied the placement of a supporting dissenter in an array of four otherwise conforming confederates preceding the naive participant. Deviants in the fourth position, who clearly dissented in the face of a majority of three, were rated the most confident, dynamic and accurate, illustrating the distinction between defiance and deviance introduced in the first section. A dissenter who responds first is merely a deviant, perhaps even an unintentional one, who does not yet realise that a group norm counter to his own position will emerge after he responds. In contrast, dissenters who speak after the majority, especially if it is known that the majority will hear them (Morris & Miller, 1975), are seen as more dynamic and confident because their 'dissenting response could plausibly be seen as being made in defiance of group pressure' (p.335).

The link between liking principled deviants and their liberating power is ambiguous. Participants flatly deny that rebels had any effect on their own decisions even if they report liking them (e.g., Asch, 1955), and some researchers are inclined to believe that liking deviants and being liberated by them are indeed separate processes (e.g., Darley *et al.*, 1974). Furthermore, 'extreme dissenters' (Asch, 1955) manage to liberate others while being extremely disliked for giving a response at odds with the participant's (Allen & Levine, 1969). Other researchers, however, report that liking for the partner predicts rates of non-conformity (Morris, Miller & Spangenberg, 1977), suggesting a possible link between these two processes.

In contrast to the model of deviants as passive victims sketched out in the first section, in this section we reviewed how defiance offers individuals some deliverance from the pressures of majorities and authorities. The greatest point of contrast may be in the interpersonal reactions to defiance. Whereas we initially documented rejection responses ranging from ostracism to hostility, we closed the present section by describing how rebels can also be embraced and ascribed numerous positive qualities.

Heroes or Heretics? The Role of Defensiveness

When is defiance revered, and when is it reviled? We saw first that deviants tend to be rejected, disliked and ostracised, and because we defined defiance as a type of deviance, it should elicit the same repressive treatment. Yet we also saw that defiant rebels can have liberating effects on their peers, who therefore tend to like and admire them. How can the same rebels sometimes be despised and sometimes be embraced? We propose that the major difference between the studies presented in the first part of the chapter (where defiance is rejected) and the ones in the second part (where defiance is appreciated) lies not in the behaviour of the rebels, but instead in the involvement of the perceivers, and therefore in the defensiveness triggered in them.

Moderation by personal involvement

A common feature of studies where participants liked the rebel was that the participant had not acted yet (e.g., Allen & Levine, 1971). In the typical partner effect paradigm, a majority opinion is expressed, the deviant opines, and only then does the experimenter turn to the naive participant for his response. The rebel here defies the majority, but this gesture says nothing about the participant, as he has not responded yet. It is therefore unlikely to trigger defensiveness, and defiance can be admired. In contrast, studies that look at the rejection of deviants occur in the context of an ongoing interaction (e.g., Schachter, 1951), or in social contexts with a long history, in other words in situations in which the deviant is judged by individuals who are already committed to the choice or opinion questioned by the deviant. No one considers one's attitude towards vegetarians *a priori*, but instead one does so in the context of a lifetime of meat eating. When participants have already made their own choice, the rebel's gesture not only questions the validity of the majority/authority claim, it questions the validity of the participants' own choice – and thus is likely to trigger defensiveness.

Thus a crucial moderator of reactions to defiance appears to be personal involvement, or how much one is already committed by one's actions to the claim of an authority or majority. The more one has supported this claim by going along with it, thus legitimising an authority or perpetuating a group norm, the more one has to lose from the deviant's challenge to the claim. It is of course somewhat obvious that concrete investment in a norm would make one reluctant to see it overturned, as when members of a corrupt company fear that a whistle-blower would make them lose their livelihood. The more interesting hypothesis is that it takes very little to be implicated, and that even passivity in the face of a problematic authority figure, or consenting silence in the face of a misguided majority, can make individuals feel retrospectively uneasy when confronted with a vocal deviant.

A straightforward operationalisation of involvement is whether individuals are actors or observers in the problematic situations. Upon reading about the Milgram (1963) experiments, it is easy to side with the minority who rebelled, and to appreciate their resistance as a token of human decency. One can imagine that this is harder for participants who have been in the experiment, because the defiance directly questions their decision to go along.

Defiance and the threat to bystanders

We propose that defiance elicits resentment instead of admiration when perceivers are *de facto* complicit with the claim being questioned, because rebels represent a threat to them which triggers defensiveness. What is the nature of this threat? Three candidates arise: imagined reproach; doubting one's choices; and being reminded of one's freedom.

Imagined reproach In this version the threat is simply that someone is in a position to morally reproach you, whether they actually do so or not. Their defiance is seen as a claim for moral superiority. When confederates refuse to go along in the Milgram experiment, they are not just questioning the morality of the experimenter; they are also implicitly questioning the morality of anyone who mindlessly obeyed him. This reproach, real or imagined, is a slap in the face to anyone who accepted the authority or the majority's claims. They now have to face the fact that someone else seized the moral high ground and could therefore be looking down on them. Individuals are reluctant to accept moral reproach from others, especially if they don't have any legitimate moral authority – and deviants typically do not. Note that in this interpretation, moral reproach is unpleasant, independent of whether you deem it warranted, that is, whether you agree that your own choice was immoral. Thus, a promiscuous bachelor may resent the condemnation of fornication by religious figures, despite feeling no compunction about premarital sex. An omnivore might be perfectly comfortable eating meat, yet be irked that vegetarians look down on her.

The validity of defiance Defiant rebels may also be resented not just because they implicitly claim the moral high ground (and insult you by doing so) but instead because you come to recognise the validity of their claim. Instead of the interpersonal sting of feeling put down by a peer, this would lead to something more akin to dissonance, whereby their gesture makes you realise that your own choice was problematic, and you now have to deal with it. To go back to our example of premarital sex, a promiscuous bachelor may feel especially threatened by virginity-pledge zealots if they elicit in him misgivings about sex before marriage. Note that this is quite different from the mere imagined reproach described above. On the one hand, this second process is more powerful, because the threat is no longer experienced as an external, interpersonal one ('I hate it when people take the moral high ground') but instead takes a much more internal, intrapersonal tone ('I guess I'm not such a great person after all'), which is likely to be more threatening to individuals – potentially triggering a much more vicious response. On the other hand, by requiring that the participant agree with the defiant rebel's condemnation, this interpretation significantly narrows the scope of the effect, making defiant rebels unthreatening in the vast majority of cases. This does not account for the many cases where we do not agree with the defiant rebel's stance, yet still resent what we perceive as ethical grandstanding. A more reasonable model most likely includes both components, with imagined moral reproach the active ingredient when we do not subscribe to the principled deviant's principles, and dissonance when we do.

A reminder of freedom A third possibility builds on the existential notion of denial of freedom (Fromm, 1941; Sartre, 1956). In this view, individuals recognise that going along has negative consequences, but they tell themselves that they did not have any other choice, perhaps because an authority figure wields considerable constraining power, or because they did not even realise that there existed an alternative to the mainstream path advocated by the majority. In this interpretation defiant rebels, by exercising their freedom, remind us of our own. By showing us that authorities can only constrain our behaviour so much, and by revealing alternative paths that we did not even consider or realise existed, defiant rebels remind us that we were free all along, and we now have to live with our choices.

Summary of the threat of defiant rebels We identified three mechanisms by which defiant rebels can threaten obedient others and elicit resentment. First, their stance implies reproach of the authority or the majority, and by proxy of anyone who went along; this reproach itself is resented. Second, the defiant rebel elicits dissonance by making conformers question the very validity of their choices, and forcing them to reconcile their positive self-image with their problematic behaviour. Third, when conformers found solace in the perception that they had no other choice but to conform, defiant rebels reveal the flimsiness of that conceit, and by reminding conformers that they were free all along, introduce existential angst as well as the necessity to account for past misdeeds.

Empirical evidence of defensive resentment Experiments on reactions to defiance conducted in our laboratory demonstrate the moderating role of personal involvement and the mediating role of imagined reproach. To establish moderation by involvement, we varied whether participants were first asked to engage in a problematic task (making them 'actors') or whether they were not ('observers') before being asked to react to a defiant confederate who refused to go along. Actor participants told to record a speech in favour of comprehensive exams (something they did not support) preferred a confederate who also obeyed to a rebel who refused to misrepresent his or her true attitude. However, observer participants who encountered a rebel without having to record the speech beforehand preferred him or her to an obedient counterpart (Monin, Sawyer & Marquez, 2008, Study 1). In a second version of the paradigm, participants role-playing a detective reviewing suspects for a burglary discovered that the most likely culprit was African American. Observers agreed that a defiant confederate who refused to make a choice and called the task 'offensive' was more moral than someone who obediently accused the lone black man, and also liked and respected this rebel more. This pattern was reversed when participants had engaged in the task themselves – in which case most participants accused the African American suspect, and then resented the defiant stance of the rebel (Study 2).

Supporting the imagined reproach mechanism, the rejection of these defiant rebels was mediated by the anticipation of rejection – participants seemed to assume that since the rebel defied the experimenter, he would also reject them for going along, and they pre-emptively rejected the rebel (Study 3). This rejection stems from a threat to the self, as demonstrated by two findings: first, self-affirmed participants (who were asked to write about one of their important traits or values prior to the threat) did not resent defiance (Study 4); second, when actor participants were invited to keep their initial choice a secret (thus removing the concern that the rebel's defiance just made them look bad in the eyes of the experimenter), they still disliked the defiant rebel (O'Connor & Monin, in preparation).

These data support our proposed resolution of the apparent inconsistency identified earlier in this chapter between the rejection and the appreciation of defiance. Mirroring the diverging reactions to defiance documented between published reports, we were able to elicit completely contrasting reactions to the same defiant behaviour in the laboratory, simply by changing the ego involvement of participants. This suggests that published studies of the rejection of principled deviants might focus on involved actors, whereas studies where participants appreciate defiance and may even be inspired by it focus on uninvolved observers. The typical appreciative participant in partner effect studies is the subject at the end of the table, who has witnessed the claims of a majority or an authority figure, and then the countervailing defiance of the rebel, all before having to commit to either position. As in our experiments, actors resent defiance, whereas observers appreciate it.

The reactions to defiance described so far were primarily assessed through attraction scales, such as how much participants would like the rebel as a friend, as a roommate, as a collaborator, or how much they respected the target. We also asked participants to rate rebels on a battery of personality traits, which aggregated into a communion dimension (e.g., kind, warm) and an agency dimension (e.g., strong, independent). Observer participants typically rated rebels as significantly more agentic, and in one instance as more communal than obedient targets. In contrast, actor participants did not grant rebels any superiority on these dimensions, sometimes even rating them as less communal than obedient targets (Monin, Sawyer & Marquez, 2008). The positive qualities ascribed to rebels in the work reviewed previously (Asch, 1955, etc.) included both dimensions, with frequent mentions of warmth, closeness, likeability (communion) as well as intelligence, leadership ability and accuracy (agency). The defensive nature of actors' reluctance to grant rebels any positive qualities is demonstrated by the consequences of self-affirmation (Monin, Sawyer & Marquez, 2008, Study 4). When self-affirmed, actor participants no longer put down rebels on the communion dimension, and started even to recognise their superior agency.

The liberating effect of moral rebels Above we reviewed how rebels were not only appreciated by individuals who had yet to pronounce themselves, but also served to liberate these individuals from the shackles of conformity and obedience (e.g., Asch, 1955). Would we observe the same kind of moderation described here on these liberating 'partner' effects? Can we expect participants to stand up to the experimenter after seeing a rebel? In Study 2 of Monin, Sawyer and Marquez (2008), we used an order manipulation so observer participants actually made their own choice in the burglary line-up task after witnessing the confederate's response. Whereas over 85 per cent of participants accused the African American suspect with no prior model, only 33 per cent did so after seeing a rebel, and 50 per cent did not respond.

This suggests that rebels did have a liberating role, freeing observer participants from the demands of a racist task. It is not possible to evaluate the liberating effect of rebels on actor participants in this study, because their choice was already made when they witnessed the rebellion. However, suggestive evidence was collected in Study 4 of Monin, Sawyer and Marquez (2008), where participants reported their happiness with their choice of the African American as the most likely suspect at the end of the procedure. Actor participants who expressed the least happiness with their initial choice (and the least tendency to blame the situation) were the self-affirmed actors who had seen a rebel, perhaps suggesting the 'validity of defiance' mechanism discussed earlier and an admittance of regret about complying with the racist task. Assuming that they would take this regret to heart and be less likely to comply with a similarly problematic task in the future, this suggest that rebels can have a liberating effect even on actors, provided the latter are self-affirmed. In the absence of self-affirmation, participants did not express more regret after seeing a rebel than after seeing an obedient other. Thus it seems that self-defence mechanisms come in the way of learning from the rebel's defiance, unless one is made secure in one's self-worth. It remains to be seen, however, if their newfound wisdom carries over to novel situations, that is, whether affirmed actors who witness a defiant rebel would take the same defiant stand if a similar situation presented itself in the future. It seems important for investigators to pursue these questions as the rebel studies may paint an overly negative picture of reactions to defiance. It is even possible that rebels are disliked but influential (see Rink & Ellemers, this volume); such a pattern is familiar in social comparison research, where superior others may be annoying but push us to excel.

Conclusion: Defiance Revered, Defiance Reviled

This chapter documents diverging reactions to principled deviants. We started the first part with a broad discussion of models of deviance in social science, then narrowed our investigation to the specific case we called defiance. Whereas social scientists often emphasise the negative consequences of deviance for the deviants, in the second part we documented how, in social psychology, rebels have played a special role for those around them, providing deliverance from social pressures to bystanders who witness their defiance, and appreciate them as a result. In the third part we tried to resolve the apparent inconsistency between rejecting deviance and embracing defiance. We proposed that personal involvement in the claim rejected by the defiant rebel moderates the defensiveness exhibited by bystanders, and presented some of our work showing that the same defiance can be embraced by uninvolved observers and rejected by involved actors, for whom it feels like a personal reproach. At the end of the day, whether defiance is revered or reviled seems to depend on defensiveness. Given the powerful liberating role of rebels in classic social psychology, it seems unfortunate that defensive processes can prevent rebels from getting through to actors who feel too involved in a situation to tolerate even implicit criticism. Future research should determine how defiance can be framed so that rebels can stand for their principles, avoid resentment from peers and bypass defensiveness to inspire others to stand for what is right, even if it means admitting they were wrong.

References

Allen, V.L. & Levine, J.M. (1968). Social support, dissent and conformity. *Sociometry, 31* (2), 138–49.

Allen, V.L. & Levine, J.M. (1969). Consensus and conformity. *Journal of Experimental Social Psychology, 5*, 389–99.

Allen, V.L. & Levine, J.M. (1971). Social support and conformity: the role of independent assessment of reality. *Journal of Experimental Social Psychology, 7*, 48–58.

Asch, S.E. (1951). Effects of group pressure upon the modification and distortion of judgments. In H. Guetzkow (ed.), *Groups, Leadership and Men: Research in Human Relations* (pp. 177–90). Pittsburgh, PA: Carnegie Press.

Asch, S.E. (1955). Opinions and social pressure. *Scientific American, 193* (5), 31–5.

Asch, S.E. (1956). Studies of independence and conformity: 1. A minority of one against a unanimous majority. *Psychological Monographs: General and Applied, 70* (9), no. 416, 1–70.

Bateson, G. (1944). Cultural determinants of personality. In J. McV. Hunt (ed.), *Personality and the Behavior Disorders* (Vol. II) New York: The Ronald Press Co.

Bragg, B.W. & Allen, V. (1972). The role of public and private support in reducing conformity. *Psychonomic Science 29* (2), 81–2.

Darley, J.M., Moriarty, T., Darley, S. & Berscheid, E. (1974). Increased conformity to a fellow deviant as a function of prior deviation. *Journal of Experimental Social Psychology, 10*, 211–23.

Erikson, K.T. (1966). *Wayward Puritans: A Study in the Sociology of Deviance.* New York: John Wiley & Sons.

Erikson, K.T. (2003). On the sociology of deviance. In D.H. Kelly & E.J. Clarke (eds), *Deviant Behavior: A Text-Reader in the Sociology of Deviance* (6th edition, pp. 85–92). New York: Worth.

Festinger, L. (1954). A theory of social comparison processes. *Human Relations, 7,* 117–40.

Foucault, M. (1995). *Discipline and Punish: The Birth of the Prison* (Alan Sheridan, Trans.). New York: Random House Vintage Books. (Original work published 1975.)

Fromm, E. (1941). *Escape from Freedom.* New York: Rinehart.

Goffman, E. (1963). *Stigma: Notes on the Management of Spoiled Identity.* New York: Simon & Schuster.

Jodelet, D. (1989). *Folie et Représentation Sociales* [Madness and social representations]. Paris: Presses Universitaires de France.

Jones, E.E. (1972). *Attribution: Perceiving the Causes of Behavior.* London: General Learning Press.

Kelly, D.H. & Clarke, E.J. (2003). *Deviant Behavior: A Text-Reader in the Sociology of Deviance* (6th edition). New York: Worth.

Leary, M.R. (2004). The sociometer, self-esteem, and the regulation of interpersonal behavior. In R.F. Baumeister & K. Vohs (eds), *Handbook of Self-Regulation.* New York: Guilford.

Lewin, K. (1936). *Principles of Topological Psychology.* New York: McGraw-Hill.

Lidz, C.W. & Walker, A.L. (1980). *Heroin, Deviance, and Morality.* Beverly Hills, CA: Sage.

Matz, D.C. & Wood, W. (2005). Cognitive dissonance in groups: the consequences of disagreement. *Journal of Personality and Social Psychology, 88,* 22–37.

Meeus, W.H.J. & Raaijmakers, Q.A.W. (1986). Administrative obedience: carrying out orders to use psychological-administrative violence. *European Journal of Social Psychology, 16,* 311–24.

Milgram, S. (1963). Behavioral study of obedience. *Journal of Abnormal and Social Psychology, 67,* 371–8.

Milgram, S. (1965). Liberating effects of group pressure. *Journal of Personality and Social Psychology, 2,* 127–34.

Monin, B., Sawyer, P. & Marquez, M. (2008). The rejection of moral rebels: resenting those who do the right thing. *Journal of Personality and Social Psychology, 95,* 76–93.

Morris, W.N. & Miller, R.S. (1975). Impressions of dissenters and conformers: an attributional analysis. *Sociometry, 38* (2), 327–39.

Morris, W.N., Miller, R.S. & Spangenberg, S. (1977). The effects of dissenter position and task difficulty on conformity and response conflict. *Journal of Personality, 45* (2), 251–66.

Moscovici, S. (1985). Social influence and conformity. In G. Lindzey & E. Aronson (eds), *Handbook of Social Psychology* (3rd edition, Vol. 2). New York: Random House.

O'Connor, K. & Monin, B. (2010). *Moral Rebels: Addressing Some Alternatives.* Manuscript in preparation.

Powers, P.C. & Geen, R.G. (1972). Effects of the behavior and the perceived arousal of a model on instrumental aggression. *Journal of Personality and Social Psychology, 23* (2), 175–83.

Rosenhan, D. (1969). Some origins of concern for others. In P. Mussen, J. Langer & M. Covington (eds), *Trends and Issues in Developmental Psychology.* New York: Holt, Reinhart & Winston.

Sartre, J.P. (1956). *Being and Nothingness: An Essay on Phenomenological Ontology.* New York: Philosophical Library.

Schachter, S. (1951). Deviation, rejection, and communication. *Journal of Abnormal and Social Psychology, 46,* 190–207.

Szasz, T.S. (1974). *The Myth of Mental Illness: Foundations of a Theory of Personal Conduct.* New York: Harper & Row.

Williams, K.D., Cheung, C.K.T. & Choi, W. (2000). CyberOstracism: effects of being ignored over the Internet. *Journal of Personality and Social Psychology, 79,* 748–62.

Worchel, S. & Brehm, J.W. (1971). Direct and implied social restoration of freedom. *Journal of Personality and Social Psychology, 18* (3), 294–304.

15

The Dissenter's Dilemma, and a Social Identity Solution

Dominic J. Packer

On 3 June 1989, after weeks of demonstrations by thousands of citizens, Chinese troops entered Tiananmen Square and made quick work of the protestors. Many were killed, many others were arrested, the rest scattered. The following day as tanks tried to exit the square, a lone man positioned himself in front of the long mechanical column and for a few moments refused to let the army move on. A famous photograph was snapped and the man, by popular account at least, disappeared and was not seen again.

A tattered poster bearing the image of the still nameless man who chose to pit himself against the might of the Chinese army used to hang on my office wall. I bought the poster at a university sale and it was named 'Human Spirit'. I could never quite make up my mind, however, whether the title best referred to the lone dissenter or to the tanks representing conformity to the vast power of the state. I suspect that conformity and dissent are equally human responses, but that the latter is likely to be the more difficult, the less common and, as such, to stand in particular need of attention and explanation.

The Dissenter's Dilemma

This chapter examines factors that might motivate someone to express non-conformist and potentially unpopular opinions, and will suggest that decisions regarding whether to dissent often pose group members with a social dilemma. Social dilemmas of all kinds possess a common basic structure: group-level benefits that may motivate behaviour in a collectively

Rebels in Groups: Dissent, Deviance, Difference and Defiance Jolanda Jetten and Matthew J. Hornsey

oriented direction are counteracted by individual-level costs that motivate behaviour in a personally oriented one (e.g., Hardin, 1968; Kollock, 1998; Messick & Brewer, 1983). The dissenter's dilemma stems from the fact that, as La Rochefoucauld (1665) put it, 'Few men are wise enough to prefer helpful censure to treacherous praise'. Applied at a group level, this simple maxim posits that although dissent can be a social good, it is unlikely to be appreciated by one's fellows and may in many cases be met with sanctions (we will return to the notion that its inverse, praise, can be treacherous later). Thus, as with other social dilemmas, dissent can be characterised as an act that may benefit the collective while entailing costs to the individual actor (see also Sunstein, 2006).[1]

Before continuing, it is worth pausing to ask to whether these characterisations of dissent are valid. First, is dissent really a social good, a behaviour beneficial to collectives? The current volume is testament to the fact that this is frequently the case. A growing literature is documenting contexts in and processes by which the expression of divergent viewpoints enhances group decision making, reduces polarisation and allows for more creative, productive and ethical outcomes (e.g., Butera, Darnon & Mugny; Nemeth & Goncalo; Rink & Ellemers, all this volume, see also Brodbeck *et al.*, 2002; De Dreu, 2002; Hornsey, 2006; Postmes, Spears & Cihangir, 2001). From the opposite perspective, adverse group outcomes are often attributed to an absence of dissent – a failure to elicit, respect and heed competing ideas (e.g., Janis, 1972). Dissent is, by this formulation, important to the healthy functioning of social groups (see also Spreitzer & Sonenshein, 2004; Warren, 2003), and a failure to allow for dissent may result in difficulty adapting to changing circumstances. Of course, the extent to which one believes that any particular dissenting perspective is helpful depends on one's own perspective, and there are almost certainly costs in terms of group disruption and disunity that can occur as a consequence of dissent in addition to the benefits it may have in terms of improved decision making.

Second, do expressions of dissent really carry costs for dissenters? Both anecdotal and empirical evidence indicates that this can often be the case (e.g., Abrams *et al.*, 2000; Emerson, 1954; Marques & Yzerbyt, 1988; Noelle-Neumann, 1974; Schachter, 1951; Tata *et al.*, 1996). To take but one example of each kind, the harried life of Nelson Mandela, imprisoned for 27 years for protesting South Africa's apartheid regime, and the classic finding that deviant members of cohesive groups are subject to heightened attention and rejection (Emerson, 1954; Schachter, 1951) illustrate (to wildly disparate degrees) the negative consequences that can accompany dissent. The current volume affirms this point, but offers an important qualification to any blanket assertions about the negative consequences of collective critique. Recognising that dissent is likely to be important for healthy group functioning, researchers have recently suggested that groups may not be as allergic to criticism as has often been supposed. In particular, certain forms of (constructive) dissent coming from certain types of (upstanding) members may be tolerated, even welcomed by groups (e.g., Jetten & Hornsey, this volume; Hornsey, 2005; Hornsey *et al.*, 2007). Thus, if one is the right sort of person saying the right sort of things (in the right sort of group; Hornsey *et al.*, 2006), one's non-conformity may be accepted and may have an influence on group behaviour (see also Hollander, 1958; Moscovici & Faucheux, 1972). Nevertheless, if you are the wrong sort of person and/or saying the wrong sorts of things, there will likely be costs and they may well be severe.

Frequent failures to provide or protect public goods suggest that social dilemmas are often resolved in favour of individual rather than collective interests (Hardin, 1968). An influential analysis by Mancur Olson (1965) posited two reasons why groups of individuals making rational choices will typically fail to advance their collective interests and thereby fail to attain outcomes that would benefit everyone. First, the fact that collective benefits are by definition shared by all members of a group means that any individual member will benefit whether or not he personally acts to advance the collective interest – knowing that personal gains are not contingent on effort, he lacks an incentive to contribute. Second, recognising that others are similarly unlikely to contribute, an individual in a sizeable group is further deterred from action in support of the collective interest by the realisation that a lone contribution (if one were made) is likely insufficient to effect the necessary change – knowing that her efforts are unlikely to be successful given the predictably selfish responses of others, she lacks the sense of efficacy necessary to contribute. From Olson's rational choice perspective, there are only two mechanisms by which groups can ensure that the collective interest is served. One is to make contributions non-voluntary, as when nation states require by law that their citizens pay taxes (see also Hardin, 1968). The other solution is to provide rewards to individual contributors beyond the collective gains incurred by pursuing the group interest; that is, to reward individuals for their work on behalf of the group, thus providing personal-level incentives for collectively-oriented behaviour.

Unfortunately, neither solution is likely to be particularly viable when it comes to motivating dissent in service of collective interests. Dissent is by definition a lonely, minority act; it cannot therefore be mandated of all group members. Further, although the virtues of dissent may be valued in the abstract, generally speaking it is likely too much to ask that groups bestow rewards on their internal critics (but see Jetten, Postmes & McAuliffe, 2002). Some groups may set up structures to protect dissenters (e.g., whistle-blower protections), and it is common in many groups to create officially sanctioned outlets for opinion expression (e.g., surveys, editorials, suggestion boxes, etc.). Nevertheless, few are the groups that honour their dissenters (particularly the truly challenging ones), at least initially. From Olson's (1965) perspective, then, we are thus more or less forced to conclude that few rational individuals would ever choose to engage in dissent.

A Social Identity Solution

Into the explanatory gap left by rational choice perspectives on collective behaviour stepped social identity theory. This approach developed by Henri Tajfel and his colleagues posits that human identity is not just instantiated at an individual level, but also includes collective senses of self (e.g., Hogg & Abrams, 1988; Tajfel, 1981; Tajfel & Turner, 1979). Groups are not simply collections of individuals who happen to have interests in common, but rather serve as the basis for identities of their own, with all the cognitive, motivational and emotional consequences that accompany idiosyncratic self-conceptions. Not every group membership becomes the basis for a social identity, but when a valued membership is salient, one's sense of self is thought to shift from 'I' to 'we', from 'mine' to 'our', and from 'me' to 'us' (see also Brewer & Gardner, 1996). Outcomes, evaluated in terms of individualistic consequences at a personal level of identity, are instead evaluated in terms of their implications for the group.

Critically, shifts in identity from personal to collective alter individuals' responses to social dilemmas, such that they are more willing to incur personal costs in order to achieve collective gains (e.g., Brewer & Kramer, 1986; Kramer & Brewer, 1984). By recognising that people will, under certain circumstances, make decisions as representatives of a group rather than as autonomous individuals (i.e., with collective rather than individual interests at heart), a social identity analysis moves beyond the standard rational choice solutions to social dilemmas (Messick & Brewer, 1983). Strongly identified group members need not be required to contribute (they are likely to do so voluntarily), and they need not be individually rewarded for doing so (indeed, they are willing to incur personal costs on behalf of the group; see also Tajfel & Turner, 1979; Van Vugt & Hart, 2004; Zdaniuk & Levine, 2001). Note that this approach does not suggest that identified group members are any less self-interested, simply that the sense of self has shifted from the individual to the collective level, such that one becomes less concerned with 'my' outcomes and more worried about 'our' outcomes (De Cremer & Van Vugt, 1999).

Thus, it appears that social identity theory can account for collectively oriented behaviour in the absence of the positive and negative incentives posited by rational choice theory as necessary to motivate individual-level actors to behave in the collective interest in social dilemmas. This is fortunate because, as we saw, requiring and/or rewarding dissent were unlikely to prove particularly viable solutions to this particular dilemma. However, before we can declare the problem solved, a not insignificant snag remains to be dealt with – namely the fact that past research has posited and observed exactly the opposite: strongly identified group members are more (not less) likely to conform to group norms (e.g., Bond & Smith, 1996; Hovland, Janis & Kelley, 1953; Spears, Doosje & Ellemers, 1997; Terry & Hogg, 1996). The mechanics underlying the shift from personal to collective identity, as articulated by self-categorisation theory, illuminate why this is the case. When a valued social identity is salient and someone shifts from a personal to a collective level of identity, they are thought to depersonalise, adopting the group's prototype as the basis for their identity. As outlined above, this process involves a shift in one's sense of self from 'my' unique traits, habits and concerns to 'our' shared characteristics, norms and values (Turner, 1982; Turner *et al.*, 1987; Turner *et al.*, 1994). The more identified a group member is, the more they depersonalise, and the more depersonalised they are, the more likely they are to behave in conformity with group norms because those norms have, quite literally, become part of who they are (Hogg & Turner, 1987; Terry & Hogg, 1996; White, Hogg & Terry, 2002).

The solution to this snag, I believe, lies in recognition of the fact that identities are more than catalogues or repositories of pieces of information about the self, which when active or salient serve as guides to action (e.g., Abrams *et al.*, 1990; Wheeler, DeMarree & Petty, 2007; Wood, Quinn & Kashy, 2002). This is certainly one element of identity, but the self is not a passive entity and it also provides the basis or reference point for continuous evaluation of actions and outcomes (e.g., Fishbein & Ajzen, 1975; Higgins, 1996; Louis, Taylor & Neil, 2004; Louis, Taylor & Douglas, 2005). The value or utility of relevant objects and events are assessed (not necessarily consciously) in terms of their implications for the self – 'is this good or bad for me/us?'. There is likely no object more relevant to the self than the self and, as such, it should come as no surprise that the self is subject to its own evaluative processes. In other words, the self can reflect on its own patterns of behaviour (traits at an individual level and norms at a group level) and can, if so disposed, come to the conclusion that these patterns are not ideal – that who I am is not who I should be, that how we are behaving is not in our interest (e.g., Prochaska, DiClemente & Norcross, 1992).[2]

The capacity to evaluate one's own identity means that strong identifiers can come to view their group's behaviour as unproductive, harmful or immoral, and the fact that they care about the group means that they may be motivated to do something about it. As Charles Taylor (1989) puts it, 'My identity. . .provide[s] the frame or horizon within which I can try to determine from case to case what is good, or valuable, or what ought to be done, or what I endorse or oppose. In other words, it is the horizon within which I am capable of taking a stand' (p. 27). The manner in which one takes a stand is likely to differ somewhat between levels of identity. Whereas attempting to change suboptimal individual behaviours involves convincing oneself of the necessity for change (e.g., Aronson, 1999), changing behavioural patterns within a social group necessarily involves convincing others to change as well (e.g., Reicher, 2004; Taylor & McKirnan, 1984) – that is, it involves dissent. As noted above, the expression of dissent is likely to impose personal-level costs, and it is those members who identify most strongly with the group who should be most willing to make these sacrifices (see also Haslam *et al.*, 2006).

In sum, if we accept that identified group members are capable, at least on occasion, of evaluating the merits of their groups, a shift from a personal to a collective level of identity may solve the dissenter's dilemma after all. Dissent probably makes little sense to a rational individual-level actor, but it may make sense to the same individual making decisions as an identified group member. Further, the processes by which decisions are made at this level of identity may be just as rational as individualistic decisions; identified group members may evaluate the pros and cons of different courses of action and choose the one deemed most likely to maximise collective utility. This is not, of course, to say that they necessarily do make rational decisions, merely that they might be able to. The same sorts of biases that influence personal decisions are likely to influence cognitions regarding the group interest, and the nature of self-evaluation at all levels of identity is likely to reflect a tension between enhancement, verification, accuracy and improvement motives (e.g., Sedikides, 1993; Sedikides & Strube, 1995).

The Normative Conflict Model

All of this boils down to the assertion that willingness to bear the costs of dissent is not intrinsically opposed to recognition of its necessity. As a result, taking on a social identity need not entail blind conformity to one's group's norms (see also Crane & Platow, in press; Hirschman, 1970; Hornsey, 2006; Hornsey, Smith & Begg, 2007; Kelley & Shapiro, 1954; Moscovici & Faucheux, 1972; Nail, MacDonald & Levy, 2000; Roccas, Klar & Liviatan, 2006). In order to account in a systematic way for instances of dissent within social groups, I have recently proposed a 'normative conflict model', which attempts to predict the manner in which members will respond to normative pressure from their groups under a variety of conditions (see Packer, 2008; Packer & Chasteen, 2010). The model predicts the likelihood of several responses as a function of three psychological factors: collective identification, normative conflict, and estimates regarding the likely costs and benefits of conformity versus non-conformity. Combining the first two factors allows a social identity solution to the dissenter's dilemma. As outlined above, the extent to which a member identifies with a group is conceptually independent from his/her evaluation of group norms. Treating these variables as orthogonal highlights the fact that group members at all levels of identification may experience feelings of conflict regarding group norms, and gives rise to four rough cells within which we can expect to observe different responses to normative pressure. The model predicts, in particular, that considering the interaction between identification and perceptions of normative conflict allows us to account for both the commonly observed positive relationship between identification and conformity to group norms, as well as instances of dissent by strongly identified group members.

As outlined in the top portion of Table 15.1, the interaction of identification and normative conflict is predicted to give rise to four dominant responses to group norms. When perceptions of normative conflict are low (norms are evaluated positively or perhaps not evaluated at all), dominant responses are likely to evidence a positive relationship between identification

Table 15.1 Responses to group norms predicted by the normative conflict model

		Low identification	High identification
Dominant responses	Low normative conflict	*Indifference*	*Loyal conformity*
	High normative conflict	*Disengagement*	*Collectively oriented dissent*
		Low Identification	High identification
Strategic alternate responses	Low normative conflict	*Strategic conformity*	*Strategic non-conformity*
	High normative conflict	*Personally oriented dissent*	*Uneasy conformity*

and conformity (e.g., Johnson & White, 2003; Terry & Hogg, 1996; Terry, Hogg & White, 1999), which can be characterised as a transition from *indifference* regarding group norms among weak identifiers to *loyal conformity* among strong identifiers. Whereas strong identifiers in this situation exhibit conformity to group norms because they are considered (if only tacitly) to be in the collective interest, the term indifference reflects the prediction that the behaviour of weak identifiers at low levels of normative conflict is likely to be essentially unrelated to group norms – these members are not reacting against or trying to change group norms, but are simply unconcerned with or perhaps even unaware of collective standards.

Things change, however, when group members experience normative conflict, perceiving group norms as suboptimal, harmful or even immoral. In this situation, strongly identified members are not expected to conform more than weak identifiers. Rather both may behave non-normatively – strong identifiers expressing *collectively oriented dissent* in an attempt to change their group in ways that they perceive as being better for the collective (see also Crane & Platow, in press), and weak identifiers engaging in *disengagement* behaviours in order to distance themselves from a norm (or perhaps even an entire group) they consider problematic (see Ellemers, Spears & Doosje, 1997; Haslam *et al.*, 2006; Hirschman, 1970; Merton, 1968; Prislin & Christensen, 2005; Sani & Reicher, 1999; Sani & Todman, 2002; Van Vugt & Hart, 2004). Importantly, although both dissent and disengagement entail non-normative behaviour, the former succeeds only to the extent it is able to influence fellow group members. Disengagement, however, carries no such constraint and may therefore involve less politic and more divisive expressions of discontent.

The four responses outlined above are posited as dominant in the sense that they reflect what group members are most inclined to do – how they would generally prefer to behave if no other considerations weighed in their decisions. Critically, however, group members' behaviour may be moderated and altered by perceptions that the dominant response is likely to be associated with costs and/or that a different behaviour is likely to be accompanied by benefits (see also Jetten *et al.*, 2010). Thus, as shown in the bottom portion of Table 15.1, group members in each of the four quadrants may, under certain circumstances, engage in alternate patterns of behaviour that reflect strategic responses to external contingencies. Take, for instance, the behaviour of weakly identified group members experiencing low levels of normative conflict. These members are generally expected to exhibit indifference to group norms. However, if they believe it to be in their personal self-interest to conform to group norms, they may instead engage in *strategic conformity*, either because they expect to be rewarded for doing so or punished for not. Absent these contingencies, however, strategic conformity disappears (recall La Rochfoucauld's (1665) 'treacherous praise'; see also Jetten *et al.*, 2003; Jetten, Hornsey & Adarves-Yorno, 2006). Similarly, strongly identified group members experiencing high levels of normative conflict may also engage in a type of strategic behaviour, in particular if they believe that the costs associated with dissent are likely to be too great to bear. This response is termed *uneasy conformity* in reflection of the hypothesis that anxiety regarding the costs of non-conformity suppresses the expression of concerns regarding norms that individuals believe to be counter to the collective interest (see also Hirschman, 1970; Kelman, 1958; Nail, MacDonald & Levy, 2000).

The original model (Packer, 2008) articulated only these six responses, but it is worth considering possible strategic alternate responses in the two remaining cells. Although strongly identified group members experiencing low levels of normative conflict are generally expected to exhibit loyal conformity, are there situations in which they might display non-conformity? There are at least two possibilities: first, these members might not publicly conform to the norms of a group with which they identify if there are likely to be severe costs for doing so – if, for instance, signs of identifying with the group are likely to result in discrimination or persecution by other more powerful groups (e.g., Goffman, 1963). Second, strong identifiers might express opinions contrary to a norm that they privately endorse if they believe that doing so will benefit the group – if, for example, they believe that playing the role of devil's advocate is likely to improve collective decision making. As such, strong identifiers experiencing little conflict with group norms might nevertheless exhibit *strategic non-conformity.*

Finally, weak identifiers experiencing high levels of normative conflict, who are generally expected to disengage from the group might, on occasion, instead engage with their collective in an attempt to change the norm(s) they oppose. Dissent, though predicted as most likely among strong identifiers perceiving high levels of normative conflict, is not necessarily limited to this quadrant. There are multiple reasons why members might try to influence their groups and, as such, there are multiple possible forms of normative conflict. Group members might, for instance, perceive a particular group norm as harmful to the collective as a whole and/or harmful to themselves personally, and personally oriented normative conflict may motivate attempts to change group norms among weak identifiers (Hirschman, 1970, 1974). It is for this reason that I have said throughout that dissent is often but not always a social dilemma. However, given that groups' reactions to dissent that is perceived as motivated by personal gain are likely to be significantly less friendly than their reactions to dissent in general (rendering this form of dissent, if nothing else, less effective), I anticipate that this is likely to be a relatively uncommon response among weak identifiers concerned about the personal implications of group norms (i.e., disengagement is likely to be the easier and more efficacious response). Nevertheless, weakly identified group members may well engage in *personally oriented dissent* if they believe that there is likely to be personal benefit to doing so.

All things considered, then, weakly identified group members are expected to behave more or less like rational individuals, generally choosing not to conform to or dissent from group norms except when they expect to be personally rewarded for doing so or punished for not. If forced to choose between the two, weak identifiers will presumably opt for the less costly response. In contrast and just as with other social dilemmas, strong identifiers are more likely to overcome personal-level costs associated with conforming to group norms or expressing dissent if they believe it to be in the collective interest to do either.

Empirical Evidence

Dominant responses in three of the model's four quadrants are relatively uncontroversial. In particular, the positive relationship between collective identification and conformity to norms that are (presumably) perceived as unproblematic is robust and well established. Generally speaking, patterns of group behaviour are likely perceived as collectively beneficial, and strongly identified (and more depersonalised) group members are, as such, more likely to conform. In order to test the normative conflict model's account of dissent, my colleagues and I have recently focused on situations in which a group's status quo may be perceived as non-functional or harmful, with particular attention to how this affects the relationship between collective identification and willingness to express opinions contrary to group norms. A series of studies has investigated how group members with different levels of identification respond to perceptions that a particular group norm is harmful to the collective (Packer, 2009, in press; Packer & Chasteen, 2010; Packer, Fujita & Chasteen, 2010). The influence of perceived collective harm is contrasted with the effect of perceptions of individualistic forms of harm (e.g., that a norm is personally harmful). As elaborated above, it is the former form of perceived harm that is expected to trigger expressions of dissent among strongly identified group members.

Our studies typically present group members (often members of a university) with a particular group norm (e.g., binge drinking), and either manipulate or measure different forms of normative conflict. In experimental designs, we randomly assign members to conditions that ask them to spend few minutes thinking about: (a) the potential harm the norm could cause the collective; (b) the harm the norm might cause individuals (including, in some cases, their personal selves); or (c) issues that do not draw their attention to negative aspects of the norm. In correlational studies, we usually ask participants to rate the extent to which they perceive the group norm as collectively and personally harmful. Participants are then asked to indicate their willingness to express contrarian opinions regarding the norm in a variety of ways (e.g., by signing a petition, writing to a newspaper, giving a speech, etc.) and/or are provided with an opportunity to actually express their opinion to fellow group members.

The pattern of findings across studies provides consistent evidence in support of the contention that strongly identified group members approach dissent as they do other social dilemmas. In each case, perceptions that a group norm is harmful (versus not harmful) to the collective increase non-conformist expressions of opinion among strong identifiers (Packer, 2009; Packer & Chasteen, 2010). Perceptions of collective harm do not appear to affect opinion expression among weakly identified group members and, critically, perceptions of personal harm do not increase expressions of dissent among strong identifiers (Packer & Chasteen, 2010). Interestingly, in our studies to date, perceptions of personal harm rarely increase dissent among weakly identified members, a finding which is circumstantially consistent with the idea that group members recognise that personally oriented forms of dissent are unlikely to be efficacious or well received and are thus not worth it.

Further, our studies indicate that in situations of high normative conflict, strongly identified members tend to express greater dissent than weak identifiers; that is, there is a positive relationship between identification and dissent in these circumstances. This pattern is consistent with the social dilemma account of dissent I have proposed, such that it is those members who identify with a group who prefer the potential collective benefits of opinion expression over its personal costs without compulsion or individual-level incentives to do so. Weak identifiers do not appear to muster the effort or initiative to publicly express contrarian opinions, presumably because they care little about group outcomes and/or it is less costly for them to go along with the uncontroversial modal opinion than to express dissent. There is little evidence to date of strong identifiers responding to normative conflict with uneasy conformity; however, the social dilemma analysis of dissent suggests that this should be a common response only when the costs of dissent are quite high, perhaps significantly higher than in our studies.

Final Thoughts

A great deal remains to be learned about the psychological motives and processes that underlie the expression of dissenting opinions in groups. I will close with a few questions that I find particularly intriguing.

- *If it is valuable, why do groups impose costs on dissent?* One potential answer has to do with the fact that there is such a thing as a silly idea. By making it difficult, groups may be able to ensure that those who do dissent are serious and committed to their positions, and thereby suppress expression of uninformed opinions and self-centred complaints. A corollary of this prediction is that reducing the costs of dissent may make it less effective; an anonymous comment deposited in a suggestion box, for instance, may carry less weight and exert less influence than a public articulation because the dissenter is not willing to stand behind it and take the flak.

- *Is dissent a high risk/high reward pursuit?* As noted throughout, dissent often triggers negative reactions. Nevertheless, some dissenters are successful and do manage to effect change within their groups. Such a display of influence is likely to be a mark of prestige, and dissenters who succeed in bringing the group in line with their own vision may subsequently become leaders (Levine & Kerr, 2007). Recognising that they will likely be denigrated in the present, but that if successful they may be honoured in the future, a savvy dissenter may take the long view and thereby overcome the immediate costs of opinion expression. Taking an even longer view, some dissenters may believe that even if they are not successful in their own lifetimes, they are on the side of history and will eventually be recognised for their contributions. Concern for the collective interest does not necessarily eliminate an identified group member's personal-level interest (see De Dreu, 2006), which may manifest itself in terms of wanting to (ultimately) secure status and recognition within the group.
- *Are successful dissenters reborn as authoritarians?*[3] According to the current perspective, group members do not dissent because they believe dissent itself to be of intrinsic value. Rather they dissent because they have a strong conviction that something about the group should be other than it is. As suggested above, their willingness to incur costs in order to effect change is likely testament to their commitment to an ideal. As a result, having achieved success, ex-dissenters may be intolerant of new, upstart dissenters coming along and challenging or changing the gains they believe they have made (see Prislin, Davenport & Michalak, this volume). Similarly and somewhat ironically given its collectively oriented nature, dissent might be considered an act of ego; although they are motivated by the collective interest, dissenters may believe that they (potentially alone) know what is best for the group and that their perspectives should prevail.
- *Is dissent hardest when everything is going well?* Groups are presumably more open to change when it is widely recognised among members that things are not going well. It is before the fall, when things are seemingly going according to plan (e.g., everyone making lots of money before the current financial crisis) that naysayers are likely to have particular difficulty convincing anyone to beware of lurking danger (e.g., Churchill languishing in the political wilderness for most of the 1930s). This raises several obvious follow-ups: who are these pessimists looking ahead to darker days, what causes them to perceive problems when others do not,

and how can they increase their chances of convincing others that there are problems to be addressed? Which bring us to the final question.

- *How important is a sense of efficacy for dissent?* Recall that Olson (1965) posited two reasons why individuals making rational choices will tend not to pursue the collective interest. The first, that individuals lack an incentive to work for the collective interest (given that they will benefit to the same extent whether they contribute or not) can, I have suggested, be overcome if people identify with the collective. However, the second reason, that individuals lack a sense of efficacy (given that they should assume that others are unlikely to act in the collective interest), remains a potential issue. At the very least, this analysis suggests that would-be dissenters need to assume that other group members are identified with the group and would be willing to act in the collective interest if they could be persuaded that change is necessary. More generally, the normative conflict model's assumption that group members are influenced by perceived costs and benefits means that the potential benefits ascribed to dissent are likely to be weighted in some way in terms of their probability. Even if a strong identifier thinks that a particular change would increase the group's utility a hundredfold, if she also assumes that the probability of the group making that change is near zero, she may be unwilling to expend the social capital involved in agitating for change.

Postscript

We will likely never know what motivated the lone protester in Tiananmen Square. Despite the logic of the above argument regarding the necessity of a sense of efficacy for dissent, I wonder how much efficacy he can possibility have felt facing that long, impenetrable line of tanks. Beyond explanation in terms of social dilemmas, levels of identity, normative conflict and cost/benefit considerations, what this man highlights above all is that dissent is often a courageous act. No manner how right or wrong-headed, rational or irrational it may be, dissent takes guts. If you want to call it human spirit, that's fine with me.

Notes

1. More specifically, I propose that decisions regarding whether or not to express dissent can pose group members with an unusual type of public goods dilemma or social fence (see Kollock, 1998).

2. Just as theories regarding personal-level identity posit that these sorts of evaluations can arise from discrepancies between current/actual selves and chronically held ideal/ought/future selves (e.g., Higgins, 1996), at a group level they may stem from discrepancies between actual group behaviour (descriptive norms) and normative conceptions of ideal group behaviour (prescriptive norms; Cialdini, Reno & Kallgren, 1990; Hogg & Abrams, 1988; Kallgren, Reno & Cialdini, 2000 – see Crane & Platow, in press). However, I would go a step further and suggest that the standards against which current behaviour is typically judged can themselves come under scrutiny and be deemed suboptimal (Packer, 2008).
3. Thanks to Wil Cunningham for posing this question.

References

Abrams, D., Marques, J.M., Bown, N. & Henson, M. (2000). Pro-norm and anti-norm deviance within and between groups. *Journal of Personality and Social Psychology, 78*, 906–12.

Abrams, D., Wetherell, M., Cochrane, S., Hogg, M.A. & Turner, J.C. (1990). Knowing what to think by knowing who you are: self-categorization and the nature of norm formation, conformity and group polarization. *British Journal of Social Psychology, 29*, 97–119.

Aronson, E. (1999). The power of self-persuasion. *American Psychologist, 54*, 875–84.

Bond, R. & Smith, P.B. (1996). Culture and conformity: a meta-analysis of studies using Asch's (1952b, 1956) line judgment task. *Psychological Bulletin, 119*, 111–37.

Brewer, M.B. & Gardner, W. (1996). Who is this 'we'? Levels of collective identity and self-representations. *Journal of Personality and Social Psychology, 71*, 83–93.

Brewer, M.B. & Kramer, R.M. (1986). Choice behavior in social dilemmas: effects of social identity, group size, and decision framing. *Journal of Personality and Social Psychology, 50*, 543–9.

Brodbeck, F.C., Kerschriter, R., Mojzisch, A., Frey, D. & Schulz-Hardt, S. (2002). The dissemination of critical, unshared information in decision-making groups: the effects of pre-discussion dissent. *European Journal of Social Psychology, 32*, 35–56.

Cialdini, R.B., Reno, R.R. & Kallgren, C.A. (1990). A focus theory of normative conduct: recycling the concept of norms to reduce littering in public places. *Journal of Personality and Social Psychology, 58*, 1015–26.

Crane, M.R. & Platow, M.J. (in press). Deviance as adherence to injunctive group norms: the overlooked role of social identification in deviance. *British Journal of Social Psychology.*

De Cremer, D. & Van Vugt, M. (1999). Social identification effects in social dilemmas: a transformation of motives. *European Journal of Social Psychology, 29*, 871–93.

De Dreu, C.K.W. (2002). Team innovation and team effectiveness: the importance of minority dissent and reflexivity. *European Journal of Work and Organizational Psychology, 11*, 285–98.

De Dreu, C.K.W. (2006). Rational self-interest and other orientation in organizational behavior: a critical appraisal and extension of Meglio & Korsgaard (2004). *Journal of Applied Psychology, 91*, 1245–52.

Ellemers, N., Spears, R. & Doosje, B. (1997). Sticking together or falling apart: in-group identification as a psychological determinant of group commitment versus individual mobility. *Journal of Personality and Social Psychology, 72*, 617–26.

Emerson, R.M. (1954). Deviation and rejection: an experimental replication. *American Sociological Review, 19*, 688–93.

Fishbein, M. & Ajzen, I. (1975). *Belief, Attitude, Intention, and Behavior: An Introduction to Theory and Research.* Reading, MA: Addison-Wesley.

Goffman, E. (1963). *Stigma: Notes on the Management of Spoiled Identity.* New York: Simon & Schuster.

Hardin, G.J. (1968). The tragedy of the commons. *Science, 162*, 1243–8.

Haslam, S.A., Ryan, M.K., Postmes, T., Spears, R., Jetten, J. & Webley, P. (2006). Sticking to our guns: social identity as a basis for the maintenance of commitment to faltering organizational projects. *Journal of Organizational Behavior, 27*, 607–28.

Higgins, E.T. (1996). The 'self digest': self-knowledge serving self-regulatory functions. *Journal of Personality and Social Psychology, 71*, 1062–83.

Hirschman, A.O. (1970). *Exit, Voice and Loyalty: Responses to a Decline in Firms, Organizations, and States.* Cambridge, MA: Harvard University Press.

Hirschman, A.O. (1974). 'Exit, voice, and loyalty': further reflections and a survey of recent contributions. *Social Science Information, 13*, 7–26.

Hogg, M.A. & Abrams, D. (1988). *Social Identifications: A Social Psychology of Intergroup Relations and Group Processes.* New York: Routledge.

Hogg, M.A. & Turner, J.C. (1987). Social identity and conformity: a theory of referent informational influence. In: W. Doise & S. Moscovici (eds), *Current Issues in European Social Psychology* (Vol. 2, pp. 139–82). Cambridge: Cambridge University Press.

Hollander, E.P. (1958). Conformity, status, and idiosyncrasy credit. *Psychological Review, 65*, 117–27.

Hornsey, M.J. (2005). Why being right is not enough: predicting defensiveness in the face of group criticism. *European Review of Social Psychology, 16*, 301–34.

Hornsey, M.J. (2006). Ingroup critics and their influence on groups. In T. Postmes & J. Jetten (eds), *Individuality and the Group: Advances in Social Identity* (pp. 74–91). Thousand Oaks, CA: Sage.

Hornsey, M.J., Grice, T., Jetten, J., Paulsen, N. & Callan, V. (2007). Group-directed criticisms and recommendations for change: why newcomers arouse more resistance than old-timers. *Personality and Social Psychology Bulletin, 33*, 1036–48.

Hornsey, M.J., Jetten, J, McAuliffe, B.J. & Hogg, M.A. (2006). The impact of individualist and collectivist group norms on evaluations of dissenting group members. *Journal of Experimental and Social Psychology, 42*, 57–68.

Hornsey, M.J., Smith, J.R. & Begg, D. (2007). Effects of norms among those with moral conviction: counter-conformity emerges on intentions but not behaviors. *Social Influence, 2*, 244–68.

Hovland, C.I., Janis, I.L. & Kelley, H.H. (1953). *Communication and Persuasion.* New Haven: Yale University Press.

Janis, I.L. (1972). *Victims of Groupthink: A Psychological Study of Foreign-Policy Decisions and Fiascos.* Oxford: Houghton Mifflin.

Jetten, J., Branscombe, N.R., Spears, R. & McKimmie, B.M. (2003). Predicting the paths of peripherals: the interaction of identification and future possibilities. *Personality and Social Psychology Bulletin, 29*, 130–40.

Jetten, J., Hornsey, M.J. & Adarves-Yorno, I. (2006). When group members admit to being conformist: the role of relative intragroup status in conformity self-reports. *Personality and Social Psychology Bulletin, 32*, 162–73.

Jetten, J., Hornsey, M.J., Spears, R., Haslam, S.A. & Cowell, E. (2010). Rule transgressions in groups: the conditional nature of newcomers' willingness to confront deviance. *European Journal of Social Psychology, 40*, 338–48.

Jetten, J., Postmes, T. & McAuliffe, B.J. (2002). 'We're all individuals': group norms of individualism and collectivism, levels of identification and identity threat. *European Journal of Social Psychology, 32*, 189–207.

Johnson, K.L. & White, K.M. (2003). Binge-drinking: a test of the role of group norms in the theory of planned behavior. *Psychology and Health, 18*, 63–77.

Kallgren, C.A., Reno, R.R. & Cialdini, R.B. (2000). A focus theory of normative conduct: when norms do and do not affect behavior. *Personality and Social Psychology Bulletin, 26*, 1002–12.

Kelley, H.H. & Shapiro, M.M. (1954). An experiment on conformity to group norms where conformity is detrimental to group achievement. *American Sociological Review, 19*, 667–77.

Kelman, H.C. (1958). Compliance, identification and internalization: three processes of attitude change. *Journal of Conflict Resolution, 2*, 51–60.

Kollock, P. (1998). Social dilemmas: the anatomy of cooperation. *Annual Review of Sociology, 24*, 183–214.

Kramer, R.M. & Brewer, M.B. (1984). Effects of group identity on resource use in a simulated commons dilemma. *Journal of Personality and Social Psychology, 46*, 1044–57.

Levine, J.M. & Kerr, N.L. (2007). Inclusion and exclusion: implications for group processes. In A.E. Kruglanski & E.T. Higgins (eds), *Social Psychology: Handbook of Basic Principles* (2nd edition, pp. 759–84). New York: Guilford.

Louis, W.R., Taylor, D.M. & Douglas, R.L. (2005). Normative influence and rational conflict decisions: group norms and cost-benefit analyses for intergroup behaviour. *Group Processes and Intergroup Relations, 8*, 355–74.

Louis, W.R., Taylor, D.M. & Neil, T. (2004). Cost-benefit analyses for your group and yourself: the rationality of decision-making in conflict. *International Journal of Conflict Management, 15*, 110–43.

Marques, J.M. & Yzerbyt, V.Y. (1988). The black sheep effect: judgmental extremity towards ingroup members in inter- and intra-group situations. *European Journal of Social Psychology, 18*, 287–92.

Merton, R.K. (1968). *Social Theory and Social Structure.* New York: Free Press.

Messick, D.M. & Brewer, M.B. (1983). Solving social dilemmas: a review. In L. Wheeler & P. Shaver (eds), *Review of Personality and Social Psychology* (Vol. 4, pp. 11–44). Beverly Hills, CA: Sage.

Moscovici, S. & Faucheux, C. (1972). Social influence, conformity bias, and the study of active minorities. In L. Berkowitz (ed.), *Advances in Experimental Social Psychology* (pp. 149–202). New York: Academic Press.

Nail, P.R., Macdonald, G. & Levy, D.A. (2000). Proposal of a four-dimensional model of social response. *Psychological Bulletin, 126*, 454–70.

Noelle-Neumann, E. (1974). The spiral of silence: a theory of public opinion. *Journal of Communication, 24*, 43–51.

Olson, M. *The Logic of Collective Action: Public Goods and the Theory of Groups.* Cambridge, MA: Harvard University Press.

Packer, D.J. (2008). On being both with us and against us: a normative conflict model of dissent in social groups. *Personality and Social Psychology Review, 12*, 50–73.

Packer, D.J. (2009). Avoiding groupthink: whereas weakly identified members remain silent, strongly identified members dissent about collective problems. *Psychological Science, 20*, 546–8.

Packer, D.J. (in press). The interactive influence of conscientiousness and openness to experience on dissent. *Social Influence.*

Packer, D.J. & Chasteen, A.L. (2010). Loyal deviance: testing the normative conflict model of dissent in social groups. *Personality and Social Psychology Bulletin, 36*, 5–18.

Packer, D.J., Fujita, K. & Chasteen, A.L. (2010). Construal-Level Effects on Opinion Expression within Groups. Manuscript in preparation.

Postmes, T., Spears, R. & Cihangir, S. (2001). Quality of decision making and group norms. *Journal of Personality and Social Psychology, 80*, 918–30.

Prislin, R. & Christensen, P.N. (2005). The effects of social change within a group on membership preferences: to leave or not to leave. *Personality and Social Psychology Bulletin, 31*, 595–609.

Prochaska, J.O., DiClemente, C.C. & Norcross, J.C. (1992). In search of how people change: applications to addictive behaviors. *American Psychologist, 47*, 1102–14.

Reicher, S. (2004). The context of social identity: domination, resistance, and change. *Political Psychology, 25*, 921–45.

Roccas, S., Klar, Y. & Liviatan, I. (2006). The paradox of group-based guilt: modes of national identification, conflict vehemence, and reactions to the ingroup's moral violations. *Journal of Personality and Social Psychology, 91*, 698–711.

Sani, F. & Reicher, S. (1999). Identity, argument and schism: two longitudinal studies of the split in the Church of England over the ordination of women to the priesthood. *Group Processes and Intergroup Relations, 2*, 279–300.

Sani, F. & Todman, J. (2002). Should we stay or should we go? A social psychological model of schisms in groups. *Personality and Social Psychological Bulletin, 28*, 1647–55.

Schachter, S. (1951). Deviation, rejection, and communication. *Journal of Abnormal and Social Psychology, 46*, 190–207.

Sedikides, C. (1993). Assessment, enhancement, and verification determinants of the self-evaluation process. *Journal of Personality and Social Psychology, 65*, 317–38.

Sedikides, C. & Strube, M.J. (1995). The multiply motivated self. *Personality and Social Psychology Bulletin, 21*, 1330–5.

Spears, R., Doosje, B. & Ellemers, N. (1997). Self-stereotyping in the face of threats to group status and distinctiveness: the role of group identification. *Personality and Social Psychology Bulletin, 23*, 538–53.

Spreitzer, G.M. & Sonenshein, S. (2004). Toward the construct definition of positive deviance. *American Behavioral Scientist, 47*, 828–47.

Sunstein, C.R. (2006). *Infotopia: How Many Minds Produce Knowledge.* New York: Oxford University Press.

Tajfel, H. (1981). *Human Groups and Social Categories.* Cambridge: Cambridge University Press.

Tajfel, H. & Turner, J. (1979). An integrative theory of intergroup conflict. In W.G. Austin & S. Worchel (eds), *The Social Psychology of Intergroup Relations* (pp. 33–48). Monterey, CA: Brooks-Cole.

Tata, J., Anthony, T., Lin, H., Newman, B., Tang, S., Millson, M. & Sivakumar, K. (1996). Proportionate group size and rejection of the deviate: a meta-analytic integration. *Journal of Social Behavior and Personality, 11*, 739–52.

Taylor, C. (1989). *Sources of the Self: The Making of the Modern Identity.* Cambridge, MA: Harvard University Press.

Taylor, D.M. & McKirnan, D.J. (1984). Theoretical contributions: a five-stage model of intergroup relations. *British Journal of Social Psychology, 23*, 291–300.

Terry, D.J. & Hogg, M.A. (1996). Group norms and the attitude-behavior relationship: a role for group identification. *Personality and Social Psychological Bulletin, 22*, 776–95.

Terry, D.J., Hogg, M.A. & White, K.M. (1999). The theory of planned behavior: self-identity, social identity and group norms. *British Journal of Social Psychology, 38*, 225–44.

Turner, J.C. (1982). Towards a cognitive redefinition of the social group. In H. Tajfel (ed.), *Social Identity and Intergroup Relations* (pp. 15–40). Cambridge: Cambridge University Press.

Turner, J.C., Hogg, M.A., Oakes, P.J., Reicher, S.D. & Wetherell, M.S. (1987). *Rediscovering the Social Group: A Self-Categorization Theory.* Oxford: Blackwell.

Turner, J.C., Oakes, P.J., Haslam, S.A. & McGarty, C. (1994). Self and collective: cognition and the social context. *Personality and Social Psychology Bulletin, 20*, 454–63.

Van Vugt, M. & Hart, C.M. (2004). Social identity as social glue: the origins of group loyalty. *Journal of Personality and Social Psychology, 86*, 585–98.

Warren, D.E. (2003). Constructive and destructive deviance in organizations. *Academy of Management Review, 28*, 622–32.

Wheeler, S.C., DeMarree, K.G. & Petty, R.E. (2007). Understanding the role of the self in prime-to-behavior effects: the active self account. *Personality and Social Psychology Review, 11*, 234–61.

White, K.M., Hogg, M.A. & Terry, D.J. (2002). Improving attitude-behavior correspondence through exposure to normative support from a salient ingroup. *Basic and Applied Social Psychology, 24*, 91–103.

Wood, W., Quinn, J. & Kashy, D. (2002). Habits in everyday life: thought, emotion, and action. *Journal of Personality and Social Psychology, 83*, 1281–97.

Zdaniuk, B. & Levine, J.M. (2001). Group loyalty: impact of members' identification and contributions. *Journal of Experimental Social Psychology, 37*, 502–9.

16

Integrating Models of Whistle-Blowing and Wrongdoing

A Proposal for a New Research Agenda

Janet P. Near and Marcia P. Miceli

Recent corporate scandals raise the inevitable question as to how wrongdoing in organisations can be prevented and corrected. Whistle-blowing represents one possible mechanism for correcting wrongdoing and it has received quite a lot of research attention. But the question as to how wrongdoing can be prevented in the first place is deeper and the answers are less well understood. In this chapter we develop an integrated model of wrongdoing and whistle-blowing. We draw from complementary literatures that have traditionally focused on answering two different questions and have developed relatively independent of one another: (a) what conditions cause employees to engage in wrongdoing themselves or ignore it when their colleagues commit wrongdoing; and (b) what conditions cause some employees to blow the whistle when they observe wrongdoing, rather than ignoring it?

Our purpose is to develop propositions that will provide a research agenda for more comprehensive empirical investigation of how the pressures to engage in wrongdoing lead directly and indirectly to the pressures on organisation members not to blow the whistle when they observe the wrongdoing. In short, we believe that pressures encouraging wrongdoing and discouraging whistle-blowing are opposite sides of the same coin and that research focused on examining both parts of the process would lead to fuller understanding than earlier research based largely on predicting wrongdoing and whistle-blowing as separate entities.

We begin by explaining the key definitions that have been developed in each of these literatures: what constitutes organisational wrongdoing and

Rebels in Groups: Dissent, Deviance, Difference and Defiance Jolanda Jetten and Matthew J. Hornsey

deviance, and what constitutes whistle-blowing in the workplace. After reviewing these definitions, we review theoretical frameworks for predicting both the labelling of wrongdoing and subsequent whistle-blowing and develop propositions based both on these theories and past empirical results in this area. Next we summarise a model describing conditions under which normalisation of wrongdoing arises in the work group or organisation and develop propositions predicting the influence of these conditions on whistle-blowing. Finally, we develop propositions about the moderating influence of normalisation of wrongdoing on predictors of whistle-blowing.

Definitions

Whistle-blowing has been defined in various ways (Miceli, Near & Dworkin, 2008), but one definition is believed to have been most widely used (King, 1997) in social science research: 'Whistle-blowers are organization members (including former members and job applicants) who disclose illegal, immoral, or illegitimate practices (including omissions) under the control of their employers, to persons or organizations who may be able to effect action' (Near & Miceli, 1985: 4). Examples include white-collar crime (e.g., Sutherland, 1949), corporate criminal behaviours (e.g., Clinard, 1979) and illegal corporate behaviour (e.g., Baucus & Baucus, 1997; Baucus & Near, 1991), but the definition includes wrongdoing other than crime. For example, an employee may consider acts such as managers treating employees arbitrarily or grossly misallocating resources (e.g., spending millions of dollars on replacement parts for obsolete machinery) to be immoral or illegitimate, even if not illegal in a given society.

Defining something as wrongful only if it violates organisational norms is inadequate, because organisational norms sometimes support fraud, pollution or other bad behaviour that conflicts with norms of other groups, such as society (Spreitzer & Sonenshein, 2004; Warren, 2003). But declaring behaviour wrong only if it violates the laws or norms of the society in which the organisation operates also is inadequate, because that standard fails to consider behaviour more universally thought of as immoral (e.g., apartheid), or conflicts between nations' laws (Warren, 2003). Warren proposed using the construct of 'hypernorms' (Donaldson & Dunfee, 1994, 1999), which are 'globally held beliefs and values . . .(that). . .encompass basic principles needed for the development and survival of essential background institutions in societies' (Warren, 2003: 628). They are more broadly shared than societal norms, which may tolerate practices that are unacceptable globally. Many instances of whistle-blowing should be viewed as 'beneficial deviant behaviour' in response to norms of silence about wrongdoing, in the sense that the behaviour may deviate from organisational norms but be beneficial for persons inside or outside the organisation (such as consumers or ethnic minorities), or for society or the world in the longer run (e.g., by improving the environment) (Warren, 2003). This idea of conflict between hypernorms and organisational norms highlights one difficulty that organisation members often have when trying to decide whether organisational actions they have just witnessed were actually wrong, a point to which we will return.

The definition of whistle-blowing cited above provides that, if wrongdoing occurs but the observer does not label it as illegal, immoral or illegitimate, then whistle-blowing by definition cannot occur. Labelling an act of commission or omission as wrongdoing is thus a prerequisite to whistle-blowing. But there has been little research on how people come to label wrongdoing. We define 'labelling' to be the designation by an observer of questionable activity as wrongful within the organisation. For example, someone subjected to racist comments or jokes may not define them as a hostile racist environment (that is illegal, immoral or illegitimate), until a certain level of frequency is reached or until the organisation has provided information suggesting that such behaviour is contrary to organisation standards or goals. The individual may or may not internalise the standards. This definition differs from the focus of labelling theory, widely applied within the discipline of sociology to refer to the 'labelling' of an individual as a deviant (Merton, 1957); here our focus is on the labelling of the behaviour as wrongdoing, not the individual who behaves in a wrongful way.

We now turn our attention to predicting and understanding what causes labelling of organisational activities as wrongdoing and, for those people who have labelled something that they have observed to be wrongdoing, whether they will blow the whistle on it. Perceiving wrongdoing is a necessary but not sufficient condition for whistle-blowing; therefore, it is important to understand why two organisational members observing the same activities or omissions may not label them as wrong. If truly wrongful activities are not observed or are mislabelled, observers will not act on them, and one critical mechanism for correcting organisational wrongdoing does not operate.

We begin with models that examine antecedents of whistle-blowing, in which early decisions are concerned with observation and interpretation of questionable activity or omissions, which could then result in labelling the situation as wrongdoing. We next offer potential improvements to those models by integrating ideas from a model that explores how wrongdoing becomes normal and routine in organisations. We believe that a comprehensive model of whistle-blowing needs to include all of these variables, to facilitate the design of better research that may explain more variance in whistle-blowing.

Propositions Based on a Model of Whistle-Blowing

Why do employees who observe wrongdoing decide to blow the whistle? Two models of whistle-blowing predictors, the prosocial organisational behaviour (POB) model (Dozier & Miceli, 1985) and the social information processing (SIP) model (Gundlach, Douglas & Martinko, 2003), have evolved. In the POB model, whistle-blowing is viewed as prosocial organisational behaviour (Brief & Motowidlo, 1986; Dozier & Miceli, 1985), in which the potential whistle-blower moves through up to three phases in the whistle-blowing process: observing questionable activity and labelling it as wrongdoing; reacting to the wrongdoing, for example by becoming demoralised; and deciding what action to take in response. In this section of the chapter, we focus primarily on the first phase; research testing other phases of the POB model is discussed elsewhere (e.g., Miceli, Near & Dworkin, 2008).

The authors of the SIP model (Gundlach, Douglas & Martinko, 2003, p. 111) 'assume that the whistle-blowing decision process begins with the potential whistle-blower's awareness of a wrongdoing act and that the level of perceived importance of this act is sufficient to motivate the individual to engage in more systematic cognitive processes (e.g., attributional processes)'. Consequently, the SIP model does not address how observers come to label or react to the activity as wrongdoing to begin with, but focuses on the phase of deciding whether to blow the whistle. Thus, we do not discuss it further, because our concern here is primarily with the initial phase of observing wrongdoing and its effect on subsequent phases of response.

We begin by discussing previous research results pertinent to the first phase of the POB model and develop propositions for an integrated model based on these results. Predictors of observing and labelling of wrongdoing are listed in Figure 16.1 and predictors of whistle-blowing in Figure 16.2.

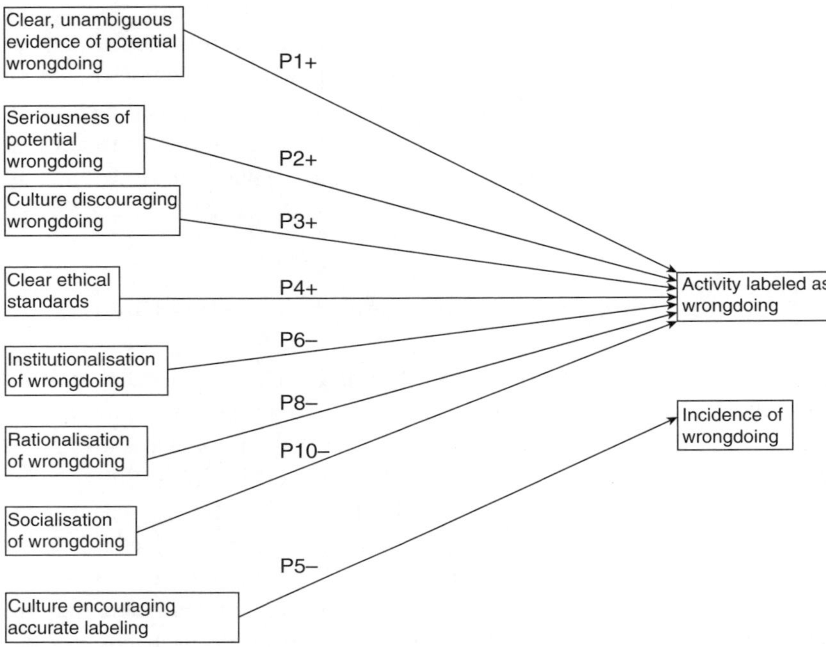

Figure 16.1 Predictors of labelling of whether wrongdoing occurred, among organisation members

POB model propositions related to the labelling of wrongdoing

In phase 1 of the POB model, employees who have encountered questionable activity decide whether it constitutes wrongdoing and whether someone is obliged to act on it (Dozier & Miceli, 1985; Miceli, Near & Dworkin, 2008). We propose that one step in this phase is labelling. Some employees remain silent in the face of clear evidence of organisational problems (e.g., Morrison & Milliken, 2003), but others are silent because they are not sure that a problem really exists – or at least, not a problem of such magnitude as to warrant mentioning. Employees may find the situation ambiguous, and need to discuss it with co-workers or search for confirming evidence before deciding that it constitutes wrongdoing.

A critical research question, then, is what factors cause organisational members to label questionable activity as wrongdoing? We have found little theory or empirical research on this question, with one important exception: sexual harassment research. Two categories of situational variables

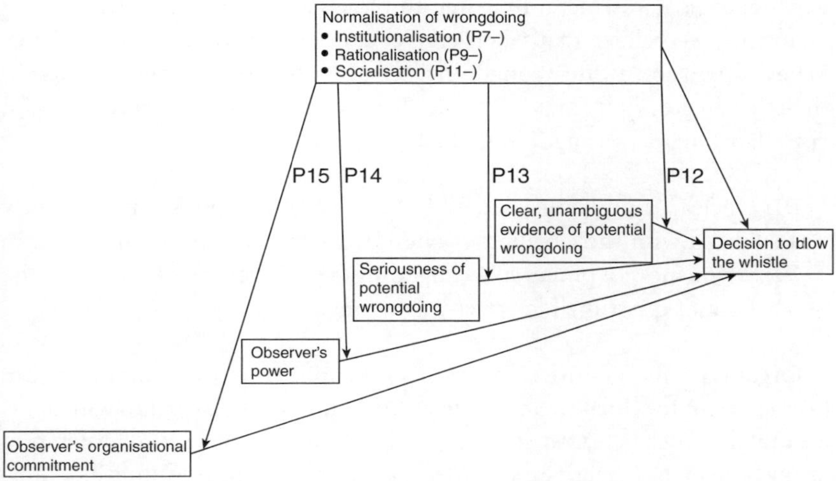

Figure 16.2 Predictors of whistle-blowing and moderated effects among organisation members who observed wrongdoing

seem to be consistent predictors of the labelling of actions as harassing: characteristics of the wrongdoing itself, specifically its explicitness and seriousness; and characteristics of the organisation, especially the organisational climate either supporting or discouraging wrongdoing.

The sexual harassment literature implies that indicators of clear evidence and seriousness may reduce ambiguity for organisation members trying to determine whether some action is harassing. More explicit and extreme sexual harassment – where evidence was clear – was found to be related to the perception that harassment occurred (e.g., Fitzgerald & Ormerod, 1991; Gutek, Morasch & Cohen, 1983). Frequency of sexually harassing behaviour increased perceived offensiveness, a mediating variable which directly predicted reporting of the harassment (e.g., Bergman *et al.*, 2002). Frequency and length of sexual harassment was related to whether respondents labelled their experiences as either felonious (more serious) or non-felonious (less serious) sexual harassment; organisational level of the harasser was also related to whether respondents labelled their experiences as non-felonious harassment (Lee, Heilmann & Near, 2004). Experimental studies indicated that the wrongdoer's intent and the harm they cause a target influence the target's judgements of prejudice and discrimination (Swim *et al.*, 2003). These findings suggest that both the quality of evidence and the perceived seriousness of the actions cause employees to label their experience as harassing, a first step to blowing the whistle. Extrapolating from this, we believe that when employees observe some event that they believe might constitute wrongdoing (termed 'potential wrongdoing here'), then they make a judgement as to whether they believe it is actually wrongful (i.e., 'labelling' as wrongdoing). Thus:

P1: Unclear, ambiguous evidence of potential wrongdoing is negatively associated with the labelling of questionable activity as wrongdoing.
P2: Seriousness of potential wrongdoing is positively associated with the labelling of questionable activity as wrongdoing.

Organisational culture is a second potential situational influence on: (a) the extent to which wrongdoing occurs, and (b) the extent to which it is accurately labelled as wrongdoing. For example, a culture tolerating cronyism (or non-merit-based selection) in hiring, promotions and sub-contracting causes hiring of less qualified candidates. Ultimately this leads to poor individual and organisational performance, as seen in the case of the US Federal Emergency Management Agency's mismanagement of the Hurricane Katrina disaster (e.g., Committee on Government Reform – Minority Staff, 2006).

Such a culture may also influence employees to label cronyism inappropriately as acceptable, which may in turn perpetuate or increase its practice. This notion will be explored in greater depth later in this chapter. Thus, the culture may directly or indirectly (through its influence on labelling) increase actual wrongdoing, though the reported perceived wrongdoing may appear lower because of mislabelling.

A fair and ethical culture, which helps employees recognise what is viewed as globally wrongful and objectionable (i.e., activity that violates hyper-norms), may reduce the *actual* incidence of wrongdoing. In this case, the labelling would be more accurate. For example, as the culture is improved, employees become more aware of harassment and label it more correctly, which may lead to a short-term *apparent* increase in perceived harassment, but ultimately employees will be less likely to engage in *actual* wrongdoing. Less fair and ethical cultures can be reinforced by passive behaviour: as suggested by a model of sexual harassment (Bowes-Sperry & O'Leary-Kelly, 2005), non-intervention by others who have observed but have not been personally targeted contributes to ambiguity and, over time, creates an environment that encourages more actual wrongdoing. A less fair and ethical culture could encourage employees to redefine actually bad behaviour as acceptable, labelling may be less accurate, and thus the long-term *apparent* incidence of wrongdoing may seem low, even though actual wrongdoing is high.

Studies generally have not focused on the role of culture in labelling accuracy – i.e., to compare organisation members' judgements about the wrongdoing to some other, valid measure of the extent to which the focal activity is wrongful – but instead on culture's effects on wrongdoing. There is research suggesting that organisational culture can ultimately reduce the incidence of wrongdoing, perhaps through encouraging better labelling (to the extent that the study measures of perceived wrongdoing reflect accurate labelling). Survey data from more than 1700 members of four business firms showed organisation members' perceptions that the organisation was generally fair and followed through on its ethics programme were associated with their *not* observing wrongdoing (Treviño & Weaver, 2001). Similarly, an organisational culture discouraging sexual harassment was related to lower levels of perceived occurrence of harassment (e.g., Bergman *et al.*, 2002; Fitzgerald *et al.*, 1997).

There is further evidence that other aspects of culture (or climate or work environment) can influence the incidence of actual wrongdoing. Sexual harassment against women was more prevalent when: (a) organisations tolerated it (Fitzgerald, Drasgow & Magley, 1999); (b) the working environment created an overall 'gender context' in which supervisors were male, more men than women worked there, and the job types represented were normally held by men (Fitzgerald, Drasgow & Magley, 1999); (c) where women performed stereotypically male tasks (Coles, 1986; Gutek, 1985; Gutek & Dunwoody, 1987; Koss *et al.*, 1994; LaFontain & Tredeau, 1986; U.S. Merit Systems Protection Board, 1988); and (d) when women worked in a mostly male environment (Coles, 1986; Ellis, Barak & Pinto, 1991; Fain & Anderton, 1987; Fitzgerald et al., 1997; Fritz, 1989; Gutek & Cohen, 1987; Martin, 1984; Schneider, 1982) or worked with male supervisors (Gutek, 1985). This may have occurred because male domination, particularly in leadership ranks, may produce an organisational culture that is more tolerant of sexual harassment than does more gender-balanced or female-dominated leadership.

These results suggest that various measures of organisational culture, indicating tolerance for wrongdoing, influence whether organisation members label actions as wrongful. And, a culture where wrongdoing is tolerated or commonplace encourages further wrongdoing. In contrast, an organisational culture that explicitly supports a credible ethics programme provides clearer guidelines as to what actions should be labelled as wrong and ultimately discourages wrongdoing.

P3: An organisational culture encouraging wrongdoing is negatively associated with the labelling of questionable activity as wrongdoing.
P4: Unclear organisational ethical standards are negatively associated with the labelling of questionable activity as wrongdoing.
P5: In the long run, organisations in which the culture encourages accurate labelling of wrongdoing have lower incidence of wrongdoing than do other organisations.

Propositions Based on a Model of Normalisation of Wrongdoing

As noted above, research on whistle-blowing generally has not considered the role of labelling in the early stages of the POB model. A recently proposed model of normalisation of wrongdoing (Ashforth & Anand, 2003) provides a potential theoretical basis for understanding not only how wrongdoing comes to be accurately labelled as such, but also the factors that influence whether it recurs or becomes more widespread. This model elucidates the process by which wrongdoing becomes routine in an organisation; under such conditions we propose that – when confronted with an instance of wrongdoing – most organisation members do not label it as wrong and, by definition, cannot then blow the whistle. By better understanding how and why wrongdoing becomes routine in organisations, we gain a stronger basis for understanding why organisation members label some actions as wrong and ultimately decide to blow the whistle on those actions.

Firms that engage in illegal corporate behaviour are likely to do so again (Baucus & Baucus, 1997), perhaps because wrongdoing has become so accepted that it seems 'normal'. The model of 'normalisation of collective corruption' explains how it can 'become *normalized*, that is, become embedded in organizational structures and processes, internalized by organizational members as permissible and even desirable behavior, and passed on to successive generations of members' (Ashforth & Anand, 2003: 3). In this model, corruption is defined as 'misuse of an organizational position or authority for personal or organization (or subunit) gain, where misuse in turn refers to departures from accepted societal norms' (Anand, Ashforth & Joshi, 2004: 40). We believe that normalisation processes could apply to other types of wrongdoing as well, so we will use the term 'wrongdoing' rather than 'corruption' in our discussion.

Normalisation of wrongdoing is important in understanding whistle-blowing, because it can have two key effects. First, it can cause observers of wrongdoing to not even 'see' the wrongdoing when it occurs, when they have become accustomed to the organisation's norms of what constitutes wrongdoing. Second, normalisation can cause a 'self-censoring' effect: observers of wrongdoing do not take action, because they believe that doing so would be useless or dangerous. That is, they believe that the organisation will do nothing to rectify the wrongdoing or that it will take punitive actions against people who blow the whistle.

Ashforth and Anand argued that normalisation of wrongdoing is more likely when the wrongdoing is collective rather than individual. When multiple wrongdoers are involved, a normative culture evolves where individual members become habituated to wrongdoing and desensitised to it such that they do not see it (Ashforth & Anand, 2003). Further, we interpret this model to mean that involvement by multiple people encourages, but does not automatically lead to, normalisation of wrongdoing. Instead, the model proposes that normalisation encourages inappropriate acceptance of wrongdoing through three interdependent mechanisms: institutionalisation, rationalisation and socialisation (Ashforth & Anand, 2003).

A review of these three normalisation mechanisms shows that they may cause employees to perceive that wrongdoing has not occurred, when in fact it has. The labelling of organisational actions as wrongdoing is a necessary but not sufficient pre-condition to whistle-blowing. Once an action has been observed and labelled as wrongdoing, then the organisation member must decide whether to blow the whistle. We believe that mechanisms of institutionalisation of wrongdoing, rationalisation of wrongdoing and socialisation for wrongdoing affect both phases of the POB model, and we develop propositions for empirical research derived by integrating mechanisms from the normalisation of wrongdoing model into the POB model. To our knowledge, no research testing these notions has been completed to date.

Propositions related to institutionalisation of wrongdoing

Institutionalisation begins when the collective corruption is initiated; as it continues, it is embedded in organisational memory, structures and processes, and is routinised in ongoing operations, becoming accepted as part of the normative culture of the organisation, adapted to and enacted 'mindlessly' (Anand, Ashforth & Joshi, 2004). Thus, the key difference between an institutionalised culture and a culture that is less ingrained is that employees adapt their behaviour to the institutionalised culture without awareness that they are doing so. Institutionalisation is more likely when organisation norms against the deviant (wrongful) behaviour are not strong, rigid, obvious or unambiguous (Robinson & Kraatz, 1998). One effect of institutionalisation is that organisation members do not even see the wrongdoing, and hence don't correctly label it, because they have become inured to it through institutionalisation; in whistle-blowing field studies, some of the respondents who claim not to have observed wrongdoing instead may have observed wrongdoing (Miceli & Near, 1992; Near & Miceli, 1996) but didn't label it as such because of institutionalisation. In terms of the POB model, they incorrectly judge that the focal activity is not wrongful and that no one has the responsibility to stop it. Therefore:

P6: Institutionalisation of wrongdoing is negatively associated with the labelling of questionable activity as wrongdoing.

As noted above, a second impact of institutionalisation is that it can cause some organisation members to self-censor. For example, 'minding your own business', working to a narrow or rigid job description, and not challenging management even to offer a positive new idea, may be part of the culture. Observers of wrongdoing in such groups or organisations believe that even strong evidence would be ignored when presented to management, reducing the expected benefits of whistle-blowing. Therefore, they take no action.

P7: Institutionalisation of wrongdoing is negatively associated with whistle-blowing.

Propositions related to rationalisation of wrongdoing

The second normalisation mechanism ensues when organisation members do not see themselves as wrongdoers because they use *rationalisation* mechanisms (Anand, Ashforth & Joshi, 2004; Ashforth & Anand, 2003), 'mental strategies that allow employees (and others around them) to view their corrupt acts as justified. Employees may collectively use rationalizations to neutralize any regrets or negative feelings that emanate from their participation in unethical acts' (Anand, Ashforth & Joshi, 2004: 39). For example, members may persuade themselves that: (a) the action is not really illegal, and therefore not wrong; (b) no one is injured by their actions; or (c) if injury occurred, the victim deserved it for some reason. Members may also: (d) refocus attention towards their good works and away from their misdeeds through 'instrumental rationalizing' (e.g., Robinson & Kraatz, 1998); or (e) use a 'metaphor of the ledger' (Ashforth & Anand, 2003), meaning that they deserve to engage in this 'minor' deviant behaviour because of accrued credits for good behaviour. In terms of the POB model, the first and the second of these rationalisations suggest that the action was not really wrong or important enough to oblige anyone to act, and therefore no labelling of the wrongdoing ensued; all other rationalisations could apply to the second phase, whistle-blowing, because organisation members recognise that wrongdoing has occurred, but believe that they personally need not act on it.

Rationalisation enables observers as well as those involved directly in the wrongdoing to believe that the activity does not constitute wrongdoing. As with institutionalisation, perhaps some 'non-observers' in prior whistle-blowing studies did witness wrongdoing but rationalised it away or engaged in denial (e.g., Wasti & Cortina, 2002), labelling it as acceptable. Thus:

> **P8**: Rationalisation of wrongdoing is negatively associated with the labelling of questionable activity as wrongdoing.

Some rationalisations could affect the likelihood of whistle-blowing where the observer believes wrongdoing has occurred. For example, co-workers who heard a sales executive brag about padding expense accounts may rationalise it away because they think that the sales executive is a high performer or that the infraction was minor relative to this performance. This rationalisation of wrongdoing reduces the chance of whistle-blowing. Therefore:

> **P9**: Rationalisation of wrongdoing is negatively associated with whistle-blowing.

Propositions related to socialisation for wrongdoing

Socialisation for wrongdoing is a normalisation mechanism through which 'newcomers entering corrupt units are induced to accept and practice the ongoing unethical acts and their associated rationalizations' (Anand, Ashforth & Joshi, 2004: 39). It is more likely in organisations in which there is high turnover, weak culture and socialisation practices that do not prescribe clear norms against wrongdoing (Robinson & Kraatz, 1998). Four socialisation methods come into play (Ashforth & Anand, 2003): (a) *co-optation* by rewards linked to their collusion with the wrongdoing, sometimes with rewards that are so subtle that they are not even aware that their initial attitudes towards the wrongdoing have changed; (b) *incrementalism*, in which they escalate commitment to the wrongdoing over time; (c) *compromise* by selecting the wrongdoing that represents the 'lesser of two evils' (e.g., when polluters rationalise that their actions allow the firm to survive, thereby preventing layoffs of employees); or (d) *coercion* into wrongdoing through fear.

Survey findings from organisational members imply that socialisation influences their view of organisational wrongdoing. For example, some studies (e.g., Miceli & Near, 1992; Near *et al.*, 2004) show that the majority of inactive observers said either that nothing could or that nothing would be done about the wrongdoing they witnessed. Presumably they reached these judgements after witnessing organisational reactions to past wrongdoing or by being advised by co-workers about such organisational reactions, suggesting that incrementalism or compromise reflective of socialisation processes occurred. Or perhaps organisation members were co-opted or coerced into wrongdoing in the past, leading them to believe that the organisation will not do anything about the current problem.

In part this belief may reflect a correct assessment of the likely organisational response, and results from the employee's past socialisation. Alternatively it may reflect the organisation members' rationalisation of their own inaction even though the organisation would actually be responsive. Many organisations seem not to react to allegations of wrongdoing, despite the reality that at least some of these allegations must be valid. Empirical evidence (reviewed by Miceli & Near, 2005) indicates that many complaint recipients (e.g., human resources staff, managers, ombudspersons, inspectors general) believe a large proportion of complaints have no merit (in some cases as high as 90 per cent), and obviously they would not take action under these circumstances. Similarly, in the United States the Sarbanes–Oxley Act of 2002 was passed to encourage whistle-blowing on financial wrongdoing, through prohibition of retaliation. But most cases alleging retaliation in violation of Sarbanes–Oxley have been dismissed (Day, 2006), indicating again that whistle-blowers are often not supported. Certainly some complaints are not valid, but other evidence (reviewed by Miceli & Near, 2005) implies that many complaints have merit – probably more of them than these statistics suggest. Similarly, in most cases of serious organisational wrongdoing reported in media outlets, the journalist describes at least one futile internal whistle-blowing attempt, e.g., in the Challenger disaster or in the Enron case. Obviously, since whistle-blowing failed to stop the wrongdoing, at least one authority within the organisation judged the whistle-blowing to be without merit; ultimately, more objective third parties judged the whistle-blowing as valid.

These findings suggest that complaint recipients often do not correct wrongdoing. So at least some observers of wrongdoing witness little or no response from their organisations to earlier wrongdoing, and are thereby socialised to accept wrongdoing and not blow the whistle. For this reason, we propose:

> **P10**: Socialisation for wrongdoing is negatively associated with the labelling of questionable activity as wrongdoing.
> **P11**: Socialisation for wrongdoing is negatively associated with whistle-blowing.

Additional Proposed Interrelationships between Normalisation Processes and Some Variables Found Previously to Predict Whistle-blowing

Interrelationships among predictors from the models: main effects

The POB model of whistle-blowing and the normalisation of wrongdoing model were developed for two essentially different purposes: the former focuses on predicting labelling of wrongdoing and whistle-blowing while the latter focuses on describing mechanisms of institutionalisation, rationalisation and socialisation by which wrongdoing becomes normalised or routine in a work group or an organisation. We propose that two of the variables explored in research on labelling of wrongdoing and whistle-blowing appear to be interrelated with the normalisation processes: organisational culture or climate supporting wrongdoing, and lack of clear ethics programmes for discouraging wrongdoing. It is difficult to envision an organisation whose culture supported wrongdoing where the mechanisms of institutionalisation, rationalisation and socialisation around wrongdoing were not present; similarly, it seems unlikely that an organisation with a clear and strongly enforced ethics programme would engender normalisation of wrongdoing. The only situation we could think of where culture might support wrongdoing without the presence of institutionalisation, rationalisation and socialisation is represented by young organisations where wrongdoing is not actively discouraged but also is not yet taken for granted. For example, in young organisations without clear norms wrongdoing might slip by unnoticed but – when pointed out to managers – elicit effective change programmes to take active steps to discourage wrongdoing. For example, some organisations clearly define wrongdoing and role requirements for observing and reporting wrongdoing. They orient and train new organisation members in ethical values and hold them accountable for the means they use to achieve goals, not just the goals. Future research could examine the extent to which normalisation accounts for the effects of culture, climate and ethics programmes.

Interrelationships among predictors from the models: proposed interaction effects

Four variables that have been shown to have fairly consistent effects in whistle-blowing research refer to characteristics of the whistle-blowing situation or of the individual whistle-blower: clarity of evidence of wrongdoing; the seriousness of wrongdoing; the power of the potential whistle-blower in the organisation; and the level of commitment of the potential whistle-blower to the organisation. But a substantial amount of variance is unexplained. We propose that the normalisation variables partially moderate the effects of these variables on both labelling and whistle-blowing, as shown in Figure 16.2. Research is needed to test all remaining propositions.

Empirical research cited previously (for P1 and P2) has shown that where the evidence of wrongdoing is unclear or the wrongdoing is not serious, few observers blow the whistle. We propose that where (a) the evidence of wrongdoing is clear, (b) the wrongdoing is serious and (c) there is no normalisation of wrongdoing because the organisational culture discourages wrongdoing, then many observers would blow the whistle. But where normalisation of wrongdoing is strong in an organisation, (a) and (b) have much weaker effects, because of the pressures created by the organisational culture of wrongdoing. Thus:

P12: Normalisation of wrongdoing moderates the association of clarity of evidence of wrongdoing with whistle-blowing.

P13: Normalisation of wrongdoing moderates the association of seriousness of wrongdoing with whistle-blowing.

In the same way, we propose that the potential whistle-blower's individual characteristics will interact with normalisation of wrongdoing in the organisation to predict whether that individual will actually blow the whistle. Previous research (reviewed in Miceli, Near & Dworkin, 2008) has shown that where observers of wrongdoing have low power they are less likely to blow the whistle. We propose that the effects of power on whistle-blowing would be greater where the organisation has *not* normalised wrongdoing. Where confronted with a culture in which wrongdoing has been normalised, we would expect that the whistle-blower's power would not matter much.

P14: Normalisation of wrongdoing moderates the association of the power of the wrongdoing observer with whistle-blowing.

Finally, we propose that organisational commitment also interacts with the effects of normalisation of wrongdoing on whistle-blowing. If wrongdoing is not normalised, high commitment to the organisation may encourage whistle-blowing, because the wrongdoing is clearly at odds with business as usual. In all other situations, we would expect less whistle-blowing. Where the wrongdoing has become normalised, organisational members who are highly committed to that organisation will self-censor. They can anticipate no success in getting change made, and expect high costs of action (Morrison & Milliken, 2000), such as the time involved in making the case, the risk of becoming a pariah in the eyes of co-workers (Milliken, Morrison & Hewlin, 2003), or the fear of isolation from others (Noelle-Neumann, 1993), which would be very painful for those with substantial investment in an organisation. The less committed observer is unlikely to blow the whistle regardless of normalisation, since they may not see themselves as responsible for action, have little reason or motivation to take on risks, and can easily withdraw instead.

This phenomenon has also been discussed in terms of social identification theory (Hornsey, 2006) and a normative conflict model (Packer, 2008). Specifically, we would expect that employees with low identification with the organisation are less likely to blow the whistle; in Packer's terms they are 'disengaged' or 'strategically conforming'; if they choose to deviate from the organisation's norms, they will do so passively. In contrast, individuals who identify strongly with the organisation and also find that the norms conflict with their sense of what should be correct will feel compelled to dissent (Packer, 2008). If they are members of the ingroup, have longer tenure in the organisation and frame their dissent carefully in language that shows concern for the welfare of the organisation itself (rather than criticism in terms that an outsider might use) they are more likely to be successful in gaining commitment to reform from others (Hornsey, 2006). It is interesting that the few empirical studies of the conditions under which whistle-blowing is most successful (Miceli, Near & Dworkin, 2008) have largely supported these theoretical arguments.

> **P15**: Normalisation of wrongdoing moderates the association of the organisational commitment of the wrongdoing observer with whistle-blowing.

Conclusions

We integrated the POB model of whistle-blowing with the normalisation of collective corruption model, to produce a series of propositions. Although the normalisation model was originally developed to predict collective corruption, we argue that its basic tenets can be extended to most cases of collective organisational wrongdoing (not just corruption) and that most cases of organisational wrongdoing are collective, including those cases that involve collusion as well as active involvement of the group in the wrongdoing. Adding the construct of normalisation of wrongdoing (and its mechanisms of institutionalisation, rationalisation and socialisation for wrongdoing) to whistle-blowing models provides a stronger theoretical framework for predicting when organisation members are likely to label organisation activities as wrongdoing, and then to blow the whistle. The resulting integrated model provides a clearer depiction of the mechanisms by which characteristics of the wrongdoing, the organisation and whistle-blower influence the outcomes of labelling of wrongdoing, followed by the subsequent act of whistle-blowing.

A second benefit of this integration is that it provides explicit recognition of group effects on the individual decision to blow the whistle – since normalisation of wrongdoing is by definition a group variable. In contrast, many of the variables in whistle-blowing models would be measured at the individual level. The integrated model proposes that the individual's decision to blow the whistle was a function of her or his assessment that wrongdoing has occurred, which in turn was affected by both individual assessments of what has transpired and group influences on those assessments. As a result, any test of our proposed model would require a method that would simultaneously account for individual-level and group-level effects (e.g., a hierarchical linear modelling technique).

The refined and extended model provides a series of propositions which, if tested, should explain greater variance in whistle-blowing behaviour than has been possible in the past. And predicting whistle-blowing behaviour is important. Whistle-blowing represents the best and sometimes only solution to many cases of organisational wrongdoing (Miethe, 1999), so we need to better understand what conditions encourage whistle-blowing. From a theory standpoint, we will gain a greater appreciation of organisational processes of compliance and dissent. From a policy standpoint, we may gain a greater understanding of how to root out corporate wrongdoing more effectively, at a time when the costs of such wrongdoing harm societies in countless ways. We hope the extended model of whistle-blowing provided here informs future research, consistent with the goal of enhancing our understanding of the processes of labelling organisational actions as wrongdoing and subsequently blowing the whistle on those actions.

Acknowledgements

Support for this work was provided in part by the Dale M. Coleman Chair in the Kelley School of Business at Indiana University, and by the Dean's Leadership Fund of the McDonough School of Business, Mr Carlos M. de la Cruz for the de la Cruz Family Fellowship, and the Graduate School of Arts and Sciences, at Georgetown University.

References

Anand, V., Ashforth, B.E. & Joshi, M. (2004). Business as usual: the acceptance and perpetuation of corruption in organizations. *Academy of Management Executive, 18* (2), 39–53.

Ashforth, B.E. & Anand, V. (2003). The normalization of corruption in organizations. In R.M. Kramer & B.M. Staw (eds), *Research in Organizational Behavior* (Vol. 25, pp. 1–52). Amsterdam: Elsevier.

Baucus, M.S. & Baucus, D.A. (1997). Paying the piper: an empirical examination of longer-term financial consequences of illegal corporate behavior. *Academy of Management Journal, 40*, 129–51.

Baucus, M.S. & Near, J.P. (1991). Can illegal corporate behavior be predicted? An event history analysis. *Academy of Management Journal, 34*, 9–36.

Bergman, M.E., Langhout, R.D., Cortina, L.M. & Fitzgerald, L.F. (2002). The (un) reasonableness of reporting: antecedents and consequences of reporting sexual harassment. *Journal of Applied Psychology, 87* (2), 230–42.

Bowes-Sperry, L. & O'Leary-Kelly, A.M. (2005). To act or not to act: the dilemma faced by sexual harassment observers. *Academy of Management Review, 30* (2), 288–306.

Brief, A.P. & Motowidlo, S. (1986). Prosocial organizational behaviors. *Academy of Management Review, 4*, 710–25.

Clinard, M.B. (1979). *Illegal Corporate Behavior.* Washington, DC: National Institute of Law Enforcement and Criminal Justice.

Coles, F.S. (1986). Forced to quit: sexual harassment complaints and agency response. *Sex Roles, 14*, 81–95.

Committee on Government Reform – Minority Staff. (2006). Waste, fraud, and abuse in Hurricane Katrina contracts. In S.I. Division (ed.) (Vol. August) Washington, DC: US House of Representatives.

Day, K. (2006, April 23). Whistle-stop campaigns: some firms are trying to limit protection of workers who expose wrongdoing. *Washington Post*, pp. F01, F09.

Donaldson, T. & Dunfee, T. (1994). Toward a unified conception of business ethics: integrative social contracts theory. *Academy of Management Review, 19*, 252–84.

Donaldson, T. & Dunfee, T. (1999). *The Ties that Bind* (Vol. 19). Boston: Harvard University Press.

Dozier, J.B. & Miceli, M.P. (1985). Potential predictors of whistle-blowing: a prosocial behavior perspective. *Academy of Management Review, 10* (4), 823–36.

Ellis, S., Barak, A. & Pinto, A. (1991). Moderating effects of personal cognitions on experienced and perceived sexual harassment of women at the workplace. *Journal of Applied Social Psychology, 21* (16), 1320–37.

Fain, T.C. & Anderton, D.L. (1987). Sexual harassment: organizational context and diffuse status. *Sex Roles, 17*, 291–311.

Fitzgerald, L.F., Drasgow, F., Hulin, C.L., Gelfand, M.J. & Magley, V.J. (1997). The antecedents and consequences of sexual harassment in organizations: a test of an integrated model. *Journal of Applied Psychology, 82* (4), 578–89.

Fitzgerald, L.F., Drasgow, F. & Magley, V.J. (1999). Sexual harassment in the Armed Forces: a test of an integrated model. *Military Psychology, 11* (3), 329–43.

Fitzgerald, L.F. & Ormerod, A.J. (1991). Perceptions of sexual harassment: the influence of gender and academic context. *Psychology of Women Quarterly, 15* (2), 281–94.

Fritz, N. R. (1989). Sexual harassment and the working woman. *Personnel, 66*, 4–8.

Gundlach, M.J., Douglas, S.C. & Martinko, M.J. (2003). The decision to blow the whistle: a social information processing framework. *Academy of Management Review, 28* (1), 107–23.

Gutek, B.A. (1985). *Sex and the Workplace: The Impact of Sexual Behavior and Harassment on Women, Men, and Organizations.* San Francisco: Jossey-Bass.

Gutek, B.A. & Cohen, A.G. (1987). Sex ratios, sex-role spillover, and sex at work: a comparison of men's and women's experiences. *Human Relations, 40*, 97–115.

Gutek, B.A. & Dunwoody, V. (1987). Understanding sex in the workplace. In A. Stromberg, L. Larwood & B.A. Gutek (eds), *Women and Work: An Annual Review* (Vol. 2). Newbury Park: Sage.

Gutek, B.A., Morasch, B. & Cohen, A.G. (1983). Interpreting social-sexual behavior in a work setting. *Journal of Vocational Behavior, 22*, 30–48.

Hornsey, M.J. (2006). Ingroup critics and their influence on groups. In T. Postmes & J. Jetten (eds), *Individuality and the Group: Advances in Social Identity* (pp. 74–91). London: Sage.

King, G., III (1997). The effects of interpersonal closeness and issue seriousness on blowing the whistle. *Journal of Business Communication, 34* (4), 419–36.

Koss, M.P., Goodman, L.A., Browne, A., Fitzgerald, L.F., Keita, G.P. & Russo, N.F. (1994). *No Safe Haven: Male Violence against Women at Home, at Work, and in the Community.* Washington, DC: American Psychological Association.

LaFontain, E. & Tredeau, L. (1986). The frequency, sources, and correlates of sexual harassment among women in traditional male occupations. *Sex Roles, 15*, 433–42.

Lee, J.-Y., Heilmann, S.G. & Near, J.P. (2004). Blowing the whistle on sexual harassment: test of a model of predictors and outcomes. *Human Relations, 57* (3), 297–322.

Martin, S.E. (1984). Sexual harassment: the link between gender stratification, sexuality, and women's economic status. In J. Freeman (ed.), *Women: A Feminist Perspective* (pp. 54–69). Palo Alto, CA: Mayfield.

Merton, R.K. (1957). *Social Theory and Social Structure* (2nd edition). Glencoe: IL: Free Press.

Miceli, M.P. & Near, J.P. (1992). *Blowing the Whistle: The Organizational and Legal Implications for Companies and Employees.* New York: Lexington.

Miceli, M.P. & Near, J.P. (2005). Whistle-blowing and positive psychology. In R. Giacalone, C.L. Jurkiewicz & C. Dunn (eds), *Positive Psychology in Business Ethics and Corporate Responsibility* (Vol. 1, pp. 85–102). Greenwich, CT: Information Age Publishing.

Miceli, M.P., Near, J.P. & Dworkin, T.M. (2008). *Whistle-Blowing in Organizations.* New York: Routledge.

Miethe, T.D. (1999). *Whistle-Blowing at Work: Tough Choices in Exposing Fraud, Waste and Abuse on the Job* (2nd edition). Boulder, CO: Westview Press.

Milliken, F.J., Morrison, E.W. & Hewlin, P.F. (2003). An exploratory study of employee silence: issues that employees don't communicate upward and why. *Journal of Management Studies, 40* (6), 1453–76.

Morrison, E.W. & Milliken, F.J. (2000). Organizational silence: a barrier to change and development in a pluralistic world. *Academy of Management Review, 25* (4), 706–25.

Morrison, E.W. & Milliken, F.J. (2003). Guest editors' introduction: speaking up, remaining silent: the dynamics of voice and silence in organizations. *Journal of Management Studies, 40,* 1353–8.

Near, J.P. & Miceli, M.P. (1985). Organizational dissidence: the case of whistle-blowing. *Journal of Business Ethics, 4* (1), 1–16.

Near, J.P. & Miceli, M.P. (1996). Whistle-blowing: myth and reality. *Journal of Management, 22* (3), 507–26.

Near, J.P., Van Scotter, J.R., Rehg, M.T. & Miceli, M.P. (2004). Does type of wrongdoing affect the whistle-blowing process? *Business Ethics Quarterly, 14* (2), 219–42.

Noelle-Neumann, E. (1993). *The Spiral of Silence: Public Opinion – Our Social Skin* (2nd edition). Chicago: University of Chicago Press.

Packer, D.J. (2008). On being both with us and against us: a normative conflict model of dissent in social groups. *Personality and Social Psychology Review, 12,* 50–78.

Robinson, S.L. & Kraatz, M.S. (1998). Constructing the reality of normative behavior: the use of neutralization strategies by organizational deviants. In R.W. Griffin, A. O'Leary-Kelly & J.M. Collins (eds), *Dysfunctional Behavior in Organizations* (Vol. 1, pp. 203–20). Stamford, CT: JAI Press.

Schneider, B.E. (1982). Consciousness about sexual harassment among heterosexual and lesbian women workers. *Journal of Social Issues, 38,* 75–98.

Spreitzer, G.M. & Sonenshein, S. (2004). Toward the construct definition of positive deviance. *American Behavioral Scientist, 47* (6), 828–47.

Sutherland, E.H. (1949). *White Collar Crime.* New York: Holt, Rinehart & Winston.

Swim, J.K., Scott, E.D., Sechrist, G.B., Campbell, B. & Stangor, C. (2003). The role of intent and harm in judgments of prejudice and discrimination. *Journal of Personality and Social Psychology, 84* (5), 944–59.

Treviño, L.K. & Weaver, G.R. (2001). Organizational justice and ethics program 'follow-through': influences on employees' harmful and helpful behavior. *Business Ethics Quarterly, 11* (4), 651–71.

U.S. Merit Systems Protection Board. (1988). *Sexual Harassment in the Federal Government: An Update.* Washington, DC: U.S. Government Printing Office.

Warren, D.E. (2003). Constructive and destructive deviance in organizations. *Academy of Management Review, 28* (4), 622–32.

Wasti, S.A. & Cortina, L.M. (2002). Coping in context: sociocultural determinants of responses to sexual harassment. *Journal of Personality and Social Psychology, 83* (2), 394.

17

Beyond Conformity

Revisiting Classic Studies and Exploring the Dynamics of Resistance

S. Alexander Haslam and Stephen D. Reicher

Conformity Bias in Social Psychology

As they open up their textbooks for the first time, students who are new to social psychology are confronted with a bleak and depressing picture of human nature. Humans, they are repeatedly told, are victims of their own mental processes, and are prisoners of cognitive forces that not only limit their thinking but also have tragic consequences for society. They soon read that people will go against the seemingly undeniable evidence of their own senses if this seems to be at odds with the judgements of their peers (Asch, 1955); that people will obey the most destructive orders of those in authority (Milgram, 1963, 1974); and that people conform willingly to the demands of oppressive roles that they are assigned within a given social system (Haney, Banks & Zimbardo, 1973).

Of these various demonstrations, it is the last that is often the most easily and frequently recalled. This is because it is based on exposure to Zimbardo and colleagues' Stanford Prison Experiment (SPE; Haney, Banks & Zimbardo, 1973) – a study that provides a particularly memorable 'journey into the heart and mind of darkness' (Zimbardo, 2007: xiiii). As every reader of this chapter will almost certainly know, the SPE assigned 24 young men to roles as prisoners and guards and placed them in a 'prison' that had been constructed in the basement of the Stanford University Psychology Department. Thereafter, they began what Zimbardo (2007: 39) describes as a rapid 'descent into hell'. After only a few days, the guards began subjecting the prisoners to extraordinary abuse and degradation. In turn, the prisoners

Rebels in Groups: Dissent, Deviance, Difference and Defiance Jolanda Jetten and Matthew J. Hornsey

conformed to their role as passive and compliant victims. Indeed, several began to show signs of serious psychopathology and so the study (which had been scheduled to last two weeks) had to be terminated after only six days. All this occurred despite the participants having been recruited for the study on the basis of their being representative of 'normal' college students (but see Carnahan & McFarland, 2007). In explaining these findings, Zimbardo makes much of this point, as well as of the unmediated emergence of these toxic behaviours.

> Participants had no prior training in how to play the randomly assigned roles. Each subject's prior societal learning of the meaning of prisons and the behavioural scripts associated with the oppositional roles of prisoner and guard was the sole source of guidance (2004: 39).

On this basis, the researchers advanced the view that acts of guard aggression were 'emitted simply as a "natural" consequence of being in the uniform of a "guard" and asserting the power inherent in that role' (Haney, Banks & Zimbardo, 1973, p. 62). Their depressing conclusion was that, far from being the product of human agency and choice, tyranny is the natural expression of a Luciferian psychology that we all share and whose clutches most of us are powerless to resist (Zimbardo, 2007). If decent, well-adjusted, well-educated young men can turn so easily into monsters, what hope is there for humanity at large?

This depression is echoed by journalists, social commentators and researchers in other disciplines who have taken the message of the SPE and other classic studies of social psychology very much to heart, and used them as a basis for making sense of the large number of atrocities, genocides and abuses that have blighted recent world history (e.g., see Browning, 1992; Stanley, 2008). Certainly, when one reflects on these events, it is not hard to see why one might be inclined to see them as grim manifestations of psychological processes that lead people naturally towards error, injustice and oppression.

Nevertheless, as Moscovici (1972; Moscovici & Faucheux, 1972) observed, this general tendency to focus on processes of conformity, obedience and repression whilst at the same time overlooking a range of countervailing processes, can be seen as a clear example of *conformity bias* in social psychology – that is, the discipline's tendency to generate theories and data that show only how the status quo is reproduced. As Moscovici and others (e.g., Tajfel, 1972; Turner, 1991, 2006) have remarked, this bias is problematic for a number of reasons. The first is that, by suggesting that social problems are the product of irresistible social psychological forces, the consumers of social psychological knowledge are encouraged to think that those problems are insurmountable. In line with the observations of Marx (1895), it is easy to see how such interpretations of the world can blind us to the task of understanding and explaining how it might be changed.

This, though, leads to a second point. The pessimism of conformity bias is profoundly ahistorical. The social world does not simply reproduce itself *ad nauseam*. On the contrary, it is prone to frequent, and often very dramatic, change. Indeed, the seeds of such change can be seen within all of the classic studies alluded to above. Thus while 65 per cent of the participants in Milgram's (1963) 'standard' obedience paradigm showed total obedience to the experimenter, 35 per cent did not. Moreover, recent evidence suggests that when the experimenter in this paradigm presents the instructions to administer shocks in the form of an order (saying 'you have no other choice, you *must* continue' rather than 'please continue') *all* participants display resistance (Burger, 2009). Likewise, although Asch's (1955) studies of line judgement are now typically understood as demonstrating the power of the peer group, Asch himself stressed that, despite all the pressure he could muster, most people did not conform (so that, on critical trials, 67 per cent of participants' responses were correct). And although approximately one-third of Zimbardo's guards responded enthusiastically to their role, the remaining two-thirds either tried to be fair or actually sided with the prisoners. Moreover, at some point in all these research programmes there was evidence of resistance that was both more substantial and more systematic. The simple fact, then, is that people do not appear to accede mechanically to the wishes of others.

This point can be reinforced by considering the most repressive sites of two of the most repressive regimes of recent history. Apartheid South Africa specially designed a prison on Robben Island in order to crush those who resisted the system. However, over time, the prison came to serve as a crucible for the liberation movement, for the development of liberation politics and for the creation of a 'government in waiting' (Buntman, 2003). As the most famous of the inmates observed, by the end: 'the inmates seemed to be running the prison not the authorities' (Mandela, 1994: 536).

More notoriously still, the Nazi regime set up a whole carceral universe of concentration camps and death camps in order to destroy those it considered foes. Yet even here, people resisted. As Langbein (1995) has documented, this took many forms including open revolts in Auschwitz,

Treblinka and Sobibor. Even here, at the limit of the human capacity for oppression, the voice of opposition was never entirely silenced. To cite David Rousset, himself an inmate, 'in all the cities of this strange universe, men resisted' (1965: 182–3; author's translation).

In light of suggestions that people tend only to 'go along' with the social systems in which they find themselves, what are we to make of this? More particularly, how can we explain people's propensity not only to challenge injustice but to transform whole societies in the process?

This is the central question that we address in this chapter (see also Haslam & Reicher, 2009). In attempting to do so, we draw on two central resources. The first is the range of ideas concerning the dynamics of resistance that are provided by social identity theory (SIT; Tajfel & Turner, 1979). The second is empirical evidence from an experimental case study that we conducted in order to provide an integrated test of SIT's key hypotheses – the BBC Prison Study (Reicher & Haslam, 2006a; see also Haslam & Reicher, 2005). Building on these resources, we also outline a more thoroughgoing model of large-scale social resistance. This incorporates three interrelated concepts that are central to the social identity literature: shared *social identity*; *cognitive alternatives*; and *leadership*. Putting these together, resistance is seen primarily as a process of *mobilising oppositional social identity* that provides group members with a basis for working together to challenge the perceived failings of a given social system.

In developing these ideas, and in keeping with the overall aims of this volume, our intention is to clarify why the topic of resistance needs to occupy a more prominent place in the research agenda of social psychology. At the same time, we aim to show how this agenda can itself be a vehicle for change and progress in the field as a whole. In particular, by taking us beyond the received wisdom of the discipline's classic studies, it invites us not only to theorise about change, but also to become participants in change ourselves.

Social Identity Theory as a Theory of Social Resistance

Although conformity bias can be identified in a great deal of the theorising that has dominated social psychology for the last half century, it is nevertheless the case that there are a number of theoretical traditions that have advanced an alternative view. Two that are particularly noteworthy are

Brehm's (1966) work on reactance and Moscovici's research into minority influence (e.g., Moscovici, Lage & Naffrechoux, 1969). Work on reactance points to the fact that people tend to resist attempts by others to influence them when this appears to compromise their sense of free will; work on minority influence demonstrates that minorities are able to stand up to, and change, the views of majorities when they consistently advance a different position. In relation to the present discussion, an interesting feature of the latter work was that it turned the conventional explanation of the Asch studies on its head. What is generally taken as conformity to the majority in these studies is in fact nothing of the sort. After all, the majority of people in society would not see lines of two very different lengths as the same. Rather, the studies show the power of an active and consistent minority in the experimental setting to change apparently stable perceptions. The findings are therefore testament to the fact that social influence is a force for change as much as for stability (see Moscovici, 1976; see also Monin & O'Connor, this volume).

This focus on change is equally central to the work of Henri Tajfel – who was, along with Moscovici, one of the twin pillars of an emergent 'European' social psychology in the 1970s. As Tajfel saw it:

> The crucial problem of social psychology, . . . is that of relations between Man and social change. . . [for] change is the most fundamental characteristic of the social environment, and, as such, is the most basic problem presented by this environment to the human organism (1978: 39).

Tajfel's most influential work – the development of social identity theory, on which he collaborated with John Turner – seeks to address this problem at the level of collective processes. Ironically, however, the theory is often represented in conformity bias terms. For many, it is about an inherent desire to see our group memberships positively and hence an inevitable tendency to debase other groups in comparison with our own. While Tajfel and Turner certainly do propose a desire for positive ingroup evaluation, they see this as a starting point – not the end point – of analysis. As social psychologists, their aim is to examine how such psychological tendencies operate in the social world. And the reality of our unequal world is that, much as people might desire to be seen positively, many (perhaps most) people belong to groups that are defined negatively: women in a sexist world; black people in a racist world; gay people in a homophobic world . . . the litany is sad and long. So the question is, what do people do about this?

When do they accept the status quo, when do they try to side-step it, and when do they confront it? The issue, for social identity theory, is *change*. And the core assumption is that change occurs when people embrace devalued group memberships and act together in order to challenge the status quo.

Whether or not people act collectively, as well as how they act in relation to the status quo, depends largely upon their perceptions of the nature of relations between the groups in a particular social system. Two factors are identified as being particularly important here: the system's perceived *permeability* and its perceived *security* (Tajfel, 1978; Tajfel & Turner, 1989).

Permeability relates to individuals' perceptions of the overall fluidity of group memberships with a given social system. If people embrace *social mobility beliefs* so that they see group memberships as fluid and as presenting no barrier to personal progress (i.e., so that group boundaries are seen as permeable and social mobility is seen as possible), then they are likely to try to improve their standing within that system by pursuing strategies of personal self-enhancement such as 'passing' into a more positively evaluated group.

However, if group boundaries are seen to be *im*permeable – so that, however hard the individual works, his or her group membership is inescapable – then this strategy makes much less sense. Under these circumstances, individuals are more likely to embrace *social change beliefs* which lead them to work with others to try to transform the system in some way.

Exactly what form this attempt at transformation takes is seen to depend upon the perceived *security* of intergroup relations within a given social system. This has two further components: perceived *legitimacy* and perceived *stability*. If people perceive group relations to be either fair or stable then the likelihood of their wanting to work together to bring about radical change to that system is low. Under these conditions, if they are unhappy with their group membership then social identity theory suggests that they are likely to adopt a strategy of *social creativity*. This will lead them to *redefine* group relations so that they are more advantageous to the ingroup – for example, by invoking comparisons with different outgroups, by reconstruing the meaning of the dimensions on which disadvantage is defined, or by defining the ingroup in terms of new dimensions on which it is not disadvantaged. However, although this strategy engages individuals as a group, like the strategy of individual mobility, it does not challenge the existing social system directly. As transformation goes, social creativity avoids unpleasant realities rather than confronting them.

In contrast, if, as well as being impermeable, relations between groups are seen to be *both* unfair (illegitimate) *and* liable to change (unstable), then those who are dissatisfied with their group membership are much more likely to embrace a strategy of *social competition* that leads them to directly challenge the superiority of relevant outgroups. Importantly too, the combination of the system's perceived impermeability and insecurity is likely to lead individuals to define themselves and other ingroup members in terms of a *shared social identity* – as 'us' (Tajfel, 1978). Rather than acting alone to address their grievances, they are therefore more likely to work together with fellow group members to try to transform the system to their advantage.

A key question here, though, is exactly what form this transformation takes – and indeed, *whether* it has an exact form. For in order for group members to work to right the perceived wrongs of a given social system, they need not only to have a sense that change is possible, but also to have a clear sense of *how* the system, and the outcomes it produces, might change in ways that will be to their advantage. In the terms suggested by Tajfel and Turner (1989: 45), 'the crucial factor . . . is whether *cognitive alternatives* to the actual outcome are available' (see also Reicher & Haslam, in press; Turner & Brown, 1978). In other words, in order for social change to be maximally effective, those who are participating in it need to have a shared understanding of what type of change they are trying to produce and what they need to do in order to produce it. In this regard, just as a shared sense of social identity turns a collection of individuals into a group (Turner, 1982), so a shared sense of cognitive alternatives turns a group that is ready to compete into a group that knows what it is competing for – turning its members from 'rebels without a clue' into 'rebels with a cause'.

Social Resistance under the Microscope: The BBC Prison Study

In the 30-year period since their original formulation by Tajfel and Turner 1979, a large body of experimental work has been conducted that provides strong support for these various predictions. In particular, it has been shown that collective protest depends upon disadvantaged group membership being seen both as illegitimate and as inescapable (e.g.,

Ellemers, 1993; Kelly & Breinlinger, 1996; Wright & Taylor, 1998; Wright, Taylor & Moghaddam, 1990). Studies of this form have been important in providing controlled tests of social identity theory's core hypotheses. They have allowed researchers to demonstrate causal links between relevant independent variables (e.g., status, permeability, legitimacy) and individuals' willingness to engage in particular forms of behaviour (e.g., compliance, dissent). At the same time, though, the analysis of social behaviour that they provide tends to be relatively two-dimensional or 'flat' rather than multidimensional and 'lived' (Haslam & Reicher, 2006a). For example, experimental studies of the factors that lead to collective protest tend to look at the impact of particular variables in isolation and involve non-interacting participants (Haslam & McGarty, 2001). Also, despite looking at patterns of change over time (e.g., in participants' willingness to endorse particular strategies of self-enhancement), they rarely offer diachronic examination of what actually happens *between* given measurement points (Levine, 2003). For both reasons, then, although resistance and social change are core concerns for social identity theorists, the unfolding process of change itself is rarely under the experimental microscope (see Jetten, Iyer, Hutchison & Hornsey, this volume, for a similar point).

Yet, alongside this experimental work, processes of resistance *have* been the explicit focus of number of field studies. For example, Reicher's (1996) study of the 'Battle of Westminster' looked at the way in which a crowd of student protestors collectively defied the police after they had been united around a shared oppositional identity as a result of hostile police action that treated all protestors alike (see also Stott *et al.*, 2007; Stott, Hutchison & Drury, 2001). Along related lines, Cocking and Drury (2004) explored the way in which collective self-efficacy – grounded in a sense of shared social identity that was built up through participation in acts of resistance – underpinned environmental protestors' willingness to persevere with disruptive action designed to halt the construction of a major road (see also Drury & Reicher, 1999).

Like experimental work, field studies of this form point both to the reality of collective resistance and to its grounding in an emergent sense of shared social identity (see also Kelly & Breinlinger, 1996; Simon & Klandermans, 2001). However, while they have the advantage of exploring these processes as they develop over time, they provide no control over the variables in which researchers are interested and have limited capacity to measure key constructs *in situ* (for obvious reasons). For this reason, the causal and predictive status of relevant variables is hard to establish. Moreover, it is clear that, despite emerging from the same theoretical stable, field research into resistance and change has a different emphasis to that which emerges from the laboratory. Specifically, while experimental work tends to focus on the causal impact of social-structural variables such as permeability and legitimacy on individuals (and treats those variables as stable and non-negotiable), field research tends to emphasise the emergent character of such variables and their impact on *shared* psychological experience (e.g., a sense of collective empowerment and common purpose).

Although social identity theorising is supported by both experimental and field research, we have therefore argued that there is much to be gained from research which attempts to bring these two traditions together – providing *both* quantitative and qualitative analysis and attempting to marry the benefits of experimental manipulation and measurement with those of fine-grained analysis of unfolding group dynamics. On the one hand, this provides an opportunity to assess the compatibility of (and potentially integrate) the various insights that these distinct traditions provide. On the other, it also allows us to identify (and potentially fill in) some of the gaps (or blind spots) that exist in the space between the two approaches.

It was with these goals in mind that we were motivated to design and conduct a large-scale study in collaboration with the British Broadcasting Corporation in 2001 – the BBC Prison Study (BPS; Reicher and Haslam 2006b; for full details and resources see also www.bbcprisonstudy.org). This took the form of an experimental case study that was designed to test and explore the key hypotheses advanced by social identity theory – specifically as they relate to the dynamics of oppression and resistance. Importantly, the study did this by revisiting the paradigm of the prison with a view to pitting the analysis that social identity theory provides against that advanced by Zimbardo's SPE. Our key questions were: (a) whether oppression would be a product of unquestioning conformity to role or else of active processes of social identification; and (b) whether social identification might also be a basis for resistance and, if so, how this might emerge.

In the study 15 participants were randomly assigned to groups as either guards or prisoners and their behaviour was studied closely over a period of eight days. This involved systematic observation and measurement using psychometric and physiological instruments as well as filming (with key events subsequently edited into four one-hour documentaries that were broadcast on the BBC in 2002).

In contrast to the SPE, a key feature of the study's design was that it also incorporated a series of planned interventions. In line with social identity theory, these involved the manipulation of three factors: (a) the permeability of group boundaries; (b) the legitimacy of intergroup relations; and (c) participants' awareness of cognitive alternatives to the status quo. More specifically, on Day 1 of the study participants were led to believe that the boundaries between high- and low-status groups were permeable and that – subject to appropriate conduct – it was possible to be promoted from prisoner to guard. Following the principles outlined in the previous section, it was expected that prisoners would pursue a strategy of individual mobility and attempt to enhance their status by working individually to gain favour with the guards and prove themselves worthy of promotion. However, on Day 3, opportunities for promotion were ruled out (i.e., group boundaries were made impermeable). This was expected to increase prisoners' sense of shared social identity and encourage them to develop a more collective response to their situation. Finally, on Day 5 a trade union leader was introduced as a new prisoner in the expectation that he would propose an alternative vision of existing conditions within the prison. Specifically, it was anticipated that he would encourage the prisoners to redefine their current situation as illegitimate and unstable (i.e., providing a set of cognitive and practical alternatives that would lead them to see their status position as insecure; Tajfel & Turner 1979), and unite them around a collective identity and a plan for social change.

Broadly speaking, the findings of the study provided support for these various predictions. Most obviously, this was apparent in the fact that while the prisoners largely complied with the guards and the strictures of the prison system in the study's early days, they became increasingly unwilling to do so as the study progressed. Indeed, they started to engage in increasingly audacious acts of resistance. On Day 6 of the study these culminated in an organised breakout by the prisoners in one cell. This ultimately led them to take over the guards' quarters and bring their regime to an end. Indeed, just as the SPE exceeded Zimbardo's expectations in demonstrating the capacity of groups in authority to brutalise and oppress those in their charge, so the BPS surpassed our expectations in demonstrating the power of subjugated groups to defy and resist those in authority.

Because it is so clearly central to the purposes of this volume, it is worth looking more closely at the unfolding sequence of events that took the participants to this point. Here we want to focus on three key dynamics: (a) the increasing willingness of the prisoners to challenge the guards' authority; (b) the increasing reluctance of the guards to act as a group to uphold that authority; and (c) the role that emergent *leadership* (or lack thereof) played in taking the groups down these paths.

Mounting resistance: Strength through shared social identity

As the foregoing summary suggests, the behaviour of prisoners in the BPS was highly consistent with predictions, but very different from that observed in the SPE. From the outset the prisoners were unhappy with their low status – objecting in particular to their cramped living space, restricted movement, poor quality food and lack of privileges such as the right to hot drinks and cigarettes. However, when the boundary between guard and prisoner groups was permeable, the prisoners adopted individual strategies for dealing with the guards and with these privations. Some were hostile, some adopted a stance of detached indifference, and some worked hard to improve their situation in the hope of gaining promotion. Thus, while discontent was rife, social identification was low (as confirmed by psychometric testing) and there was an absence of any organised resistance.

However, once promotion was ruled out, it was apparent that the prisoners' orientation towards the guards, their regime and each other changed dramatically. In part, this was an anticipated consequence of the fact that the barrier to promotion rendered group boundaries impermeable. At the same time, though, it was reinforced by the prisoners' sense that this barrier was unjustified and hence illegitimate. Indeed, although we had planned an independent manipulation of illegitimacy, it became apparent that none was actually needed. Now the prisoners clearly embraced a much stronger sense of shared social identity and, on this basis, their attitudes and behaviour became much more consensual (Haslam *et al.*, 1998). Moreover, a key feature of this social identity was that its content was *oppositional*, in the sense that it defined the prisoners' ingroup ('us') as set against the now-rejected guard outgroup ('them'; see Figure 17.1).

In this situation, then, the prisoners recognised that the best way to improve their position was to work as a unit to challenge both the guards and the prison system. Accordingly, they plotted together about how best to achieve this. This was particularly apparent in one cell where, in the space of just a few hours, participants went from disagreeing over whether they wanted to become a guard or not, to agreeing on a scheme to kidnap one of their jailers. Collective action entirely usurped personal solutions to their predicament.

Figure 17.1 Resistance in the BBC Prison Study
Source: Reicher, S.D. and Haslam, S.A. (2006). Rethinking the psychology of tyranny: the BBC Prison Experiment. *British Journal of Social Psychology*, *45*, 1–40; for relevant video clips see www.bbcprisonstudy.org

Yielding to resistance: Weakness through fractured social identity

Faced with mounting resistance from the prisoners, it was clear that if the guards were going to hold on to their power this was going to require an equal concentration of collective will and endeavour. However, contrary to our expectations, this never materialised. A key reason for this was that, from the outset, several of the guards were uncomfortable with their role and expressed doubts about taking on the responsibility and demands it brought with it. Not all the guards shared these concerns. Nevertheless, as with the prisoners in the early days, the absence of a common orientation towards their predicament was associated with a failure to develop a strong sense of shared identity. This proved fatal to the guards' capacity to organise themselves and impose their authority on the system.

The key reason why the guards failed to form a shared social identity was primarily to do with the fact that they recognised that their role might involve the application of force. They also feared that power might make them tyrannical. This was a problem for those who held identities with more liberal values in their everyday lives. The problem was exacerbated by the filmed surveillance and the fact that their peers in these other groups would later be able to view them on television. If one had a cherished liberal identity, how could one risk being exposed as a tyrant?

Far from conforming blindly to the oppressive demands of their role, the upshot of these dynamics was that the guards were never able to develop a strong sense of shared social identity and consequently proved incapable of enacting their role with any force. They became increasingly disorganised and ineffective at maintaining order; increasingly depressed, stressed and burned-out (Haslam & Reicher, 2006b; Reicher & Haslam, 2006a). As long as the prisoners were not organised against them, this resulted in a weak system, but not yet a system in crisis. Yet once the prisoners began to unite in opposition, their days in power became inevitably numbered.

The decline and fall of the guards' regime raises important points about the dynamics of social change. Most importantly, change cannot be understood by reference to the subordinate or the dominant groups alone but must also take account of the balance of forces between them. Hence, although shared identity and coordinated collective action amongst the subordinated group may be necessary to achieve change, it is not sufficient. One also needs to take into account the ability of the dominant group to act in a coherent and efficient way to suppress change. Where the dominant group has both superior resources and the will to employ them, the most determined resistance may still fail, as is clear in the example of Nazi Germany (Levi, 1958/1987; Rees, 2005). However, where the dominant group is fractured, where its members work against each other and where they lack the will to deploy their repressive resources, then even relatively weak resistance can succeed. That is not only the case in our BBC study. A key moment in virtually every revolutionary process has been discord amongst the ruling classes. This is true of the French Revolution of 1789. It is also true of the Russian Revolution of 1917. By the time the Bolsheviks stormed the Winter Palace in October, the old regime was a mere husk. The key moment came earlier, in the so-called 'July days' when the Cossacks refused to charge against the massed workers. At that point the balance of power began to tilt decisively towards the revolutionaries (Trotsky, 1981).

We can take the argument about balance of power one step further. Subordinate and dominant groups rarely interact in isolation. Generally they exist in a wider world where both are trying to recruit third parties to their side (Saroyan, 2009; Subasic, Reynolds & Turner, 2008). The stance of these third parties can therefore be crucial to the success or failure of resistance. In the SPE, for instance, the experimenters worked hard to ensure that third parties would not intervene on the side of the prisoners. They did this both by hiding evidence of abuse from them and also by alternatively charming or challenging them into quiescence.

Zimbardo, for instance, relates how, on the parental visiting day, the prison was cleaned up and attractive young women were deliberately used to greet the visitors. When parents still voiced concern for the plight of the prisoners, Zimbardo intimated that this was an acknowledgement that their sons were weak and vulnerable. The parents (especially, it seems, the fathers) quickly backed off. This failure to intervene told the prisoners that they were completely alone, and this further contributed to their demoralisation.

In the BBC study, by contrast, the TV cameras ensured constant surveillance and this made the participants – particularly the guards – constantly aware of the sanctions that they might face from third parties. This time it was the dominant group that was demoralised and hence resistance that thrived. A full understanding of resistance, then, must include an analysis both of the existence of third-party structures (e.g. human rights legislation, war crimes tribunals) and of the tactics used both by dominant and subordinate groups to invoke or prevent the intervention of these third parties (see, for instance, McEvoy, McConnachie & Jamieson, 2007).

Organising resistance: The importance of leadership

As with much of the experimental research in this area, our analysis thus far can be seen to characterise the path of resistance as one whose course is a straightforward function of the relative strength of the social identities associated with dominant and subordinate groups. In these terms, resistance will be successful to the extent that those who participate in it are more identified with their group cause than their opponents are with theirs. While this should generally be true, when it comes to resistance, this analysis neglects the active *leadership* role that individual group members play both in cultivating a shared sense of social identity and in mobilising group members around a specific set of cognitive alternatives (Haslam, Reicher & Platow, 2010; Reicher, Haslam & Hopkins, 2005).

As the BBC study progressed it was clear (both observationally and from psychometric data; Haslam & Reicher, 2007a) that the dynamics described in the previous two sections were reinforced both by an emerging leadership among the prisoners and by a corresponding lack of leadership on the part of the guards. For the prisoners, leadership both helped to build a sense of shared identity but was also made possible by it; for the guards, failures of leadership undermined their sense of social identity but this lack of social identity in turn undermined the possibility of leadership.

Following the promotion, there were numerous occasions where the prisoners acted together and followed the lead of others, whereas individual guards all tried to exert leadership but were spurned or contradicted by their peers. Each time this happened, the prisoners prevailed over the guards, and the prisoners went away feeling exhilarated, empowered and more united while the guards were left bitter, dejected and more divided. However, perhaps the clearest example came after one of the prisoners stole a set of guard keys. After the guards failed to recover the keys, they agreed to meet with prisoner representatives in order to negotiate a handover. At this point the prisoners were able to develop and follow an orderly process in order to arrive at a consensus concerning who should represent them and what stance he should take. But there was no such agreement amongst the guards when they met. Consequently, in the negotiating meeting itself, the prisoner representative spoke confidently knowing that he spoke for all his group. The guards, by contrast, spoke across and against each other and quickly conceded ground.

The importance of the prisoners' leader, though, was not simply that he further empowered the group by ensuring coordination around an existing consensus. He also played a role in developing a new consensus. In particular, he helped his fellows imagine an alternative to the existing regime of inequality. That is, he was instrumental both in creating an alternative vision and in creating the common action that could realise that vision in practice. Both of these components are crucial for the development of a *specific* cognitive alternative with the potential to underpin and drive forward social change.

Conclusion: Can We Escape from the Stanford Prison?

> Those of us who have never found the SPE picture at all plausible as a historical or political story can now point to the BBC study and say 'look, when one gives people a chance to act reasonably naturally, with some choice, as they might in reality, over time, then there are instances when far from conforming to imposed roles they reject or change the roles, they reject and change the social structure' (Turner, 2006: 42).

Whatever else it does, one of the key contributions of the BPS is to break from the tradition of a long line of classic studies in social psychology which appear to suggest that human beings are instinctively inclined towards conformity and obedience, and that these instincts take them down an inevitable path towards conflict, abuse and tyranny. This is not to deny that we live in a world where these phenomena are all too prevalent. But where they occur, they are the product not of thoughtlessness and zombie-like followership, but of individuals' active identification and engagement with the groups of which they are part (Haslam & Reicher, 2007b; Reicher & Haslam, 2006b). The ultimate proof of this point is that, like the guards in our study, people can *and do* refuse to conform to role and, like the prisoners, they can *and do* rebel against the system.

The questions that the BBC study raises, and that we have sought to address in this chapter, concern the conditions under which people strive to resist those in authority, and to fight against a given social system. As we have noted, these are questions which served as a catalyst for the development of social identity theory (Tajfel & Turner, 1979). Our analysis builds on work in this tradition to suggest that resistance is most likely to occur, and most likely to succeed in effecting social change, when members of disadvantaged groups come to define themselves in terms of an oppositional identity whose content is oriented towards achieving that change. As well as being contingent on social structural and social psychological factors specified within social identity theory (specifically, the impermeability and insecurity of group boundaries, and group members' sense of cognitive alternative), we have also argued that the development and impact of such identities is structured by other factors: notably, the strength of social identity within the group one is challenging, the involvement of third parties, and leadership. And, as we saw in the BPS, when these factors are in alignment, the resistance that ensues not only challenges social systems, but can also topple them.

In sum, we are faced with a choice between two different psychologies, two different understandings of history and two different stances in society. The dominant one, informed by conformity bias, strips people of choice and strips change out of history. From such a perspective our emphasis on resistance and revolt is unthinkable and possibly laughable. Thus Zimbardo remarks of the BBC study:

> The rather remarkable conclusion of this simulated prison experience is that the prisoners dominated the guards! . . . The prisoners soon established the upper hand, working as a team to undermine the guards . . . What is the external validity of such events in any real prison anywhere in the known universe? In what kind of prisons are prisoners in charge? How could such an eventuality become manifest? (2006: 49).

In response, one might do well to recall Robben Island and Nelson Mandela's observation that here 'the inmates seemed to be running the prison not the authorities'. Yet our concern with Zimbardo's position, and with approaches that are infused with conformity bias more generally, is not simply empirical. It is normative as well. The danger is that those who deny (or scoff at) the very possibility of resistance and change thereby deny alternatives to the status quo in general. Hence, they are not merely advocates for an analysis from which the possibility of social change is excluded, but also part of the process whereby social change is itself rendered unimaginable. In this sense, they suppress *our* cognitive alternatives.

It is high time, then, that we escape the *real* Stanford Prison (Turner, 2006). This is not the one that was constructed in the basement of a Californian psychology department, but the one we perennially reconstruct in our classrooms. This is not the one in which a handful of carefully chosen college students were incarcerated, but the one in which we are the unwitting prisoners.

Acknowledgements

Work on this chapter was supported by the Economic and Social Research Council (RES-062-23-0135).

References

Asch, S.E. (1955). Opinions and social pressure. *Scientific American, 193*, 31–5.

Brehm, J.W. (1966). *A Theory of Psychological Reactance.* New York: Academic Press.

Browning, C. (1992). *Ordinary Men: Reserve Police Batallion 101 and the Final Solution in Poland.* London: Penguin.

Buntman, F.L. (2003). *Robben Island and Prisoner Resistance to Apartheid.* Cambridge: Cambridge University Press.

Burger, J. (2009). *In their Own Words: Explaining Obedience through an Examination of Participants' Comments.* Paper presented at the Meeting of the Society of Experimental Social Psychology, Portland, ME, 15–17 October.

Carnahan, T. & McFarland, S. (2007). Revisiting the Stanford Prison Experiment: could participant self-selection have led to the cruelty? *Personality and Social Psychology Bulletin, 33*, 603–14.

Cocking, C. & Drury, J. (2004). Generalization of efficacy as a function of collective action and intergroup relations: involvement in an anti-roads struggle. *Journal of Applied Social Psychology, 34*, 417–44.

Drury, J. & Reicher, S. (1999). The intergroup dynamics of collective empowerment: substantiating the social identity model. *Group Processes and Intergroup Relations, 2*, 381–402.

Ellemers, N. (1993). The influence of socio-structural variables on identity enhancement strategies. *European Review of Social Psychology, 4*, 27–57.

Haney, C., Banks, C. & Zimbardo, P. (1973). A study of prisoners and guards in a simulated prison. *Naval Research Reviews* (September, pp. 1–17). Washington, DC: Office of Naval Research [Reprinted in E. Aronson (ed.), *Readings about the Social Animal* (3rd edition, pp. 52–67). San Francisco: W.H. Freeman].

Haslam, S.A. & McGarty, C. (2001). A hundred years of certitude? Social psychology, the experimental method and the management of scientific uncertainty. *British Journal of Social Psychology, 40*, 1–21.

Haslam, S.A. & Reicher, S. D. (2005). The psychology of tyranny. *Scientific American Mind, 16* (3), 44–51.

Haslam, S.A. & Reicher, S.D. (2006a). Social identity and the dynamics of organizational life: insights from the BBC Prison Study. In C. Bartel, S. Blader & A. Wrzesniewski (eds), *Identity and the Modern Organization* (pp. 135–66). New York: Erlbaum.

Haslam, S.A. & Reicher, S.D. (2006b). Stressing the group: social identity and the unfolding dynamics of responses to stress. *Journal of Applied Psychology, 91*, 1037–52.

Haslam, S.A. & Reicher, S.D. (2007a). Identity entrepreneurship and the consequences of identity failure: the dynamics of leadership in the BBC Prison Study. *Social Psychology Quarterly, 70*, 125–47.

Haslam, S.A. & Reicher, S.D. (2007b). Beyond the banality of evil: three dynamics of an interactionist social psychology of tyranny. *Personality and Social Psychology Bulletin, 33*, 615–22.

Haslam, S.A. & Reicher, S.D. (2009). *The Social Psychology of Resistance: Prison Studies and the Case for a More Expansive Theoretical Imagination*. Unpublished manuscript, Universities of Exeter and St Andrews.

Haslam, S.A., Reicher, S.D. & Platow, M.J. (2010). *The New Psychology of Leadership*. London: Psychology Press.

Haslam, S.A., Turner, J.C., Oakes, P.J., McGarty, C. & Reynolds, K.J. (1998). The group as a basis for emergent stereotype consensus. *European Review of Social Psychology, 8*, 203–39.

Kelly, C. & Breinlinger, S. (1996). *The Social Psychology of Collective Action: Identity, Injustice and Gender*. London: Taylor & Francis.

Langbein, H. (1995). *Against all Hope: Resistance in the Nazi Concentration Camps 1938–1945*. London: Constable.

Levi, P. (1958/1987). *If This is a Man.* London: Abacus.

Levine, R.M. (2003). Times, theories and practices in social psychology. *Theory and Psychology, 13,* 53–72.

Mandela, N. (1994). *Long Walk to Freedom: The Autobiography of Nelson Mandela.* London: Abacus.

Marx, K. (1845). Theses on Feuerbach. In K. Marx. & J. Engels (eds), *Basic Writings on Politics and Philosophy* (pp. 243–5; trans L. S. Feuer). Garden City, NY: Doubleday.

McEvoy, K., McConnachie, K. & Jamieson, R. (2007). Political imprisonment and the 'war on terror'. In Y. Jewkes (ed.), *Handbook of Prisons* (pp. 293–323). Cullompton: Willan.

Milgram, S. (1963). Behavioral study of obedience. *Journal of Abnormal and Social Psychology, 67,* 371–8.

Milgram, S. (1974). *Obedience to Authority: An Experimental View.* New York: Harper & Row.

Moscovici, S. (1976). *Social Influence and Social Change.* London: Academic Press.

Moscovici, S. & Faucheux, C. (1972). Social influence, conformity bias, and the study of active minorities. In L. Berkowitz (ed.), *Advances in Experimental Social Psychology* (pp. 149–202) New York: Academic Press.

Moscovici, S., Lage, E. & Naffrechoux, M. (1969). Influence of a consistent minority on responses of a majority in a color perception task. *Sociometry, 32,* 365–80.

Rees, L. (2005). *Auschwitz: The Nazis and the 'Final Solution'.* London: BBC Books.

Reicher, S.D. (1996). 'The Battle of Westminster': developing the social identity model of crowd behaviour in order to explain the initiation and development of collective conflict. *European Journal of Social Psychology, 26,* 115–34.

Reicher, S.D. & Haslam, S.A. (2006a). Rethinking the psychology of tyranny: the BBC Prison Experiment. *British Journal of Social Psychology, 45,* 1–40.

Reicher, S.D. & Haslam, S.A. (2006b). On the agency of individuals and groups: lessons from the BBC Prison Experiment. In T. Postmes & J. Jetten (Eds), *Individuality and the Group: Advances in Social Identity* (pp. 237–57) London: Sage.

Reicher, S.D. & Haslam, S.A. (in press). Change we can believe in: the role of social identity, cognitive alternatives and leadership in group mobilization and social transformation. In B. Wagoner, E. Jensen & J. Oldmeadow (eds), *Culture and Social Change: Transforming Society through the Power of Ideas.* London: Routledge.

Reicher, S.D., Haslam, S.A. & Hopkins, N. (2005). Social identity and the dynamics of leadership: leaders and followers as collaborative agents in the transformation of social reality. *Leadership Quarterly, 16,* 547–68.

Rousset, D. (1965). *L'Univers Concentrationnaire.* Paris: Editions de Minuit.

Saroyan, S. (2009). *The Impact of Third Parties on Resistance amongst Oppressed Groups.* Unpublished manuscript, University of Exeter.

Simon, B. & Klandermans, B. (2001). Politicized collective identity: a social psychological analysis. *American Psychologist, 56,* 319–31.

Stanley, A. (2006, June 1). 'The human behavior experiments': What can be done in the name of obedience. *The New York Times.* www.nytimes.com/2006/06/01/arts/television/01huma.html (Retrieved 7 June 2006).

Stott, C., Adang, O., Livingstone, A. & Schreiber, M., (2007). Variability in the collective behaviour of England fans at Euro2004: 'hooliganism', public order policing and social change. *European Journal of Social Psychology, 37,* 75–100.

Stott, C., Hutchison, P. & Drury, J. (2001). 'Hooligans' abroad: intergroup dynamics, social identity and participation in collective 'disorder' at the 1998 World Cup finals. *British Journal of Social Psychology, 40,* 359–84.

Subasic, E., Reynolds, K.J. & Turner, J.C. (2008). The political solidarity model of social change: dynamics of self-categorization in intergroup power relations. *Personality and Social Psychology Review, 12,* 330–52.

Tajfel, H. (1972). Some developments in European social psychology. *European Journal of Social Psychology, 2,* 307–22.

Tajfel, H. (1978). Interindividual behaviour and intergroup behaviour. In H. Tajfel (ed.), *Differentiation between Social Groups: Studies in the Social Psychology of Intergroup Relations* (pp. 27–60). London: Academic Press.

Tajfel, H. & Turner, J.C. (1979). An integrative theory of intergroup conflict. In W.G. Austin & S. Worchel (eds), *The Social Psychology of Intergroup Relations* (pp. 33–47). Monterey, CA: Brooks/Cole.

Trotsky, L. (1981). *History of the Russian Revolution.* London: Pluto.

Turner, J.C. (1982). Towards a cognitive redefinition of the social group. In H. Tajfel (ed.), *Social Identity and Intergroup Relations* (pp. 15–40). Cambridge: Cambridge University Press.

Turner, J.C. (1991). *Social Influence.* Milton Keynes: Open University Press.

Turner, J.C. (2006). Tyranny, freedom and social structure: escaping our theoretical prisons. *British Journal of Social Psychology, 45,* 41–6.

Turner, J.C. & Brown, R.J. (1978). Social status, cognitive alternatives and intergroup relations. In H. Tajfel (ed.), *Differentiation between Social Groups: Studies in the Social Psychology of Intergroup Relations* (pp. 201–34). London: Academic Press.

Wright, S.C. & Taylor, D.M. (1998). Responding to tokenism: individual action in the face of collective injustice. *European Journal of Social Psychology, 28,* 647–67.

Wright, S.C., Taylor, D.M. & Moghaddam, F.M. (1990). Responding to membership in a disadvantaged group: from acceptance to collective protest. *Journal of Personality and Social Psychology*, *58*, 994–1003.

Zimbardo, P. (2007). *The Lucifer Effect: How Good People Turn Evil.* London: Random House.

Index

Rebels in Groups: Dissent, Deviance, Difference and Defiance Jolanda Jetten and Matthew J. Hornsey